Entrepreneurs in the Southern Upcountry

BRUCE W. EELMAN

Entrepreneurs in the Southern Upcountry

Commercial Culture in Spartanburg, South Carolina, 1845–1880

THE UNIVERSITY OF GEORGIA PRESS

Athens & London

© 2008 by the University of Georgia Press
Athens, Georgia 30602
All rights reserved
Set in Adobe Caslon by BookComp, Inc.
Printed and bound by Thomson-Shore
The paper in this book meets the guidelines for
permanence and durability of the Committee on
Production Guidelines for Book Longevity of the
Council on Library Resources.

Printed in the United States of America
12 11 10 09 08 C 5 4 3 2 1

Library of Congress Cataloging-in-Publication Data

Eelman, Bruce W., 1967–
Entrepreneurs in the southern upcountry : commercial
culture in Spartanburg, South Carolina,
1845–1880 / Bruce W. Eelman.
p. cm.
Includes bibliographical references and index.
ISBN-13: 978-0-8203-3019-8 (hardcover : alk. paper)
ISBN-10: 0-8203-3019-1 (hardcover : alk. paper)
1. Industries—South Carolina—Spartanburg—History—
19th century. 2. Industrialization—South Carolina—
Spartanburg—History—19th century. 3. Entrepreneurship—
South Carolina—Spartanburg—History—19th century. I. Title.
HC108.S797E35 2008
381.09757'29—dc22   2007037370

British Library Cataloging-in-Publication Data available

For Rens Eelman and Evelyn Eelman

and

for Lori Jancik

Contents

List of Tables *ix*

Acknowledgments *xi*

Introduction *1*

One. "The Rising Generation": Commerce and Class in Antebellum Spartanburg *9*

Two. "We Must Manufacture": Textiles and Transportation in the Antebellum Era *38*

Three. "An Educated and Intelligent People Cannot Be Enslaved": The Struggle for Common School Reform *70*

Four. "Moral and Industrial Reform May Be United in One System": Modernizing Law and Morality *88*

Five. "We Have No Union Now": Secession and War *113*

Six. "To Pay Our Debts and Build Up Our Fallen Fortunes": Economic Recovery and Commercial Expansion in Postwar Spartanburg *134*

Seven. "A Great Commercial and Railroad Centre": Textiles, Transportation, and Trade in the Postwar Era *163*

Eight. "Educate Your Sons, They Will Build Reservoirs and Railroads": Race, Class, and Postwar Public Education *189*

Nine. "The Timely and Judicious Administration of the Laws": Law, Vigilantism, and the Business Community of Postwar Spartanburg *213*

Conclusion *243*

Notes *247*

Bibliography *283*

Index *303*

Tables

1. Slaveholding in Spartanburg District, 1860 *15*
2. Spartanburg Population, 1850–1860 *15*
3. Farm Value and Agricultural Production, Spartanburg District, 1850–1860 *33*
4. Value of Merchandise, Professions, and Land in Spartanburg District *33*
5. Spartanburg State Legislators, 1850–1860 *35*
6. Textile Mills in Spartanburg District, 1850 *46*
7. Textile Mills in Spartanburg District, 1860 *46*
8. Cases before the Spartanburg District Court of General Sessions, 1850 and 1860 *101*
9. Spartanburg State Legislators, 1870–1880 *143*
10. Farm Value and Agricultural Production, Spartanburg County, 1870–1880 *156*
11. Rural and Town Property Values in Spartanburg County, 1873–1878 *176*
12. Textile Mills in Spartanburg County, 1870 *182*
13. Textile Mills in Spartanburg County, 1882 *183*
14. Textile Mills in South Carolina, 1884 *184*
15. Cases before the Spartanburg Court of General Sessions, 1870 and 1880 *237*

Acknowledgments

WRITING A BOOK is at one and the same time a solitary endeavor and a community effort. I am indebted to many people for their intellectual and personal generosity.

This work, and my life as a scholar, has been immeasurably influenced by my undergraduate mentor and friend, Dan Crofts, at the College of New Jersey. Dan's passion for history, his skills as a teacher, and his humanity have shaped my approach to the discipline. He also read an early version of the manuscript and made valuable suggestions.

At the graduate level Whit Ridgway directed my work with the ideal combination of intellectual criticism and unflagging encouragement. Other readers at the University of Maryland offering important critiques were David Grimsted, James Henretta, George Callcott, and Herman Belz. The history department at the University of Maryland facilitated early trips to southern archives with two William Randolph Hearst Travel Grants. A Littleton-Griswold Grant from the American Historical Association permitted a more extended stay in Columbia, South Carolina, to examine court records.

I have benefited from the assistance of numerous librarians and archivists at Duke University, the University of North Carolina at Chapel Hill, Harvard Business School, the Library of Congress, and the National Archives. Anyone fortunate enough to do research in Columbia, South Carolina, knows of the wonderful staffs at the area repositories. At the South Caroliniana Library Allen Stokes, Henry Fulmer, and Robin Copp deserve special mention. A number of archivists at the South Carolina Department of Archives and History were patient in guiding me toward important government sources.

The Institute for Southern Studies at the University of South Carolina offered both an intellectual community and a refuge from solitary research. Director Walter Edgar and Assistant Director Tom Brown are incredibly supportive of visiting researchers.

Fred Holder was exceptionally generous in sharing important sources, his own command of South Carolina history, and ceaseless encouragement to complete the book. John Hammond Moore graciously shared his home, his manuscripts, and, most important for anyone spending long hours at an archives, good conversation and strong drink.

Siena College provided important assistance along the way. Reassigned time permitted critical hours of writing. A fellowship from the Committee on Teaching and Faculty Development helped fund a final research trip. I could not ask for better colleagues than Siena's history department. In particular, Jim Harrison has always been supportive of my scholarship.

Portions of this book have appeared as papers at a host of conferences, and I received tremendously helpful comments from David Carlton, Angela Lakwete, Scott Nelson, and Mark Rose. Parts of chapters 2 and 7 originally appeared as "Entrepreneurs in the Southern Upcountry: The Case of Spartanburg, South Carolina, 1815–1880," *Enterprise & Society* 5 (March 2004): 77–106. Much of chapter 3 first appeared as "'An Educated and Intelligent People Cannot Be Enslaved': The Struggle for Common Schools in Antebellum Spartanburg, South Carolina," *History of Education Quarterly* 44 (Summer 2004): 250–70.

Editor Derek Krissoff at the University of Georgia Press has been terrific in moving this book through the review and production stage with lightning speed. The reviewers themselves provided prompt, wonderful critique of my work.

Family and friends have been a vital source of support. My parents' love and support throughout the years made this work possible. I can never repay them for all they have given me, but I hope they view this work as a testament to their success as caring parents who let their children choose their own paths in life.

Finally, my wife, Lori Jancik, has been the most important source of strength over the many years this book took shape. Her love and support continue to astonish me.

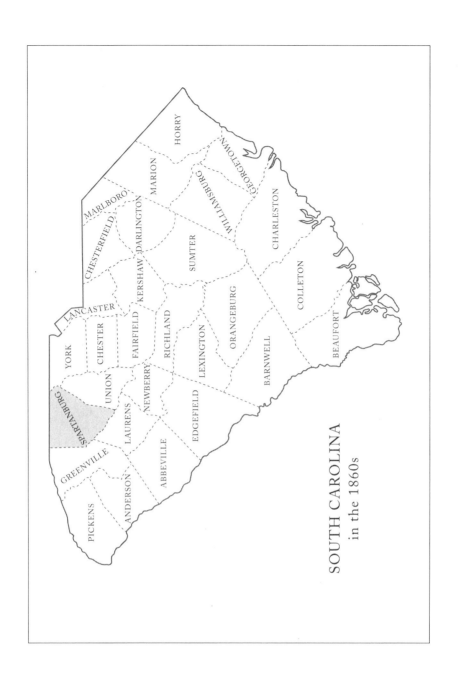

SOUTH CAROLINA in the 1860s

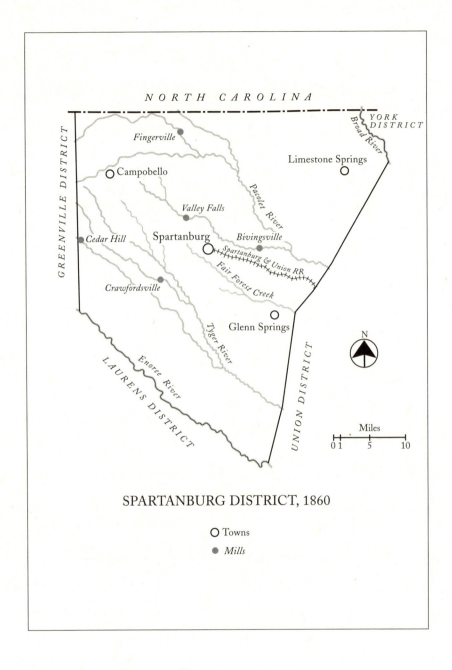

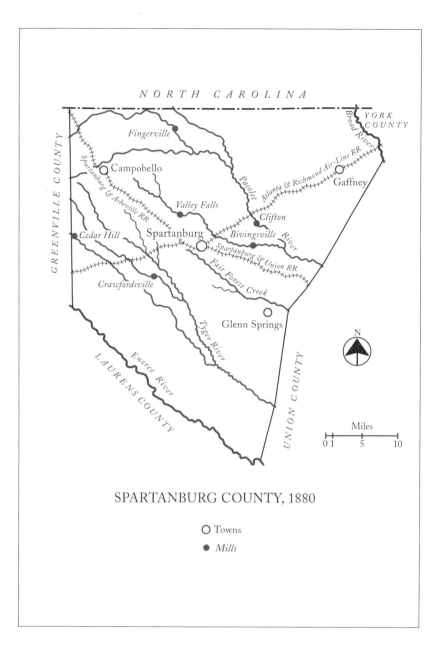

SPARTANBURG COUNTY, 1880

Entrepreneurs in the Southern Upcountry

Introduction

CONTINUITY VERSUS DISCONTINUITY. Precapitalist versus capitalist. Race versus class. Oppositional interpretations such as these have been the mainstay of historical work on the American South over the past century. This intellectual sparring has often been most intense over socioeconomic issues. Although historians have generally agreed that the antebellum American South lagged behind the North in terms of economic diversification and industrial development, disagreements emerge over the causes for this lag.[1] Some argue that slavery ensured the persistence of a pre-bourgeois, paternalistic culture at odds with the individualistic free-market capitalism of the North.[2] Other scholars have found that differences in industrial development between North and South were much more the product of rational economic choices than cultural aversions to diversification and industrialization. These historians argue that planters generally embraced modernization as long as it complemented the staple-crop economy. However, this agricultural dominance discouraged town-centered networks of the merchants and entrepreneurs necessary for innovation.[3] The apparent lack of diversification and industrial activity prior to the Civil War is often contrasted with the lightning pace of commercialization and factory development following the war and through the late nineteenth century. In his seminal study *Origins of the New South, 1877–1913* C. Vann Woodward emphasized this sharp break with an agrarian past throughout the entire postwar South and identified the rise of a new entrepreneurial business elite that embraced railroads, industry, and mercantile development.

Recent scholarship, however, has questioned the use of such sharp dichotomies in studying the southern past. Instead, these historians focus on the nineteenth-century South as a region in transition. Important work comparing the southern economy with other countries has revealed that planters were active players in the changing market of the Atlantic world and that global forces affected the South's economic fortunes.[4] Mark Smith's innovative study on clock time, *Mastered by the Clock: Time, Slavery, and*

Freedom in the American South, suggests that planters looked to secure profits through greater discipline and order and thus embraced at least some elements of modernity. In his study of Civil War–era Georgia Chad Morgan finds that antebellum planters "supported at least a moderate degree of industrialization."[5] Although these studies have corrected the stereotype of backward-looking planters maintaining a single-minded focus on cotton production, plantation owners were not the driving force behind efforts to modernize the southern economy. The recent work of Jonathan Wells clearly traces a self-conscious middle class of professional and commercial people emerging in the antebellum South to challenge planter control. Wells argues that southern businessmen imbibed northern middle-class culture and looked to "remake southern society with all the tangible signs of progress."[6] However, their efforts were impeded by opposition from planters and poor whites. In his study of southern merchant culture in the Civil War era, *Becoming Bourgeois: Merchant Culture in the South, 1820–1865,* Frank Byrne finds a growing commercial middle class that laid the groundwork for a postwar liberal capitalist ideology. Similarly, Tom Downey finds that by 1860 the South Carolina communities of Edgefield and Barnwell were in the midst of a "transition from merely being a society with capitalist features toward becoming a capitalist society."[7] Merchants and industrialists were central to this transition.

This is not to suggest, however, that increasingly diversified commercial activity signified a rejection of traditional southern institutions. Instead, this activity was largely adjusted to embrace slavery. Adhering to a republican ideology that cherished independence for all whites, southern businessmen argued that factories, new villages, and more commerce via railroads would further delineate white opportunity from black slavery. Thus, businessmen advocated a distinctly southern variant of modernization.

Through an analysis of business activity in Spartanburg County, South Carolina, from 1845 to 1880 this book adds to the growing scholarship on the nineteenth-century South's transitional economy and expands upon it in important ways. Far from experiencing a sharp break between prewar planters and postwar industrialists, Spartanburg was a center of commercial and industrial entrepreneurs in both the antebellum and postwar eras. What changed was not the modernizing spirit but rather the political context that allowed this spirit to flourish. During the antebellum era a group of Spartanburg's business leadership worked hard to overcome political and cultural biases against nonagricultural entrepreneurial activity. In this sense, the findings here challenge those who emphasize economic discontinuity while complementing the work of those who find increasing economic diversity over the course of the antebellum era.

Although the scholarship on the South's transitional economy has been pathbreaking, few of these studies have taken the long view of the South from the antebellum period through the Civil War and Reconstruction.[8] This broader time frame reveals with greater clarity the importance of the role of local professionals and merchants in the transition to a more diversified, integrated market economy. In the case of Spartanburg, political and social realignments largely allowed town-based entrepreneurs from the antebellum era to wrest power from rural elites and implement much of their economic initiatives. Without this base of nonagricultural entrepreneurial activity prior to the Civil War, the commercial development of the postbellum era would have been very different.

The fledgling business class of the early-nineteenth-century South recognized that they could not control the course of the region's economy without both accommodating and altering aspects of their society. As already noted, business plans were carefully crafted to dovetail with the institution of slavery. However, there were also significant efforts to reshape important aspects of the southern landscape. Remarkably few works have examined the activities of southern professionals and commercial folks within the context of broader cultural and institutional efforts at reform.[9] Spartanburg businessmen pushed for public education, a more structured legal system, and reforms in social behavior to create an environment more conducive to diversified market activity.

Spartanburg's location as an upcountry community magnifies the importance of this study. Located in far northwestern South Carolina about fifty miles from the North Carolina hillcountry made famous in Charles Frazier's novel *Cold Mountain*, Spartanburg would seem a good candidate for the southern backcountry stereotype of economic and social isolation. Historians of the southern upcountry have contributed to this generalization of the region as insulated from socioeconomic change until the late nineteenth century. Some historians explain that geographic isolation conspired against upcountry involvement in the market until northern-sponsored transportation links reached the area after the Civil War.[10] Other scholars contend that yeoman farmers of the upcountry consciously resisted the market until the late Reconstruction period, when a group of new entrepreneurs joined with wealthy farmers to draw the region into the market's web.[11] Lacy Ford's work offers an important challenge to this historiography by arguing that important market forces extended into the South Carolina upcountry during the late antebellum era. However, Ford's main focus is on the lower piedmont and less on northwestern communities like Spartanburg.[12] A focused examination of Spartanburg permits an opportunity to rethink generalizations about the nineteenth-century upcountry and the pace of socioeconomic change.

Studying the upcountry also lays bare the ways in which economic change contributed to intrastate sectional tensions. Since early colonization along the eastern seaboard, older villages have jealously guarded their power from newer frontier communities. These tensions accelerated with market expansion during the antebellum era.[13] In the case of South Carolina, lowcountry dominance of the general assembly slowed state support for interior development. Spartanburg's town-oriented merchants and professionals also had to face resistance from rural areas within their own county. Local planters viewed the rising town influence as a challenge to their authority in the region, and poorer farmers saw little to be gained from the consolidation of money and power in towns. As both Michael Johnson and Frank Towers have demonstrated, many leading secessionist planters in the South feared destabilization of their world if interior cities developed. According to Towers, these men advocated disunion "as a preventive measure against social changes that would destroy slavery and southern society."[14] This study of Spartanburg amplifies the turbulent nature of economic change within the nineteenth-century South.

These intrastate tensions, combined with interest in developing stronger commercial relations with the rest of the South and the North, led many of Spartanburg's business leaders to be slow in supporting South Carolina's immediate secession movement. They feared economic isolation if South Carolina seceded on its own without cooperation from other southern states. Spartanburg representatives ultimately supported the 1860 secession ordinance when the results were a foregone conclusion and thus reflected ambivalence more than secessionist radicalism.

This ambivalence would quickly turn to disaffection during the Civil War. Wartime shortages, high prices, and heavy demands imposed by the state and Confederate governments led to widespread destitution and military desertion throughout the South Carolina upcountry. Although most farmers accumulated substantial wartime debts, a number of wealthy men who had diversified in manufacturing and mercantile activities prior to the war sustained fewer economic losses, and some grew rich fulfilling military needs. The war also disrupted community institutions. Finances that would have been earmarked for schooling were diverted toward the war effort. Normal operations of law atrophied as many of those involved in the judicial process left for the front. Slaves and free blacks suffered most as the absence of constituted authority combined with the war's shifting emphasis toward emancipation led discontented whites to discard any pretense of a fair legal process. Harsh punishments were meted out on those blacks merely accused of crimes.

The war's end brought important changes to the political and economic structure of Spartanburg. With the end of plantation slavery, the power of rural planters gave way to town-based businessmen. This critical power shift meant that antebellum Spartanburg's champions of commercialization and diversification could implement much of their longstanding vision for the region. Although Democrats quickly regained local control in Spartanburg, Democratic town leaders often looked to the business-friendly Republican state government for assistance in the release of creative financial energy through such initiatives as railroad subsidies and tax breaks for industry.

Over the course of the 1870s Spartanburg experienced unprecedented railroad expansion, dramatic factory development, and a quadrupling of cotton production. In many ways this was a realization of a quest begun well before the Civil War. However, many did not experience the increased independence and prosperity promised in the booster rhetoric. The changes in the postwar economy brought greater inequalities between rich and poor, town and countryside.[15] Attempting to recover from wartime losses, rural farmers went further into debt by borrowing on credit from merchants and landlords. By 1880 the railroads crisscrossing Spartanburg were controlled by northern-led corporations, and textile factories were becoming corporate industrial villages. The incorporation of boomtowns like Spartanburg and Gaffney further strained the unity of town and country interests in economic development.

The central players in this study represent the developing middle class of the nineteenth-century South. These included merchants, lawyers, doctors, bankers, manufacturers, and other professionals. Some of these people also owned sizeable farms and utilized slave labor; others did not. Most were closely linked to the success of the developing towns in the region, especially Spartanburg village. In this sense, the people who are the focus of my study are similar to the group Wells defines as the southern middle class.[16]

Byrne has challenged this definition, arguing that the business experience of merchants was distinct from that of manufacturers.[17] Although each occupation had its own peculiarities, I contend that the businessmen studied here all shared the experience of being rising entrepreneurs.

Entrepreneur and entrepreneurship have had many definitions over time. Eighteenth-century economist Richard Cantillon viewed the entrepreneur simply as someone who was self-employed and therefore open to greater financial risk. One hundred years later Jean-Baptiste Say found that the entrepreneur needed managerial competence. In the early twentieth century Joseph Schumpeter emphasized innovation as central to entrepreneurial activity. As Wayne Long has noted, these three themes of risk, managerial competence, and innovation remain the critical elements in defining the entrepreneur.[18] Some historians of the American South may argue that plantation owners were as much entrepreneurs as merchants and industrialists because they looked for new ways to expand production, assumed risk with investments in new agricultural methods, and even supported some industrial development.[19] My use of the term *entrepreneur*, however, aligns more with Schumpeter's definition by placing emphasis on the initiation of new commercial enterprises and the use of resources in innovative ways. Although planters looked to new agricultural methods, the focus remained on similar staple crops. Likewise, interest in industry only extended as far as it would clearly benefit the market for staple crops. The middle-class businesspeople of Spartanburg looked to utilize the natural resources of their region for new industrial mills and to exploit their geographic location for a web of rail lines that would transform the area into a market hub. In addition, Spartanburg entrepreneurs were innovative in their use of human resources. A comprehensive effort at moral, intellectual, and legal change was designed to create a commercial culture championing new opportunities for whites while sustaining black slavery. As a group, these people looked to modernize the southern upcountry. The term *modernization* is employed here to mean the effort to create an integrated and diverse economic system complemented by widespread educational opportunities, a formal rationalized legal system, and social reform. As Richard D. Brown noted many years ago, modernization should not imply specifically positive or negative change, but it does include "technological development, complexity, specialization, and rationality."[20]

Given the paternalistic nature of society in nineteenth-century America, it is hardly surprising that most of the entrepreneurs discussed here are male. However, it is important to recognize that women played active roles in the commercial culture of the region.²¹ As part of an emerging middle class, Spartanburg entrepreneurs expected that their families would conform to the bourgeois ideal of the man on the make and the woman at the hearth. Women would therefore contribute to their middle-class families as consumers, domestic caregivers, social educators of children, and the moral center of the community. However, financial realities and social needs would necessitate that some of these women work from their homes at jobs such as dressmakers, laundresses, and music teachers. Some wives would at times function as clerks and store managers when their husbands were away on business. Middle-class women from the North would also influence the region as schoolteachers at new female academies.

Although the central focus of my work is on the modernizing leadership of Spartanburg, race and class are essential parts of this story. By sheer numbers, yeomen dominated Spartanburg's landscape. Representing over half of inhabitants in antebellum Spartanburg, yeomen could not be ignored in any plans for development. In seeking to prevent class division over the benefits of commercialization and the introduction of new industries, Spartanburg's businessmen argued that diversification would bring uplift to all whites while strengthening the institution of black slavery. A number of historians have skillfully identified the interconnection between white liberty and black slavery in the Old South.²² Class tensions were muted, these scholars find, by a central ideal that all whites shared a basic equality as independent individuals while black slaves performed the hard labor ill suited to citizenship. Spartanburg's leadership emphasized the importance of this racial divide in justifying economic and institutional change. Slavery, they argued, was not only consistent with economic diversification but actually permitted whites to pursue new avenues of development. Common school reform was justified both as a means of opening doors for whites and as a way to reinforce the separation between whites and blacks. Similarly, legal reform reflecting the complexity of the market economy coincided with the continued use of separate, less formal courts for slaves and free blacks.

At the same time Spartanburg leaders encouraged racial division, they also looked to challenge one of the South's ideological by-products of black slavery. Antebellum observers noted that southerners tended to view most manual labor as dependent "nigger's" work. Eager to develop the region's economic infrastructure, Spartanburg's political and business leaders recognized the need for white labor in industry and town building. Through newspapers and public pronouncements these men worked to convince their community that free and slave labor could coexist in a modernizing

South without blurring racial separateness. Supporting white manual labor also was a means by which the rising middle class could challenge planter dominance without advocating social revolution. In her study of white artisans in Georgia, Michele Gillespie finds that "the promotion of mechanics proved a useful means of critiquing the old agricultural society and the people who perpetuated it. Accordingly, Whig newspapers . . . attacked planters for not supporting the wealth-producing work of free laborers."[23]

The connection between racial inferiority and the ideal of white progress had important implications for post–Civil War Spartanburg. Many yeomen and poor whites in the county reacted violently to black independence because they feared both economic competition and the elimination of an important indication of their political and social freedoms. Looking to preserve economic and political power, Spartanburg leaders temporarily suspended their commitment to stronger legal structure and supported racial violence, particularly through Ku Klux Klan organizations. These men publicly condemned Klan operations only after the threat of federal intervention. Whites also joined in resisting biracial education. Having called upon the state to adopt compulsory white schooling in the antebellum period, county leaders rejected Reconstruction plans for universal education and instead looked to continue instruction for whites only. In postwar Spartanburg race continued to define community and limit class tension between whites.

Spartanburg's story merits attention because it reveals much about economic development and political economy in both the antebellum and postbellum upcountry. It challenges generalizations that antebellum southerners failed to appreciate that the worldwide market revolution required economic diversification and a larger investment in human capital in order for the region to retain its financial health and compete with the North. In Spartanburg's case the same entrepreneurial leadership promoted commercial and industrial expansion both before and after the Civil War. In this sense it was a story of continuity rather than revolutionary change. At the same time, however, a revolution in political climate permitted town-based entrepreneurs to eclipse the power of rural elites and help the region transition to a more fully capitalistic New South economy. This is neither the story of planters who refashioned themselves as New South industrialists nor the story of the persistence of the old plantation regime. Instead, it is a richer, more complicated story of businessmen struggling over the course of the nineteenth century to reshape politics and economics in the South.

CHAPTER ONE

"The Rising Generation"
Commerce and Class in Antebellum Spartanburg

ASSESSING THE PEOPLE of Spartanburg in 1847, Presbyterian minister Zelotus Holmes found "the old stock generally not very intelligent, but the rising generation vastly improving & numbers entering the various professions from all parts of the District." As evidence of this improvement, Holmes noted the district's "three cotton factories[,] 3 or 4 foundries[,] two rolling mills & nail factories[,] & . . . twenty to forty merchant mills."[1] Although the minister was correct in observing a growing business and entrepreneurial class in the district, the developmental impulse he found in "the rising generation" actually owed much to the early settlement of the region. Migrants to the colonial southern frontier came with the dual purpose of establishing new homesteads and deriving economic profits from untapped resources.[2] The balance between these twin aspirations varied, naturally, according to the individual. Some of the earliest arrivals were squatters primarily interested in the quiet enjoyment of private land, while others were speculators looking for profit maximization above all else. Most, however, combined a commitment to a strong family farmstead with an interest in developing market opportunities when possible. This duality in the motives for frontier settlement ensured that agitation for the expansion of social and economic institutions persisted longer than in the established planter regions of the lowcountry and Black Belt.

Concern over individual farm development and improved connections to the wider web of the market economy informed the rise of two influential groups in Spartanburg. Some early settlers gained title to substantial plots in the southern stretches of the district where fertile soil supported the development of staple-crop agriculture. By expanding investments in land and slaves, a handful of families emerged as a rural planter elite. Like plantation owners throughout the South, this group's primary interests were in preserving both the financial strength of staple-crop agriculture and the political strength of the slave institution necessary for large-scale production. The generation after initial settlement saw the formation of a second influential group—this one of merchants, entrepreneurs, and town professionals—that was less dependent on staple-crop agriculture and more interested in combining a commitment to the slave economy with diversification in agricultural, industrial, and mercantile markets.

Although some elites defied easy categorization by maintaining both nonagricultural entrepreneurial interests and plantation estates, subtle differences in the priorities of rural and town professional elites had important implications for the district. These differences were highlighted during South Carolina's first secession crisis of 1849–51. Spartanburg's rural elite politicians, with their substantial investments in slave labor for staple-crop production, feared northern attempts to control the expansion of slavery and advocated immediate secession from the Union with or without the cooperation of other southern states. However, town-oriented economic leaders, with their interests in maintaining and expanding market connections outside the state, urged cooperation with other southern states as a prerequisite to disunion. By the 1850s a professional class had emerged in Spartanburg as an influential and active force working to mobilize support for economic diversification and infrastructural improvement. This quest to implement change would clash with the interests of the state's political machinery and local rural farmers.

Located at the foothills of the Blue Ridge Mountains in the northwestern corner of South Carolina, antebellum Spartanburg District left a favorable impression on travelers to the region. One of the South's most gifted antebellum writers, William Gilmore Simms, found Spartanburg's climate "temperate and salubrious" and the landscape "agreeably diversified by hill and dale, mount and plain." Simms joined many lowcountry planters who vacationed in the district as an escape from the miasmas of the summer coast. Planters were particularly attracted by a series of mineral springs that were believed to bring about relief from "rheumatisms, agues and fevers, ulcers, &c." While touring South Carolina in 1843, Virginia agricultural reformer Edmund Ruffin sought the "cathartic effects" of Spartanburg's Glenn Springs resort.[3]

Spartanburg town, the local seat of justice, represented an important demarcation line in the district's landscape. South of town a rich, red clay soil permitted cotton agriculture along with a variety of food crops. To the north gray soil scattered with small stones restricted farming to the principal provision crops of corn, wheat, and oats. Throughout the district cropland and pastures were interspersed with forests of oak, pine, poplar, chestnut, walnut, and maple. Four rivers flowed through Spartanburg: the Enoree and Tyger in the south and the Pacolet and Broad to the north. Each of these watercourses and their tributaries afforded enough waterpower to sustain both community gristmills and larger factory operations.[4] It was this diversified setting that first attracted colonial migrants in search of new opportunities.

Colonial migration to the Spartanburg region of the Carolina upcountry bore little resemblance to settlement patterns along the coast. Many lowcountry settlers arrived from plantations in the West Indies and brought a substantial population of African slaves with them. A wealthy elite emerged quickly, setting up extensive rice, indigo, and long-staple cotton plantations during the first half of the eighteenth century. This elite exercised substantial social, political, and economic control over a relatively small group of poor to middling white farmers and laborers as well as a majority population of black slaves.[5] Aware of their virtually unchallenged power, lowcountry planters showed little interest in investing in social institutions and infrastructural development beyond what was necessary for financing and promoting staple-crop agriculture. Throughout the antebellum era, then, lowcountry South Carolina came closer to historian Eugene Genovese's image of a hegemonic, prebourgeois society than any other southern region.[6]

Most upcountry settlers, however, came not from slave-based plantation communities but rather from modest farms and mercantile establishments in the upper South and the North. The first white settlers reached the Spartanburg area in the early 1760s and were composed primarily of Scotch-Irish and German farmers who had migrated from Pennsylvania through the Shenandoah Valley to the frontiers of Virginia and the Carolinas. A few families made the journey directly from Northern Ireland looking to escape religious and political persecution in their homeland.[7] The primary goal of most of these early emigrants was to ensure household prosperity and peaceful enjoyment of family and friends. In this regard, they were not much different from most rural settlers in early America who looked to build strong communities through mutual support.[8] This community development, however, was not contradictory to furthering economic opportunity.

In fact, most of these settlers made the decision to uproot because of declining prices for tobacco and increasing land pressures in the mid-Atlantic region. Bradley Bond has noted that the very act of migration to the South and West revealed a quest to find more fertile land and better prices indicative of market interest. Likewise, Joyce Chaplin finds in migrants to the colonial South Carolina backcountry "overtly commercial ambitions" and a "self-awareness in their schemes for settling the upcountry."[9]

Although these more recent studies offer an important corrective to those historians who suggest a general desire among upcountry farmers to remain free of outside economic connections, not all market involvement signaled "progressive" financial ambitions. Some settlers, in fact, had little choice but to plant marketable crops. At times, agricultural laborers and tenant farmers had to plant cash crops so that they or their landlords could sell or exchange the produce to pay their rent. A series of disastrous crop years could plunge tenants into deeper debt and leave a legacy of tenantry to succeeding generations. By 1860 about 44 percent of Spartanburg farmers were tenants, and about 35 percent of all tenants grew cotton for the market.[10] Assessing the degree to which these tenants viewed the market as merely a necessity or as an opportunity for future growth is nearly impossible due to scant written testimony left by the poorer classes. However, the fact that some had to grow commercial crops undoubtedly made participation in the market economy a source of tension in these farmers' lives.

Agriculturalists who owned their own land had more choices in how and when to participate in market exchange. Throughout the antebellum period, slightly above 50 percent of household heads owned land. Of these landholders, 66 percent owned under one hundred acres, while less than 1 percent held over five hundred acres.[11] This yeoman majority often combined self-sufficiency in foodstuffs with active interests in commercial production. In a study of the South Carolina upcountry, Steven West finds that 69 percent of yeomen in Spartanburg maintained self-sufficiency in grain through the end of the antebellum period. In this regard, yeomen fared better than the less than 40 percent of tenants who maintained independence in provision-crop production but not quite as well as the 87 percent of large landowning and planter households who achieved self-sufficiency.[12]

Although yeoman farmers stressed self-sufficiency, they also worked very hard to keep active in the market. James F. Sloan, a farmer of sixty improved acres in eastern Spartanburg District, sought to balance his resources between cotton and provision crops. In the 1850s Sloan labored in his fields almost ceaselessly alongside his wife, daughter, and son. Together they averaged four to six bales of cotton per year in addition to wheat, corn, and oats. Sloan relied heavily on a local store owner for his farm supplies and every winter took his cotton to Columbia, where he solicited merchants for the best price. By 1859 Sloan had enough cash to hire a slave woman named Manda to assist in field work.[13]

Cotton was not the only marketable crop for Spartanburg farmers. As Sloan's experience reveals, yeomen involvement in cotton production was an exhaustive prospect, and even some middling farmers in the generally cotton-favorable soil of southern Spartanburg avoided significant production of the staple and instead looked to market provision crops. David Golightly Harris offers one such example. In 1860 Harris farmed 100 of his 550 total acres and owned ten slaves in the Fair Forest neighborhood, about eight miles southeast of Spartanburg village. Despite having a significantly larger workforce than Sloan, Harris never produced more than two or three bales of cotton a year, and he usually made only one bale.[14] Instead, he put his slaves to work on what seemed the most dependable and marketable crops: corn, wheat, and oats. Harris's customers were primarily local small producers. Although he at times took payment in the form of labor or in kind, Harris preferred cash for his produce and refused to extend credit.

Harris's journal reflects the middle-class farmer's attempts at profit maximization through means other than staple-crop production. With corn scarce in May 1855, the Fair Forest farmer "sold out my corn . . . a[t] $1 per bu[shel]." One year later, Harris sold six bushels at sixty cents per bushel, but he "refused to sell" all of his corn because he thought it was worth at least seventy-five cents. The following spring Harris's corn was in such demand that in March alone he sold over 120 bushels to at least ten people at seventy-five cents per bushel. With such demand, Harris began to "think that I must rase my prices," and on March 28 he raised his corn to one dollar per bushel. In one spring day in 1859 Harris's business exchanges provide a classic example of the laws of demand, supply, and prices. "Today I have sold the last corn that I can sell this summer," Harris recorded. "I sold the first at 60 c[ents], the most of the other at 75 cents, the last at 85 cents & one dollar." He could also occasionally find good prices for wheat, selling the grain for as much as $1.30 per bushel in March 1861.[15] Although Harris's economic transactions remained local and profits modest, his constant concern with getting the best prices for his crop while avoiding the less-reliable cotton crop reveals the workings of a rational business mind.

The example of David Golightly Harris's farming practices reveals much about the economy of antebellum Spartanburg District. Despite cotton's rising importance in the region, it had yet to become "king." In fact, cotton production actually declined in Spartanburg by almost four hundred bales between 1850 and 1860, most likely due to the economic depression of 1857. Grains and cereals dominated the district's agricultural production. In 1860 Spartanburg was the state's leading producer of wheat and rye, while its corn production ranked third. The district also maintained a healthy share of the state's livestock, including the second largest number of swine. John Earle Bomar recalled that "driving cows to 'pasture' was a regular part of life" in antebellum Spartanburg. According to the antebellum fence law, anyone with stock was permitted to drive his or her animals onto designated grazing grounds, and it was the responsibility of landowners to keep their crops protected from livestock. For many whites in the northern half of the district, livestock production represented the most important form of commerce. Spartanburg was located on a major route for upper South drovers looking to sell their stock in the markets of Charleston and Savannah. As North Carolina herdsmen made their way through the district, local stock owners would sell them their animals, thus avoiding the long trip themselves. Some enterprising residents set up small slaughterhouses for ducks and turkeys, which would then be sent to markets farther east and south.[16]

Overall, then, most Spartanburg residents were white yeoman farmers rather than men of means. In 1860 the district's white population ranked second highest in the state behind only Charleston. Throughout the antebellum period Spartanburg's nonslaveholders numbered between 60 and 70 percent of heads of households, while slaves never constituted more than one third of the total population. Slave owners accounted for slightly above 5 percent of the total white population, and planters—those owning twenty or more slaves—represented just one half of 1 percent of the district's white inhabitants. Among slave owners just 9 percent were planters owning more than twenty slaves.[17]

Although most white farmers remained yeomen throughout their lives, a select few were able to move from small producers into a rural elite over a relatively short span of time. In 1765 Pennsylvania farmer William Smith moved his family to Spartanburg in search of better agricultural opportunities. Smith would serve as a captain in the Revolutionary War and later was chosen as one of the district's first judges. In 1797 he was elected to Congress

Table 1. Slaveholding in Spartanburg District, 1860

No. of slaves owned	No. of slave owners	% of all slave owners in district	% of all slaves in district	% of total white population in district
1–5	530	52.6	15.4	2.8
6–19	378	37.5	48.6	2.0
20–49	90	8.9	28.5	0.4
50–200	9	0.89	7.5	—
TOTAL	1,007			5.4

Source: U.S. Bureau of the Census, *Population*, 237.

Table 2. Spartanburg Population, 1850–1860

	1850		1860	
	No. of persons	% of district population	No. of persons	% of district population
White	18,311	69.4	18,537	68.9
Free black	50	0.2	142	0.3
Slave	8,039	30.5	8,240	30.6
TOTAL	26,400		26,919	

Sources: U.S. Bureau of the Census, *Seventh Census*, 334–35, and *Population*, 448–50.

and served the South Carolina upcountry for several terms. By the early 1800s Smith owned a substantial tobacco and cotton plantation that would serve as a base of wealth and power for his ambitious sons. His eldest son, Isaac, served as a state senator from 1818 to 1826 and as a state representative from 1828 to 1830. Eber, Smith's second son, became a physician as well as a farmer and was a state representative from 1818 to 1822. His third son, John C. Winn Smith (who later changed his name to Winsmith), was also a respected physician and planter, and he was a state legislator from 1856 to 1858 and 1860 to 1862. By 1860 Winsmith had amassed real estate in Glenn Springs worth $41,000 and used most of his ninety-nine slaves to produce 193 bales of cotton. Winsmith's younger brother, Elihu Penquite Smith, was also a planter-politician, serving in the state legislature from 1842 to 1850 and operating a plantation with forty-three slaves producing eighty-three bales of cotton.[18] The Smith family's involvement in state politics and their dominant role in the agrarian economics of the region placed them on an even footing with many prominent lowcountry planters.

Other rural elites emerged in the generation after settlement when the increased viability of cotton production offered new opportunities. B. F. Kilgore, grandson of the family's first settlers to the region, practiced medicine before purchasing valuable farmland on the Enoree River, Spartanburg's southernmost border. By the 1840s Kilgore had served as commissioner of roads, and he later won election to the state legislature in 1854 and 1858. Possessing real estate worth $32,000 and owning sixty-three slaves in 1860, Kilgore had solidified his reputation as a respected planter-statesman. At about the same time that the first Kilgores arrived in the colonial upcountry, the Foster family made their way into Spartanburg from Amelia County, Virginia. Although the family had established stable, moderate-sized farms during the early republic, grandson B. B. Foster looked to capitalize on the westward expansion of cotton cultivation and establish his own substantial plantation. Foster first made his money as a physician before purchasing and developing a cotton plantation near Glenn Springs in southern Spartanburg, where he utilized the labor of forty-three slaves to produce thirty-four cotton bales. Like other prominent area planters, Foster served the district as a state legislator from 1844 to 1850.[19]

During the first half of the nineteenth century, however, planter political and economic influence was matched by another group that was less heavily involved in staple-crop agriculture and centered around the emerging town of Spartanburg. Although viewing land and slaves as essential to success in the South, this second group tied the region's future prosperity to economic diversification and internal improvements. Composed of lawyers, merchants, industrialists, and entrepreneurial farmers, this developing professional class advanced programs designed to fulfill their vision of a stable, law-abiding, educated community of productive commercial farms with improved transportation routes to markets in all directions and an important industrial sector.[20]

Some came to Spartanburg with the express goal of utilizing the area's virgin resources to establish profitable industrial enterprises. Maryland native William Wofford looked to tap one of the region's primary mineral resources by erecting an ironworks on the Tyger River in the 1760s. Although the factory was burned during the Revolution and Wofford himself moved to Georgia shortly after the war, his early interest in manufacturing was matched by subsequent settlers and natives to the region. In the fifteen years following the War of 1812 a group of Rhode Islanders set up four textile operations in the district. James Edward Henry was among these early Rhode Island immigrants to Spartanburg. Henry initially arrived as an administrative clerk in one of the first factories before studying to become a lawyer in the 1830s. By the 1840s Henry had gained a reputation as the district's most influential representative in the state legislature, and he became a major supporter of and investor in manufacturing, railroads, land, and slaves.[21]

Other businessmen were the children and grandchildren of early farm families looking to develop opportunities emerging out of expanded settlement and increased production of marketable crops. Leading antebellum entrepreneur and politician Gabriel Cannon offers an important example of Spartanburg's homegrown business leadership. The grandson of a Virginia farmer who migrated to the upcountry around the time of the Revolution, Cannon apparently had little enthusiasm for farm life and began his career as a clerk at Cowpens Iron Foundry in the mid-1820s. Within a few years he opened his own store in New Prospect, and by the 1840s Cannon and his partner, Joseph Finger, owned and operated a cotton mill, gristmill, and store at Fingerville. Cannon's star rose higher during the last antebellum decade, when he served as the district's state senator from 1848 to 1860, president and director of the Spartanburg and Union Railroad, trustee of Reidville High School, and lieutenant governor of South Carolina. By 1860 he had amassed $77,500 in personal and property wealth, including twenty-two slaves. Cannon owed his fortune, however, not to heavy investment in a staple crop—in fact, he reported having produced just five bales of cotton in 1860—but to shrewd investments in manufacturing, mercantile operations, and railroad development.[22]

Population growth and increased market production during the 1840s aided in the rise of an important town mercantile elite. In 1842 Massachusetts native David Cook Judd arrived in Spartanburg town to open his own merchandising business after having clerked in Boston. By the late 1840s Judd was able to increase business after entering into a partnership with his brother-in-law Joseph Foster. Throughout the antebellum era creditors recognized the firm of Foster & Judd as "First Class traders" who were "G[oo]d as gold" and the best merchants in the district. Also in the 1840s Spartanburg native William T. Wilkins opened a successful mercantile business in New Prospect near the district's northern border. Gabriel Cannon and his brother Aaron operated a country store "embracing a little of everything." Existing firms also benefited from increased market activity. Jesse Cleveland's business had been in operation since he immigrated to Spartanburg town from Wilkes County, North Carolina, in 1810. By the 1830s and 1840s Cleveland was purchasing goods from a variety of locations in both the upper and lower South, including Charleston, Baltimore, and Augusta.[23]

As they expanded their sources of goods, merchants like Jesse Cleveland brought new products to Spartanburg and helped shape the consumer culture of the emerging middle class in the South. By the early 1850s merchants were advertising their stock of the latest fashions from the North. Hiram Mitchell touted his "Spring stock of goods" from New York, including "Ladies['] and gentlemen's dress goods" that were "entirely new and very desirable." The firm of Lee & Twitty advertised that they had "just returned from New York and Philadelphia" with a "careful selection of a stock of goods."[24] Wives and daughters of the rising middle class became important consumers of these products as they looked to define themselves as more cosmopolitan than many of the traditional farmers in the region. Contracts with suppliers outside South Carolina also meant that merchants would occasionally have to travel for extended periods. These merchants would have to rely on clerks to run the stores in their absence, or, in some cases, wives would gain direct experience in the mercantile business by running stores in their husbands' absence.[25] Either through consumer behavior or as helpmeet in their husbands' work, women in entrepreneurial families played an increasing role in the commercial culture of the antebellum South.

Commercial exchange and mercantile activity necessitated legal wranglings, especially in the areas of debt collection and contractual arrangements. Consequently, lawyers became more conspicuous and more influential in Spartanburg over the course of the 1840s. Among the most prosperous and oldest law practices in the district was the firm of Bobo & Edwards. Simpson Bobo founded the firm in the 1830s and by 1852 was identified as the "oldest mem[ber] of the Bar" in Spartanburg. Oliver E. Edwards joined as Bobo's partner in the late 1840s and earned Greenville lawyer-legislator Benjamin F. Perry's respect as a man of "fine bus[iness] hab[its]." An attorney in Spartanburg since 1829, Hosea J. Dean found a host of new opportunities in the 1840s after he entered into partnership with James Edward Henry. By 1850 Dean owned fifteen thousand dollars in real estate and nineteen slaves and had won a seat in the state legislature. Dean, Henry, and Bobo were leading investors in local industry and helped lead the drive for a railroad connection to eastern and western markets.[26]

A few wealthy Spartanburg residents could be counted as members of both the rural and professional elites since they applied equal energy to extensive staple-crop production and nonagricultural entrepreneurial enterprises. Town lawyer H. H. Thomson combined his legal practice with investment in an early textile operation, ownership of a mercantile business, and title to an extensive cotton plantation worth ninety thousand dollars, including ninety-one slaves. In addition to his work as an attorney, Simpson Bobo owned a substantial plantation, invested in a local textile mill, and was the largest stockholder in the South Carolina Manufacturing Company, the region's most productive iron factory. Although few Spartanburg residents made such substantial commitments to both staple-crop agriculture and economic diversification, there did exist an important area of common interest between elites. Whether focusing more heavily on staple-crop expansion or investing in the development of a mercantile and industrial base, elites wanted better market connections to the East and West. In order to accomplish this, Spartanburg leaders argued, the upcountry needed better and easier access to credit and enough political influence to force the lowcountry-dominated state legislature to address their concerns.

Soon after Spartanburg County was laid out by a 1785 act of the South Carolina legislature, residents located threats to their newfound freedoms not in the federal government or in an overseas empire but in their own newly formed state. The South Carolina Constitutions of 1778 and 1790 ensured the continued dominance of lowcountry elites. Coastal planters in parishes with some of the smallest white populations and a tiny fraction of land controlled both houses of the state legislature.[27] These elites not only withheld political equality but also restricted participation of the interior regions of the state in the market economy. Upcountry petitioners responded by repeatedly urging the legislature to support economic development of their area through improved river navigation and the appointment of local officers charged with facilitating commercial exchange. In 1789, for example, 156 citizens from Spartanburg, Union, Greenville, Chester, and York counties cited "their extreme remoteness from a Tobacco inspection" in their petition to the legislature for a tobacco inspector at Union County Courthouse. Legislative committees often rejected such requests for increased powers and infrastructural changes both because they were reluctant to share political and economic control of the state and because they were ambivalent about economic "progress." Joyce Chaplin finds that lowcountry planters, who clung to a nostalgic view of isolated farming communities even as they became further engaged in the capitalist economy, "wanted to freeze newer areas at a stage of development behind that of the coast, at a phase that avoided the lures of the market and of slavery."[28]

The upcountry's struggle for equal representation in the state continued through the 1790s and into the first decade of the 1800s until the lowcountry elite agreed to a compromise in 1808. By this compromise each election district (the local government designation had changed from county to district in 1800) or coastal parish was given one state senator, while the house of representatives would be apportioned according to a formula that weighed white population and taxable property equally. In theory, the numerous parishes of the coast and the expansion of the Black Belt into the piedmont would ensure lowcountry control of the senate, while the white majority population of the upcountry would confirm that region's dominance in the house of representatives. In reality, however, giving wealth equal consideration with white population guaranteed the continued power of the lowcountry in the lower house as well.[29]

By the early 1800s lowcountry elites were willing to grant a limited compromise, and leading citizens of the upcountry were able to tolerate the meager gains of the agreement because the two regions were becoming increasingly similar in their socioeconomic commitments. The introduction of the cotton gin in the mid-1790s permitted much of the upcountry to grow the short-staple variant of the cotton crop profitably, thus bringing a large group of farmers into the web of the market economy rather quickly. To cultivate the cotton, more farmers bought more slaves and thus forged a lasting bond with lowcountry elites in their commitment to the peculiar institution. The remarkable influx of slaves to the upcountry tells the story. William Freehling estimates that while about five-sixths of South Carolina's slaves resided in the lowcountry in 1790, by 1830 over three-fourths lived in the state's upcountry.[30] Spartanburg's gains were more modest but still reveal an increased commitment to a slave economy by the early antebellum period. In 1790 the district's white population stood at 7,907, with just 898 blacks. By 1810 the black population had more than doubled to 2,424, while the white population had increased 67 percent. The vast majority of newly purchased bondsmen and bondswomen went to toil on the farms of yeomen who owned fewer than five slaves.[31]

Despite growing agreement between regions of the state on the importance of slavery, upcountry leaders still squabbled with lowcountry politicians over the legislature's failure to assist in the creation of an adequate credit system and the improved transportation facilities necessary for market expansion. Since few farmers had cash on hand at the beginning of a crop season, merchants often sold to them on credit with an informal agreement that the debts would be paid when the commercial crops were sold. Merchants themselves would purchase from wholesalers on credit, expecting to pay up when the farmers paid for their purchases. Lacking an antebellum crop-lien law, merchants had little security for their advances. As historian Frank Byrne notes, "Credit and debt concerns plagued the everyday working lives of southern merchants."[32] Faced with such financial risk, merchants complained that the state's usury law limiting interest rates to 7 percent hurt their profit-making abilities and restricted access to credit for farmers and merchants alike. By the mid-1850s the district's newspaper, the *Carolina Spartan*, came out in favor of a slow rise in interest rates to ensure greater access to credit for farmers and more profits for merchants, arguing that "the whole political philosophy of usury laws is becoming obsolete." John Earle Bomar, one of the paper's co-owners and editors, was familiar with the economic concerns of merchants, having clerked in Alfred Tolleson's store in the late 1840s. The statewide clamor among merchants and planters for repeal of the usury law was only silenced by the economic panic of 1857, which farmers blamed on greedy creditors.[33]

In addition to "obsolete" usury laws, merchants, professionals, and commercially oriented farmers complained that the upcountry suffered from a shortage of capital because private banking interests were restricting the state bank's ability to open branches in South Carolina's interior. Opened in 1813, the Bank of the State of South Carolina (BSSC) was unusual among state banks throughout the country in two ways. First, the BSSC retained financial stability throughout the antebellum period due to the conservative management of a series of skilled presidents.[34] Second, the BSSC was one of the few state banks in the country in which the state held exclusive ownership. As a result, all private financial institutions were effectively in competition with the BSSC.

Antebellum South Carolina had no general banking law for the incorporation of private banks, and, until 1852, the legislature chartered each bank individually. These charters imposed high financial qualifications for the directors of each bank, and no bank was permitted to incur a total debt in excess of three times its capital stock. Stockholders were usually liable for twice the amount of their stock in the event the bank failed, and charter privileges were limited to a specified number of years, after which time the board had to seek a recharter from the legislature. Beyond these initial charter regulations, however, private banks in South Carolina were relatively free of heavy-handed state control through the 1830s. The state had no board of commission to supervise private banks, and the comptroller of the treasury rarely exercised his power to examine a bank's books. After the panic of 1837, however, many farmers criticized private banks for issuing paper currency without a sufficient supply of specie to back it up. When bank members looked to trade in their notes for specie, many private banks simply suspended all specie payments. In 1840 the legislature responded to such criticism with an act requiring private banks to submit monthly financial reports detailing available specie and notes in circulation. The act also penalized banks that suspended specie payments with a fine of 5 percent on all notes in circulation for each month that specie was not paid out. Private bankers who looked to take advantage of the financial needs that would come with an expanding market did not welcome these new regulations. By the late 1840s officials and investors in some private banks had directed their discontent at the BSSC. Using arguments similar to those employed against the Bank of the United States during Andrew Jackson's presidency, private bankers complained that the state's involvement in banking led to corruption and the creation of a privileged elite who legislated for their own profit to the detriment of the state's financial health. As evidence, some pointed to the fact that only the BSSC was allowed to issue bills valued at less than five dollars. One typical criticism attacked the BSSC's "Partiality, Favoritism, and Partyism."[35]

In 1848 Bank of Hamburg president Hiram Hutchinson became the principal upcountry organizer of a legislative attempt to prevent renewal of the BSSC's charter in 1856. With no banking operations nearby, however, Spartanburg representatives argued that unregulated private banks were only acting to draw capital away from the district, while the legislatively controlled BSSC could be made to serve the whole state equally. James Edward Henry, a leading opponent of the Bank of the United States during Jackson's administration, came out in favor of the BSSC in 1848. Henry, a lawyer who by the late 1840s had become an investor in Spartanburg cotton mills and railroads, argued that the bank served a positive function in bringing more currency to capital-starved regions of the state. In fact, Henry cited this probank position as the reason for his failure to win the speakership of the state house of representatives in 1848. After leading the first four ballots, he tied the fifth and lost on the sixth, convinced that the result owed more "to the question of Bank and Anti-Bank than to the popularity of the gentleman elected. He was Anti, I Bank."[36]

Unable to secure a conclusive vote against the BSSC's recharter or for the slow withdrawal of capital from the bank, anti-BSSC forces continued to attack government sponsorship of banking in the 1850s. During the 1850 legislative campaign Spartanburg candidates looked to garner support from the varied interests of small farmers, merchants, and planters by supporting the BSSC's present operations while deferring the question of the bank's recharter to a later date. Lawyer Joseph Wofford Tucker expressed opposition to any legislative action that would liquidate the bank before the end of its charter in 1856, but he also suggested uncertainty about his views on recharter. Peter M. Wallace came out against recharter at such an early time, arguing that the uncertainty of recharter would promote the good behavior of bank managers in collecting debts. A small farmer and owner of a local textile mill, Wallace suggested a new charter granting smaller loans "so that the people, the working people, may partake of its advantages if they desire it." He also opposed liquidation of the bank, arguing that it would break pledges to foreign creditors and injure the character of the state. Fellow Spartanburg manufacturer Elias C. Leitner mirrored Wallace's position on recharter and also opposed liquidation on grounds that the elimination of the BSSC would allow private banks to take over and "create a privileged order, tending inevitably to an unfeeling moneyed aristocracy more to be deprecated than monarchy itself." Candidate John T. Kirby called the BSSC a "true and valuable friend" to the agricultural, commercial, and mechanical pursuits of the country, while Esau Price referred to bank opposition as "perfect humbugry . . . only got up by a few designing capitalists, in order to cripple the operations and put asunder the Bank, so that they could sway [the] iron rod of oppression with more perfection over the heads of the oppressed." Such reference to a "few designing capitalists" resonated with smaller farmers even though support for the bank centered around the desire for more capital development in the region. Other candidates, including dentist-merchant W. C. Bennett, lawyer-industrialist Hosea J. Dean, and manufacturer Samuel N. Evins, opposed eliminating the bank before the end of its charter. Legislative victory went to Tucker, Leitner, Dean, Elihu Penquite Smith, and T. W. Waters. Statewide, the anti-BSSC forces were defeated, and in 1852 the BSSC received a new charter valid through 1871.[37]

The economic panic of 1857 placed banking back in the forefront of politics and led many to call for greater restrictions on banking operations in the state. According to Spartanburg leaders, these restrictions were best placed on private banks, which, they argued, ran roughshod over all notions of equality in the pursuit of economic prosperity. The *Carolina Spartan* expressed hope that "the general dissatisfaction of the people with the masterly manner in which the [private] banks treat them will awaken a discussion in the Legislature touching their right to lord it over all interests but their own." In the fall of 1858 a Spartanburg grand jury identified South Carolina's private banking system as "injurious to the rights, interests, and monetary affairs of the great mass of the people." The presentment objected to the legislature granting banks the exclusive privilege of promissory notes, which were circulated at a ratio of three dollars to one of capital. In addition to "giving a treble advantage to moneyed capital over all other interests in the State," the bank charters created a glut of paper currency, which increased the capital necessary for business. The jury also viewed the private banking system as unstable, causing wild price fluctuations and reckless speculation, which retarded "progress in agricultural, mechanical and manufacturing pursuits." The legislature, they argued, had lost control over the "great moneyed power," which had concentrated their wealth to a degree "contrary to republican independence." As a solution, the jury proposed the prohibition of any new bank charters and the refusal to recharter old private banks at the end of their original grants. That Spartanburg leaders remained supportive of the BSSC while attacking private banking is rather easily explained. Lacking any private banks or, for that matter, a local agency of the BSSC until 1859, Spartanburg residents watched as banks in other localities drew capital away from their region. A state bank, as E. C. Leitner explained, was the "people's bank and could not work for one class of people alone."[38]

Rural planters and town-centered professionals found basic agreement on the banking issue because both groups needed more capital to expand their commercial operations. Through the 1840s this apparent broad consensus among elites extended to district politics as well. In the upcountry the yeoman majority embraced the populist appeal of Jacksonian Democracy with its emphasis on limited federal government interference in local economic and social institutions. Rural elites opposed the rival Whig Party due in large part to its platform of federal protective tariffs and the affiliation of its northern wing with the antislavery movement. With a cross-section of planters and yeomen supporting the Democratic Party, even those who were interested in diversification programs and who may have found common ground with much of the Whig platform saw little to gain from membership in the party. In fact, the few Whigs who sought to challenge the strength of the Democrats in Spartanburg were easily defeated at the polls. Campaigning for the state house of representatives in 1838, hotel proprietor William Walker supported the Whig platform of protective tariffs, internal improvements, and a bank of the United States. Walker was soundly defeated by a slate of Van Buren Democrats led by lawyer and large slaveholder H. H. Thomson. Two years later the Democrats again carried the district in both the state representation and the presidency. In 1840 lawyer James Edward Henry enjoyed a wide margin of victory over Whig candidate James Bivings, a textile manufacturer who voiced his full support for the party's presidential candidate, William Henry Harrison.[39] Combining a commitment to commercial agriculture with investments in internal improvements and economic diversification, Thomson and Henry could have found common cause with a number of Whig initiatives. However, their substantial investments in land and slaves and the practical realities of the district's political allegiance outweighed the Whig Party's possible appeal. The 1840 election effectively ended the Whig organization in the district and the state as a whole.

One-party politics brought an atmosphere of consensus among elites and between elites and yeoman farmers in Spartanburg. Legislative candidates voiced little in the way of substantive differences, and, once in office, incumbents faced few real challenges to reelection. During the 1840s 60 percent of the district's legislators served two or more terms, and the majority of those who served one term in the decade had not sought reelection. However, beneath this apparent consensus lay subtle yet important divergences between the interests of rural and town elites. For rural planters in the district, cotton and slavery were paramount to all other interests and made South Carolina a powerful economic and political force in the South and the nation. Town elites concurred that cotton and slaves were essential to the district and the state's prosperity but added to these interests a need to diversify commercial production and establish Spartanburg town as an important trading center with markets to the north, south, east, and west. Such development would require better coordination and cooperation with other southern states. These different economic emphases between rural and town elites became manifest in the political conflict surrounding the first secession crisis of 1849–51.

Since the early 1830s Spartanburg whites had joined most other white southerners in resisting abolitionist attempts to bring the issue of slavery to the forefront of national politics. Slavery's expansion in the district during the 1840s further heightened sensitivity to any perceived attacks on the peculiar institution. At the same time, Spartanburg residents also shared with many southerners the hope that the Missouri Compromise of 1820 would ensure slavery's protection and extension in the southwestern portion of the United States. This hope was dashed in 1847 when Pennsylvania congressman David Wilmot introduced a proviso before the United States House of Representatives designed to exclude slavery from all lands acquired in the Mexican War. The Wilmot Proviso unleashed a national debate on the status of slavery in the territories and drew universal condemnation from the white South as evidence of a northern conspiracy to destroy southern property rights. Although the Wilmot Proviso was never adopted, it did contribute to the formation of the Free Soil Party, a combination of northern Democrats and Whigs whose platform demanded that western territories be open only to free white settlers. An impressive showing of the Free Soilers in 1848 unnerved white southerners and led them to threaten secession if federal guarantees for the protection of slavery in the West were not adopted.[40]

South Carolina spearheaded the secession movement. Radicals like Robert Barnwell Rhett called for the state's immediate secession, arguing that other southern states would soon follow. Learning from his prior defeat at the hands of the federal government during the nullification crisis, elder statesman John C. Calhoun warned that too much haste in plans for secession would only create division in South Carolina. Calhoun instead supported the plan introduced by the Mississippi legislature calling for a cooperative convention of southern states in Nashville to consider resistance options.[41]

Leading Spartanburg citizens initially presented a unified front against northern interference with the South's institutions. In January a large crowd gathered at the district courthouse for a meeting to address the sectional tensions. Large planter John C. Winsmith chaired the proceedings and opened by warning the audience about the designs of the "fanatical party" in the North. The great question of the South's right to hold slave property, Winsmith contended, "cannot in fact be longer evaded—it must be met and met now." State legislator James Edward Henry and state senator Gabriel Cannon also made speeches urging a unified response to the northern threat.[42]

The *Carolina Spartan* repeatedly informed whites that resistance to northern attacks on slavery were essential because "the white man and black can never occupy the same territory in this latitude, but as master and slave." In 1849, as sectional tensions over western expansion were reaching their height, the paper was taken over by Peter M. Wallace, a trained physician and small farmer who embraced immediate secession. Wallace equated any compromise on slavery's expansion with "defeat and degradation." Another supporter of immediate secession, Samuel Otterson, served as one of two delegates from South Carolina's First Congressional District at the Nashville convention in June 1850. When Otterson returned from Nashville, he expressed some discontent that the convention had produced no decisive action but looked forward to a more productive second meeting.[43]

In fact, it was this second meeting of a southern congress that produced political divisions statewide. More radical state representatives advocated the calling of a state constitutional convention to consider articles of immediate secession rather than spending more time discussing cooperation across the South. These immediate secessionists were opposed by cooperationists who favored South Carolina's participation in a second southern convention to guarantee unified support for secession among all slave states.[44] These divisions reached Spartanburg's representatives on the motion of immediate secessionists to postpone the election of delegates to a southern congress. District representatives Elihu Penquite Smith and T. W. Waters supported the motion, while Hosea J. Dean, E. C. Leitner, and Joseph Wofford Tucker voted against it. The same split occurred when immediate secessionists put forward a bill calling for a state constitutional convention.[45]

Smith and Waters represented a similar rural, agricultural interest in preserving rights in slavery. A wealthy planter with almost twenty thousand dollars of real estate and forty-three slaves in southeastern Spartanburg, Smith had been born into agricultural wealth and influence and shared the sensitivity of many southern planters to any assaults on slavery as potential threats to their power. Waters owned land worth forty-five hundred dollars and seven slaves. Although he occupied a relatively comfortable position for an upcountry yeoman, Waters's political activity reveals his ambition to build a greater estate for himself and for his five young sons. Restrictions on slavery could hamper his efforts to pass on a secure, independent estate to the next generation.

The three cooperationists also owned land and slaves, but they were far less devoted to cotton agriculture and listed their occupations as professionals and manufacturers. Hosea J. Dean was a prominent town lawyer who owned a gristmill and a sawmill and invested in area cotton factories. Fellow town lawyer Joseph Wofford Tucker championed rail development and advocated better schooling for the state's youth as a path to improved prosperity. E. C. Leitner owned a textile factory in addition to his thirty thousand dollars worth of real estate and twenty-one slaves.[46] The fact that two out of the three men opposed to calling a secession convention were town professionals is significant. Town elites were interested in developing Spartanburg town into a center of trade not only within the South Carolina upcountry but for regions throughout western North Carolina and eastern Tennessee as well. Tucker's plans for the town were even grander, as evidenced by his and his law partner James Farrow's representation of a New York company looking to drum up northern interest in settling and/or investing in Spartanburg.[47] Leitner resided in the small mill town of Bivingsville and had done business with clients across the border in North Carolina. Immediate secession, then, would risk isolation from what were viewed in Spartanburg as important markets in the development of mill and town.

Political divisions between cooperationists and immediate secessionists continued despite a compromise act passed by the general assembly in December 1850 that called for both the election of delegates to a southern congress in Nashville and a state convention to consider secession. In February 1851 voters were asked to select delegates for the state convention, scheduled to meet in October 1852. Three out of the five successful candidates had expressed a willingness to accept immediate secession. At the same time, prominent professionals and entrepreneurs worked to sustain the cooperation movement. Leading the cause for cooperation were H. H. Thomson and Simpson Bobo. Although both men were large slave owners growing over one hundred bales of cotton each in 1850, they also were lawyers with primary residences in Spartanburg town and heavy investments in an iron foundry, gristmills, and railroads.[48] Bobo in particular may have been less sensitive to concerns over the extension of slavery westward because he witnessed firsthand the application of slave labor to nonagricultural pursuits at home. Under Bobo's management the South Carolina Manufacturing Company overwhelmingly relied on slaves to work in the factory's iron foundry.[49]

In the summer of 1851 immediate secessionists and cooperationists again clashed over the impending October election of delegates to the Nashville convention. Over three hundred citizens signed a petition calling for an antisecession meeting at Spartanburg Courthouse on August 4. District advocates of immediate secession organized their own rally for the same day. Of the twenty-four men identified with organizing the antisecession gathering, seventeen lived in Spartanburg town. Only eight men listed their occupations solely as farmers. Those supporting the immediate secession meeting were overwhelmingly slave-owning farmers from rural areas of the district. The two groups each nominated their own delegates to the Nashville convention. Immediate secessionists selected U.S. Congressman Daniel Wallace of Union and Spartanburg lawyer T. O. P. Vernon, while the cooperationists put forward Union District Judge Thomas Dawkins and Samuel Rainey of York. In August H. H. Thomson attended a regimental muster, where he was convinced that two-thirds of the men were cooperationist, but he noted that the secessionists "with Dan'l Wallace at their head [are] moving heaven and earth to carry their point."[50]

One month prior to the election Spartanburg's leading citizens looked to ease tensions between immediate secessionists and cooperationists at a public barbecue honoring Daniel Wallace. However, Wallace's support of immediate secession ensured a partisan tone to the event. Local radicals made toast after toast affirming the state's right to secede. Planter John Winsmith went so far as to honor Mississippi fire-eater John A. Quitman as the future "President of a Southern Republic." Samuel N. Evins, one of the few cooperationists present, rose to his feet and, avoiding the secession debate entirely, toasted the newly chartered—and yet unbuilt—Spartanburg and Union Railroad.[51] Evins's choice for a toast revealed the attitudes of many cooperationists in Spartanburg who saw little to be gained from immediate secession in light of the district's relative isolation from markets. In the early 1850s the district still had no railroad connections or substantial plank roads with links to trading centers in the East or West. If other southern states did not immediately follow South Carolina out of the Union, Spartanburg could be cut off from commerce to the north and west and be left at the mercy of lowcountry representatives who had already shown a consistent unwillingness to support significant improvements of the state's interior.

The October election resulted in a victory for cooperationist delegates throughout South Carolina by a vote of 24,909 to 17,471. In Spartanburg the vote was close, with cooperationists securing just under 55 percent of the ballots cast. Not surprisingly, election precincts in the cotton-producing southern half of the district overwhelmingly supported immediate secession. Interest in staple-crop agriculture had spread across this region between 1840 and 1850, attracting yeomen who planted cotton on even the smallest surplus land.[52] Looking to become more prosperous through increased cotton cultivation and the acquisition of more slaves, yeomen as well as planters in the southern half of the district found much to fear in federal restrictions on slave property. James Oakes makes a forceful case that by the late antebellum period slave ownership had become the principal measure of success for many slaveholding and nonslaveholding whites alike. Although some yeomen might disapprove of the aristocratic haughtiness of planters, they nevertheless looked forward to a time when they could purchase their own slaves. This interest in slave ownership as a path to prosperity went hand in hand with the special allure of western lands for southern yeomen. By the late 1840s upcountry farmers faced the problem of exhausted soil, and many had already left the state in search of more fertile lands to the west.[53] Movements to restrict slavery in the western territories thus appeared to threaten the future success of slaveless and small slaveholding yeomen.

While planters and farmers in Spartanburg's southern region generally embraced immediate secession, people in the town of Spartanburg and precincts near the district's northern border constituted the core of cooperationist strength. Townsmen, residents of mill villages along the Pacolet River, and hardscrabble provision crop farmers in the northernmost stretches of the district saw little to be gained from a rash, independent action on secession. Although town merchants, professionals, and entrepreneurs opposed the Wilmot Proviso and any efforts to restrict slavery, they felt less direct emotional and economic connection to the western territorial issue. These men were more concerned with development over time, not space.[54] Merchants, manufacturers, and professionals wished to build an infrastructure that would create greater links to market centers and attract more people and business to the district. In fact, rather than look to the West exclusively as a land of opportunity, these men often complained about the westward drain on Spartanburg's population and looked for ways to keep families in the district.

During the nine years between the 1851 cooperationist victory and South Carolina's secession from the Union in December 1860, Spartanburg town's position and influence within the district increased significantly.⁵⁵ This expansion was in part a reflection of increased focus on marketable crops in the surrounding region. Between 1840 and 1850 cotton production in the district increased 40 percent, while the slave population experienced a 71 percent jump.⁵⁶ Although the annual yield of staple crops leveled off during the 1850s, the accelerated need for a local center of trade and stores to supply the requirements of more substantial farming operations boosted town development. During the 1850s wheat production experienced an increase of almost 38 percent. Considering that the district population remained stagnant through the last antebellum decade, this increase reflects accelerated production of wheat for the market.⁵⁷ The bulk of this market exchange remained local, and Spartanburg town acted as the central point for most transactions.

During the 1850s town population also increased. In 1850 Spartanburg claimed 1,176 residents, of which 504 were white. All of the black inhabitants were listed as slaves, with approximately 20 percent being owned by H. H. Thomson and Simpson Bobo. Ten years later the town's white population had more than doubled to 1,187. Total figures for the 1860 slave population are unavailable, but it is likely that the numbers followed the districtwide trend of a 2–3 percent increase. Overall, white residents of Spartanburg town accounted for 6 percent of the white population in the district. Although these numbers might appear small, it is important to recognize that only Greenville had a larger white population than Spartanburg in the South Carolina upcountry of 1860.⁵⁸ As a result, Spartanburg was one of the few centers of commercial, legal, and social activity.

Mercantile business boomed over the course of the last antebellum decade as the demand for farm supplies and general necessities increased. Some skilled businessmen amassed considerable fortunes as a result of skillful trading and careful bookkeeping. Albert Bivings and Robert E. Cleveland maintained a thriving business worth about one hundred thousand dollars by 1860. B. F. Bates's success with his Batesville general store helped him acquire at least twenty thousand dollars in valuable real estate and slaves.

Others were a bit too ambitious and speculative in their transactions. Merchant and hotel keeper Alfred Tolleson overextended himself by "taking anything that [came] his way" and became indebted to wholesale distributors in major cities. A "considerably embarrassed" Tolleson had to sell the Palmetto House hotel to settle claims against him. The determined businessman rebounded quickly and by 1858 owned another hotel and a dry goods store that he operated with his sons. Creditors identified Tolleson as "a thriving bus[iness] man" who had made his fortune from "comparatively little."[59]

Between 1850 and 1855 the value of town lots catapulted from $44,175 to $122,968.[60] Area newspapers commented on the construction of "new and elegant" brick businesses replacing wood frame houses on the public square. With an increasing demand for new construction, Spartanburg witnessed an influx of coach makers, cabinetmakers, brick masons, stonemasons, carpenters, and mechanics. The *Carolina Spartan* reported that Spartanburg town had in operation

> thirteen dry-goods establishments; two saddlery and harness establishments; two confectionary and druggist stores; one furniture room—any articles manufactured here; three carriage manufactories; five blacksmith shops; two shoe and boot making rooms; three tailoring establishments; three excellent hotels; three commodious churches, and another in progress of construction; two Academies, male and female; two day-schools for smaller pupils; lawyers and doctors a-plenty, and lots and cords of kind, courteous and excellent people![61]

Recognizing that commercial business and industry could not develop solely through local investment and initiative, town leaders encouraged outside investments through public advertisements and special incentives. Lawyers Joseph Wofford Tucker and James Farrow jumped at the chance to represent a New York real estate firm interested in the "inducements to invest capital in Manufacturing, Mechanical, Mercantile and other pursuits" in Spartanburg. Tucker and Farrow urged those selling or leasing their property to consider the tens of thousands of New Yorkers seeking investments in the South. Since a large portion of surplus capital in the country was centered in New York and thousands of the "better classes" of immigrants—those with industrial wealth—were arriving in that state's

Table 3. Farm Value and Agricultural Production, Spartanburg District, 1850–1860

	1850	1860	% change
Total farm acres	561,947	612,549	+9.0
Value of farmland	$2,659,146	$4,388,642	+65.0
Value of livestock	$657,161	$865,620	+31.7
Wheat produced	102,993 bu.	141,648 bu.	+37.5
Corn produced	873,654 bu.	800,960 bu.	−8.3
Oats produced	153,562 bu.	48,145 bu.	−68.6
Cotton produced	6,671 bales	6,279 bales	−5.9
Wool produced	22,348 lb.	21,639 lb.	−3.2
Potatoes produced	92,880 bu.	112,632 bu.	+21.3

Sources: U.S. Bureau of the Census, *Seventh Census*, 345–47, and *Agriculture*, 128–31.

Table 4. Value of Merchandise, Professions, and Land in Spartanburg District

Year	Value of goods and merchandise	Value of professions	Value of lots	Value of land	Total taxes
1846	$42,132	$8,085	$54,195	$266,977	$4,672.66
1850	$42,821	$10,030	$44,175	$263,818	$5,433.39
1855	$199,535	$17,576	$122,968	$267,205	$6,652.36
1860	$295,099	$16,289	$162,640	$261,340	$13,285.18

Source: Compiled from "Reports of the Comptroller General," in *Reports and Resolutions of the General Assembly of the State of South Carolina*, 1846–60.

harbors every day, it was logical to attract these men to the district that could offer "greater facilities for manufacturing and mechanical enterprize" than any other section in the South or West. "Nothing," Tucker and Farrow proclaimed, "can contribute more to advance the physical prosperity of our section" than such northern investment.[62]

This clear connection between Spartanburg's success and northern investment is reflective of the prewar business and cultural ties that historian Jonathan Wells identifies between the northern and southern middle class. Wells finds that travel, migration, and news kept each region aware of events and opportunities in the other region.[63] As already demonstrated in this chapter, some of Spartanburg's early entrepreneurs were from New England. Continued interest in and awareness of northern commercial and cultural life would influence the plans of Spartanburg's entrepreneurs.

Although most business leaders viewed the increasing property values around Spartanburg as a positive change, some feared it would act as a double-edged sword. On the one hand, rising real estate costs signified a growing economy. However, if prices inflated too quickly, investment in the region might stall. The *Carolina Spartan* reported that "gentlemen of highest respectability, and possessed of large fortunes" were considering buying improved and unimproved lots in the district but that the high price of real estate might tip the scales against their decision to make any purchases. Such a loss of investment would deprive Spartanburg of men who would "contribute a great deal to [the town's] social and pecuniary improvement and importance."[64]

With property values on the rise and the prospect of Spartanburg town becoming an important upcountry trading center, some townsmen looked to increase the town's revenue while obtaining greater control over town growth. In 1853 a group of forty-four town residents petitioned the legislature to amend the town charter so that an annual tax could be levied on "all Lots[,] Lands[,] and Buildings, Merchandise[,] stock in trade of all kind, and Negroes within the corporate Limits of the Town, not exceding Ten Cents on every one hundred dollars of the Value thereof." The petitioners also wanted the state to give the town council the power to tax carriages, horses, saloons, cockfights, and bowling alleys and the right to own real estate. Finally, the petitioners requested that the town council be granted the authority to force owners of town lots to keep them in "*good Repair*" and ensure that all sidewalks were of sufficient width. Before the Committee on Incorporations took up the matter, however, some of the petitioners expressed second thoughts about granting such a large expansion of the council's powers, and the petition was not adopted.[65]

Town leaders also became increasingly influential in districtwide affairs. Most of the proactive initiatives sponsored by Spartanburg legislators during the 1850s came from town professionals. Between 1848 and 1860 manufacturer and town resident Gabriel Cannon served as Spartanburg's sole state senator and championed a host of initiatives for infrastructural and institutional development in the upcountry. In the state house of representatives Tucker and Farrow led a drive for state funding of upcountry railroads and reforms in education and law. Other Spartanburg town professionals in the state legislature during the 1850s included lawyers Dean, Edwards, and J. V. Trimmier.[66]

The substantial rise of town influence over the last antebellum decade drew concern from people in the rural countryside that there was an emerg-

Table 5. Spartanburg State Legislators, 1850–1860

Name	Occupation	1850 Real estate	1850 Slaves	1860 Real estate	1860 Slaves
Gabriel Cannon	Manufacturer	n.a.	14	$15,000	22
Elias C. Leitner	Manufacturer	$30,000	22	—*	—*
Joseph Wofford Tucker	Lawyer	$3,000	4	—*	—*
T. W. Waters	Farmer	$4,500	7	n.a.	n.a.
Elihu Penquite Smith	Merchant-farmer	$19,300	44	$43,200	41
Hosea J. Dean	Lawyer	$15,000	19	deceased	—
John C. Winsmith	Farmer-physician	$35,000	61	$41,000	99
B. F. Bates	Merchant-farmer	$6,000	6	$14,500	22
J. V. Trimmier	Lawyer	$0	0	n.a.	n.a.
J. W. Miller	Farmer	$11,000	22	n.a.	48
W. M. Foster	Farmer	$0	0	$2,500	8
Oliver E. Edwards	Lawyer	$0	0	$12,000	12
James Farrow	Lawyer	$0	0	$6,800	0
O. P. Earle	Farmer	$0	0	$11,000	12
Benjamin F. Kilgore	Physician	$10,000	51	$32,000	63
AVERAGE		$9,557	17	$19,778	33

Source: Manuscript Census Returns, Population and Slave Schedules, Spartanburg District and County, 1850 and 1860, NA.
*Leitner and Tucker left Spartanburg District in the 1850s.

ing polarization of interests in the district. Evidence of rural suspicion of town initiatives is revealed in public pronouncements designed to preserve district unity. "Viewed in the relation of producers and consumers," an article in the *Carolina Spartan* proclaimed, "there is a much greater identity of interest between the people of a Town and the surrounding country than many might first imagine." The article assured that "the prosperity which may come to our town will not—cannot be confined to the contracted limits of our corporation; but will go—must go—by the unerring and uncontrollable laws of Providence to every nook and corner of our District." These providential laws linked the destinies of town and country "even though for the moment our attitude to each other may seem that of opposition."[67]

Laurens District, to the immediate south of Spartanburg, encountered similar town-country conflicts. The *Carolina Spartan* reprinted a column from the *Laurensville Herald* urging country people to see their welfare connected to the town's prosperity. Acknowledging country prejudices toward the town of Laurensville, the article called for a "spirit of reconciliation." The column maintained that since the town was the center of market activity, "the more business is concentrated at this point, the better market it will afford the farmers and planters; but when the people of the country permit prejudices toward each other to bias them, they inflict injuries to the interests of each party." Villagers were defended as those "looked to to subscribe most of the money and provide the fountain to set in motion" any new enterprise for the good of the district. The article then condemned those farmers who saw no benefit in towns as illiberal old fogies who "would have all the lawyers, merchants, mechanics, and men of science and literature put between the plow handles and made to till the soil." Only when town and country recognized mutual interests could the district truly prosper.[68]

The town-country division in Spartanburg threatened to open wider over the issue of taxation. In early 1857 a change in the distribution of town taxes stipulated that all funds accruing from the town's taxable property would be applied exclusively to the benefit of the town. A group of citizens from Grassy Pond—a neighborhood in the northeastern corner of the district— objected to this change, arguing that "the Town and District ought to be mutually dependent, each upon the other, and that the funds accrued from each should enure reciprocally to the benefit of both." Since the incorporated town had a greater concentration of wealth, it seemed only equitable that the taxes be used on roads, schools, and watercourses throughout the district. The Grassy Pond group expressed frustration that "under the present arrangement it appears the ancient maxim 'Private interest must give way to the public good,' has entirely lost its validity, and in this instance the public good is clearly yielding to what is comparatively private interests."[69]

A supporter of the town taxation method replied that the Grassy Pond group had gotten their facts wrong. In 1855 an act of the legislature amended the town charter so that taxes for roads and bridges would be spent within the town. All other taxes, however, went to either the state or the district treasury. As such, the town supporter argued, it was really the town that had the legitimate complaint of unequal tax distribution, not the countryside.[70]

Recognizing that animosity between town and country threatened overall development, some Spartanburg residents urged townspeople to make tangible signs of commitment to the district. One important overture, the *Carolina Spartan* suggested, would be for the wealthy townspeople to remain in Spartanburg during the summer months rather than head northward to

Saratoga Springs, Newport, and similar resort towns. Spartanburg District had several well-respected resort springs that, if patronized by local residents, would promote the "distribution of the surplus the wealthy have at their disposal among our own people, to foster enterprise and promote homogeneity, without which there can scarcely be stability of institutions."[71]

In the early stages of Spartanburg's settlement and growth, a rural elite emerged and exerted primary influence on the district's economy and polity. By the early 1800s an embryonic town-based elite also began to take shape that was composed primarily of merchants, lawyers, doctors, and other professionals. Initially, rural and town elites shared a common interest in developing the commercial opportunities of the district. As the town developed and professional interests increased, however, subtle differences emerged in the economic and political interests of the two groups. These distinctions became readily apparent in political conflicts surrounding the first secession crisis. Through the 1850s the influence of Spartanburg town in the district's economy and polity increased, drawing suspicion from rural elites and yeoman farmers regarding the overall community benefits of town-led developmental initiatives. This suspicion would present one important challenge to town leaders looking to expand the region's infrastructure and institutions. Plans for diversification and change were also hindered by the state legislature's general reluctance to support upcountry development. The precise nature of town-led plans for diversification through internal improvements is explored in the next chapter.

CHAPTER TWO

"We Must Manufacture"

Textiles and Transportation in the Antebellum Era

IN APRIL 1849 young Spartanburg lawyer Joseph Wofford Tucker warned his community that they faced a critical moment in history. While speaking in support of the proposed Spartanburg and Union Railroad, Tucker argued that the line was "*the only means* of increasing the future prosperity of our District—the only means to prevent its impoverishment and agricultural decay and ruin." The competing railroad interests of the surrounding districts, he noted, left Spartanburg little choice but to fight for a route through its own lands. "Has Spartanburg lost its independent spirit—its proud unbending soul?" Tucker inquired. "Has the Old Iron District bowed its head? Does it bite the dust in token of prostration and submission to inferiority?"[1]

Tucker used language that the southern yeoman could clearly understand. Among the nineteenth-century southern yeoman's most sacred principles were independence, individual strength and power, and a revulsion to anything that would place him in an inferior position.[2] Tucker linked the railroad and resulting market opportunities directly to these principles. If Spartanburg residents refused to support a railroad, they would relinquish their independence and declare their inferiority to the world. Tucker and other railroad supporters went even further. Railroad development, market expansion, and diversification were crucial not only to their society's progress but to their society's very survival. By turning their heads away from development, people would not merely be standing still, they would be regressing to a lesser stage of civilization. Citing the potential to tap the enormous cotton region to the south and east and the timber and mineral resources to the north and west, a *Carolina Spartan* editorial urged the people to "build up our stupendous temples of *labor* and worship at their altar. In a word, we must *manufacture*. We must do *handi-work*. We must make of Iron, Cotton, Wool and Flax, of Wood and Stone, Leather, &c., the things that men need, and which they must have or go down into barbarism."[3]

The hyperbole of Spartanburg's booster rhetoric was not especially unusual in the nineteenth century. In a time when speeches and broadsides were the dominant form of persuasion, politicians and economic promoters pushed their agendas as if society's very future depended upon the outcome. What was a bit more distinct was the sustained and comprehensive nature of Spartanburg's booster rhetoric in the antebellum South. As town-oriented professionals and merchants increased their local political and economic influence, they looked to mold the community toward their interests. These interests, supporters of diversification argued, would forward the interests of all white Spartanburg residents while strengthening the foundations of black slavery. However, not all Spartanburg citizens agreed with booster rhetoric that the community's salvation would be in railroads and industry. Instead, divisions over the district's economic future would emerge between rural and town elites and between town elites and a portion of the yeomanry.

Interest in diversification through industrial development derived in large part from the topographical and geological features of Spartanburg's landscape. Four swift-moving rivers with a series of shoals and their tributaries offered a seemingly unlimited power source for machine operations. The northern portion of Spartanburg's geology held its own potential for prosperity with significant veins of precious minerals, including granite, gold, silver, copper, limestone, graphite, and, most abundantly, iron ore.[4] Small limestone quarries and gold and silver mines were opened early in the district's settlement, but it was iron ore that offered the most promise for large-scale industry.

The Spartanburg region was particularly well suited to the iron industry because it contained the five natural resources necessary for production: iron ore, extensive hardwood forests for fuel, fast-flowing rivers for power, limestone as a fluxing agent in iron production, and building stone for the factories. In 1773 William Wofford of Maryland began the first foundry operations on Lawson's Fork, a tributary of the Pacolet River and an important source of water power. The ironworks continued production until it was burned during the American Revolution.[5] A series of small foundries followed until the South Carolina Manufacturing Company emerged as the most successful iron factory in the antebellum upper piedmont. Chartered in the 1820s, the South Carolina Manufacturing Company began operations in the 1830s with investments from manager Simpson Bobo, Gabriel Cannon, William Clark, and Vardry McBee. With one hundred thousand dollars in capital investment by 1860, the factory produced nails and iron castings in rolling mills, forges, and furnaces on about twenty-five thousand acres adjacent to the Pacolet River. Creditors estimated that the South Carolina Manufacturing Company paid out at least a 7 percent return on investments in the late 1850s. Other area iron foundries included the Nesbitt Iron Works and Coopersville Iron Works, with its main factory in Union District and substantial land in Spartanburg, as well as the Kings Mountain Iron Company in western York District.[6]

Beyond the notable exception of the South Carolina Manufacturing Company, however, the iron industry in the upcountry struggled and declined over the course of the 1840s and 1850s. On a visit to the Nesbitt Iron Works in 1843 Edmund Ruffin was impressed by the factory's rolling mill, extensive nail factory, large flour mill, and "workshops of every kind necessary." Ruffin added, however, that half of the several hundred thousand dollars invested in the factory was already gone, and the Virginian predicted no profits due to "the intoxication of paper-money banking."[7]

The experience of James S. M. Davis reflects the struggles encountered by iron makers in the Spartanburg region. Davis moved from the North in the early 1840s to take over management first of the Susan Furnace in Union District and then of the Glen Furnace in Spartanburg. Once at Glen Furnace, Davis found the company in serious debt due to the high cost of labor, both slave and free, and the limited availability of coal. "[Y]ou know it take[s] coal & men to carry on a furnace," Davis wrote his wife, Marion, in 1845, "& it takes meal & bred to feed them [and] a grate many other things & you know I had none of these things." He was all the more frustrated because he had "a considerable metal on hand yet which if I had time I could turn into mony after it is maid into nails." A somber Davis concluded that "the Furnace will blow out in a few days & I shall have nothing [to] do but to settl up & come home."[8]

The two main reasons for the decline of iron manufacturing were increasing labor costs and competition from Pennsylvania anthracite regions. Since iron work required heavy labor and involved the use of dangerous machinery, managers most often relied on slave workers. Indeed, the potential dangers were very real, as one ex-slave recalled a worker being drawn into a rolling mill at Coopersville. The machine mangled the slave's body to such a degree that a special elongated coffin had to be made for his burial. Such a reliance on slaves placed the iron companies at a disadvantage when slave prices rose in the 1850s.⁹

When a Swedish company purchased the Nesbitt Iron Works in July 1850, the management attempted to reduce the factory's dependence on slave labor. Recognizing that iron work now had the same stigma as slave's work from the perspective of white southerners, the Swedish Iron Manufacturing Company's president, C. W. Hammerscold, wrote to Sweden "to engage experienced and competent workmen" for the factory. In January 1851 about forty Swedes "of stalwart frames and intelligent countenances" arrived at the foundry.¹⁰ Other iron entrepreneurs, however, had to either pay the rising costs of slave labor or scale back operations.

Competition from the anthracite coal regions of Pennsylvania dealt a severe blow to upcountry foundries. Anthracite furnaces provided a much cheaper fuel for iron production than the charcoal used in South Carolina. These savings allowed northern iron manufacturers to ship their products to major southern cities, including Columbia and Charleston. However, transportation remained difficult and costly for entrepreneurs in the Spartanburg region. Iron producers closer to home like Simpson Bobo saw their factories remain isolated from transportation lines. Indeed, an oft-repeated justification for railroad development was its potential to free the state from dependence on northern iron while generating healthy profits for manufacturers.¹¹

The second major industry to employ the abundant water power found in the district was the textile industry. Such manufacturing interest in Spartanburg dated back to the period of economic expansion following the War of 1812. From 1816 to 1830 textile factories in the Spartanburg area were akin to a colonial outpost of Rhode Island manufacturers, as four such ventures were launched by Providence natives. Providence was the site of mills belonging to Samuel Slater, America's first textile factory owner. Slater had completed his first mill at Pawtucket in 1793. The British-born industrialist employed women and children from nearby farms to spin yarn. The yarn was then sent to local homes, where men and women would weave the yarn into cloth. This combination of factory and home production was well suited to the agrarian nature of the early republic. By 1815 competition from several new mills in the Providence area as well as a flood of new British goods led enterprising businessmen to look for virgin territory suitable for factory operations.¹² Spartanburg appeared adaptable to the Providence system since it afforded rivers surrounded by yeoman farms.

The first factory, the South Carolina Cotton Manufactory, commenced textile production in 1816 with five hundred spindles on the banks of the Tyger River. Another group of Rhode Island immigrants brought heavy machinery with them to set up their factory in 1819. By 1825 this mill was operating with 432 spindles and 8 looms. Ten years later, Leonard Hill, then sole proprietor of the factory, sought to expand the mill's operations and entered into partnership with lawyer and fellow Rhode Island native James Edward Henry.[13] By the 1840s Henry would emerge as the district's most prominent politician and booster of industrial expansion. These northern middle-class immigrants would continue to influence the commercial culture of Spartanburg throughout the antebellum era.[14]

This early activity of New England industrialists intertwined with native interest in the district's manufacturing potential. Early native investors included Simpson Bobo, H. H. Thomson, and Hosea J. Dean. Bobo's and Thomson's substantial slaveholdings and staple-crop production fit some historians' assessments that manufacturing investment in the antebellum South came from large planters whose interest in industry was ancillary to agricultural production.[15] Yet both Bobo and Thomson were also town lawyers with diversified interests in ironworks, gristmills, and railroads. Likewise, Dean was a Spartanburg lawyer with an array of commercial investments.[16]

By the 1840s and early 1850s the shock of an agricultural depression combined with growing sectional tensions to produce public campaigns for crop diversification and industrial expansion throughout South Carolina.[17] The economic panic of 1837 and its aftermath revealed to many the potential perils of cotton monoculture. Sectionalism growing out of the Mexican War alerted prescient Carolinians to the South's overreliance on northern manufactured goods. These men argued that southern self-sufficiency in manufacturing would permit the region to end commercial ties with the North, if necessary, and still maintain a healthy, independent economy.

In order to achieve this independent economy, however, southern industrial promoters would first have to ape northern mill technology and culture. Although the Providence system served as an important stage in America's factory development, its reliance on coordination between factory workers, domestic producers, and merchants to provide raw cotton and market the finished goods limited profitability and opportunities for expansion. In the 1820s a group of investors in Massachusetts, including Francis Cabot Lowell, created a central textile complex on the Merrimac River. By the

1830s the Lowell system had integrated all aspects of textile production—from raw cotton to finished cloth—in one place. The Lowell system also shifted ownership from a simple partnership to a limited liability corporation of investors.[18] Some Carolinians interested in expanding the region's industrial base, the most notable of whom was William Gregg, recognized the advantage of the Lowell system.[19] These same southerners were well aware, however, that the Lowell system required enormous initial investment, which meant a substantial economic risk as well.

By the mid-1840s Gregg had emerged as the leading proponent of industrial development in South Carolina. Having acquired considerable wealth as a Charleston jeweler, Gregg and his brother-in-law bought the Vaucluse Manufacturing Company in the early 1840s. A four-story cotton mill employing fifty workers in Barnwell District, Vaucluse was one of the largest textile operations in South Carolina at the time. Although Gregg revealed an aptitude for managing industry by bringing Vaucluse out of significant debt, he was hampered by the limited machinery and the factory's focus on local rather than national markets.[20] In 1844 Gregg toured New England textile mills and found the Lowell system with its corporate structure, company towns, and wider market connections to be the preferred industrial future for South Carolina.[21]

In a bid to create a new Lowell-oriented approach to southern manufacturing, Gregg divested himself of Vaucluse and worked with partners to gain a charter for the Graniteville Manufacturing Company in 1845. Located in Edgefield District, Graniteville began with a substantial initial investment of three hundred thousand dollars. Historian Tom Downey notes that the nature of this investment marked an important change in the region's approach to factory development. "The primary Graniteville investors," Downey argues, "were not 'men of property,' but rather 'men of capital.'... Men of property operated on a small-scale and individual basis, but men of capital pooled resources in highly capitalized, corporate ventures."[22] These investors included bankers, merchants, and entrepreneurs who invested in a host of nonagricultural ventures. Graniteville's success would have an important influence on similar "men of capital" in Spartanburg.

Factory operations began at Graniteville in 1849 with over three hundred employees, nine thousand spindles, three hundred looms, and an annual value of almost $275,000. Following the Lowell system, the factory relied exclusively on white labor and provided housing, churches, and schools for employees.²³ In the mid-1850s Graniteville stood as South Carolina's singular example of a successful, well-integrated, corporate textile factory. Spartanburg's residents interested in expanding industry found promise in Graniteville's example. The *Carolina Spartan* devoted its front page to Gregg's 1855 annual report to Graniteville's stockholders. In analyzing the report, editor Peter M. Wallace felt certain that if Spartanburg investors followed Gregg's advice, "a great and wonderful advancement, in all the elements of wealth and happiness would be the result." Spartanburg's geography beckoned new factories with its rivers "ever rolling and thundering down their rugged declivities . . . inviting the appliances of our skill and industry." Indeed, despite Gregg's report that Graniteville stockholders had received an 18 percent profit, Wallace asserted that an existing cotton factory in Spartanburg "pays a much better percentage than even Graniteville itself." Wallace could hardly understand why district residents, with such facts before them, continued to put their funds into land and slaves "when a far more pleasant and profitable business and equally respectable, may be found in the manufacture of Cotton and the making of cotton cloth."²⁴

Despite the seeming potential offered by Graniteville's example, however, difficulties in securing necessary capital and machinery and poor transportation links to markets hamstrung many industrial efforts in Spartanburg. Wallace's characterization of cotton manufacturing as a "pleasant and profitable business" was betrayed by his own struggles with the industry. In 1853 Wallace bought a Spartanburg factory for $150,000. Two years later he owed creditors almost $9,000 despite having almost $3,000 worth of yarn on hand. As one creditor explained, Wallace found it difficult to unload the yarn "due to hard times." By January 1859 he had developed a reputation for drunkenness, separated from his wife, and watched his property sold at public auction.²⁵

Wallace was not alone in his struggles to make textile manufacturing profitable. James L. Hill's cotton factory on the Tyger River in the southern portion of the district suffered indebtedness throughout the 1850s, and creditors were predicting the company's failure by 1860. At the Bivingsville factory owner Elias C. Leitner faced a dire situation by the mid-1850s. Listed as "hopelessly insolvent," with outstanding judgments against him totaling over fifty thousand dollars, a desperate Leitner apparently committed forgery to obtain the necessary cash from a variety of banks in the state. By January 1855 Leitner had fled to the West, with law enforcement "after him with a sharp stick."²⁶

Not all textile firms faced such profound economic difficulties. Prior to Leitner's economic fiasco at Bivingsville, original owner James Bivings ran the factory profitably in the 1830s and 1840s. Having gained experience at textile mills in Lincolnton, North Carolina, Bivings brought stonemasons, machinists, and machinery with him to the Lawson's Fork tributary of the Pacolet River. By the late 1840s, however, a bitter disagreement with stockholders, including Leitner and Simpson Bobo, led Bivings to divest himself of Bivingsville and open the Crawfordsville factory on the Middle Tyger River.[27] Crawfordsville was rated as being as solvent as any business in South Carolina, and, with forty thousand dollars in capital investment, Bivings and his son were described as "safe, close, shrewd businessmen." Samuel Morgan purchased Peter Wallace's failed Cedar Hill factory in 1859, which was found to be "as good as any firm in the State for all their contracts" just one year later. Gabriel Cannon and Joseph Finger also operated a moderately successful textile mill in Fingerville on the northern reaches of the Pacolet River.[28]

John Bomar and Company emerged as the most successful textile firm in antebellum Spartanburg. Bomar purchased the Bivingsville factory in 1855 with the help of significant investments from Greenville entrepreneur Vardry McBee, Spartanburg industrial investor Samuel N. Evins, hotelkeeper John C. Zimmermann, and Simpson Bobo. In addition to receiving strong financial backing from these wealthy investors, Bomar's factory also benefited from the arrival of an experienced mill worker from the North, Dexter Edgar Converse. Raised by his uncle, a textile manufacturer in Canada, Converse had learned the ins and outs of manufacturing by the time he was eighteen. At age twenty-one he took a position in a cotton mill at Cohoes Falls, New York, where he worked for five years before seeking new opportunities at a mill in Lincolnton, North Carolina, in 1854. A year later Converse moved to Spartanburg, where he purchased an interest in the Bivingsville factory and became its manager. The New Englander's skillful management, along with stockholders worth about $500,000, ensured that Bivingsville became "one of the strongest concerns" in Spartanburg by 1860. In that year Spartanburg's six textile mills ranked highest in South Carolina, representing a capital investment of over $140,000 and an annual product value of almost $88,000.[29]

In addition to utilizing the knowledge of northern factory managers, southern factory owners also continued to rely on the North for machinery. Bivingsville was one of a number of upcountry mills that bought equipment

Table 6. Textile Mills in Spartanburg District, 1850

Mill	Capital	Operatives	Value of products
South Tyger Manufacturing Co.	$12,000	22	$11,000
Bivingsville	$63,200	52	$32,000
Crawfordsville	$10,400	11	$10,500
Pacolet Manufacturing Co.	$10,000	15	$9,720
Hill's Factory	$4,000	14	$5,400
TOTAL	$99,600	114	$68,620

Source: Manuscript Census Returns, Schedule 5: Products of Industry, 1850, Spartanburg District and County, SCDAH.

Table 7. Textile Mills in Spartanburg District, 1860

| Mill | Capital | Machinery | | Operatives | Value of products |
		Spindles	Looms		
Fingerville	$11,000	396	0	18	$9,000
Bivingsville	$50,000	1,435	26	58	$34,070
Crawfordsville	$40,000	n.a.	n.a.	26	$16,340
Hill's Factory	$15,000	500	0	16	$6,260
Cedar Hill	$12,475	800	0	19	$12,777
Valley Falls	$12,000	420	0	14	$9,500
TOTAL	$140,475	3,551	26	151	$87,947
% OF STATE TOTAL	17.5	n.a.	n.a.	17	12.3

Sources: Manuscript Census Returns, Schedule 5: Products of Industry, 1860, Spartanburg District and County, SCDAH; U.S. Bureau of the Census, *Manufactures*, 559.

from P. Whitin & Sons of Whitinsville, Massachusetts. Converse corresponded with Whitin for the purchase of looms. Other South Carolina industrialists engaged with Whitin included McBee and Sons of neighboring Greenville and Graniteville's William Gregg.[30] These business relationships with northern suppliers were crucial to the success of southern factories.

Although upcountry mill activity was rather impressive by South Carolina's standards, it paled in comparison to agrarian interests. For example, the value of animals slaughtered, just one important element of the Spartanburg rural economy, exceeded the product value of the district's textile mills by nearly 200 percent in 1860. Likewise, a 22 percent increase in mill product values between 1850 and 1860 did not keep pace with the nearly 38 percent rise in wheat production over the same decade. As long as agricultural products commanded good prices, districtwide interest in industrial investment remained low. Agrarian interests were also labor intensive, leaving few workers for nonagricultural pursuits. Some early textile operations may have used slave labor, but steadily rising prices for cotton and marketable provision crops in the late 1840s and 1850s pushed slave prices beyond a profitable investment for most textile factory owners. The costs of raw materials also increased, leaving even less available capital for wages.[31] These considerations led mill owners to use white labor in the factories. However, late antebellum expansion in important areas of agricultural production meant competition for white labor from enterprising farmers.[32]

Spartanburg's cotton mills, like those in New England, relied on women and children for labor both to help keep labor costs down and to utilize more delicate hands for threading operations. In 1860 the district's textile mills employed eighty-seven women and sixty-five men. Mill owners like James Bivings advertised their preference for young women employees and even offered homes for some families.[33] For poor families the mills offered a means by which women and young girls could contribute to the family income. In 1860 day laborer Zecheriah Tennison's four daughters—ages twelve to nineteen—worked as factory hands alongside Tennison's eleven-year-old son. Fellow day laborers Drewry McMakin, James Turner, John Hymin, and William Henry Stone all had daughters employed at area mills. A young woman's mill work could be essential to widows with little or no estate. Forty-eight-year-old Mary Groning, for example, relied on the factory work of her three daughters, who ranged in age from fifteen to twenty-six.[34] Although these examples make clear that some poorer white families in Spartanburg turned to factory employment as an important source of supplemental income, mill promoters would continue to face difficulties in expanding production as long as the appeal of industrial labor did not extend to wider segments of the white population.

In addition to competition for labor from relatively profitable farming operations, manufacturers faced a cultural bias against factory wage labor. Throughout the South a prevailing ideology held that only those who controlled productive property were free of exploitation and able to enjoy the full fruits of citizenship. Thus, independent landownership was the ultimate form of freedom. Landless whites viewed agricultural work as the primary path to acquiring real estate. Through the first several decades of the nineteenth century the North shared this basic emphasis on private landownership as essential to independence. However, increased urbanization and industrialization as well as a dearth of arable farmlands brought about a shift in the rhetoric of many northern political leaders. This new rhetoric argued that dependent labor was often a stage toward independent control of property.[35] Some southern visitors to the North recognized the potential for such a shift in free-labor ideology to make the white worker no better than a slave. Spartanburg resident Thomas John Moore received a letter from a relative traveling in New York who seemed shocked that he could "tell a white man to black his boots with impunity."[36] Factory work, then, was dependent labor in a region where anything less than independent mastery meant compromising one's rights in the republic.

Northern abolitionists compared the productivity and advancement of free wage laborers in the North with what they argued was an inefficient manual labor force in the slave South. These reformers maintained that the South's reliance on slave labor made whites despise any manual wage work and thus inhibited industrial development. The southern economy was inefficient and unhealthy, the abolitionists continued, because slavery effectively removed one of the key stages that enabled individual prosperity and independence in a republic—hard work.[37]

This outside criticism of the southern labor system, combined with a native ideology resistant to dependent work, necessitated southern counterattacks to show that white labor enjoyed full dignity while slavery produced the greatest possible prosperity for all.[38] An 1853 *Carolina Spartan* newspaper article entitled "Dignity of Vocation" assured that "no impression prevailing in society, is more false or fatal to the manhood of a people, than that which gauges a man's worth or respectability by the field of labor or profession he occupies, so long as that labor or profession is honest." The article's author found it to be the community's conviction that "he is more of a true man, who turns chimney-sweeping to an honest, independent account, than he, who scorning the rough toils of the humble and needy, is willing to live an idler—how ever proudly caparisoned upon the industry, sweat and blood of his fellow men."[39] Therefore, the chimney sweep or any laborer who worked hard could find independence in the pride of being a producer.

While traveling in New England a Spartanburg correspondent found it necessary to correct a general opinion that "the white population at the South, and particularly in South Carolina, regard labor—personal, manual labor, as degrading." The writer argued that, rather than degrade labor, southerners "were disposed to regard a man who did not labor in some useful mode, a drone in society."[40] While it was always best to be an independent landowner, one could still find more respect and dignity as a manual laborer than as an "idle drone."

The campaign to dignify manual labor extended across gender lines in an attempt to promote domestic as well as corporate labor. In 1853 a Spartanburg woman drew praise when she garnered a Royal Commission Medal at the World's Fair for her own manufactured cloth. "Is not the example of the lady," the paper queried, "sufficient to inspire our ladies generally with an honorable ambition to do likewise? . . . Is there not an ineffable happiness in the thought of the winner, that, although she toiled hard to secure such an amiable distinction, she has done much to honor those of her sex and to give to our village a pre-eminence in this wide world competition, for the last specimens of domestic manufacture?" The woman's accomplishments were enhanced further by her position in society. Despite her marriage to a wealthy gentleman, she "refused to court the case and enjoyments of her position and circumstances, and with her own hands and loom manufactured the very articles to which this rich . . . offering has been made, thus rebuking that sickly sentiment which prevails, that manual labor is degrading."[41]

Mechanics and artisans were also championed as important contributors to diversification and development, particularly in towns. Michele Gillespie's study of white artisans and mechanics in antebellum Georgia finds that politicians promoting business dynamism publicly praised mechanics as critical to a balanced economy independent of the North.[42] Similarly, the *Carolina Spartan*'s editors argued that no town or village could flourish without the aid of mechanics who lived and worked in their own communities. "There is no truth more undeniable," they asserted, "than that it is the bounden duty of every community to support its mechanics." Spartanburg had shown its progressive spirit by continually adding to its community "a large number of mechanics and artisans of every description." It was only the "ignorant and heartless" aristocrats, the editors continued, who used the derogatory expression, "HE IS ONLY A MECHANIC."[43] Such boosterism of nonagricultural workers reflects an appreciation among supporters of economic diversification that development was dependent on the coexistence of free labor and slave labor in the South.

Just as bringing greater recognition to the dignity of free labor might encourage laborers to work in the mills, so too the expansion of mills might correspondingly reinforce the dignity of free labor. Not surprisingly, northern visitors to the South were quick to note the social benefits of industrial expansion. New England poet William Cullen Bryant saw factory development in the South as an important civilizing process, since, he explained, "it both condenses a class of population too thinly scattered to have the benefit of the institutions of civilized life, of education and religion—and it restores one branch of labor, at least, to its proper dignity, in a region where manual labor has been the badge of servitude and dependence."[44] Spartanburg natives touted factories for enabling those people who were "doing little or nothing for either themselves or their country [to] obtain good employment and adequate means of support." In addition, more manufacturing would give rise to more schools and churches, thus promoting intelligence and good morals.[45]

The promise of manufacturing villages acting as centers of morality seemed to be reaching fulfillment in Bivingsville by the early 1850s. Located on Lawson's Fork, about five and a half miles from Spartanburg town, Bivingsville employed twenty-two men and thirty women. On the first anniversary of the Lawson's Fork Division of the Sons of Temperance, factory operations shut down for the day, and the "little girls and young ladies were dressed in holiday style, the young men were promenading in small companies, the elderly gentlemen were seated in social mood around the thoroughfares." Exercising both his economic and moral leadership, none other than factory owner Elias C. Leitner acted as marshal of the temperance parade.[46]

Although suggestive of the paternalistic attitude that mill owners of later decades would adopt, the temperance effort at Bivingsville may have affected few beyond those who lived a short radius from the manufacturing community. The various industrial operations scattered about the area, however, had an impact on many individuals within the district. This is particularly true because most factory production in antebellum Spartanburg stayed local despite the hopes of manufacturers to develop transportation networks that would allow profitable long-distance trade. Textile factories, for example, offered farmers a selling point for their cotton as well as work to the unemployed, and the factory store provided basic necessities as well as an opportunity to go into debt. The Bivingsville cotton factory hired agents from surrounding districts to market their products on commission. Andrew Feaster, a merchant and farmer from Fairfield District, negotiated sales for Bivingsville at between 5 and 10 percent commission.[47] Customers often found it difficult to meet their contractual obligations for payment. Bivingsville kept local magistrate James F. Sloan busy with file after file of debt cases. Many of these cases involved area residents who purchased yarn, shirting, and calico from the factory on credit. Often these debts were repaid in agricultural products like wheat and cotton, or the debtor would provide the factory with necessary services such as horseshoeing, wagon repair, and fence and building repair.[48]

In addition to affecting the rhythms of work for yeomen, the growth in textile factories and mercantile operations also affected the commercial activity of area planters. Recognizing the need for more infrastructure to market crops, plantation owners initially supported the construction of local textile mills. As Tom Downey notes, planters tolerated the growth of merchants and manufacturers as long as they played a "subordinate role in their political economy."[49] However, as mills and mercantile firms expanded, planters often found themselves in an interdependent relationship with these rising entrepreneurs. Elihu Smith, one of the wealthiest planters in the district, incurred debts to Hosea Dean in Dean's dual role as lawyer and manufacturer. Dean represented Smith in the planter's quest to recover outstanding debts. In the process, Smith accumulated his own debts in legal fees. Smith also owed money for the processing of his cotton at Dean's textile mill. When Dean needed to make repairs to his mills in 1848, he informed Smith that he was "compelled to call on my friends who are indebted to me for money." When Smith set up his own merchandising business on the plantation a year later, he turned to the textile mill operated by Gabriel Cannon and Joseph Finger for supplies of cotton yarn. Through the 1850s Smith depended on Cannon and Finger for yarn and, at times, incurred debts to them. In addition, Smith purchased the plowing equipment for his farm from the South Carolina Manufacturing Company.[50] Planter Catherine Stone also depended on both textile mills and merchants and often ran up significant debts to them. Having taken over control of the plantation after her husband died in 1844, Stone used the Bivingsville factory to have her cotton spun into yarn and purchased a host of goods from several local merchants. Throughout the 1850s Stone received numerous magistrates' summonses for debts. Merchant Hiram Mitchell sent Stone a form letter indicating the gendered notions of business: "Dear Sir: As money has been scarce in the country for the last two years, I have been disposed to wait on my Customers as long as my Creditors would wait on me. But necessity now *Compels* me to collect all my debts *Immediately*."[51] As the examples of Smith and Stone demonstrate, Spartanburg planters found that instead of performing merely ancillary roles to staple-crop production, mills and merchants forged an increasing interdependence between middle-class business people and plantation owners.

Elihu Smith's and Catherine Stone's transactions with area manufacturers also reveal the localized nature of the market in the 1850s. This system of local exchange also persisted in transactions involving the growing collection of smaller-scale manufacturing enterprises such as flour mills, gristmills, carriage factories, tanneries, and sawmills. Because they farmed in a substantial grain-growing region, farmers relied on local gristmills to prepare their produce for home consumption or sale. In 1860 the district's thirty-four gristmills ranked second only to Greenville, and total capital investments amounted to sixty-two thousand dollars.[52] Area carriage makers enjoyed prosperous times in the local market as well. James Fowler's carriage factory accepted lumber as payment for his goods, but Fowler offered a 10 percent discount to those paying cash.[53] Fowler's discount reflected a desire among area businessmen to develop a stronger cash economy in Spartanburg. Yet the only way for the district to enter the cash nexus more completely was to go beyond local exchange and tap into the major markets of the North and East as well as the developing areas of the West. To do this, Spartanburg needed a much more developed transportation system, which, local leaders argued, would only be possible with state aid.

Town professionals and commercial farmers viewed better connections to trading centers as essential to expanding prosperity and avoiding economic stagnation. These men not only appealed for local support of transportation initiatives but also urged the South Carolina legislature to provide financial and legal aid for projects aimed at developing the state's interior. This legislative assistance was justified as a means of ensuring equal economic opportunity to all regions of the state. Despite an extended public campaign, Spartanburg's entrepreneurs enjoyed only moderate success in convincing local voters and statewide politicians of the importance of a substantial transportation network in the upcountry.

Interest in transportation links to established market centers followed closely on the heels of settlement in the upcountry frontier. Early in the nineteenth century, state legislators made overtures to upcountry residents by making significant appropriations for interior canal projects. However, the few waterways that were built soon fell into disrepair.[54] Spurred on by the discussions over agricultural diversification and industrial development in the 1830s and 1840s, politicians from Spartanburg and the surrounding districts looked to secure more effective avenues for commerce and manufacturing. Of particular interest to Spartanburg and neighboring York and Union districts was the navigability of the Broad River. Skirting what was then Spartanburg's northeastern corner, the Broad was a wide waterway extending from southern North Carolina through South Carolina's upcountry to the state's capital, Columbia, where the river converged with the Saluda to form the Congaree, a main tributary of the Santee River. The Santee River then continued eastward to a canal that ran directly to Charleston. It is little wonder that these three districts recognized the Broad, a link to the state's biggest commercial cities, as a key to the region's economic development. The problem lay in a series of falls beginning in Union District. Petitioners urged the government to aid in the construction of dams and sluices, since the improvement of the river was crucial to "the conveyance of [the area's] produce & manufactures to market & for receiving by it in return such surplus & articles of commerce as the wants of thousands of families require." Too much energy, one petition argued, was expended on conquering "miserable" roads. Not only would improved navigation permit increased trade with Columbia, it would also finish the connection to the "hart of provision country" in North Carolina. The Nesbitt Iron Works had already made the Broad navigable to within two miles of the North Carolina border, and the North Carolina legislature had supported projects aimed at opening the river's tributaries to boat traffic. As a result, the petitioners explained, South Carolina's government had only to incur minimal costs "to aid and perfect what already has been done by private Enterprize and Capital."[55]

Beyond the trade in agricultural provisions, improved navigation would also develop the region's industrial interests. Rich minerals, particularly limestone and iron, were abundant above the falls, and power harnessed from the falls could drive several factories. The Spartanburg region, one petition instructed, had "all those elements out of which industry & enterprise can work up a great prosperity if they only had the means of communicating with markets. No country in all our Land could manufacture to more advantage; they would exchange the produce of their soil their Iron & their manufactures of wool & cotton for the merchandize of Charleston & the cotton of the State."[56] Improved navigation, in short, would help create a strong, diversified market economy encompassing the whole state.

Although the rhetoric supporting better navigation seemed to tout universal benefits, conflicting interests emerged over water rights. Sawmill and gristmill owners wanted rivers for the exclusive use of their local industries, which meant a series of dams and little navigability. Subsistence farmers tended to support these millers to ensure local sources for turning their wheat to flour and for building materials. Commercial farmers, however, desired unimpeded navigation to bring their produce to market. Finally, budding industrialists wanted to preserve shoals and waterfalls to power their factories, but they also wanted downriver navigation to markets.

Two rival petitions to the state legislature in 1846 demonstrate this riparian conflict. A group of 313 petitioners from both Spartanburg and Union districts asked the state either to make an appropriation sufficient to make the Pacolet River navigable up to Easterwood Shoals at the Spartanburg/Union District line or to let the river be used exclusively for machinery, "which latter use we beleave to be by far the most advantageous to all interested." By machinery, the petitioners largely meant sawmills and gristmills. Many of the signers likely hailed from Union District, which operated more sawmills and gristmills than Spartanburg until the 1850s. Three of the Spartanburg residents identified on the petition would be sawmill and gristmill owners during the 1850s. The support of millers and small farmers is not surprising. However, by offering the legislature the choice of mill use *or* increased navigation, the petition contained signatures of men with competing interests. Of the 313 signers, two included this note next to their names: "to make the river navigable." These men were Spartanburg residents Elias Leitner and James Sloan. As noted earlier, Leitner owned the Bivingsville textile factory from the mid-1840s through the mid-1850s. Since the factory was located on the Lawson's Fork tributary of the Pacolet River, Leitner looked to bring navigation closer to his business. Sloan was a commercial farmer and a debt collector for the Bivingsville factory.[57] Improved navigation would serve to better market Sloan's produce and, importantly, serve the interests of his employer. Thus, within one petition the conflicting interests of millers, subsistence farmers, commercial farmers, and industrialists surfaced.

A separate petition signed by 162 people from the Grindal Shoals neighborhood a few miles downriver in Union District urged the legislature to keep the river navigable to its current limits. The petition noted that a particular owner of sawmills and gristmills had enjoyed exclusive rights to a dam at Grindal Shoals and that this operation was beneficial to all in the immediate community. Particularly objectionable to the petitioners was the proposal that the Pacolet be used exclusively for mill use, since this would bring competition from other mills and alter the local economy of Grindal Shoals. Once again, however, what seemed like a competition between mill owners and farmers extended to Spartanburg's industrial entrepreneurs. One of the signers of the petition was Simpson Bobo.[58] Like Leitner, Bobo had investments in textile operations as well as the extensive iron factories of the South Carolina Manufacturing Company. Bobo recognized that the rival petition looked to end navigation in favor of mill dams. For those looking to harness the power of shoals and waterfalls for larger factory operations, dams could alter a river's force and disrupt downriver navigation to markets. This underlying conflict over water usage never accelerated, however, since all of the Spartanburg-area petitions regarding river navigation in the 1840s were rejected by the senate committee on internal improvements. Most likely, the lowcountry-dominated legislature saw little to be gained from such projects, especially in light of the potential profitability of railroads by the late 1840s.[59]

Spartanburg leaders joined a growing chorus of voices throughout the state urging construction of new rail lines in the 1840s and 1850s. The idea of railroad development in the upper piedmont dated back at least to 1832, when South Carolina politicians suggested a line from Charleston to the Ohio Valley. Charleston leaders supported a transmontane project because they wanted to regain trade lost to port cities like New York, Boston, Philadelphia, and Baltimore. After the organization of the Louisville, Cincinnati, and Charleston Railroad Company in 1836, surveyors mapped possible routes, including one through the middle of Spartanburg. However, a series of financial difficulties led supporters to abandon efforts at a transmontane route by 1839 and focus instead on completing a line between Charleston and Columbia. The completion of the South Carolina Railroad to Columbia in 1842 renewed optimism among commercially oriented Spartanburg residents of a trunk-line connection between the upcountry and the state capital.[60]

The state legislature granted a number of charters for new railroad construction in the mid-1840s. Most important for Spartanburg residents were two trunk lines slated to run from Columbia up through the northeastern portion of the upcountry. The Greenville and Columbia Rail Road Company was chartered in 1845 and given exclusive right to build a line between the state capital and Greenville District, Spartanburg's neighbor to the west.

A year later a charter was granted to the Charlotte and South Carolina Rail Road Company to run between Charlotte, North Carolina, and Columbia. The prospect of two major trunk lines excited interest in a feeder line to Spartanburg.[61]

By the late 1840s Spartanburg entrepreneurs were convinced that a railroad would bring unbounded prosperity to their region. In November 1848 Simpson Bobo informed relative James Saye that it was "the object of our people to have a Rail Road to Spartanburg Village." Bobo expressed his preference for a road from Union District Courthouse that would connect with either the Greenville or the Charlotte line. It was already well known throughout the upcountry, Bobo observed, that Spartanburg's resources were "immense and only need a facility of transportation to devellope them." Citing the abundant rivers and tributaries that produced rich bottomlands, the wealthy entrepreneur promised, "If we had a market that would enable us to get a fair price for it we should be an extensive grain & flour Exporting people." The fast-flowing rivers were also ideal for factories, and Bobo predicted that a railroad would foster "extensive manufacturing establishments" in Spartanburg. Indeed, Bobo envisioned a doubling of both iron and textile production following the arrival of the locomotive. Steam trains would also open a mutually beneficial market exchange with western North Carolina and eastern Tennessee. In sum, Bobo assured Saye that a railroad through Spartanburg "would stimulate labor & industry[,] cause the farmers to improve their lands [and] draw an increased amount of capital & labor."[62]

Wealthy investors like Bobo, Gabriel Cannon, and John Winsmith worked with their counterparts in Union District to secure enough capital for a state charter of the Spartanburg and Union Railroad in 1847. The charter granted the company exclusive right to a rail connection between Spartanburg town and either the Greenville and Columbia or the Charlotte and South Carolina. The act further stipulated that incorporation would be granted once the company sold eight thousand shares of stock.[63] Shortly after state authorization, committees were formed in Spartanburg "for the purpose of agitating the Railroad question, and enlightening the public mind on the utility of Railroads." The key goal of railroad boosterism, of course, was to get district residents to purchase stock in the Spartanburg and Union Railroad. When books of subscription were opened at Spartanburg Courthouse on sales day in May 1849, much of the town's business shut down for the day, and railroad supporters sought signatures from "every man who has got an acre of land and a pony—every man who has got two ponies and a hundred acres . . . [and] wealthy planters who have land, negroes and money." Among those speaking in favor of liberal subscriptions were textile factory investors James Henry, H. H. Thomson, Gabriel Cannon, and James Bivings. Battalion musters were also used to spread the gospel of railroads. Henry and town lawyer James Farrow stumped for support of the railroad following a muster parade in April 1849.[64]

Railroad advocates argued that support of internal improvements would prevent a dangerous overreliance on cotton production. In a letter to the *Carolina Spartan* "Strong Faith" argued that price fluctuation combined with inhospitable soil and climate made cotton dependency a potentially disastrous course for Spartanburg farmers. The cheap transportation provided by a railroad, however, would allow farmers to send whichever crop brought the most profit, perhaps corn one time, flour the next, then cotton, potatoes, pumpkins, or a combination of produce. "Strong Faith" also argued that a rail line would eliminate market costs to Columbia merchants. With poor means of transportation, farmers wishing to market their surplus crops had to pay these merchants to find buyers. Spartanburg farmers, the writer explained, currently paid more every year "TO SUPPORT THIS UPPER TEN ARISTOCRACY, THAN YOU PAY IN STATE AND DISTRICT TAXES TO SUPPORT THE STATE GOVERNMENT."[65] A railroad would both prevent perilous dependence on monocrop agriculture and allow true independent action in the market economy.

In a series of promotional articles for the *Carolina Spartan* a writer using the pseudonym "Elmore" argued that geology had marked the district as "a *manufacturing* country—her soil is suited only for grain—she cannot raise cotton—she is too far from market to sell grain—and much of her land is unproductive even for grain." Comparing Spartanburg's five watercourses to only three in the entire manufacturing state of Rhode Island, Elmore saw the promise of "limitless water power" if the railroad would bring a market for industrial products. With three iron foundries, two potteries, eight tanneries, and eight cotton factories, Spartanburg was already asserting its claim as "the Manufacturing District of Upper South Carolina." Relying on the 1840 census, Elmore noted that Spartanburg invested more capital in manufacturing than in any other district, and only a railroad was needed to increase the value and output of the district's industries. "Other Districts may have soil suited to Rice and Cotton and Corn and Wheat," Elmore observed, "but the products intended by nature for Spartanburg are *Sheetings*,

Calicoes, Carpets, Cassimeres, Broadcloths and the like. Not only these, but Shoes, Hats, Chairs, Fire Irons, indeed everything in the shape of manufactures from a horn button up to the Steam Engine. Give Spartanburg a Rail Road and in thirty-five years she will have more than one Lowell."[66]

The primary goal behind Elmore's articles was to drum up support for state aid to the Spartanburg and Union Railroad. In justifying such assistance Elmore employed the sanctified principle of equal opportunity used earlier by advocates of improved water transportation. Elmore announced that it was "the duty and policy of the State to see that the [railroad] shall not fail. That the State will extend to Spartanburg and Union the same generosity so wisely extended to other Districts, there can be no doubt." The state-supported improvements of lowcountry rivers and government assistance to roads throughout the state's other districts were "guaranties that the Spartanburg and Union Railroad Company will be aided to a proportionate degree." Again, the government could not lend its support to one region or one type of improvement without providing such assistance to all who asked for it. To do so would admit favoritism and a return to aristocratic tendencies supposedly overthrown by the bourgeois revolutions of the eighteenth century.[67]

Elmore had a ready answer to those who would argue that state funding of internal improvements should only be in proportion to the money raised within each district. Although Spartanburg's individual railroad subscriptions were not as high as elsewhere, Elmore argued that the state should still assist the road for egalitarian reasons. The writer explained that districts should not be penalized simply because their soil and their distance from the market resulted in less wealth. "We cannot believe that being poor, in the case of either an individual or a community," Elmore continued, "is such conclusive evidence of criminality as would be implied in the opinion of those who would expect all men by equal industry to gain equal wealth." Spartanburg's relative inaccessibility to markets meant less money in circulation, which, in turn, resulted in lower wages for skilled laborers. Comparing carriage manufacturing in Spartanburg and Union districts, Elmore argued that the "labor of twelve men in Spartanburg will only sell for half the money that the labor of *six* men in Union will!" Thus, to deny Spartanburg aid in developing transportation networks was to keep the district at a distinct disadvantage in the state.[68]

When stockholders of the Spartanburg and Union Railroad petitioned the legislature for state aid in December 1850, they employed much of

Elmore's rhetoric. Having raised the two hundred thousand dollars necessary for the company's organization, the stockholders urged the legislature to accept a smaller proportion of individual subscriptions than the normal three-fifths of the total necessary capital. Spartanburg, the petition explained, "is situated further from the market, than any other in the whole State," and its principal product, grain, was too heavy for horsepower transportation. As a result, "a subscription of one hundred thousand dollars, is really much more for Spartanburg, than the same amount would be for districts growing marketable products." Like Elmore, the petition also highlighted Spartanburg's "inexhaustible beds of iron and lime" and "boundless water power" in discussing how easing access to the district would benefit the entire state.[69]

Arguments for liberal state aid in completing a railroad to Spartanburg found at least some receptive ears in the lowcountry. The *Charleston Mercury* agreed that it was unreasonable to expect substantial local subscriptions since the district was "far removed from the stimulus of commercial enterprize." Spartanburg's people, the *Mercury* explained, were "for the most part poor, and hesitate at risking the most of what they have, in an enterprize of which they have no experience." Concurring with Spartanburg developers that the district had great manufacturing potential, the paper added another reason for the railroad of particular importance to the lowcountry during the 1850 sectional crisis. "This road is the last in a system of works," the *Mercury* noted, "that is to bind the up country to the seaboard, in sympathy, interest and daily association. We need not dwell upon the importance of securing this community of feeling and interest. The strength and security of the State depend on it."[70] In 1851 the Spartanburg and Union was capitalized at $750,000.[71]

Since much of the discussion surrounding the expected benefits of a railroad centered on Spartanburg town, farmers in the district's countryside expressed concern over whether or not they would share equally in the prosperity of a rail line. This would mark the early stages of a town-rural divide that would only widen as commerce and industry expanded.[72] In 1849, on one of the first sales days to solicit subscriptions for the Spartanburg and Union, men from the countryside criticized town residents for not raising their share of the subscriptions. The *Carolina Spartan* responded that in the few days following the sales day the town subscribed an additional forty-five thousand dollars with assurances to reach at least sixty thousand dollars within a short time and played down the potential profits for the town in comparison to the district as a whole. While town lots would increase in value, many would stay in town and not sell their lands. Increased competition among businessmen would actually reduce profits. The paper also argued that, aside from five or six persons, "the great majority of the rest [of the townspeople] are poor men, and in some cases scarcely able to support their families." Far from isolating commerce to the town limits, the railroad would bring "an inexhaustible market . . . at the very door of each farmer."[73]

Joseph Wofford Tucker rejected the notion that a railroad would only benefit wealthy townspeople, arguing that competition would drive merchants' prices down while increasing demand for produce and craft goods. "The truth is," Tucker explained, "that while a Railroad would benefit the whole people as a body—every member of it, however great or small—the farming and mechanical interests would be most eminently benefitted." Asking each man to subscribe what he could, the town lawyer and magistrate set himself as the example. While only owning three and a half acres of land, Tucker subscribed five hundred dollars to the great enterprise.[74]

While railroad proponents continued to sell the community-wide benefits of the project, Spartanburg and Union company officials struggled to pay for the route's construction. In August 1854 the scarcity of money in the upcountry contributed to a high percentage of delinquent payments among railroad stockholders. While understanding the "stringency of the money market," the company urged legal action against delinquent subscribers, arguing that it was a question of continuing the work or suspending it. Suspension of work would be a blow to the districts involved and to the honor of each individual involved. "Having put your hands to the plow," a committee report read, "do you intend to look back? Do you intend to fail in the accomplishment of this great enterprise, which has been so well begun?" By early 1855 the *Unionville Journal* estimated that subscribers were falling short on their dues by an average of three thousand dollars monthly.[75]

Having expended about $800,000 on the Spartanburg and Union by August 1856, the company estimated that it would cost another $400,000 to complete the road to Union Courthouse. With a glut of bonds on the market from other railroad projects throughout the state, company officials knew they had to offer incentives if any new bonds were to be sold. As a result, $500,000 in bonds were issued payable in ten, twenty, twenty-two, and twenty-four years with interest paid semiannually. In addition, $150,000 in bonds were offered to stockholders and creditors at eighty cents on the dollar. Acknowledging this policy as a loss to the company, officials felt it better to "let the profits be made by the Stockholders, than to go into the market to sell."[76]

When the legislature granted additional aid to the Spartanburg and Union in late 1857, prospects brightened that the railroad would reach Spartanburg town before the decade's end. In October 1859 commercial farmer David Golightly Harris recorded that the railroad was within ten miles of Spartanburg Courthouse and would be completed by Christmas. Harris added that the railroad's arrival would "be a long look[ed]-for Jubille."[77] Finally, on November 25, 1859, the first railroad cars steamed into the town, much to the delight of "thousands of anxious persons who surrounded the Depot and lined the road on every side." The crowds were treated to a barbecue and lengthy speeches praising Spartanburg's new era of rail.[78] James Sloan estimated that ten thousand people attended the event. Sloan and his family rode the train but found "the *accomodations* and fare was not very good." On the return trip the engine stalled two or three times, and another engine had to be summoned to assist in pushing the cars.[79]

As much as the arrival of the railroad brought cause for celebration, Spartanburg and Union supporters were eager to have the line extended westward through the mountains toward Asheville, North Carolina, and eastern Tennessee. As early as 1853 Simpson Bobo and fellow town lawyer James Farrow spoke of the necessity to cooperate with citizens of North Carolina in completing a western rail line. A committee of twenty-one was appointed to represent the district at the proposed railroad convention in Asheville on August 25, and a separate committee was formed to memorialize the legislature for incorporation acts supporting the road's extension, to be known as the French Broad route. Shortly thereafter, the state authorized the Spartanburg and Union to extend its line to the North Carolina border using any funds the company might raise by subscriptions.[80]

Looking for state support and lowcountry subscriptions, advocates of the Spartanburg and Union Railroad waged a campaign to assure Charleston of the multiple benefits of a western extension. A rail line to the upcountry, western North Carolina, and eastern Tennessee would bring a bounty of goods that would eliminate competition from New York, Wilmington, Augusta, and Mobile. One supporter informed *Charleston Standard* readers that the "district of Spartanburg alone could supply the city of Charleston with a large amount of grain and other elements of subsistence and export, if once possessed of the means of railroad transportation, and which her people doubtless would in a great measure exchange for merchandise." The road would also have reciprocal benefits for western neighbors as it would provide "the safest and most rapid outlet to the markets of the world for their produce." In May 1855 the North Carolina legislature passed a charter for the connection of railroads in South Carolina with those in eastern Tennessee. An Asheville committee then called for a convention in July to complete the rail link between Lexington, Kentucky, and Charleston, South Carolina.[81]

At the conclusion of the July convention, a committee formed to petition the South Carolina legislature for substantial funding for the completion of the railroad. Spartanburg's Gabriel Cannon and prominent Greenville residents Benjamin F. Perry and Vardry McBee were among the seven committee members. The petition itself provides an important example of what Spartanburg leaders like Cannon viewed as the government's role in promoting the release of creative energy for internal improvements. Legislators were informed that "the functions of Government, are not merely repressive." Beyond the necessary duties of suppressing crime and collecting taxes, the general assembly should also assume "the active function of direction, assistance & guidance." Whenever a proposed project was calculated to further the public good, the petitioners argued, such a project required the state's enthusiastic support. If the government refused assistance, however, it could "claim but little preeminence above the repressive polity of barbarism."[82]

The upcountry petitioners called upon the legislature to levy state property taxes for railroad development, assuring the politicians that this call came from "the public voice & the public intelligence." Proper state aid would enable the Spartanburg and Union Railroad and the Greenville and Columbia Rail Road to extend their lines to the North Carolina border to link up with the Greenville and French Broad line. Steam locomotion, the petitioners professed, had become "the prince & ruler over the industrial & social fortunes of our race" and would continue to be "the one supreme law of progress to human society." Recognizing this truism, the legislature "*must and will, by stern necessity conform to it.*" If the legislature chose to ignore these facts, the petitioners prophesied Charleston's demise as the commercial, social, and political center of the South. Failure to make a link to the west would also mean the continuation of the state's ruinous dependence on cotton. The petitioners argued that the only way to escape stagnation and decline was "*to make by its system of Rail Roads, the population, capital, & agricultural resources of other States, tributary to its own wealth & prosperity.*"[83]

For models of the successes wrought by interstate railroads, the petition pointed northward. The great coastal commercial cities of Boston and New York had strengthened their positions through connections to the northwestern states and the Great Lakes. To this "rule" of opening western tributaries via locomotives, the petitioners explained, "South Carolina must conform." In this way, upcountry promoters linked a stronger South Carolina to following the pattern of northern development. Unconvinced by the need for substantial state support and perhaps wary of taxing real property to fund internal improvement projects, the legislature refused to grant aid to the western extension.[84]

The legislature's refusal to aid the Spartanburg and Union's extension stemmed largely from another major hurdle facing upcountry entrepreneurs: competition. Since the state issued numerous charters without a clear plan of integration, competing lines had to clamor for the legislature's favor. In one sense, this competition was a powerful stimulus to internal improvements, since local railroad supporters would want to complete lines before their competitors. In the case of South Carolina, however, those rail lines with close ties to lowcountry legislators had a distinct advantage. This was the case with Spartanburg's chief competitor for a western route, the Blue Ridge Railroad Company. In 1853 the Blue Ridge Railroad Company proposed a route that would extend west from Charleston, well south of Spartanburg, and skirt the western border of South Carolina through the Rabun Gap of the Blue Ridge Mountains into Tennessee. The Blue Ridge had support from a number of prominent legislators as well as the governor. In fact, Governor John L. Manning urged the state to subscribe $750,000 of capital stock to the company, and he equated the significance of the Blue Ridge with the Baltimore and Ohio or the western railroads to New York.[85]

When a bill to grant aid to the Blue Ridge came before the legislature in December 1853, Spartanburg's John C. Winsmith rose to oppose the measure. As a substantial commercial planter from south of Spartanburg town, Winsmith looked to lower his costs for transporting cotton by bringing a railroad to the district. He argued that the potential costs and the "stupendous difficulties" in laying track for the Blue Ridge made the state's investment unwise. In addition, the proposed route through the Rabun Gap of the Blue Ridge Mountains would only skirt the western border of South Carolina, bringing the benefits of western produce to Charleston at the expense of the upcountry. Winsmith argued that since the proposed Blue Ridge line ran far to the south, the upcountry would have to pay the costs of shipping western products to Charleston and then reshipping them to the interior of the state. Not surprisingly, Winsmith found the more central route through Spartanburg the most logical choice for a rail link to the west. Winsmith portrayed the Blue Ridge investors as a group of elites who would continually return to the legislature for more funds without producing a profitable railroad. Gabriel Cannon, who in 1854 was the Spartanburg and Union's president, expressed anger that the state bank refused to loan his company four thousand dollars while telling legislators that it could advance four hundred thousand dollars to the Blue Ridge Railroad Company.[86]

The *Carolina Spartan*'s editors joined the fight against the Blue Ridge Company, explaining that, while they believed "the State should aid, judiciously, in works of Internal Improvement," the Blue Ridge project had become too costly, with no definite prospect of a completed railroad. The paper also suggested that Blue Ridge supporters reneged on an agreement that the company would not ask for any stock subscriptions from the state after receiving a 1.2-million-dollar grant from the legislature. The *Charleston News* found Spartanburg's challenge to the Blue Ridge route "a vein of illiberal prejudice and sneer against Charleston." Echoing these sentiments, the *Charleston Mercury* found the charges against the Blue Ridge baseless and disputed the *Carolina Spartan*'s comparative cost estimates for the two roads.[87]

In 1856 all of Spartanburg's candidates for the state legislature came out against any further state aid for the Blue Ridge Railroad.[88] Two and a half years later, Gabriel Cannon spoke against yet another bill in aid of the Blue Ridge Railroad. Cannon argued that the company was not sound, based on its prior errors in estimating costs and general incompetence in securing private subscriptions. The Blue Ridge Railroad bill was defeated in the senate in December 1858.[89]

Spartanburg and Union Railroad officials had no problem justifying state aid to their enterprise even while they fostered suspicion of legislative involvement in other routes. In his report to the stockholders, railroad president Daniel Wallace of Union named the state government as the railroad's "most powerful ally." Wallace found it "the duty of the State to contribute by her legislative action to such schemes of internal improvements as are calculated to elevate the standard of her civilization, and confer lasting benefit to the community." Criticizing the "antiquated policy of standing still," Wallace urged active involvement by the legislature.[90]

The political ideal of equal opportunity to market access played a key role in attempts to complete the railroad to Spartanburg. The district's railroad project required active state support, it was argued, because the government had assisted internal improvements in other districts. Likewise, the Blue Ridge was opposed on grounds that it would only benefit a small elite. While serving as an important defense of railroad development, this political ideal of equal market opportunity also hurt Spartanburg and Union supporters. With the approved rail line following a roughly diagonal path from Union Courthouse to Spartanburg Courthouse, there was little doubt of the future financial benefits for Spartanburg town. The challenge, however, was to convince country farmers that the road would substantially enhance their market opportunities as well.

This underlying concern that the western rail route provide equally shared benefits broke into political conflict. In January 1860 upcountry leaders succeeded in getting the legislature to pass a Railroad Tax Act authorizing the boards of commissioners of roads for Spartanburg, Union, Fairfield, and Richland to subscribe to the capital stock of the Greenville and French Broad Railroad. Since these subscriptions would necessitate a tax increase, the act stipulated that the question of subscription should be submitted to the legal, taxpaying voters of each district. Adhering to the wording of the act, Spartanburg's road commissioners set a date in May for an election on the issue of railroad subscription to be open to the district's taxpayers only. In addition, Spartanburg and Union directors passed a resolution to receive as cash payment for railroad taxes all tax receipts from those persons with an annual tax of under five dollars. In this way, the vote was opened only to those paying the subscriptions while guaranteeing no increase in burden on the smaller taxpayers.[91]

In early March 1860 a public meeting convened at Spartanburg Courthouse to invite speeches and discussion on the proposed subscription. Gabriel Cannon was among the speakers in favor of the one-hundred-thousand-dollar subscription. Cannon warned that plans for other rail lines through neighboring districts were already under way and would take trade away from Spartanburg if the district failed to pay for the French Broad. The legislator-entrepreneur also argued that more direct trade with the North and West would produce enough of an annual savings in the price of pork alone to far outweigh the interest on railroad bonds.[92]

One of the few prominent voices raised in opposition to the subscription was a powerful one. Planter John C. Winsmith invited his fellow citizens to reject the proposed tax as antithetical to the principles of republican equality. As a commercial cotton grower, Winsmith recognized the importance of a rail center where his cash crop could be expedited to eastern markets. Therefore, he supported the Spartanburg and Union's completion to Spartanburg town. He had also joined with other local entrepreneurs in opposing state support of the Blue Ridge, arguing that such a line would bypass the upcountry entirely. However, Winsmith likely had less enthusiasm for a westward line, since small farmers of upcountry North Carolina and eastern Tennessee would have limited demand for raw cotton. In addition, his Glenn Springs plantation was at least fourteen miles south of the proposed rail extension, suggesting he would reap little immediate reward from the line. As an important member of a politically and socially influential family, Winsmith also had to worry about the increasing power of entrepreneurs like Gabriel Cannon, James Farrow, and Dexter Edgar Converse as well as older rivals like Simpson Bobo. Although by the 1850s all South Carolina politicians professed devotion to the one-party rule of the Democrats, the dispute over the railroad tax vote revealed contests of power between town elites and rural elites.

Winsmith argued that Spartanburg's payment of the railroad tax would represent a regional inequality, as the district would bear a heavier burden than other areas for a railroad that would benefit the entire state. He also questioned the purported benefits to his own district, noting that a western extension would bring the competition of cheaper grains from North Carolina and Tennessee. Winsmith strongly objected to restricting the eligible voters to taxpayers only. Such a restriction deprived "many of the freemen of our district of the privilege which was intended to be given to them by the constitution of our State." Winsmith argued that the very idea of a restricted franchise "effaces all the old republican *land marks* which have been *notched-out*, and *blazed-out*, by the *toil*, and *treasure*, and *blood* of the Revolution." If the railroad tax was approved, any nontaxpayers who later bought land would adopt a tax instituted without their approval. Winsmith also portrayed the tax-receipts-as-cash scheme as a rather sinister means of buying poorer farmers' votes.[93]

Lawyer James Farrow stepped forward as the primary respondent to Winsmith's charges. A member of Spartanburg town's emerging entrepreneurial leadership, Farrow countered that Winsmith's version of equality would "arrest civilization and unhinge society." The key question, Farrow explained, was not whether or not someone else was benefiting from a tax but rather "whether I will be benefited to the amount I will have to pay." In other words, it mattered little if Charleston and Columbia prospered as a result of the western extension so long as Spartanburg did as well. Rejection of the railroad tax would prevent Charleston from accruing benefits, but it would also deny Spartanburg any commercial progress. To remain stagnant in an ever-changing world was, in effect, to regress.

Farrow also attacked Winsmith's criticism of the voting limitations for the tax. It was only fair to leave the issue of taxation to those who would be paying the proposed taxes. Regardless, Farrow had not heard of "the first non-tax-payer who has expressed any dissatisfaction at not having been given the power to vote in this question." As far as those who would become future landholders and taxpayers, Farrow argued that individuals make a free choice to buy taxable property. When buying property, informed citizens would consider tax costs in determining the price they were willing to pay for a piece of property.[94]

When the final votes were tallied on May 14, it was clear that Winsmith's rhetoric had carried the day: the proposed railroad tax to raise a stock subscription of one hundred thousand dollars was easily defeated 766 to 431.[95] The tax failed for a combination of reasons. To begin with, the timing of such a tax could not have been worse. By early 1860 the Deep South was convinced that the northern Republican Party wished to dismantle the cherished rights of southerners one by one. These Yankee demagogues were making a mockery of the South's equality in the nation by attempting to force policies on the region without its consent. Therefore, any attempt to narrow political participation was cause for considerable alarm. Spartanburg's rural farmers were concerned that benefits would be restricted only to neighborhoods directly located on the railroad's path. Town prosperity seemed assured by the railroad's extension; the district's country residents, however, feared they might be passed over by western competition. In the May 14 vote Spartanburg town favored the subscription by a margin of more than three to one, while almost all of the rural precincts voted in opposition.[96] One of the few exceptions of a rural precinct favoring the railroad tax was the Campobello neighborhood, which lay in the northeastern corner of the district directly on the intended route of the Spartanburg and Union's westward extension.

The feud over the railroad tax between Winsmith and Farrow continued during the fall legislative elections. Farrow complained that Winsmith used the railroad tax as a political hobby, while Winsmith stood his ground as the defender of republican rights. Yet despite the extended discussions about the tax, the issue seemed to lose the interest of voters. Farrow and Oliver E. Edwards, two of the most fervent supporters of the tax, were also the two top vote getters in the fall election. Winsmith ran a close third to win one of the five legislative seats.[97] Further discussions of the railroad's extension gave way to the politics of secession and war.

Antebellum Spartanburg's town-oriented business leaders worked hard to mold the district to their diversified economic interests. Far from relying solely on the price of land and slaves for their fortunes, these men diversified their investments to include industry and internal improvements. Both the state government and local white farmers were urged to support such a plan for diversification liberally. However, political and cultural biases limited the degree of economic change in the antebellum period.

Despite struggles with area farmers and state legislators, Spartanburg's men of capital persisted in their efforts and did achieve some success. By 1860 the district appeared poised to take advantage of full market involvement with both the East and the West in agricultural and manufactured products. The Spartanburg and Union's arrival ensured the better transport of the cotton crop in the district's southern portion, the increased sale of manufactured cotton cloth from north of Spartanburg town, and the town's development as an important trading center. A study of these antebellum conditions gets to the heart of questions concerning continuity and change in the Old and New Souths. Certainly, the postbellum explosion in cotton production and factory expansion was impressive. Yet historians have tended to overgeneralize when discussing the postwar revolution of ideas among southern white politicians and business leaders.[98] In the case of Spartanburg, the issues most often identified with the New South—town building, manufacturing, railroads, and market diversification—were already a crucial part of the district's developmental plans before the Civil War.

The same proposed transportation routes that would send out Spartanburg's native products were also expected to bring in new imported goods, more people, and, importantly, outside investment in the region. For Spartanburg leaders these were elements crucial to the district's progress. But this progress was not possible, they argued, without some basic changes in Spartanburg's institutional structure. A law-abiding, sober community was required to ensure the hard work and peaceful coexistence necessary for opportunity and outside interest. In addition, district leaders called for reform of the state's public school system so that every white child would have at least some preparation for an increasingly competitive world. Each of these changes was advocated as a means of further separating the independent opportunities of whites from the inferiority and dependence of the South's black slaves. In this way, local leaders hoped to promote their economic agenda while preserving cohesion within the white community. The course of these antebellum institutional changes will be explored in the next two chapters.

CHAPTER THREE

"An Educated and Intelligent People Cannot Be Enslaved"
The Struggle for Common School Reform

AS THE POLITICAL CONFLICT over the fate of slavery in the West intensified through the summer of 1849, Spartanburg factory owner and newspaper editor Peter M. Wallace vowed that he was "utterly opposed now and forever to all political compromises" on the issue of slavery. Significantly, Wallace connected the success of such southern resistance to the improvement of South Carolina's free schools. The *Carolina Spartan*'s columns, the editor explained, "will be open to the advocates of a more liberal but judicious appropriation of the public money" for common schooling because "an educated and intelligent people, cannot be enslaved."[1] Wallace was one of many antebellum Spartanburg leaders who linked schooling with southern nationalism and used slavery as a metaphor for dependence on northern institutions. In the process, these men espoused what historians often view as a very unsouthern idea—liberal government support for public education—and contrasted it with an image central to the definition of southern white republicanism—the ignorant slave.

Beyond the rhetoric of southern rights, entrepreneurs like Wallace looked to public education as a means to advance their program of economic diversification while creating more opportunities for Spartanburg's white community. These men were careful to argue that school reform would preserve the central institution of slavery while promoting a commercially robust economy. Although the push for public schools enjoyed broad support in Spartanburg, the state legislature resisted significant educational reform in the antebellum period.

For years, historians presented a rather clear dichotomy when discussing public schooling in antebellum America. According to this early scholarship, the North adopted centralized statewide systems of public education befitting a democratic, progressive society. The South, on the other hand, resisted public education because of its backward, premodern slave society. Revisionist historians, however, questioned the democratic notion of public schooling and instead highlighted the social control mechanisms in northern educational reform. Although this scholarship did not offer much of a revision of southern schooling, it did suggest that northern systems should not be viewed uncritically as having expanded freedom and democracy. The postrevisionists have left us with the richest, most complex scholarship on public schooling. Rather than focus on sharp distinctions between North and South, these scholars have revealed diverse and contentious ideas about public schooling in both regions.[2] Opponents of state school systems in both North and South feared the erosion of local control over their cultural institutions. Supporters of school reform in each of the regions were interested in both social control and increasing opportunities for their communities. Thus, the basic outlines of antebellum school reform were not as regionally distinct as one might initially imagine.

Despite these broad similarities, however, the cultural distinctions of the South ensured a different outcome for educational initiatives in the antebellum era. As educational historian John Hardin Best has noted, schooling was "framed for good or for ill by the culture of the South."[3] This culture was shaped to a large degree by the region's commitment to staple-crop agriculture and to chattel slavery. The land requirements for staple-crop production ensured scattered settlement patterns that made the establishment of neighborhood schools more difficult. The profitability of cash crops also gave rise to a plantation elite that exercised a disproportionate share of the power in southern state legislatures. This elite was often resistant to programs that invested in human capital, such as schooling and health care, and instead focused on increased protection of property in the form of land and slaves.[4]

Although these particular southern conditions presented important challenges to public schooling, advocates for state-supported education could be found in the region. In 1779 Thomas Jefferson introduced his now famous "bill for a more general diffusion of knowledge," which, the sage of Monticello argued, was essential to preserving republican government and preventing "degeneracy" into tyranny. In 1795 the much-revered Revolutionary War general Francis Marion called for popular education in South Carolina, arguing that men could only understand government through education, and since a significant portion of the population was too poor to afford private schooling, "it [was] plainly the duty of government to bestow it freely upon them."[5] These views, however, remained limited to a few individuals. In the 1810s and 1820s most southern states created a fund for the support and encouragement of public schooling, but there was little administrative oversight, and communities were not required to establish schools.[6]

More serious efforts at reforming and expanding the common school systems in the South began in the 1830s. This was largely the result of a nationwide reform impulse growing out of religious revivals and perfectionism. Reformers examined all aspects of society and looked to perfect America with a combination of humanitarian and self-interested goals. Although historians have traditionally tended to view the South as immune to these reforms, a small but increasing body of scholarship suggests that there were some genuine, albeit peculiarly southern, reform efforts. These scholars have focused primarily on urban centers that experienced growth in charitable institutions, temperance organizations, and increased political involvement for white women.[7] Jonathan Wells is one of the few scholars to find that this reform environment in the South extended to education, where, he argues, "modernizing forces in almost every southern state pushed hard to adopt a system of public schools on the northern model."[8]

Southern initiatives in common schooling, however, occurred in fits and starts and did not achieve great success prior to the Civil War. North Carolina had established a permanent public school fund as early as 1825, but there was little administrative oversight of how these funds were distributed. In the reform atmosphere of the 1830s, however, North Carolinians called for a more systematized plan for educating the state's children. In 1839 the legislature passed the first school law, which set up county elections on public schooling. Those counties that voted for public schools were to have boards of school superintendents and levy taxes for school construction. The state's literary fund would then match the county tax.[9] Georgians also looked to provide greater access to education during the 1830s. In 1836 the state legislature earmarked one-third of Georgia's share of the federal surplus revenue for school purposes. Seven years later each county court was given permission to levy and collect taxes for educating the poor. In practice, however, this plan was inefficient and placed a heavier burden on poorer counties.[10] Both Alabama and Mississippi had public school laws by the 1840s, but neither state did a good job of administering school funds or assessing the competency of local school commissioners. Similar stories can be repeated for Florida, Louisiana, Arkansas, Texas, Tennessee, and Virginia. In each case the state legislatures passed school laws in the 1830s or 1840s that established greater funding and organization for public education. In practice, however, these laws were ill administered. Since most of these laws looked to ensure support for poor students, common schools also developed a reputation as pauper schools, which discouraged patronage.[11]

For all of their deficiencies, however, no other southern state could match the underdeveloped nature of public education in South Carolina. During the early national period South Carolina's inattentiveness to common schooling was not unusual among southern states. When the educational reform movement filtered through the South in the 1830s, however, South Carolina resisted change.

Common schools in antebellum South Carolina operated under the guidelines of the state's Free School Act. Passed in 1811, the act conformed to early national ideas about education that mixed state public funding with local voluntary schools and private academies.[12] Under the Free School Act, the general assembly appointed commissioners for each district who were charged with establishing free schools equal to that district's number of delegates in the state house of representatives. White children could attend these schools for free, but priority was given to orphans and poor children. The state would provide three hundred dollars per school annually, and local commissioners were given discretion to reduce or increase the number of schools if they saw fit. However, the state would not increase the appropriation beyond a district's number of representatives. Further, since the act prohibited the establishment of common schools if local citizens refused to tax themselves for construction of a schoolhouse, commissioners rarely found cause to expand such services. More often, commissioners took advantage of the act's provision allowing state funds to support poorer scholars attending private schools.[13]

From its inception the South Carolina free school law never functioned effectively. Just two years after the law passed, many in the state legislature looked to abolish the school system, arguing that few schools had been established and that the appropriations were not properly monitored. Indeed, throughout the antebellum period only 20 to 30 percent of the white school-age population in South Carolina actually attended school, and those schools that were created often functioned sporadically.[14] Part of the explanation for the law's failure stems from the general association of the common schools with pauperism. Embracing an ideology of independence, nineteenth-century southerners were reluctant to accept state "handouts" like free education for fear they would be viewed as paupers. Planters and generally well-off southerners chose private schools, yeomen feared association with the poor, and the poverty-stricken either could not afford to lose their children's labor or wished to avoid confirming their status by sending their children to the free schools.[15]

As early as 1815 Governor David R. Williams had suggested reforming the school law by creating a permanent public endowment and by granting school commissioners the power to enforce compulsory attendance. Throughout the antebellum period successive governors pointed out serious deficiencies in the free school law and suggested changes. In 1839 the legislature appointed a special commission to study the plight of the common schools. In its report the commission recommended creating a state superintendent, a teacher training program, larger school appropriations, and more equitable distribution of school funds. The legislature, however, did not act on any of these suggestions. In 1847 another committee again recommended more equity in school funding, noting that by basing appropriations on a combination of wealth and population poorer districts were receiving less school funding than wealthier ones. As late as the mid-1850s Governor James Adams urged a "thorough and entire reformation" of the free school system. Yet the South Carolina state legislature made no substantive changes to the 1811 school law during the antebellum era. In fact, South Carolina was the only southern state that did not establish a permanent public school fund before the Civil War, and it joined Virginia as the only two states that had not created a state school superintendent.[16]

Historians seeking to explain the failure of public schooling in antebellum South Carolina have focused on the role played by intrastate sectionalism.[17] Since the American Revolution representatives from the South Carolina lowcountry had dominated the state legislature. Although efforts were made at providing a more equitable distribution of political power in the state during the early 1800s, lowcountry planters continued to dominate because the formula for representation was based on both population *and* wealth.[18] Further, planters generally regarded education as a privilege of the wealthy and left the fate of common schools to the voluntary spirit of local communities. "The southern aristocrat's sense of noblesse oblige," Orville Vernon Burton notes, "did not extend to the education of the common people; in fact the planters thwarted public education."[19]

Although these lowcountry planters hindered public education in the upcountry, they did assist in developing Spartanburg's reputation for fine private schools. Many planters flocked to the district's mineral springs as an escape from the humidity of the summer coast. Planters brought their children to the upcountry and helped create a demand for elite institutions. By the 1840s Spartanburg's private schools enjoyed a favorable reputation throughout the state. James Edward Henry praised the creation of new schools and expressed excitement that "our [E]nglish and classical schools promise very fair and we hope soon to have a female school of equal character." Henry, a transplanted New Englander and investor in Spartanburg textile mills, sent his own children to one of the nearby institutions. Confident of the superior quality of Spartanburg's private schools, Henry encouraged his nephew Rufus in North Carolina to come stay with him so the boy would not "lose his time at second rate schools."[20]

Spartanburg's enhanced reputation as a result of strong private schools was welcomed, but it also made the contrast of these institutions with the poor state of common schooling all the more stark. At an 1849 convention of Spartanburg magistrates the participants drafted an unusual recommendation that the legislature use the costs paid to magistrates for criminal prosecutions to increase the poor school fund, "thereby increasing the educational fund without an increase in taxation."[21] Information is available on eleven of the sixteen magistrates attending the 1849 convention. Nine of these eleven listed real estate holdings with an average valuation of $2,478. Six magistrates were slave owners with average holdings of 7.3 slaves. Occupations included seven farmers, one merchant, one tavern keeper, one lawyer, and one unknown.[22] These demographics clearly place the magistrates in the rank of prosperous farmers and professionals. While most, if not all, of these magistrates had the means to send their children to private school, public education served important social, economic, and political purposes.

The magistrates recognized that expanding the reach of common schools would help address the outside perceptions of ignorance and offer better opportunities for succeeding generations. As demonstrated in the previous chapter, the 1840s were a time of high expectations of progress in transportation and industry. Railroad charters, petitions for better roads, and manufacturing projects expanded during the decade. As men on the make, magistrates endorsed greater funds for education, in part because schooling could orient citizens toward the potential benefits of such projects.

Southern officeholders also recognized that education could socialize the less fortunate to accept and even support political leadership by wealthier professionals and farmers.[23] The office of magistrate was often a launching pad toward larger political ambitions. In fact, one of the magistrates at the 1849 convention was elected a state representative the following year, while another became intendant (mayor) of Spartanburg town.[24] Therefore, while stronger schools could secure greater opportunity for all, they could also solidify support for political authority.

The magistrates were also looking to answer charges of immorality and backwardness, which abolitionists increasingly linked to the South's peculiar institution.[25] By 1849 many whites in the district feared the arrival of abolitionist agitators. Spartanburg formed the Committee of Vigilance and Safety to deal with suspected antislavery radicals, while James Edward Henry reported numerous arrests and examinations of "suspected persons."[26] Within this atmosphere of hysteria the magistrates made their proposal for increasing the school fund. Better education for all whites not only would refute northern claims of ignorance, it could also prepare common farmers to resist abolitionist appeals.

Ultimately, the magistrate's draft recommendation never became a resolution before the general assembly. Nevertheless, the proposal for a free school tax and its printing in the *Carolina Spartan* reveal an interest in government support of education often overlooked. The tax proposal also presents a corrective to the argument that many magistrates used their position merely to collect court fees and had little interest in initiating change.[27]

Spartanburg grand juries also placed increasing focus on the need for a standardized school system. An 1850 Spartanburg grand jury found the free school system "grossly inadequate to the wants and necessities of the [district]." The jury called upon the legislature for an equal division of the free school funds among the free white population of the state and recommended that the districts be laid off in sections, or beats, with a school in each beat. The same jury also reported "the large appropriation to the South Carolina College compared with the meager appropriation for general school purposes as a state grievous and an imposition which calls loudly for reform." In 1854 yet another grand jury blamed the inefficiency of the primary school system on school patrons ill qualified to assess the competency of the teachers they hired. As a solution, the jury proposed that the general assembly adopt a general free school system with uniformity in teaching, a standard school year, and trustees to ensure competent instruction. The money for this system would, in part, come from their proposal for a poll tax on all male citizens over age twenty.[28] Grand juries repeated this call for a poll tax for common schools over the next few years, noting that "every person exercising the right of suffrage, consequently influencing the Government in making laws, should contribute something to the support of the State."[29]

These grand juries reflected the attitudes of the wealthier, more commercially oriented members of the Spartanburg community. In the fall 1849 Spartanburg grand jury, seventeen of nineteen members owned real estate at an average valuation of $3,356, and nine members were slave owners with an average ownership of ten slaves. The most powerful members of the grand juries were the foremen, who exercised proportionally higher influence over court decisions. The 1849 grand jury was under the leadership of Elias C. Leitner, a textile factory owner with $30,000 worth of real estate and twenty-one slaves. Between 1849 and 1860 grand jury foremen owned an average of $14,470 worth of real estate and sixteen slaves.[30]

Although leading residents lamented the condition of common schooling and urged reform, on paper Spartanburg had more publicly supported schools than any other district within the state in 1850, and the number of schools would double to one hundred between 1855 and 1861. In addition to receiving the state appropriation of fifteen hundred dollars in 1850, Spartanburg public schools also received ten thousand dollars from "Other sources."[31] These sources were primarily tuition and donations from those parents who could pay for their children's education.

Yet Spartanburg's seeming success in public schooling was more illusory than real. Many schools did little more than exist on paper. In addition, funding based on representation worked against Spartanburg because representation in antebellum South Carolina was based on a formula that weighed white population and taxable property equally. Districts with the greatest concentrations of wealth received the most school funds.[32] Therefore, while Spartanburg applied $11,500 to fifty schools in 1850, Charleston divided $19,549 among only twenty-eight schools, of which $10,930 came directly from state appropriations.[33]

Citing this disparity in school funding between Spartanburg and the Charleston area, a resident informed the *Carolina Spartan* that there had been "much complaint about this inequality in the upper part of the State, particularly amongst the poor and middling class." Centering the problem squarely within the context of united southern resistance to northern aggression, the writer argued that equality of education was necessary, since "large armies are composed of a majority of [the poor] class and [it] must be further admitted that the South will soon have to rely upon her own strength to defend her rights."[34] Throughout the 1850s Spartanburg proponents of school reform agitated for a switch in the basis of funding from representation to white population alone while urging that the general assembly assume greater responsibility for ensuring equal schooling opportunities throughout the state.

The idea that the state should assume responsibility for schooling clashed with older ideas about republican independence and the role of education in society. In 1849, for example, Frederick Porcher wrote an article in the *Southern Quarterly Review* repudiating "most religiously the cant of the day which calls on the State to educate the masses in order that they may preserve their liberties."[35] A lowcountry intellectual, Porcher grew up on his father's plantation in St. John's, Berkeley Parish, and received all the benefits of a private education. Porcher represented Charleston in the state legislature as a states' rights, strict constructionist before becoming chair of history and belles lettres at the College of Charleston in 1848.[36]

For Porcher, the tradition of republican civic duty seemed threatened by proposals for making the superintendent and district commissioners paid positions. A stipend would undermine "that high sense of moral obligation which so eminently characterizes our country gentlemen." By offering a salary, the state "would convert this obligation into one of law purely. We would thus have the mortification of seeing one of our most respectable associations reduced from the elevated position of gentlemen discharging a duty, not only gratuitously but lovingly . . . to a body of stipendiary ministers." Unlike lowcountry gentlemen, the common folk of the upcountry would seek these offices as "stepping-stones to others more important."[37]

While Porcher seemed content with the educational status quo, a group of Spartanburg residents took their own initiative to urge more state involvement in common schooling. In 1853 fifty-two Spartanburg citizens petitioned the general assembly to pass a school tax of fifty cents on every white male inhabitant between twenty-one and sixty years of age. The petitioners felt that the sum of this tax added to the existing school fund would provide about $125 annually to each school district of six square miles. If this money was "judiciously managed," it would provide six months of schooling for children ages seven to twenty-one in every neighborhood. The petitioners then called attention to the specific needs of upcountry yeomen: "[The tax] may be a matter that little concerns the wealthy or those who live in Cities or Villages where they can have access to good schools, but for the poor and common class of men in the upper Districts of our State, where our means are limited, and Children numerous[,] we think it would be a matter of great importance."[38]

An analysis of the free school petition's signers sheds light on just who was supporting the education of "the poor and common class of men." Thirty of the fifty-two free school petitioners could be identified in the 1850 census. Of these, nineteen listed real estate values between $200 and $10,000, with the average value at $2,909. At least thirteen of the thirty were slave owners, with average holdings of 10.5 slaves. Occupations included twenty-one farmers, three physicians, two merchants, two overseers, and two unknown. Fully twenty-five of thirty had school-age children in their households.[39]

The economic diversity of the petitioners suggests that the appeal of the school tax extended beyond elite leadership to include farmers of more modest means. Although any scale of wealth in the nineteenth-century South is rough at best, ten petitioners can be classified as lower-middle-class yeoman farmers, ten were middling yeomen, and ten were substantial farmers and/or professionals.[40] Common school expansion had somewhat different meanings for each of these groups.

In 1850 petitioner Maurice A. Moore worked as a physician in Spartanburg town, owning three thousand dollars worth of real estate and eight slaves. This wealth allowed Moore to employ Miss M. C. Hood as a live-in teacher for his fourteen-year-old son, James, and eleven-year-old daughter, Celina.[41] Moore's interest in a tax for common school expansion, then, did not derive from personal need. As a town professional, Moore's concern centered more on the cultural and economic development of the entire region.

Town residents were in the forefront of calls for expanding educational opportunities, arguing that schooling would bring progress and prosperity to all. These townspeople found the rural folk's indifference to schooling and development frustrating. "If we go into the surrounding country," *Carolina Spartan* editor Peter M. Wallace complained, "we also meet with the sad indications of a stupid indifference" to development. Wallace urged wealthy townspeople to take an active interest in "whether the country is beautiful with the neat and comfortable cottage, the spacious well filled school house, the decent and well finished church, or with decayed cabins, neglected farms or an ignorant population."[42] Town professionals like Maurice Moore, then, saw increased taxation for common schools as a means of lessening town-country divisions while creating a society of competent and successful white citizens.

For other petitioners, however, the school tax had more personal resonance. Overseer David G. Finley offers a case in point. In 1850 Finley owned two hundred dollars worth of real estate and no slaves while trying to support a wife and five children. Four of the children were of school age, yet not a single one had attended school prior to 1850.[43] Having to stretch his money thin, Finley could not afford tuition for his children, nor could he afford to lose their labor. Yet with some real estate and experience handling slaves, Finley must have had ambitions for a more comfortable life—if not for himself, then for his children. The school tax would provide a less costly way for Finley to send at least one of his sons to a common school. Armed with an education, this son might enter the growing professional class in Spartanburg, where he would earn enough money to purchase land and slaves.

It is unclear to what extent support for the tax extended to the poorest of Spartanburg's white population. Some of the petitioners listed no real estate values, although fifty-two could sign their name legibly, indicating literacy. Few of Spartanburg's poorest farmers would have been literate. Many poor residents may not have been aware of the free school petition, especially if it had been drawn up and circulated by townsmen of middling status. The poor also had to balance the future opportunities that schooling might bring to their children with the immediate needs of the agrarian economy. The landless poor were often dependent on their children's labor, making school attendance infrequent at best.[44] Thus, some of Spartanburg's poor whites had little incentive to support a tax they could not afford that paid for schools their children could hardly attend. At the same time, there were likely those poor farmers and laborers who recognized that access to education was a key divide between those with economic and political power and those without it. Indeed, just across the Blue Ridge and Appalachian mountains in eastern Tennessee a once-impoverished and illiterate tailor-turned-governor utilized the support of poor whites to secure the state's first direct school tax.[45] It is certainly conceivable that some of Spartanburg's poor would have shared Andrew Johnson's concern that class divisions would only worsen without better common schools. Regardless of support from Spartanburg's wealthy and yeoman farmers and perhaps some poorer whites, the state legislature's Committee on Education summarily rejected the petition for a free school tax.[46]

Frustrated by the government's inaction and influenced by the growing concerns over education among private citizens and officeholders, Spartanburg state representative Joseph Wofford Tucker introduced a bill before the legislature on the subject of free schools. Tucker had studied law at Cokesbury, South Carolina, and began his practice in Spartanburg town in the 1840s. Having served as a district magistrate, he entered the state legislature in 1850 and, six years later, became the first president of Spartanburg Female College.[47]

Tucker's bill called for the establishment of boards of direction for common schools in each election district. Each board would subdivide its district into school sections of five square miles, with a common school located at the center of every section. A superintendent would be elected annually by the general assembly to oversee this common school system. The bill also called for an annual appropriation of one hundred thousand dollars to be distributed among the election districts according to the number of white inhabitants only, not representation.

Promoting his bill as a solution to the stigma of public schools as pauper schools, Tucker explained that those able to pay tuition for common schooling would do so; the state would only provide for the "humbler and less fortunate pupils." Better free schools were necessary, he argued, because "the maintenance, in their strength and purity, of the Institutions of regulated liberty, depends upon the combined *virtue* and *intelligence* of the people, who are the legitimate source of power." Tucker directly countered Frederick Porcher and all who embraced the notion that "*the privileged few* must govern." The Spartanburg legislator also argued that the 1811 Free School Act had produced nothing but a "moral waste," with teachers "of the most illiterate, unworthy and undeserving character."

Tucker condemned those who objected to imitating New England's school system simply because it was northern in origin. Such derision of all things Yankee was in poor taste, he noted, for while the South talked, the North acted. "While we have been writing words of menace and defiance," Tucker observed, the northern school system had produced "the most enlightened, industrious economical and energetic people upon the face of the earth." Rather than threaten the South's peculiar institution, adopting northern ideas on education would strengthen its defense. Tucker argued that the conflict over slavery would involve "more of *moral* than of physical elements," and the conflict would be settled "not so much by the force of *Northern opinion*, as the existence or non-existence of an enlightened *Southern opinion*." Clearly, the North's superior education provided the region with a strong advantage. Southern leaders had to follow the North's example in educating the masses as the only sure way to "preserve Southern Institutions [and] promote Southern prosperity." Tucker attempted to assuage southern fears about aping northern education by assuring southerners that abolitionism was the "joint product of religious fanaticism and political licentiousness," not popular education.[48]

Tucker had counterparts in other areas of the South. The emerging, modernizing southern middle class read the latest northern literature on education reform and corresponded with leading reformers in the North, including Horace Mann. Recognizing the economic and cultural advances of public schooling, modernizing southerners viewed northern educational reformers with both competitive envy and admiration. In fact, Jonathan Wells argues that the interregional relationships formed over the quest for educational reform led middle-class southerners to identify more with the northern middle class than with southern planters.[49]

Southerners had already been using northern teachers in their private schools and likely expected to rely, at least in part, on northern-trained instructors in implementing public education reform. Teaching provided northern middle-class women one of the few opportunities to work outside the home. By the 1850s Spartanburg was home to a number of private secondary schools for women that employed many northern teachers. Foremost among these were the Limestone Springs Female High School, the Reidville Female Academy, and Spartanburg Female College. Subjects taught included music, languages, painting, and primary instruction in writing. Adeline Harlow, a Cambridge, Massachusetts, native, moved to Spartanburg in the 1840s to teach at the Limestone Springs Female High School. In 1839 Phoebe Paine arrived from Maine to teach at the Methodist Female Seminary and was an acknowledged leader in women's education in the upcountry through the 1850s. The influence of these northern educators reached girls from throughout the South. Of the 110 students enrolled at Limestone Springs Female High School in 1858, 15 percent were from Spartanburg, 42 percent from the upcountry, 24 percent from out of state, and 19 percent from the South Carolina piedmont and lowcountry.[50] Spartanburg District was most affected by these northern women, however, as they lived as well as taught in the community. These women patronized village shops and likely influenced fashions and cultural behaviors of the region. Northern women were also hired to teach children of single families. When merchant David C. Judd came to Spartanburg from Massachusetts, he brought Vermont teacher Dorothea Tapper with him to ensure that his children continued to enjoy the educational standards of New England. As sectional tensions increased over the course of the 1850s, the influence of these northern educators became a concern. By 1859 administrators at Limestone Springs Female High School assured parents that, although the school "combined the advantages of a Northern and Southern Education[,] [i]t [was] in all respects a SOUTHERN SCHOOL."[51]

Spartanburg's educational reformers knew that the implementation of northern school policies and the use of northern teachers had to serve distinctly southern goals. Employing rhetoric designed to convince the strongest supporters of slavery and elite control that education of all whites was crucial to their interests, Joseph Wofford Tucker presented his school bill as legislation to ensure that "every white man shall *feel* he is free and every negro *know* that he is a slave." He promised "no depression of the *higher*, but an elevation of the *lower* classes; no disfranchisment of the '*privileged few*,' but to do something for the *humbler multitude*; not to dispense with skillful and experienced officers, but to place an *army* with a bright and burning *esprit du corps* under their control."[52] Here lay the fruits of schooling the white masses. Expanding access to education would simultaneously strengthen slavery and reduce class tensions by creating clearer intellectual superiority of all whites over all blacks.[53]

At the time that Tucker made his proposal, a movement was afoot among the intellectual community in the South to reduce dependency on northern scholarship and northern teachers.[54] As early as 1836 South Carolinian Duff Green proposed a literary company in the South that would "prepare a new series of elementary school textbooks, elevate the general standing of literature, and 'render the South independent of Northern fanatics.'"[55] By the early 1850s a series of mass meetings in numerous southern cities advocated stronger southern schools run by southern teachers. However, most of this discussion focused on higher education, not common schooling.[56] Tucker looked to take the basic structure of northern schooling and combine it with southern principles in creating a strong system of public education.

Although the legislature initially postponed consideration of Tucker's school bill, many upcountry newspapers praised the Spartanburg legislator for bringing the issue of education to the forefront of politics.[57] Not surprisingly, the *Carolina Spartan* provided the most effusive praise of Tucker's bill and expressed full support for having "the State of South Carolina paying her money for [education], upon a system which shall extend the privilege to all."[58] A *Carolina Spartan* contributor under the pseudonym "Australis" was particularly concerned with assuring lowcountry aristocrats they had nothing to fear from the proposed common school system. Appropriation based on white population would not slight planter-dominated regions because the demand for poor school funds would be comparatively less than in the upcountry. There would, in fact, be a crucial benefit to planters from educating the masses. Schooling would make the poor more "interested as to their special relations and obligations towards the wealthier and more sparsely inhabited districts," and education would abate "those jealousies which always exist amongst the ignorant towards those whom they regard as their social and political oppressors."[59]

Recent improvements in transportation and industry seemed to highlight the need for expanded educational opportunities. Acknowledging that many people were apathetic toward common schooling, Spartanburg resident P. J. Oeland warned that "internal improvements are drawing into their luminous circle every dark shadow," and in order to protect people from being left behind, "the State [had] to provide amply for the education of every citizen." Indeed, the anticipation of a railroad in the district resulted in the creation of new academies and colleges, and common schools would have to keep pace.[60]

Other observers linked the community's progress to the education of white laborers. "[T]he mechanics of our State," Spartanburg magistrate Andrew Bonner wrote, "would scarcely arrive at anything like perfection, until the laboring classes are better educated." Indeed, a public campaign emerged to remove any preconceptions that laborers were incapable of intellectual exercise or that schooling would decrease productivity. For example, the *Abbeville Banner* ran a story about noted Scottish author and geologist Hugh Miller's early life as a stone cutter. The paper opined that this manual labor, combined with Miller's later intellectual work, accounted for his renown. Miller's story demonstrated the "natural relationship of toil and study—of literature and daily labor."[61]

In 1855 *Carolina Spartan* editors John Earle Bomar and William H. Trimmier found no better example of the important link between education and physical labor than William Gregg's Graniteville textile factory in Edgefield District.[62] The most successful manufacturer in antebellum South Carolina, Gregg set up schools at his factory, arguing that the moral and intellectual advancement of the workers was crucial to industrial prosperity.[63] According to Bomar and Trimmier, Gregg had demonstrated that "there must be a steady unfluctuating working class—and that the cohesive element, thereby securing their constant and cheerful services is the church and schoolroom." If schools were widely diffused around manufacturing establishments, the editors explained, "we can well conceive how a strong sympathetic feeling will spring up between [workers] and their benefactors." The example of the "happy condition of the working classes about Graniteville" revealed the "necessity for an enlarged and more productive system of common schools."[64]

The link Spartanburg-area leaders made between public education and economic success were the same links David Carlton found in his study of South Carolina mill towns in the 1880s. According to Carlton, these post-Reconstruction leaders viewed public education as "one of the major factors in the economic success of the northeast which, despite the conventional hatred of all things Yankee, the new town classes admired and envied."[65] These "new town classes," however, were repeating a connection made thirty years earlier in Spartanburg and neighboring upcountry villages.

When the state house of representatives took up consideration of Tucker's school bill, Charles P. Sullivan, chairman of the Committee on Education, opposed the call for a superintendency and confessed his uneasiness with fellow legislators who looked to northern school systems as models for South Carolina. Sullivan, a representative of Laurens District, which bordered Spartanburg to the south, believed abolitionism to be a fundamental teaching in common schools and likely felt any imitations would be tainted with such fanaticism. Viewing the existing system itself as sound, Sullivan suggested simply a permanent increase in free school funds. Other legislators regarded the state's educational duties as extending only to those "who are called" and argued against any general system as too much centralization.[66] In a debate described by one reporter as "long and somewhat stormy," many of the bill's opponents also objected to the proposed change in funding from taxation and representation to population. J. J. Middleton, a representative of the lowcountry Prince George Winyah Parish, offered a substitute for Tucker's bill in which support for free schools would be provided at a rate of six hundred dollars per state house member, and local school district commissioners could tax up to 25 percent of the general tax and receive matching funds from the treasury. When the vote finally came on December 15, 1855, opponents defeated Tucker's school bill by just four votes.[67]

Following the defeat of his bill, Tucker adopted a new strategy by unleashing a barrage of egalitarian rhetoric against the state's tax in support of South Carolina College. While arguing that every man should be taxed for common schools, Tucker did not see the justice in taxing everyone so that "One Four-hundredth part of the free white youth" could attend college. Worse still, the money would usually go to students of wealthy backgrounds, while the poor were denied elementary instruction. "The middle classes and poor young men of the neighborhood have to pay the tribute," Tucker argued, "and then (Heaven bless them in their good work) take care of themselves!"[68]

Tucker had an additional reason to attack taxes in support of South Carolina College. The college created a controversy in the 1820s when president Thomas Cooper denied the doctrine of immortality of the soul and thus seemingly set the college on the path of irreligion. Through much of the antebellum era evangelicals railed against South Carolina College, and the various denominations founded their own institutions. By 1856 Spartanburg maintained several denominational colleges, academies, and high schools. However, the legislature adhered to separation of church and state by rejecting any support of religious schools while funding the South Carolina College.[69] As president of the Methodist-run Spartanburg Female College, Joseph Wofford Tucker lashed out at the "twattle about 'a connection between Church and State.'" He proposed appropriating a small annual sum to *"every regularly constituted College in the State, for the education of poor young men; and this without reference to any denominational character of the Institutions."*[70] In this way, Tucker could advance his egalitarian motives while promoting private, denominational higher education.

By the late summer of 1856 the dual issues of common school reform and tax support of South Carolina College were prominent enough to be placed on a published slate of questions for the district's legislative candidates. Six of seven candidates came out in support of school reform while announcing their opposition to continuing state appropriations for the college.[71] The seventh candidate, James Farrow, also supported common school reform but expressed support for funding the college as well. Feeling that the question on college funding was put forward as part of a conspiracy to ensure his defeat, Farrow published a lengthy defense of his position. Criticizing Tucker for suggesting that the college did not benefit the poor, Farrow argued that he had "seen the poor boy from Spartanburg District entered, educated, and graduated there, *free of charge*." Farrow then turned the argument around on Tucker and his supporters. Although Tucker was correct that many parents did not feel able to send their sons to the college, many parents also did not take advantage of the free schools because they "*think* they cannot afford to send their children on account of losing their services at home." Yet, Farrow observed, nobody would tolerate the dismantling of the free school system as a result of this problem. "The man who aims a blow at the State College," Farrow warned, "is making war upon the very principles that support all free or common school progress."[72] Farrow's strategy may have paid dividends, since he won a seat in the legislature. Tucker, having failed to navigate his bill through the house, took his law practice and his public education cause west to St. Louis, Missouri, in early 1858.[73]

Secession and war diverted attention and funds away from the cause of common school reform. By 1860, however, Spartanburg's town professionals, along with many yeoman farmers, demanded greater state involvement in universal white education. The emphasis on common schooling as a unifier of all whites—whether they be operatives, day laborers, yeomen, or planters—was geared toward promoting the egalitarian nature of economic development while preserving racial slavery. Similar arguments would be made in support of legal and moral reform. However, advocates of these reforms would continue to face resistance to proposed changes in the cultural and economic landscape of the upcountry.

CHAPTER FOUR

"*Moral and Industrial Reform May Be United in One System*"
Modernizing Law and Morality

PRIOR TO 1850, visitors to Spartanburg District often found basic institutional structures of the region lacking. While riding the court circuit in 1837, Judge Charles Colcock and lawyer Benjamin Perry witnessed a Spartanburg riot that lasted well into the night, with "hundreds . . . fighting by lightwood fires." An inexperienced attorney on his first circuit, Perry feared the fracas to the point that he fled town before his casework was completed.[1]

Observations such as these by judges and lawyers were an increasing concern for Spartanburg's rising entrepreneurs. A reputation for lawlessness, drunkenness, and immorality would make the region less attractive for future investment. Recognizing this, they launched a campaign to strengthen law and order while eradicating sources of immoral behavior. However, these efforts were hindered by a cultural tradition that combined parallel systems of formal law and extralegal community action.

The parallel system of formal and informal community justice in Spartanburg was reflective of the South's distinct legal heritage.[2] An important part of this heritage involved the region's agrarianism. Historian J. G. A. Pocock noted that agrarian societies throughout history have defined justice according to a combination of written laws and unwritten customs. When societies become more centralized and bureaucratic, as occurred in much of the antebellum North, unwritten customs are either transcribed into law or abandoned. However, the South's continued adherence to an overwhelmingly agrarian economy governed by a ritualized planter elite contributed to the persistence of extralegal customs.[3]

Closely connected to the South's agrarian foundation was its localism. Power in the rural South often emanated from neighborhood planters whose primary goal was to maintain a proper balance in the local community. Therefore, these leaders often rejected legal abstractions and retained a Blackstonian view of loose construction whereby the law could be manipulated according to local demands. Bertram Wyatt-Brown has argued that the major focus of local justice on maintaining the organic structure of society meant that "exigencies of law, distant authorities, or any form of outside force could be thrust aside if necessary."[4]

The localistic nature of southern society also meant that personal, face-to-face relationships and the spoken word were far more important than written doctrines. In such intensely personal, oral cultures, honor takes on central importance. Honor-bound societies place primary emphasis on the opinions of others: each citizen is to be accorded the ritualized displays of respect appropriate for his or her station in life. If this respect was not forthcoming, the offended party might turn to violence as a means of reclaiming and retaining honor. In fact, the failure to respond to an insult could result in the loss of one's honor in the community.[5]

For some historians, the source of southern legal distinctiveness could be found in human passion. While the North came to attribute crime to a degenerate class in need of reform or permanent institutionalization, southerners believed that violence among whites emerged from the passions present in everyone. This fact, Dickson Bruce contends, led to a pessimistic view of the world which came to accept "violence as unavoidable, as an essential fact of human life somehow built in, profoundly, to human relationships." The recognition of the inevitability of extralegal violence in society helps account for the existence of vigilantism as a legitimate means of restoring social stability.[6]

The South's dual commitment to law and extralegal authority differed according to class and region. For lowcountry aristocrats, many of whom were legislators and judges, extralegal violence most often took the ritualized form of the genteel duel. Southern gentlemen generally considered brawls and fistfights an indication that one lacked self-control and refinement. The duel offered a systematic, prearranged (albeit potentially deadly) method of resolving disputes outside the courtroom. Duels were not always fought to the death. If one or both parties were slightly injured, the affair was often considered closed. Some accounts reveal that even when neither contestant hit his mark, representatives of both parties could arrange a settlement whereby each man preserved his honor and his life.[7]

By contrast, the yeoman-dominated upcountry provided a much more fertile ground for widespread violence. A number of historians contend that this was the case because upcountry communities remained in provincial isolation and had only weak attachments to the market economy.[8] Early backcountry violence was characterized by rough-and-tumble fighting, no-holds-barred physical contests that often resulted in gouged eyes, severed noses, and disfigured ears. At the commencement of an 1837 court session in the South Carolina upcountry, Judge Aedamus Burke proclaimed, "Before God, gentlemen of the jury, I never saw such a thing before in the world. There is a plaintiff with an eye out! A juror with an eye out! And two witnesses with an eye out! What a state of society you must have in this part of the country!"[9]

The nature of violence and informal community justice in the South owed much to the region's commitment to racial supremacy. Many slave crimes were considered to be under the province of masters, and, in certain situations, slave patrols had the authority to exact immediate punishment without trial. The power of planters in a slave society discouraged a strong, centralized legal structure. Desirous of maintaining autonomous control over their communities, planters opposed an independent judiciary because it would create an alternative to their authority.[10]

If historians have reached a general consensus that law was less formal in the nineteenth-century South, they are virtually unanimous that South Carolina epitomized the region's weak legal structure. Legal historian Michael Stephen Hindus finds that "extralegal and informal authority was actually encouraged as part of [South Carolina's] overall reluctance to maintain a strong system of formal authority." The lowcountry planters who dominated the legislature kept courts weak and were reluctant to grant petitions for increased legal powers at the local level. Stronger than most southerners in their devotion to personal honor and race control, South Carolina's leading planters preferred that incidents of disorder be handled within the household, church, or neighborhood rather than in the courtroom.[11]

In many ways, Spartanburg conformed to these general findings regarding the violent nature of the South. Between 1820 and 1824, for example, the Spartanburg District Court of General Sessions heard sixty-eight cases of assault and battery compared to just fourteen cases of theft. In 1850 violent crimes still accounted for 72 percent of all cases brought before the court. The next highest category of offenses, those involving issues of morality and order, constituted just over 19 percent of cases. Property crimes lagged far behind, contributing slightly more than 7 percent of the docket.[12] An examination of the workings of the juries and court officials reveals a degree of tolerance for such violent confrontations. Since charges usually originated from an individual swearing out a complaint before a magistrate, the courts could be used as an arena for private feuds. Recognizing this as well as the fact that some street scrapes were inevitable, grand juries often found "No Bill" when a case was flimsy or the charge seemed trivial.

In addition to grand juries, prosecutors or plaintiffs could enter a nolle prosequi, a decision not to proceed with the trial. In 1850 51 percent of all assault cases ended in pretrial acquittal. Of those cases that were forwarded to the petit jurors, 50 percent resulted in conviction. With half of these offenses ending with the grand jury and half of those advanced to trial found not guilty, the total conviction rate for assault cases was under 30 percent. Community opinion could play an important role in whether or not a case was brought to trial. Recognizing this, a convention of district magistrates asked the legislature for the power of discretion "in cases, when as conscientious men they did not think the public welfare demanded a public prosecution and punishment." The nature of the assault also often determined the decision to proceed and, if convicted, the sentence imposed. For example, the grand jury found "No Bill" against Calvin Cantrell for allegedly collaring Green Mitchell "and running his fist in his face." Even if the evidence in this case were strong, Cantrell's crime was little more than common fisticuffs and hardly warranted the court's attention. A jury took little time, however, in finding Hudson Vickers guilty of assaulting one Polly Hamper. Vickers's attack on a member of the "fairer sex" violated notions of honor and proper gender relations, thereby threatening the organic order of society. The convicted man's stiff sentence of four months' imprisonment and a one-hundred-dollar fine reveals the perceived seriousness of the crime. Wherever possible, however, the protection (and control) of women was the responsibility of the male household head. When Alford Smith charged Patsey O'Shields with assaulting his wife, Harriet, the jury found O'Shields guilty but limited the sentence to one month in jail.[13] Under the prevailing social ethos, Alford Smith should have either prevented the assault or settled the issue privately.

Throughout the antebellum period, then, conflicts between free white citizens in Spartanburg were resolved through both formal and informal means. As citizens of South Carolina and the United States, Spartanburg whites were entitled to the procedural guarantees of trial by jury. At the same time, however, the persistence of a traditional frontier notion of informal community justice ensured that some conflicts continued to be resolved outside the courtroom.

The parallel system of formal and informal justice converged in a distinct way when conflicts occurred between one person or group and another person's slave property. In 1740 South Carolina had created district Magistrates and Freeholders Courts, a special community-based system that handled all alleged crimes involving slaves and free blacks. Although established by state law, the procedural peculiarities of these courts made them more quasi legal in practice. The central purpose of the courts was to preserve harmony within the white community by assuring the protection of property rights while policing slave activity. Free blacks, although not legally property, were brought before a Magistrates and Freeholders Court due to their anomalous status in the South. Not recognized as full citizens with the same procedural guarantees as whites, free blacks were also not assured any protection as property and, at times, had more to fear from the courts than slaves did.

Although minor conflicts involving slaves were often settled informally between the victim and the slave's owner, more serious crimes involving a slave accused of injuring a white person or the person's property often wound up in the Magistrates and Freeholders Court. When a white person brought a formal complaint to a magistrate, the officer drew up a charge and created a list of eight freeholders to serve as potential jurors. The accused slave's owner or the owner's lawyer, or, in the case of a free black, a white guardian or his lawyer, selected five people from this list to serve as both judge and jury. Although often not well trained in the law, the magistrate served as the prosecutor.[14] Slaves and free blacks were not permitted to give sworn testimony or initiate prosecutions. The Magistrates and Freeholders Court did not meet in a courthouse but at the home of a prominent slave owner or, occasionally, at the scene of the alleged crime. Looking both to save time and retain community control over slave property, magistrates summoned men from the nearest farms and plantations to serve as jurors. One scholar's study of over 174 trials in the Spartanburg Magistrates and Freeholders Court reveals that over a third involved juries that included more than one person with the same last name. The study also found that some trials were "procedurally incestuous"; that is, jurors shared surnames with the magistrate, the owner of the accused slave, or the person alleging criminal activity by the slave.[15] Instead of following the general practice for white trials, where petit jurors were selected at random, the Magistrates and Freeholders Courts summoned neighborhood men who often served repeatedly. Such a practice preserved neighborhood justice within the context of a legally sanctioned court.

There was at least one upcountry legal reformer who recognized the problems of fairness in the loosely constructed slave courts. Circuit judge and lifelong liberal reformer John Belton O'Neall believed that the Magistrates and Freeholders Courts should work not only to preserve the rights of slave owners but to provide basic procedural fairness to slaves themselves. "Trial by a magistrate and freeholders is so liable to be influenced by prejudice and passion," O'Neall observed, "that it is not at all wonderful that gross injustice should be done." The judge argued that black trials should take place at a courthouse with a presiding judge, magistrate, and twelve-man jury picked from twenty-four.[16] O'Neall's critique of the Magistrates and Freeholders Courts was never seriously considered because to have done so would have meant an implicit recognition that slaves and free blacks shared some basic equal rights with whites.

Despite indications of procedural informality, the property concerns of slave owners ensured that accused slaves were not convicted out of hand. Since most of the jurors were slave owners themselves, they recognized the dilemma of authorizing damage to a person's slave property. If all slaves before the court were found guilty, spiteful individuals could bring a charge against a slave as part of a personal vendetta against a slave owner. Historian Philip Racine has found that, between 1824 and 1865, 49 percent of all accusations resulted in acquittals through either decisions not to prosecute or not-guilty verdicts. Of those cases that went to trial, both slaves and free blacks faced a 67 percent conviction rate. Although infrequently used due to high costs, slave owners did have the right of appeal on behalf of their slaves. In 1857, for example, an appeals judge overturned the particularly severe sentence of a Spartanburg slave accused of burglary because the presiding magistrate in the trial was hostile to both the slave and the slave's master.[17]

Southern whites used the instances of acquittals in the Magistrates and Freeholders Courts as ammunition against abolitionists who argued that slaves were at the complete mercy of tyrannical masters. When a slave named Patrick was found not guilty of poisoning another slave, the *Carolina Spartan* pointed to the trial as "another refutation of the abolition slander that a negro cannot get justice at the South."[18] In one sense, the slave's legal position as property did provide a modicum of protection when evidence of guilt was specious and the crime itself was relatively minor. However, when slaves were convicted, punishments were as harsh as the political economy of slavery would allow.

The lash was the common denominator for all convicted slaves. Although sentences averaged twenty to fifty lashes, some cases reached into the hundreds, and one topped one thousand lashes. Most cases before the court involved theft, and those convicted usually faced between twenty-five and forty lashes. Assaults accounted for 11 percent of cases and, not surprisingly, drew some of the harshest penalties. Slave assaults of whites gave the lie to the image of the contented slave and challenged the supposed hegemonic control of slave owners. Polly Burgess testified that her slave Violet had averted a beating by knocking Burgess to the ground and striking her three times. After Burgess expressed her outrage that the slave "thought she was an equal," the court found Violet guilty and sentenced her to two weeks in jail and one hundred lashes. A slave named Jim avoided an intended whipping by stabbing his master in the stomach, for which he was convicted and received an unimaginable six hundred lashes.[19]

One of the categories of slave crimes whites feared most, rape or attempted rape of a white woman by a slave man, came before the court only four times in the antebellum period. In each case, the testimony was of questionable validity, yet three of the four cases resulted in guilty verdicts. In the three cases of attempted rape, two were based on the complaints of suspected prostitutes and the third on the testimony of a woman who did not know her age or the meaning of a sworn oath. In 1851 a slave named Harry was convicted of rape despite the court's assessment that the alleged victim was an "imbecile."[20] It is unlikely that any of these cases would have been tried had the accused been white, but the mere accusation of an interracial sexual assault demanded action. Over the course of the antebellum period only four Spartanburg slaves received the death penalty: three were hanged for murder, and one was hanged for arson.

Hardly a bastion of black justice, the Magistrates and Freeholders Courts acted instead as a legitimate means of maintaining control over slaves while preserving the property rights of slave owners. As Hindus astutely observes, "Black justice may have served some bureaucratic need for certification while at the same time soothing some slaveholders' consciences, but its primary purpose was not to be just." Since its earliest colonial origins, South Carolina, and the South overall, had based greater opportunity for whites on their complete dominance over slaves. The Magistrates and Freeholders Courts, along with plantation justice, worked to ensure that there were few challenges to the exclusivity of white independence.[21] This meant that the courts policed the lives not only of slaves but of free blacks as well. In fact, free blacks had reason to fear a trial before the Magistrates and Freeholders Courts as much if not more than slaves.

Free blacks had always posed a difficult legal problem in the antebellum South. Since free blacks were not susceptible to private plantation discipline, the Magistrates and Freeholders Court served as the primary arena for whites to police free black activity in South Carolina. The emerging ideology among southern leaders during the early republic that slavery represented a positive good required that all blacks be enslaved for their own interests and the interests of white society. As such, southern politicians and writers looked to eliminate gradually the free black presence through colonization, forced migration out of the southern states, and even possible reenslavement. Following Nat Turner's infamous slave rebellion of 1831, the South adopted a general policy of repression aimed at driving away free blacks and eliminating all contact between those who remained and slaves. In the decade after Turner's rebellion, Spartanburg whites succeeded in forcing out approximately twenty-five free blacks. The South Carolina legislature passed an act in 1835 prohibiting any free black who left the state from ever returning. During the first secession crisis of 1849–50, Spartanburg whites grew particularly sensitive to the presence of free blacks in their community. Although numbering only fifty, free blacks nevertheless presented a challenge to notions of racial hierarchy and, more importantly, threatened to ally with slaves against the peculiar institution. The fall 1849 grand jury warned that free blacks were "dangerous instruments in the hands of the enemies of our Institutions inasmuch as many of them can read and write, and can always direct incendiaries to slaves."[22]

As sectional tensions waxed over the course of the 1850s, Spartanburg whites further tightened the legal controls over both free blacks and slaves. Fewer cases were dismissed, and conviction rates of free blacks increased by 8 percent. In 1858 the Magistrates and Freeholders Court prosecuted an elderly slave couple on the grounds that they were really free blacks who had come from Mississippi and thus violated the 1835 law. Apparently, the slaves had convinced a man in Mississippi to buy them and then immediately sell them to C. D. Woodruff, a Spartanburg resident who owned the couple's children. The two slaves contributed some of their own money to the sale, and Woodruff permitted them to live out their remaining years in relative freedom near their family. The court argued that the sale was merely a facade and, despite the existence of a bill of sale, found the elderly couple guilty. In an appeal Judge O'Neall overturned the verdict, arguing that the bill of sale had to be considered evidence of the couple's slave status. The lower court's prosecution of these elderly people, one over seventy and the other over eighty, puts in stark relief the level of repression and intolerance of anything other than complete control over the district's black population.[23]

New local laws also aimed at restricting black mobility. An 1857 town ordinance prohibited any slave from selling, without written permission, poultry, fruit, "or any products of the farm or poultry yard" on the Sabbath. If caught, the slave was to be imprisoned until the master paid a fine. Slaves were also not permitted to walk with a cane or stick unless infirm, nor could they smoke cigars in the street or on other public highways "on the Sabbath or any other days." For each violation a slave faced a punishment of twenty lashes. A *Carolina Spartan* contributor drew readers' attentions to "the misconduct [particularly gambling and drinking] of many negroes in our midst." This immoral combination, "reformers" noted, could turn lethal, as the case of a slave named Charles indicated. During a night of gaming and drinking Charles lost all of his money at the gaming table. He then allegedly went to the camp of a slave moonshiner from North Carolina, where he killed the slave and took his money. Convicted by the Magistrates and Freeholders Court, Charles was publicly executed in July 1853. For *Carolina Spartan* editors T. O. P. Vernon and George Trimmier, this case highlighted the importance of prohibiting slave access to card playing and whiskey. Since slaves were "morally and mentally deformed and degraded," they argued, alcohol easily excited their base passions and led to violent confrontations. Believing that nine-tenths of all slave crimes were the result of drink, the editors called for the prohibition of out-of-state liquor dealers.[24]

Fearing for their safety by the end of the decade, Spartanburg whites sought to expand their control over the black population by creating a police force. Paranoid slave owners reported having seen "the deadly rifle in the hands of blacks in the District" and noted the absence of efficient slave patrols. In 1859 the Spartanburg town charter was amended so that the town council could raise revenue for the establishment of "a night watch, guard, or police." The tax would be levied on all those townspeople eligible for slave patrol duty. Looking to prevent slave access to weapons and, equally important, access to abolitionist ideas, Spartanburg town passed an ordinance in February 1860 stipulating that all free blacks who resided in the town could not remain unless they obtained permission from the town council. Those found in violation of the ordinance were to be whipped and expelled from the town. The fall 1860 grand jury recommended that the legislature "take some measures to prevent all negroes, free negroes, and slaves from attending musters and political meetings."[25]

While the growing sectional crisis of the late 1840s and early 1850s resulted in the greater control of free blacks primarily through formal means, Spartanburg whites drew on the traditions of both formal and informal justice in addressing perceived abolitionist threats. In April 1849 the editor of the *Carolina Spartan* responded to the arrival of an abolitionist tract at the Spartanburg post office by noting that the "villain must be detected" and dressed with "a fine new coat of Tar and Feathers." Yet when J. M. Barrett of Ohio was arrested in Spartanburg for possessing and intending to distribute abolitionist literature, the same editor expressed "great pleasure in stating that the prisoner was treated with the utmost civility, and nothing like a disposition to mob, as seemed to be apprehended by the prisoner, made its appearance." Barrett had worked his way up to the district after Columbia officials issued an arrest warrant on him for violating an 1820 state law prohibiting the circulation of abolitionist material. Prior to his arrival in Spartanburg, packages arrived in the post office addressed to his attention. Suspecting an abolition campaign, a group of citizens forced Barrett to reveal the contents of the parcels upon his arrival and found numerous antislavery tracts. A public meeting was immediately called at which those present voted unanimously to prosecute Barrett for his connection to "a foul set of conspirators."[26]

Although extolling Barrett's right of trial by jury, a *Carolina Spartan* contributor made it clear that any future abolitionists would be "taken in hand by the Committee of Safety and lynched forthwith, without the ceremony of law." Spartanburg lawyer James Edward Henry confessed to a relative that, although Barrett's crime was clear, "there is some doubt whether he can *legally* be proven guilty. If not, his punishment will be a severe one. He will not be permitted quietly to leave the State, without carrying with him its sov[e]reign if not legal *marks* of displeasure."[27]

In another example of a response to abolitionism that held out both legal and extralegal remedies, the Spartanburg Committee of Vigilance and Safety formed in September 1849 to protect citizens against the cancerous spread of abolitionist writings. The committee justified its organization on a long republican heritage of citizen resistance to radical institutional change through the formation of groups *"whose powers rose superior to the Law"* to ensure peace and the protection of property rights. "In carrying out our views of the duties imposed on us," the committee's statement read, "we may in some instances have to rise above the Law, but where the Law will apply the remedy, we will resort to legal proceedings, 'and exercise that sound discretion' which is necessary under our peculiar circumstances." Among the leading officers of this committee pledged to rising above the law if necessary were three town lawyers and two local manufacturers.[28] Men who in the 1850s championed law and order as essential to civilization's moral and material progress, their support of possible vigilantism against abolitionists reveals that the dual commitment to legal formalism and extralegal authority extended throughout the community, particularly in racially charged conflicts. This long tradition of formal and informal community justice provides an important context in which to consider the prominence of the Ku Klux Klan in Spartanburg following the Civil War.

Although whites used both formal and informal methods to maintain the racial hierarchy and to preserve local autonomy over justice, during the 1850s Spartanburg entrepreneurs became more vocal about their support for the rule of law over extralegal force and called for judicial reform in the region. This campaign for law and order was closely tied to efforts at economic modernization. Spartanburg's town-oriented leadership maintained that a stable, diversified market economy would not be possible without a well-ordered civil society. To ensure such a society, these men sought to bring greater power and efficiency to local courts, convince state legislators to create a penitentiary for the incarceration and reformation of criminals, and eliminate the perceived sources of criminal behavior. An important element in crime prevention was moral reform through legal means, particularly in the regulation of alcohol. These increased attempts to legislate morality contributed to town-rural divisions. Drinking and fighting were a part of rural society and presented a challenge to town professionals in their plans for an ordered, hard-working community.

"Our court week in this country," an 1857 *Carolina Spartan* article explained, "is a sort of jubilee or festival, where our citizens meet to acknowledge the supremacy of law, and to afresh their vows . . . to its genial sway, with all its injunctions, restraints, and protection." The successful prosecution and prevention of crime was heralded as an indication of the district's progress. Touting the "argus of growth and of progress," the *Carolina Spartan* noted that the jail had "no solitary convict to pine within its walls, and if matters continue thus it will ere long be 'to rent.'" When crimes were committed, the district solicitor was recognized for his "success in ferreting out criminals and bringing the delinquent to punishment." However, law and order boosters remained vigilant against any potential backsliding into disorder. The spring 1855 court's handling of a large caseload involving assaults and illegal liquor retailing prompted calls for civility and respect for laws befitting an advanced society. "In this age of progress," *Carolina Spartan* editor T. O. P. Vernon commented, "we may reasonably hope for a dimunition of this sort of business, as well as for a smaller number of civil cases."[29]

The district's expanding population resulted in an increased need for legal representation in civil and criminal cases as well as drawing up wills, out-of-court settlements, and financial contracts. Increased market exchange is nowhere reflected more clearly than in the explosion of debt cases before the Court of Common Pleas. Between 1850 and 1860 these cases quadrupled from 35 to 143. On the criminal side of the court, the docket remained active despite a 50 percent reduction in assault cases from forty-nine in 1850 to twenty-four in 1860. The rise in property crimes more than compensated for the decline in crimes against persons. Comprising just 7.4 percent of all business before the District Court of General Sessions in 1850, property cases came to account for over 30 percent of the docket ten years later. This change in prosecution rates is most likely the result of the combination of an actual increase in these types of crimes and their more serious prosecution. More involvement in market exchange over the course of the 1850s meant more risk of indebtedness, decreased living standards, and possible foreclosure for farm owners. Some individuals under such serious economic strain undoubtedly turned to theft to alleviate their situation. In addition, commercial trade went hand in hand with accelerated interest in property accumulation and thus greater protection of private property.³⁰

An important result of this expansion in legal and economic activity through the 1850s was the ascending influence of lawyers in the community. "The business of Spartanburg is increasing," the *Greenville Southern Patriot* noted in 1854, "and the lawyers all seem to be prosperous."³¹ The firm of Bobo, Edwards & Carlisle continued to expand its business through the 1850s. The newest member of the firm, John W. Carlisle, joined the practice by way of marriage to Bobo's daughter and quickly developed a reputation as a responsible business professional. All three partners served in the state legislature at various times between the 1850s and 1870s. Other prominent attorneys included Joseph Wofford Tucker and James Farrow; both were state legislators in the 1850s, and their firm was touted by creditors as "one of the best . . . in the State for Mercantile bus[iness]." Attorneys Hosea J. Dean and George Trimmier were reportedly doing substantial business with Charleston mercantile houses, which were "well satisfied." In the last half of the 1850s young lawyers David R. Duncan and John H. Evins set up practices in Spartanburg town that would help bring them notoriety and political influence in the postwar period.³²

By the mid-1850s the wealth and influence of the district's lawyers were apparent to anyone who traveled the main streets of Spartanburg town. Hosea J. Dean was "erecting himself a sort of castle, on the main street," while Oliver E. Edwards built "a very fine house on Church street." James Farrow and Simpson Bobo both completed their residences, which "would grace any village in the State." Despite this material display of wealth and power, town boosters were quick to note that each lawyer's connection to the community along with his spirituality acted as a safeguard against any tendency toward excessive self-interest. "Sojourner" drew the attention of the *Carolina Spartan*'s readers to the "remarkable fact that of the active Bar in our court last week, no less than *eight* gentlemen are, so far as we are informed, orderly and consistent members of some branch of Christ's Church." These men, along with "a Pious Judge [and] a religious Solicitor," ensured that "the end of government [was] to be answered."³³

The desire for more local legal control in Spartanburg at times extended beyond the interests of wealthy property owners looking to secure their holdings. Laws could also offer more protection for the poor and alleviate the financial stresses on yeoman farmers. In 1846 eight hundred Spartanburg citizens signed their names to a petition requesting that the legislature

Table 8. Cases before the Spartanburg District Court of General Sessions, 1850 and 1860

Type of crime	1850		1860	
	No. of cases	% of total cases	No. of cases	% of total cases
Personal				
Murder	0	0	0	0
Assault and battery	27	39.7	14	21.2
Assault	21	30.9	10	15.2
Unlawful slave beating	1	1.5	0	0
TOTAL	49	72.1	24	36.4
Property				
Larceny	3	4.4	11	16.7
Horse theft	0	0	2	3
Malicious trespass	1	1.5	5	7.6
Attempted felony	0	0	2	3
Arson	1	1.5	0	0
TOTAL	5	7.4	20	30.3
Order/morals				
Bastardy	2	2.9	3	4.5
Liquor violations	3	4.4	9	13.6
Trading with a slave	3	4.4	5	7.6
Gaming with a slave	1	1.5	0	0
Gambling	1	1.5	1	1.5
Affray/riot	3	4.4	3	4.5
TOTAL	13	19.1	21	31.7
Miscellaneous				
Neglect of duty	0	0	1	1.5
Obstructing the highway	1	1.5	0	0
TOTAL	1	1.5	1	1.5
GRAND TOTAL	68	100	66	100

Source: Sessions Rolls, fall and spring terms, 1850 and 1860, Spartanburg Court of General Sessions, SCDAH.

"raise the jurisdiction of Magistrates to such a maximum as you in your wisdom may see fit." In particular, the petitioners urged the expansion of the magistrate's power in collecting small debts, citing the prohibitive costs of settling obligations through the Court of Common Pleas. The costs to the debtor in these cases often amounted to half the sum of the debt, forcing the sale of the poor man's property and perhaps his imprisonment, as much of the original debt went unpaid. By vesting the magistrates with the power to settle small debts, the petitioners hoped to lower court costs, thereby preventing "a loss of both property & liberty." To counter the argument that magistrates lacked legal training, the petition also requested that a bound, digested version of the statute laws be provided to all magistrates. At about the same time, the Spartanburg grand jury duplicated the petitioners' requests, noting that the mode of collecting small debts "operates oppressively upon the poor man." Despite these pleas, the judiciary committee of the general assembly displayed the legislature's continued resistance to tampering with the legal apparatus of the state by rejecting the requests.[34]

The 1846 petition's call for a well-distributed, bound volume of South Carolina's statutes reflects a growing attempt on the part of Spartanburg leaders to place more legal control in the hands of local officials. Throughout the 1840s and 1850s grand jury presentments and newspaper editorials urged the legislature to adopt a uniform edition of the statutes and the reports of appellate court decisions. The goal, one jury explained, was to present the laws of the state "in plain language before the Public."[35] Widespread printing of the statute laws would also ensure more efficiency and fairness in prosecutions. Over the course of the antebellum era, grand juries throughout the state had complained periodically that the magistrates' unfamiliarity with the law had led to inefficiency and unnecessarily high caseloads, which cost the state money. An 1855 Spartanburg jury noted the "great evil" of magistrates bringing cases to court "without sufficient evidence to warrant them in so doing[,] putting the State to immense cost."[36] Certainly, the skills and intellect of magistrates varied widely, and some yeoman farmers took the job with little concern beyond the legal fees they would collect with each prosecution. On the whole, however, Spartanburg magistrates did the best they could with little legal training and limited access to statute law.[37]

Some grand juries went beyond the calls for codified statute laws and better-trained magistrates to urge the establishment of inferior courts. By the 1850s South Carolina was the only southern state not to have a county court or justices of the peace with the power to hear most civil cases separate from circuit courts.[38] Instead, there remained just six circuit judges to handle both civil and criminal cases twice a year in all thirty districts. Not surprisingly, dockets were often too crowded for a circuit judge to clear in the limited time he had before having to move on to another district. In addition, a person accused of committing a petty crime could be forced to languish in the local jail for months before the semiannual court commenced its session. Looking to alleviate this situation and place more legal control in the hands of local leaders, an 1857 grand jury—led by foreman and textile manufacturer James Bivings—urged the establishment of inferior courts similar to those in Georgia, where five popularly elected judges heard all county civil cases except those involving land titles. If the legislative judiciary committee was hesitant to create new courts, the *Carolina Spartan* reasoned that "petty sessions business must be devolved upon the magistrates." For its part, the judiciary committee continued to resist any innovations in the state's legal structure.[39]

Delay, confusion, and overwork in the South Carolina courts also resulted from the absence of a separate appeals court in the state. Judges had to ride the circuit and hear appeals cases at the same time. Those legislators who opposed any change in the system often voiced fear that a separate appeals court would result in unchecked, "irresponsible power." Indeed, power appears to have been an important issue, as many of those who held substantial amounts of it saw little to be gained from replacing a flexible system involving personal authority with an inflexible appeals court seemingly beyond the reach of outside influence. In 1855 a proposed appeals court met with legislative defeat. Two years later the *Carolina Spartan* supported a separate appeals court as an alternative to inferior courts or more powerful magistrates. A separate court was finally created in 1859 with John Belton O'Neall as its first chief justice. However, the court's jurisdiction was quite limited. All constitutional questions, split opinions, and disagreements between law and equity were to be settled by the Grand Court of Errors, composed of all circuit judges, chancellors, and appeals judges.[40]

In addition to changes in judicial structure, Spartanburg leaders also advocated legislation designed to reform the criminal code, which would provide both swifter, more certain punishment and the prevention of crime. An increased focus on preventing violence stemmed, in part, from a shift in the way these crimes were committed. Through the early republic assaults in the upcountry most often consisted of rough-and-tumble fighting between individuals that occasionally spread to wider brawls. By the 1840s, however, the increasing availability of pistols had changed the nature of violent contests. In some cases, the yeomanry mimicked the aristocratic duel and agreed upon a meeting place and time. Constantly carrying weapons, however, also opened more possibilities for a moment of enraged passion to result in the death or disfigurement of an unprepared and unsuspecting offender. If the pistol-wielding person was a bad aim, innocent bystanders could become victims. Concealed weapons, then, posed a much greater threat to the community at large.

Looking to encourage development and outside interest in their district, Spartanburg boosters called for tougher laws against carrying firearms. Under the leadership of manufacturer Elias C. Leitner, the fall 1849 grand jury voiced its concern over "the danger to which the community is exposed by the wearing of deadly weapons, about the person. Bloody deeds are often perpetrated in a moment of haste, shocking to humanity, and the very resort to such a means is thought to be injurious and demoralizing." The grand jury urged the legislature to consider severe punishments for those carrying concealed weapons. Spartanburg jurors were not alone in their calls for weapons restrictions. Indeed, the state legislature received at least thirty-seven petitions in support of curbing the wearing of deadly weapons about the person over the course of the antebellum period. Most of these calls came from areas outside the planter-dominated lowcountry.[41] In 1854 Circuit Judge O'Neall urged upcountry residents to support a bill before the state legislature to prohibit the sale of bowie knives, revolving or pocket pistols, and other deadly weapons and to make stabbing or shooting with a concealed weapon a capital offense. Although the bill failed in the senate, interest in weapons restrictions persisted. The spring 1857 grand jury again recommended a stringent law "with a view of suppressing the practice of carrying concealed and deadly weapons, which prevails to an alarming extent in the country." In late 1858 the legislature did pass a law that stiffened the penalties for assaults committed with concealed weapons to include fines of between two hundred and two thousand dollars and imprisonment for up to six months.[42]

Legislation to prevent crime and provide for its more efficient prosecution did not address the problem of how best to punish convicted criminals. By the early national period, Spartanburg's educated citizens and their counterparts throughout the South increasingly recognized that inconsistent sentencing along with often severe physical punishments and high numbers of capital crimes only offered northerners more evidence of the region's barbarous nature. In an attempt to correct this seemingly uncivilized pattern, these men supported what had come to be the symbol of criminal justice in an enlightened age: the penitentiary.[43] As early as the 1790s northern states began erecting penitentiaries as an outgrowth of Enlightenment rationalism, which found in central institutions a precision of punishment and possibilities for humanitarian reform. Influential European legal minds like Beccaria, Blackstone, and Montesquieu supported state prisons as a means to assure equal and certain punishment and to avoid excessive cruelty. Historians have noted that such institutionalization also appealed to capitalist societies because it stressed efficiency and the removal of those who could not display the self-discipline necessary in a liberal community.[44]

The groundwork for a penitentiary system in America was laid at Philadelphia's Walnut Street prison in 1790. Having substantially reduced the number of capital crimes, Pennsylvania looked to reform criminals through solitary confinement and hard labor. Isolation, it was argued, would force prisoners to search the sinfulness of their soul and work to correct their deviant behavior. In 1816 an important change was introduced in the philosophy of institutionalization with the construction of a prison in Auburn, New York. The Auburn system rejected the practice of total isolation and instead brought prisoners together to work in silence during the day and return to separate cells at night. By the 1830s Auburn-inspired penitentiaries had been built in a number of states in both the North and the South.[45]

Despite a stronger suspicion of centralized power, many southerners nevertheless saw the benefits in removing from society those who lacked the self-control so necessary to the preservation of republican independence. Indeed, prison supporters followed a philosophy similar to that of the proslavery theorists who presented black bondage as a positive good in part because it controlled the poorest and most dangerous criminal class, thus allowing law-abiding whites to pursue prosperous independence. The penitentiary would serve to punish those whites who failed to control their passion by taking away cherished liberties and enabling free men the greater ability to enjoy their independence. In sharp contrast to the irredeemable slave, however, the prison offered the hope of reformation and the return to a successful, independent life. Penitentiary opponents in the South pointed to the dangerous precedent of state centralization and the prospect of even greater cruelty to inmates behind prison walls. In the end, penitentiary supporters held the day, as every southern state with the exception of South Carolina built an institution before the Civil War.[46]

The absence of a penitentiary in South Carolina offers a striking indication of the power of an entrenched planter elite in the state's political life. Despite widespread support for this innovation, these aristocrats resisted a prison because it presented a formal, centralized power immune to their personal authority. Calls for a penitentiary in the state can be found as early as 1797, and the first of many bills to create the institution met defeat in 1811. Prospects for a prison seemed particularly bright in the 1830s, when South Carolina professor and internationally renowned penologist Francis Lieber joined forces with Greenville lawyer-legislator Benjamin F. Perry. Perry prepared a legislative report and Lieber authored a public letter outlining the benefits of a state prison, particularly its egalitarian and efficient punishment. Despite much discussion, consideration of the matter died in the senate.[47]

The 1840s and 1850s witnessed a groundswell of support for a penitentiary, including every governor and at least eighty-two grand juries between 1846 and 1859. Not surprisingly, Spartanburg editorialists and grand jurors added their voices to the chorus of prison advocates. "Believing that certain punishment is more effective, in preventing crime, than cruel punishment, seldom inflicted, because of its cruelty," an 1849 grand jury explained, "and believing that fierce punishment, publicly exhibited, is a species of brutality, which poisons the fountain of morality at its source, and therefore involves a whole community in a form of collective guilt; and because an amelioration of the criminal code with fidelity in its administration, has every where been followed by a diminution of crime, we present the want of a Penitentiary in our State, as a grievance which cannot be too speedily remedied."[48]

Support for a penitentiary thus followed two basic lines of argument. The first of these noted that the certainty of punishment was more a deterrent to crime than the severity of punishment. In capital cases, sympathetic jurors, who often were neighbors or kin of the accused and the accused's family, would choose to acquit if the only other option was conviction with an automatic death penalty. An 1855 grand jury reported that in capital cases there were "three escapes, where one is punished." In addition to ensuring punishment, supporters also looked to the penitentiary as a means toward the criminal's reformation. Capital and corporal punishment, they argued, did nothing to restore the moral compass of the convicted. Instead, floggings only served to harden the criminal. Also, whippings and brandings too closely resembled slave punishment, which, critics feared, shamed white criminals in the eyes of both whites and blacks.[49] A penitentiary proposed to solve each of these problems by ensuring certain punishment in the form of lost liberties, the removal of white criminals from the sight of blacks, and both the prisoner's reform and contribution to the infrastructural improvement of the state through hard labor. In fact, the last issue of prison labor seemed to penitentiary supporters to clinch their arguments for the institution. The *Carolina Spartan* pushed for incarceration to be "accompanied by labor, so that moral and industrial reform may be united in one system." Editors A. T. Cavis and George Trimmier countered objections that prison labor would compete with honest workers by explaining that the inmates' work would defray the expenses of the penitentiary, and prison officials would select employment "least likely to conflict with honest home enterprise."[50]

By the late 1850s reform-minded folks in Spartanburg had grown weary of the state's resistance to legal change. After a ten-year lobbying effort on behalf of a penitentiary, reformers found the prospects "so hopeless . . . that the papers and people, as primary exponents of sentiment have ceased solicitude upon the topic and it has since passed to the grand juries." Yet session after session of grand jury appeals for the institution and for a host of other judicial changes went unheeded. The *Carolina Spartan* observed: "Term after term of our courts, the bench directs the public attention to the various subjects deemed important for the general welfare,—the reports are made—copies are ordered to be transmitted to the legislature—presented—referred—and so ends the circle. No changes or modifications are made, and the ship of state scuds along . . . to drift like a log, and be passed by the jaunty craft that hold the same course upon the sea of progress and amelioration." Legal reformers assured conservatives that they were not radical innovators but simply recognized the need for "salutary reforms when demanded by public exigency and the progress and change constantly passing over the face of society." The legislature's inaction was also blamed for the steady stream of emigration out of the state. Facing a conservative and unresponsive government, the argument followed, South Carolina's most talented and best educated citizens moved to regions more hospitable to development. "If those who make our laws will not heed popular discontent," an article warned, "that discontent will develop its potency by taking itself away from the State." One suggested solution to the legislature's inaction was to extend the assembly's term to ensure thoughtful deliberation of proposed changes.[51]

Many of Spartanburg's economic leaders also looked to moral suasion and moral legislation to ensure a society of temperate, hard-working, law-abiding citizens. Much of the interest in moral reformation derived from the evangelical revivals sweeping through the southern upcountry around the turn of the nineteenth century. These revivals emphasized new standards of piety and restraint necessary for participation in a democratic republic. Historians have clearly demonstrated that evangelical churches adapted to southern culture by eliminating much of their focus on egalitarianism and thereby removing any potential religious threat to slavery.[52] This conservative nature of southern evangelicalism appealed to whites of all classes. As Jonathan Daniel Wells demonstrates, however, modernizing southerners could draw on the evangelical message of hard work and temperance to support their calls for a diversified market economy, which necessitated a more fixed work schedule and sober employees. In addition, southern entrepreneurs could utilize the Baptist and Methodist attack on luxury to critique the excess of plantation culture.[53] In 1802 an interdenominational camp meeting of Presbyterians, Baptists, and Methodists in Spartanburg District drew over five thousand people and signaled an important step in the religious development of the area. However, it was not until the 1830s that formal church buildings and distinct congregations took shape. This was precisely the time that a business middle class of merchants, lawyers, manufacturers, and other professionals was emerging. Many of the leading middle-class entrepreneurs in Spartanburg were also leaders in local evangelical churches. For example, Simpson Bobo, Joseph Finger, and Joseph Wofford Tucker were all lay leaders in the Methodist church. In addition to important Baptist and Methodist congregations in Spartanburg town, evangelical churches also appeared near the mill villages of Fingerville and Bivingsville.[54] Therefore, Spartanburg entrepreneurs were well positioned to influence much of the religious community and play an important role in defining the place of morality and commerce within that community.

The churches were usually the first organizations to identify excessive indulgence in hard drink as the clearest moral failing leading to idleness and crime. By the antebellum period this religious influence combined with an increased focus on economic development to produce a significant temperance movement in the upcountry. In 1849 a Spartanburg grand jury identified "the tipling or spirit selling in the district, as the fruitful source of immorality, poverty and crime." Circuit Judge O'Neall spoke for many temperance reformers when he cited alcohol as responsible for nine-tenths of all crime in South Carolina and as "the parent of poverty," destroying the "activity, energy, industry, and hope" of the state.[55]

In 1829 South Carolina's first temperance society formed in Columbia with the drafting of a constitution and the election of officers. The next year Spartanburg formed its own temperance organization under the leadership of three of the district's most prominent citizens: lawyers Simpson Bobo and Hosea J. Dean and physician R. M. Young. These men expressed particular concern at the prevalent inebriation on holidays, court days, and sales days, all days when persons from outside the district were more likely to visit. The organizers initially found the crusade slow going and membership nonexistent until they enlisted the support of the Reverend John G. Landrum. Raised in neighboring Union District and ordained in the Baptist Church in 1831, Landrum was assigned to Spartanburg's New Prospect Church the following year, where he quickly developed a reputation for his eloquent sermons on the evils of liquor. Simpson Bobo later recalled that "when Mr. Landrum first came among us dram-drinking was common with members of the church, so much so that it was a matter of constant reproach to the church. Treating with whisky at elections by candidates was almost universal." Yet with Landrum's influence "in 1843 there were nearly three thousand persons in the [district] pledged to total abstinence."[56]

When the state Temperance Convention convened at Greenville in August 1842, representatives of six Spartanburg societies were in attendance. A year later, the convention met at Spartanburg, with twenty-three of the host district's temperance societies present. Interest in the temperance crusade extended throughout the South Carolina upcountry. Mary Davis Brown, a York District resident, reported "great temperance meeting[s]" in her district in 1857 and 1858. Brown heard some estimates putting the attendance at the July 1857 gathering at between three and four thousand people. In February 1860 Wofford College student Sumter Tarrant was sufficiently impressed by Professor James H. Carlisle's "excellent address" on the evils of drink to consider joining the school's Sons of Temperance organization the following week.[57]

Some temperance advocates went beyond emotional orations and testimonials on the sin of hard liquor to push for legal restrictions on its sale. In 1853 a group of Spartanburg businessmen ran for the town council on a ticket aimed at seriously curbing or even prohibiting alcohol retailing within town limits. At the September election 138 of 165 voters elected the "gentlemen [who] pledged to carry out the Anti-License principle." By the next February the new town council had passed an ordinance making it illegal to sell alcohol in quantities of three gallons or more "to be drank, or with a view to be drank" within the corporate limits of the town. Even prior to this law the court dealt rather heavily with those convicted of unlicensed liquor sales. In 1850 Thomas Spencer and his wife, Mary, were each fined one hundred dollars for illegal retailing; only one other case out of the sixty-eight before the court drew a higher fine. Ten years later prosecution of liquor law violations had tripled.[58]

In the spring of 1854 Judge O'Neall, chairman of the Central Temperance Committee, urged citizens to persuade their representatives to place a state prohibition law on the ballot. The manufacture and sale of alcohol, O'Neall observed, squandered "millions of wealth and income which otherwise might be appropriated to benevolence, education, and improvement." The judge argued against distilling as a necessity for some farmers to sell their grain. Not only were these farmers encouraging immorality, but, with little grain surplus in the State, "[e]very bushel distilled takes *that much from the mouth of the hungry, starving poor*!" O'Neall congratulated the towns of Spartanburg, Edgefield, Anderson, Greenville, Laurens, Newberry, and Sumterville for setting precedents in suppressing liquor traffic and called for a statewide prohibition law.[59]

However, attempts to reduce alcohol production and consumption faced a number of obstacles. For poorer farmers in the northern reaches of the district, distilling grain was the least costly, most easily transportable option for selling wheat. In addition, spirits were often one of the few pleasures a laborer or struggling farmer could enjoy. Beyond this, even wealthier yeoman farmers and planters found a dram of whiskey crucial to sealing friendships, business deals, and votes. Certainly, the temptation of hard drink was not limited to poor farmers. Lawyers T. O. P. Vernon and J. M. Elford both struggled to keep their inclinations toward the whiskey bottle in check. Factory owner Peter M. Wallace's financial troubles were blamed, in part, on his being "fond of strong drink." Even the *Carolina Spartan* expressed some reservations at the election of the dry ticket to Spartanburg's town council in 1853. "None can feel dissatisfied," the paper announced, "if hereafter, the social glass cannot be enjoyed or a small quantity obtained at the houses where it formerly was vended." Adopting a sarcastic tone, the article expressed its hope that the teetotalers would dry out other important elements of town life like sidewalks and streets and that men engaged in spiritual rapping might be arraigned for performing "*liquid spiritualism*."[60]

A Spartanburg resident no doubt gave voice to many countryside farmers in a letter to the *Spartanburg Express* against temperance legislation. The writer objected in principle to the idea that any legislation could bring about a great moral reformation. The government recognized the legal right to make, use, and distribute alcohol with restrictions only on the "well settled principle—*that I must so enjoy and use my rights as not to injure or infringe the rights of others*." Thus, liquor dealers could not provide drink to slaves, nor could alcohol be used in a way that would disturb scholastic, religious, or other associations. Beyond this, however, the law was impotent. The writer acknowledged drunkenness as a great problem but viewed religion and education as the only institutions capable of making men "sober and virtuous." A persistent effort on behalf of statewide legislation would close temperance supporters' access to drinking men and do the cause far more harm than good. "Let Maine have its liquor law," the writer demanded. "Let us have peace."[61]

The author of this antilegislation piece may well have been Randolph Turner, who, as a candidate for the legislature, sounded a similar philosophical approach one month later. Turner stated his opposition "to Legislation upon Liquor just as much as I am opposed to legislation upon Corn, cotton, wheat or Rice. Legislating upon Liquor in South Carolina, would cast a shade on my character which as a Caucassian and a white man, I am not willing to bear." While supporting the temperance cause and counting many temperance advocates among his friends, Turner objected to a class of prohibitionists who wished to "force people into submission." The candidate warned this class of reformers that there were "hundreds of men in this district who will shoulder their muskets and fight for individual rights, as well as State Rights."[62]

Turner's juxtaposition of the people versus oppressive legislation may not have helped his cause (he finished tenth out of ten candidates), but the notion of increasingly intrusive government was not lost on small farmers in the more rural areas of the district. These people saw their constitutional right to carry a weapon for self-preservation threatened. Temperance laws challenged their ability to market grain through distillation and to enjoy a social drink. Since poorer whites tended to make up the highest proportion of those prosecuted in courts, they feared more than most that a proposed penitentiary would remove control of their fates from "the hands of people whom they knew" and create the potential for greater abuse of their liberties. Each of these issues combined to make many smaller farmers wary of government-sponsored changes whether at the local, state, or national level. For their part, local proponents of legal and moral reform saw more at stake than the control over lower-class whites. Drinking and violence were real problems that threatened the safety of each person and kept individuals from realizing their full potential. A reputation for violence also impeded efforts to attract outside markets to the region.[63]

In their quest for stronger legal structure Spartanburg's entrepreneurial leadership faced challenges both from state government and from local residents. As sectional tensions grew over the 1850s, many whites were increasingly suspicious of any proposed changes to their society, economy, or polity. At times, the calls from Spartanburg businessmen for moral reform sounded too similar to the radicalism of northern abolitionists. However, these antebellum tensions over legal and moral changes did not produce gaping divisions in the white community largely because of a shared commitment to racial supremacy. By 1860 race and southern nationalism had trumped the designs of Spartanburg entrepreneurs and led to the region's involvement in four years of bloody civil war.

CHAPTER FIVE

"We Have No Union Now"
Secession and War

BY 1860 SPARTANBURG BOOSTERS viewed their district as a land of limitless potential. The arrival of the Spartanburg and Union Railroad in late 1859 complemented a small but growing manufacturing sector and an agricultural economy that, despite some market fluctuations, left a larger percentage of the white population better off than they were ten years earlier. This sense of peaceful, progressive development was violently interrupted by secession and the Civil War. Reaction to the initial drive for disunion in Spartanburg was varied. Large slaveholding planters tended to support South Carolina's immediate secession, fearing that slavery—their economic and cultural lifeblood—was under dire threat from Lincoln's election. Yeomen were a bit more mixed in their responses, but, as agriculturalists looking to increase their crop yields and slaveholding, many found common cause with the immediate secessionists. Spartanburg's entrepreneurs, however, largely embraced cooperation with other southern states in secession plans, fearing that if South Carolina left the Union on its own, the state would be economically and politically isolated from the rest of the South. Once it was clear that immediate secessionists had the greatest power in the state, most Spartanburg residents unified behind the decision. After the Civil War began, some entrepreneurs found opportunities to advance their modernizing goals due to the needs of the Confederate war machine. For many in the district, however, initial patriotic support turned to disaffection when wartime demands brought shortages, high prices, and unprecedented government interference in people's lives. In addition, the drain of manpower at home interrupted the institutional life of the district, particularly in the exercise of law and the operation of public schooling.[1] The war's end in 1865 brought efforts among Spartanburg's leadership to restore the economy and institutional life of the district while preserving white unity in the wake of emancipation.

Following the cooperationist victory in 1851, many in the upcountry and throughout South Carolina adopted a more moderate position on national issues. Mollified by a new fugitive slave law, the *Carolina Spartan* praised President Franklin Pierce for having "boldly announced his determination and readiness to enforce our rights to the rendition of fugitives." Spartanburg and its surrounding districts moved further in the direction of national unity following the realignment of the state's congressional districts in 1853. Prior to the change, immediate secessionist Daniel Wallace represented Spartanburg and his home district of Union. Leading cooperationist James L. Orr of Anderson served both his home district and Greenville. The realignment created a new congressional district of Greenville, Spartanburg, Union, and Pendleton, which forced Orr and Wallace to run against one another. In the ensuing election, Orr handily defeated Wallace and brought with him a commitment to participation in the national Democratic Party.[2]

Orr was the antithesis of the ideologue, looking instead to steer a practical, economically beneficial course for his state. The cooperationist praised Stephen Douglas's brainchild, the Kansas-Nebraska Act, as a peaceful resolution to the territorial conflict. He envisioned a South Carolina that was "a little less doctrinaire, a little more opportunistic, a little more like himself." In support of his cause, Orr established what one historian has labeled the "first real party organization in the State." Among the congressman's national Democratic lieutenants were prominent South Carolinians Francis W. Pickens, Arthur Simkins, and, initially, Preston Brooks. In his own Fifth Congressional District Orr found devoted followers in Greenville's Benjamin F. Perry and Spartanburg's James Farrow.[3]

As the debate over popular sovereignty in the territories heated up, Orr led the call for sending a state delegation to the Democratic National Convention for the first time in over ten years. *Carolina Spartan* editors W. H. Trimmier and A. T. Cavis gave their full support to representation at the national convention to be held in Cincinnati in June 1856. "The North is anxious for the opportunity to prove its conservatism," the editors announced confidently. "Shall we unheard condemn?" At a March public meeting the district overwhelmingly supported sending delegates to Cincinnati. In May Spartanburg representative James Farrow was one of the state delegates selected at the South Carolina Democratic Convention to attend the party's national meeting in June. Upon returning home from Cincinnati, Farrow reported his satisfaction that northern Democrats opposed abolitionism and respected the property rights of southerners.[4]

Farrow and most politically minded Spartanburg residents remained devoted to Orr's more practical, opportunistic approach through the late 1850s. Analyzing Robert Barnwell Rhett's qualifications for the U.S. Senate, the *Carolina Spartan* found the radical secessionist "totally unsuited" for the position. "No dogmatist is suited for diplomacy or statesmanship," the editors opined. "Give us, say we, a man who knows when to advance, when to recede without yielding ground, and ready at all times to be governed by circumstances." Two weeks later the newspaper argued that the radical created more excitement than the practical politician but accomplished much less. The *Carolina Spartan* compared the fire-eater to the "high mettled racer [who] is beautiful to look upon by those devoted to the sports of the turf; but plain practical men prefer the heavy built draft horse, with bone and muscle adapting him to profit in every day operations of life."[5]

The influence of national Democrats throughout South Carolina, however, was being eclipsed by events in Kansas and on the floor of the Senate. Since the passage of the Kansas-Nebraska Act in May 1854, states and local communities from the North and the South had developed and supported emigrant aid societies in an attempt to establish either a free-soil or a proslavery majority before territorial organization. By the winter of 1855–56 two rival governments existed in Kansas, and the territory was inhabited by armed camps of settlers supporting either a free or a slave constitution.[6] Some Spartanburg farmers joined men from other upcountry districts in traveling to Kansas "with a determination to see out the fortunes of a good cause." As early as February 1856 Spartanburg resident O. P. McArthur left with twenty-seven men and two slaves to find good agricultural lands and take up permanent residence. After fighting broke out on the Kansas plain, a couple of Spartanburg emigrants wrote back home of their efforts to "exterminate every one of the [Yankee] villains from the Territory."[7] For small farmers, westward migration still held out the potential for new opportunities and an escape from overused land, even though Kansas itself offered little agricultural advantages.

The day after the sack of free-soil Lawrence, Kansas, by proslavery forces, U.S. Senator Charles Sumner of Massachusetts rose in the Senate chamber to deliver a speech entitled "The Crime Against Kansas." In the speech Sumner lashed out at Senator A. P. Butler of South Carolina for having chosen "the harlot, slavery" as his "mistress." Such incendiary rhetoric, with its allusion to rape, could not stand without some retribution from the South. Butler's cousin, Congressman Preston Brooks, took it upon himself to answer Sumner's charges by repeatedly thrashing the senator with his gutta-percha cane. For many southerners the Brooks-Sumner affair was a wake-up call that northern politicians would not acknowledge the South's constitutional right to slave property and that physical confrontation had become the only way to defend the region's liberty and honor. South Carolinians showered Brooks with praise and increasingly looked to secession as the region's only option. Throughout the summer of 1856 the *Charleston Mercury* stressed that it had become "impossible for the Union to last." The *Carolina Spartan* was somewhat less certain of the inevitability of secession but did admit that no politician could object to Brooks's behavior and hope to remain in office.[8]

Over the next three years the position of national Democrats in South Carolina continued to erode. For many South Carolinians Stephen Douglas's rejection of the fraudulent, proslavery Kansas constitution in 1857 was the virtual death knell of national Democratic unity. *Carolina Spartan* editors Trimmier and Cavis appeared to abandon their nationalist position after John Brown's raid on the federal arsenal at Harpers Ferry, Virginia, in October 1859. The radical abolitionist's call to arms, they concluded, confirmed that "the safety of the South lies outside the present union." Still, despite announcing that it did not "care a fig about the convention or the election of another President," the *Carolina Spartan* joined the *Spartanburg Express* in urging state participation in the Democratic National Convention. In one sense, the district's commitment to black slavery and white independence made farmers and professionals alike sensitive to any restrictions on their peculiar institution. Yet in another sense, Spartanburg's two-thirds white majority did not lend itself to the "crisis of fear" gripping other regions of the state. In addition, the upcountry's developing economy led district leaders to be cautious in maintaining southern, if not national, unity. With a railroad having finally reached Spartanburg in 1859, men like James Farrow, Simpson Bobo, and Gabriel Cannon looked to tap into new markets to the north and west. Hasty, separate state secession could isolate South Carolina from these markets and impede the drive toward diversification.[9]

In February 1860 Spartanburg Democrats elected a delegation to the state convention, unified in their support of the state's participation in the national meeting. Two district men, Gabriel Cannon and Oliver E. Edwards, served as alternate delegates to the national convention in April. When that meeting rejected a resolution stating that Congress was constitutionally bound to protect slavery in the territories, Cannon and Edwards joined the rest of South Carolina's delegates—except die-hard Unionists Benjamin F. Perry and Lemuel Boozer—in walking out of the convention. With all hope of national unity lost, the state Democratic convention reconvened to prepare for a meeting of southern Democrats in Richmond on June 11.[10]

Benefiting from the state's system of legislative apportionment, immediate secessionists were able to control the state convention and elect a new slate of delegates in favor of separate state secession. One of the most significant indications of the new power of this radical group was the election of fire-eater Robert Barnwell Rhett to one of the four at-large positions in the convention. The southern cooperationist Democrats angrily objected to this new delegation and argued that the same group that went to Charleston should go to Richmond. When their defeat was clear, these disciples of James L. Orr, including five of Spartanburg's six delegates, announced that they could not work with Rhett and the other fire-eaters and refused to make any further nominations. Lawyer J. D. Wright, the sole Spartanburg delegate to vote with the immediate secessionists, was attacked in the local press for abandoning his district colleagues.[11]

The Richmond convention ratified John C. Breckinridge's presidential nomination to the southern Democratic Party in late June. Breckinridge would face national Democratic Party nominee Stephen A. Douglas, Constitutional Union Party candidate John Bell, and Republican nominee Abraham Lincoln in the contest for the nation's chief executive. Between July and the November election, southern states focused on the question of what course to take if the wholly northern, antislavery Republican Party won the presidency. In the upper South, where two-party competition lasted through the 1850s, this question was hotly debated, and attempts to reach assurances of slavery's protection from Lincoln and his party reveal a serious attempt to avert secession.[12] In South Carolina, however, two-party politics had disappeared, leaving a one-party system that prevented institutionalized debate over secession. Some historians also note that the state's slave majority led whites to unite behind both a republican ideology that placed slavery at the heart of white independence and a "crisis of fear" that the success of a northern antislavery party would unleash slave insurrection.[13] Manisha Sinha refutes the notion of a unified ideology and instead argues that planters forced the issue of secession as an antidemocratic movement designed to crush the increasingly democratic ideas of poor whites.[14] In secession-era Spartanburg the debate was not unionism versus secessionism, but cooperative secession versus immediate secession.

Throughout the fall of 1860 Spartanburg's newspapers joined the growing chorus of calls for secession in the event of Lincoln's election.[15] However, much of the upcountry support for secession was contingent on cooperation with other southern states, and Spartanburg's business leaders continued to oppose South Carolina's immediate secession. James Farrow, a leading proponent of district development, confided to his Charleston friend Johnston Pettigrew that he was oppressed by a feeling of dread over disunion and initially considered the benefits of delaying the calling of the South Carolina convention to give other states time to build momentum for secession. Charleston book dealer James McCarter maintained that Farrow and Spartanburg's state senator Gabriel Cannon were two of only four legislators in the entire general assembly who would even listen to those against immediate secession.[16] Despite these private concerns over state action, however, Farrow and Cannon recognized that there was only one politically practical choice, and they voted along with every other representative in favor of a state convention to begin on December 17. After the vote Farrow returned home and was joined by Spartanburg's other leading citizens in addressing a mass meeting on the decision for disunion. Farrow informed the crowd that he had carefully considered all political options and, after initial hesitation, decided that separate state secession was the right course. Lawyer-industrialist Simpson Bobo also addressed the gathering on the decision for disunion. His tone was much less one of jubilation and more a resignation to South Carolina's destiny. "We have no Union now," Bobo observed, "and with the forces arrayed against us, it is folly to hope for its restoration."[17]

District leaders were not alone in their uncertainty about immediate secession. Although yeoman farmers in the upcountry were unquestionably concerned about their rights to own slaves and the threats posed to their independence by emancipation, immediate secessionists commented repeatedly on the lethargy and apathy of the region in organizing for disunion. Politicians traveling in Pickens, York, Greenville, Pendleton, and Spartanburg districts all reported a seeming lack of interest in the secession cause. Vigilance committees and minutemen organizations were formed to awaken farmers from their slumber. In northern Spartanburg District the Limestone Southern Rights Guards organized in November because, they informed the governor, "this Section of our Dist. (& indeed, we might add, our whole Dist.) is far behind the Central and Coast Dist. in the doctrine of 'States Rights,'—& more especially, in that of 'Separate action' on the part of our State." In an examination of similar organizations throughout the upcountry, Steven West finds that members were generally owners of at least ten slaves or were the sons of planters. In Spartanburg, political leaders lent their names to minutemen organizations. Even latecomer to the secession cause James Farrow placed his name at the head of a minutemen chapter. Having felt compelled to explain his initial hesitation in supporting separate state secession, Farrow no doubt wanted to convince state secession leaders of his sincerity in the drive for disunion.[18]

These military-like organizations were an effective means of not only generating secession excitement but also suppressing the potential for dissent in the communities where they operated. Persons "suspected of being suspicious" in Spartanburg and other upcountry districts were arrested, expelled, whipped, or—a favorite antebellum punishment—ridden on a rail. In white majority districts like Spartanburg, these tactics may well have created as much fear in the white community as the threat of slave insurrection.[19]

If vigilance committees succeeded in preventing opposition to secession, they were less effective in generating enthusiasm for South Carolina's independence. This fact is most clearly revealed in the low voter turnout for the secession delegates in early December. The ballots cast at the December 1860 election were less than half those polled at both the November legislative contest and the 1851 secession vote.[20] Certainly, there may have been less incentive to venture out to the polls, since secession was a foregone conclusion in the state by election day. Yet voting in antebellum Spartanburg, the South, and the entire country had been a central form of cultural expression. South Carolina voters cast their ballots both to reaffirm their participation in the democratic process and to announce their political vision for the community despite the absence of two-party competition throughout the 1850s. Seen in this light, poor voter turnout suggests an apathetic acquiescence in immediate secession rather than confidence in the desired outcome.

The six Spartanburg delegates overwhelmingly elected to serve in the secession convention were Baptist minister John G. Landrum, Limestone Female High School president William Curtis, physician-farmer Benjamin F. Kilgore, Wofford College math professor James H. Carlisle, farmer B. B. Foster, and Simpson Bobo. On December 20 these men joined in the unanimous approval of South Carolina's ordinance of secession. Ten days later

Spartanburg farmer David Golightly Harris privately expressed the conflicting emotions of many upcountry residents. In the course of one short diary entry Harris went from finding the secession atmosphere "ominous" and admitting that he was "uneasy about the consequences" to expressing happiness that South Carolina "has commited herself, and [I] do not fear the consequences."[21]

Southern entrepreneurs had reason to be conflicted about their departure from the Union. Merchants were using northern suppliers for the latest fashions, school reformers were largely dependent on northern teachers, and factory owners relied on the North for machinery. In his study of southern merchants, Frank Byrne finds that businessmen with northern trade "viewed secession as a dire threat to their economic well-being" and that some merchants continued to trade with the North during the Civil War.[22] South Carolina piedmont industrialist William Gregg revealed the problem secession posed for southern manufacturers in his correspondence. Through the 1840s and 1850s Gregg had purchased looms, rollers, gears, engines, and other machinery for his Graniteville textile mill from P. Whitin & Sons of Massachusetts. Shortly after the firing on Fort Sumter in April 1861, Gregg wrote Whitin to continue to fill his orders and hoped that "you businessmen of the North will see the necessity of putting a stop to a war, the only purpose of which is to sustain a party—We have set up a government for ourselves and intend to sustain it at all hazards & at any cost." In the same letter Gregg also informed Whitin that he was going to the Confederate capital in Montgomery, Alabama, in an effort "to get the government to make machinery free of duty which will enable us to purchase as usual from New England which machinery suits us better than English." One month later, an exasperated Gregg wanted to know why his machinery was not being sent from New England and confessed to Whitin, "We suffer many inconveniences here now which will be a lesson to us," but he further warned his supplier that "you Northern people have to learn one thing, that is that you cannot conquer us, or get any compromise out of us, all we ask is that you let us alone."[23] Gregg's dilemma reflects the mix of bourgeois and conservative ideals among southern entrepreneurs. They wanted to be fully engaged in the Atlantic markets but left alone when it came to their cultural and economic attachments to slavery.

Less susceptible to hysterical rumors of slave uprisings and more concerned with forging new economic relationships, entrepreneurs in the upcountry recognized more clearly than lowcountry disunionists that immediate secession would likely create more problems than it would solve. Yet, as William Barney notes, upcountry whites ultimately acquiesced in immediate secession because "they could not offer a compelling vision of their own, for many of their preconceptions were the same as those of the outright secessionists." In the end, Barney argues, southerners "were united by their common vulnerability to the social consequences of emancipation."[24] Such passive acceptance of immediate secession would have broad implications for the response of upcountry whites to the trials and tribulations of a protracted civil war.

Once out of the Union, South Carolina fire-eaters and reluctant secessionists alike answered the call for volunteers. Yet some Spartanburg residents were hesitant to jump headlong into the mobilization for war. David Golightly Harris found that as the war grew more certain, "the fiery arder of the fighting men seems to cool off rapidly." On the same January day in 1861 that the Morgan Rifles, a Spartanburg militia company, volunteered their services to the state, a group of men formed themselves into a Union military company at "Lancasters Old-field" near Harris's property. The farmer expressed his regret that Spartanburg "should be the first and only District to raise the Submision flag." However, the Unionists quickly rethought their plan for organization and disbanded for "fear [of] being hanged." As southern states joined South Carolina in secession, confidence in the cause increased, and volunteer companies formed more quickly throughout the upcountry. A witness to a drilling of one such company in Spartanburg expressed his amusement at the behavior of the green recruits as they "leaped up, leaped backward, sideways, turned one way, then the other, squatted, stooped, snorted, spit, shut their eyes, bowed and scraped. And looked very monkeyish."[25]

Volunteer companies were generally organized around particular neighborhoods and thus kept the same basic community dynamics while in camp. Soldiers most often elected company officers who were well known in the community and held some sort of authority in their neighborhood. For example, Company K of the First Regiment Rifles elected young lawyer John H. Evins as captain, and the men of Company B, Holcombe Legion, selected surveyor, magistrate, and yeoman farmer James Sloan for the same rank.[26] Although these selections tended to confirm the power structure in the community, the act of voting for superiors was an important assertion of democratic action. Some evidence suggests that soldiers, having elected prominent citizens as officers, looked for these men to respond by appointing plain folk to other posts. For example, on a visit to a drill of Capt. S. F. Smith's volunteer company in August 1861, James Sloan observed that there was "difficulty in the company in consequence of appointing two Court-House gentlemen 1st & 2nd Seargents." John Carson, son of wealthy farmer Jason Hazard Carson and a member of Spartanburg's Holcombe Legion, felt that plain folk played too much of a role in his company. Carson wrote his father that "some of the officers even down to the corporals knowing their inferiority at home both in social position and influence take every opportunity at making you feel their superiority here in holding a petty office."[27]

The firing on Fort Sumter in April 1861 and the First Battle of Bull Run three months later ended all hopes for a quick and relatively bloodless separation from the Union. As district soldiers continued to march for the South Carolina coast and the Virginia countryside, those remaining at home formed relief societies to support the fighting men. Wives, daughters, elder community leaders, and Sunday schools organized fund-raisers, made uniforms, and packed supplies for the troops. Women and young girls were particularly encouraged to take up the cause on the home front. The *Spartan* called for the formation of aid societies in every neighborhood "so that every lady . . . and every little girl who can knit a pair of socks, may have the satisfaction of assisting . . . [and do] . . . all that *Woman* in her sphere, can do in these times of her Country's trials."[28] The Spartanburg Ladies Relief Association consisted largely of women from commercial families, and they put on amateur concerts to raise funds for the war effort. Performers at the September 1861 concert included wives and daughters of prominent merchants Joseph Foster, Alfred Tolleson, and William Choice, lawyer G. W. H. Legg, and manufacturer Simpson Bobo.[29]

Those organizing relief for men on the front lines would soon need aid themselves. The labor shortage caused by the absence of men reduced agricultural production, while disruptions in normal trade relationships resulted in further shortages and high prices. In October 1861 David Golightly Harris reported that money was scarce and that prices for coffee, leather, and most other commodities were "out of reach." To make matters worse, Harris observed, "we are not permitted to carry our cotton to marke[t] for fear the Lincol[n]ites will steal it."[30] These problems of high prices and interrupted trade were the source of particular distress in families where household heads were absent. In December 1861 the state legislature created a board of relief in each district with the authority to levy taxes for the support of soldiers' families.[31]

These boards of relief, however, could not keep pace with the widespread shortages that were common throughout the upcountry by summer 1862. In July Spartanburg farmer William C. Anderson could find no flour for sale in town, and he sent his slave Jim throughout the countryside in search of it. Thieves broke into Anderson's storehouse and took hams, sugar, salt, and what little flour he had. Six months later, the exasperated farmer wrote of his trip to Spartanburg town to see "a dirty scoundrel who promised a mutton & quarter of beef of which I got neither."[32] Anderson was at least fortunate to have some provisions on hand at all times throughout the war. By December 1862 a correspondent to the *Charleston Daily Courier* found that shortages had placed "thousands of the poorer people [around Spartanburg] on the verge of starvation."[33]

Early in the war, the state legislature looked to protect families from extreme destitution by passing a stay law, which prevented local courts from collecting private debts. Originally intended as a temporary measure, the law was extended throughout the entire war. Although the law undoubtedly protected poor farmers and laborers from losing their homes and livelihoods, middling yeomen who rented land or gave small loans to laborers and neighbors complained that the legislation made for hard times. "It does look hard that we are made to pay a heavey tax," David Golightly Harris wrote in January 1862, "and at the same time can make no one pay us."[34] Virtually everyone in the upcountry, then, found reasons to detest the effects of war.

Many blamed the sharp rise in prices on speculators who hoarded goods to create even more demand for limited supplies.[35] For struggling farmers whose sons were risking all for southern independence, this self-interested profiteering was unpatriotic and challenged the very notion of community welfare. Some wealthier yeomen and planters in the upcountry clearly recognized the potential for wartime profiteering. Just six months after the war began, Eliphus Smith, a soldier encamped near Fairfax, Virginia, and the son of wealthy Spartanburg planter Elihu Penquite Smith, urged his father "to hold on to his corn for it will be worth something after awhile."[36] Other farmers who did not stockpile goods used the same business sense they employed during the antebellum period to garner the best profits while ensuring their own self-sufficiency in food. Writing from a Confederate camp in Alabama, Andrew Charles Moore advised his mother in Spartanburg that "when beef is 3 1/2 cts. per lb. & pork 15 cts, it is better to use the beef & sell pork."[37]

Some of the wealthier farmers and leading officials in the upcountry recognized the damage to the community wrought by speculation and resisted the temptation of high prices. "If you sell to a poor soldiers wife hereafter anything of mine," farmer Thomas John Moore informed his overseer, "let her have it very cheap. A man who imposes upon helpless women and children should be drummed out of the Country." Soon after the Confederate and state governments issued legislation authorizing the impressment of private property valuable to the war effort in 1863, Confederate captain S. C. Means, a wealthy Spartanburg physician-farmer, instructed commissioning agent George Larsen that "in making impresments, it is desirable you should class your subjects as follows, 1st the speculator, 2nd the man who encourages the speculator, 3rd the man who sells to anyone for more than government price, and in the same class, I would include those who refuse to sell."[38]

Spartanburg's manufacturers looked to avoid the charge of war profiteer while still experiencing a wartime boom as a result of demands for uniforms, weaponry, and ammunition. The Coopersville Iron Works, which straddled both Spartanburg and Union districts, was under contract to supply iron to the Confederate arsenal at Charleston. Spartanburg's South Carolina Manufacturing Company also manufactured iron war materials for the Confederacy. Textile factories in the district produced essential clothing for the military while it continued to provide for the local community. By January 1863 the demand for products from the Bivingsville textile factory were reportedly "so extended that neither the machinery nor operative force [were] adequate to supply it." James L. Hill's textile operation and James Bivings's Crawfordsville factory increased production and helped make both men rich by the war's end.[39]

Military demands and civilian shortages also resulted in a greater diversification of products made at the mills. In 1864 John Bomar's Bivingsville factory was reportedly turning out six hundred wooden shoe soles per day. When the need for military clothing peaked, the mills ran short in production for local consumers, driving up prices for yarn and cloth. "The yarn fever is quite as high now as ever," Elizabeth Lipscomb reported to her sister in October 1863. David Golightly Harris found factory yarn selling for $1.50 to $2.00 per bundle "& not much to be had."[40]

Wartime production demands also drove up the value of skilled and unskilled factory labor. When a Confederate lieutenant took workers from the Coopersville Iron Works to a "camp of instruction" in October 1862, factory superintendent A. M. Latham convinced Governor Francis W. Pickens to return the men "to avoid future interruption in work so important to the Government." Even those looking to make their own cloth were dependent upon skilled mechanics to provide looms. In February 1863, for example, nineteen residents from a community in neighboring Greenville District petitioned the Confederate army for the release of J. B. McDowel "for the purpos of supplying this Beat with looms as he is a good mechanic an says he will furnish the great demand for looms at a uniform Price of ten dollars a peace." Fourteen of the nineteen petitioners were women, who stressed the need to "make clothes for our children and Friends in the army."[41]

The wartime success of the textile and iron factories suggested to both local and Confederate leaders the necessity of industry and wage labor in the South as an effective means to adjust to downturns in the agricultural economy and to prevent future dependence on the North. Confederate president Jefferson Davis had long supported a stronger industrial capacity for the South and through the Civil War viewed internal improvements as "an integral part of his program of southern resistance." Fire-eater Robert Barnwell Rhett agreed with Davis that industrial self-sufficiency was necessary "to rid ourselves of Yankee domination."[42] In his study of Confederate Georgia, Chad Morgan argues that "industrial mobilization consolidated rather than weakened the power of planters because it eliminated what had been the slaveholding regime's Achilles' heel: dependence on the North and foreign countries for finished goods." Mary DeCredico has also noted that some of Georgia's planters embraced wartime industry, but she finds "strains of both Yankee entrepreneurship and traditional hostility toward manufacturing pursuits . . . in Georgia during its experience with supply mobilization."[43] South Carolina had far fewer urban centers of industry, and therefore direct planter involvement in wartime manufacturing was limited.

The war confirmed the antebellum views of most Spartanburg leaders that white community progress was only possible with economic diversification. A contributor to the *Carolina Spartan* found in the Bivingsville factory one of the few successes of the war. "In these days, cheerless and gloomy," the commentator noted, "it is a matter of gratification that the improved water power of our district is doing so much to alleviate the evils of war." Besides providing for all the "temperal wants" of the district and surrounding states, the factory also provided good employment for over sixty operatives, "all of whom seem to be cheerful, and exceedingly happy."[44]

Although generally commended for their operations, factory managers were not ones to ignore market advantages resulting from war emergencies. With Sherman's army advancing on the Carolina piedmont in early April 1865, Bivingsville's John Bomar and Dexter Edgar Converse urged their agents to buy as much cotton as possible, since desperate planters were unloading their crops at bargain prices. "Cotton is the first thing to [be] burn[ed] by the Yankees when on a Raid," Bomar and Converse informed one of their agents, "& this is becoming a matter of alarm to the planter and it will induce many to sell to get it out of the way."[45] Yet these calculations of profit were overshadowed by a general view of manufacturing as a contributor to the war effort and employer of needy families.

The apparent success of the district's wartime manufacturing was not shared by the Spartanburg and Union Railroad. One of the last lines built before the war, the Spartanburg and Union was one of the first to shut down operations during the war. Wartime inflation, cancellation of further construction, and the military priorities for rails in the Virginia theater of war all conspired against the Spartanburg and Union's success.[46] Despite inactivity at the local level, however, the Confederacy initiated changes in the South's approach to rail development that would have far-reaching consequences for the entire region.

The critical need to move troops and supplies resulted in unprecedented governmental support of interstate rail traffic. Early in the war the Confederacy's efforts to construct an interstate line through the southern piedmont were stymied by states' rights advocates. However, the Union army's destruction of rail centers along the Mississippi forced the War Department to make an end run around traditional notions of federalism. With the approval of the Confederate Congress, the War Department gave its financial support to three new corporations with the goal of establishing a systematic interstate rail network in the South. Most important for Spartanburg's future was the creation of the Piedmont Railroad. Although authorized and partly funded by the Confederacy, the Piedmont was under the control of the Richmond and Danville Railroad. The Piedmont Railroad would effectively extend the operations of the Richmond and Danville from Danville to Greensboro, North Carolina. At Greensboro the Piedmont would link with another rail line to Charlotte. War brought rail traffic from the north that much closer to Spartanburg. This would lead Richmond and Danville stockholders to move to extend its line through Spartanburg and on to Atlanta in the postwar period. Historian Scott Nelson has demonstrated that these wartime corporations depended on the Confederate War Department for supplies, used Confederate bonds to pay contractors, and looked to the Confederate army to provide labor in the form of impressed slaves. In this way, the Confederacy, which many states' rightists argued was destroying the very principles for which the South fought, laid the groundwork for corporate control of railways.[47]

Manufacturing and rail transport meant little, however, to most Spartanburg residents struggling through the privations of war. Farmers blamed much of their problems on policies implemented by the state and Confederate governments. On April 24, 1863, the Confederate Congress passed a tax law that collected one-tenth of most farm produce from every farmer. This tax in-kind was particularly burdensome, since it asked yeomen and poor farmers already suffering from shortages to surrender a portion of their corn, wheat, oats, peas, cotton, wool, tobacco, meat, and most other forms of produce.[48] "I am taxed upon all I sell, or have to sell," David Golightly Harris complained in 1863, "and still have to buy at these extravagant prices while the Government only gives me eleven dollars per month [for military service]." In March 1864 Harris reported a corn crop of forty-five bushels out of which he had to pay the government thirty-three bushels for taxes. The remaining thirteen bushels would have "to feed my family, 5 horses & hogs and two oxens."[49]

In addition to the tax in-kind, slave owners were required to send a percentage of their slaves to the Carolina coast for work on fortifications. Since owners were allowed to pay a fine instead of sending their slaves, this system of slave impressment discriminated against small slaveholders. Planters often preferred to pay the fine of $1.50 per day in lieu of sending their slaves, a fine far too steep for most yeomen.[50] One writer to the *Charleston Daily Courier* recognized the danger of making such demands on the poorer areas north and west of Columbia. Before upcountry residents could be called upon to make patriotic sacrifices, he warned, "the strong hand of the law" had to crush "the speculative spirit" in order to prevent "disaffection, distrust of Government, and open defiance of the laws." The writer continued, "You may preach religion and loyalty, and talk of the duties of good citizens to those whose waistcoats are filled with the fat of the land, but appeals like these will no more affect an empty stomach than drops of water effect the ocean."[51]

By the beginning of the war's second year, disaffection had indeed become a problem in the upcountry. In addition to impressment, taxation, and high prices, the Confederate government passed a conscription act in March 1862 to provide replacements for the volunteers whose terms of service were expiring. One Spartanburg observer noted that conscription was "a bitter pill" to the eligible men who had yet to enlist, "for they are the crew that does not want to fight for their country." The removal of so much more manpower from the home front led soldiers to worry about the safety of their households and farms. By summer 1862 Capt. James Sloan saw a desperate need for more men at home to provide for Spartanburg's families and preserve the safety of the community. "How can I stay in servis[?]" Sloan inquired of his wife. "You are not able to do everything [and] it will take a man person" to care for the household.[52]

As soldiers read letters detailing the increasingly desperate situation on the home front, desertions rose precipitously.[53] In early September 1862 the *Columbia Daily Southern Guardian* reported eighty-one delinquent conscripts in Spartanburg, the fifth highest number of delinquencies in the state. By August 1863 the official in charge of state conscripts, Maj. C. D. Melton, reported an ever-increasing number of deserters in Greenville, Pickens, and Spartanburg districts who were receiving aid from the local community. "The tone of the people is lost," Melton informed his superior officer. "It is no longer a reproach to be known as a deserter; all are ready to encourage and aid the efforts of those who are avoiding duty." The conscription officer noted that Spartanburg deserters were occupying "their farm-houses in the valleys and on the hills, and by a well-arranged system of signals give warning of the approach of danger." Melton also suggested that a few "persons of property and some social standing" were encouraging new desertions.[54]

Military officials sent company officers back to their home districts to find neighbors who had deserted or were escaping the draft. In November 1862 David Golightly Harris was sent to Spartanburg "for some of our company who had not reported themselves for duty." Toward the war's end Capt. James Sloan applied for permission to go to the district to arrest deserters and absentees, "there being 39 of the former and some 50 or 60 of the latter most of whom have never reported and are nearly all known to me."[55]

Wealthier and higher-ranking soldiers also looked to escape the war, but few of these men were willing to risk their political and professional futures on being labeled a deserter. Instead, they looked to hire substitutes and thus use their class position to absent themselves legally from the fighting. In upcountry areas like Spartanburg, however, discontent had reached levels where even willing substitute soldiers were hard to locate. By November 1862 young planter Thomas John Moore had seen enough of the war and informed his sister Ann that he would be willing to pay a thousand dollars for a substitute. Moore found that many in his company were looking for substitutes and that he was "as tired of the war as they are and as able to pay for one as they are." Although he periodically asked his overseer to look for willing replacements throughout the remainder of the war, Moore never succeeded in finding a substitute.[56]

In addition to shortages, discontent, and desertion, the Civil War also brought a general disruption to Spartanburg's institutional life. Throughout the South, the absence of community leaders, potential jurors, and magistrates interfered with the operation of courts and basic law enforcement. Although courts continued to convene in Spartanburg, business was anything but usual. Of fifty-seven cases heard in Spartanburg's Court of General Sessions between 1862 and 1864, only one resulted in conviction, while two other defendants pled guilty.[57] The ineffectiveness of the court is revealed in the experiences of farmer David Golightly Harris. In 1862 Harris was called as a witness in the trial of accused murderer Benjamin Finch. According to court records, Finch believed that a Dr. G. H. King had circulated rumors among South Carolina soldiers that Finch was harboring his son William, a Confederate deserter. At some point King and Finch met on a road, where King proceeded to draw a pistol. Finch quickly raised and fired his shotgun, killing King. Just why Harris was a witness is unclear, but the farmer dutifully arrived in Spartanburg town the night before the court session began in April. The next day the court was dismissed "without trying any case whatever," and Finch was discharged on five thousand dollars bail. Harris again traveled to town on June 2 only to find that court was canceled because there was no judge. When the November court term began, the Fair Forest farmer returned to serve as a witness, but this time the Finch case was postponed to another court session. By the spring of 1864 the court must have had great difficulty in finding enough men eligible for jury duty, since Harris was now called to serve both as a witness in the Finch case and as a juror. On April 4 Harris went to Spartanburg "through rain, mud & mire to attend Court, but [when] I got there I learned there was no Court."[58] Harris's experience demonstrates that the normal functions of trial law were all but suspended in the district. Most lawyers, judges, and potential jurors and witnesses were serving on the front lines. Not all of those who were able to serve were as conscientious as Harris and instead took advantage of the power vacuum created by war to avoid their civic duties. Defendants benefited the most from this breakdown in criminal prosecution, as the courts either bought them more time or acquitted them without much of a trial.

If disintegration of the normal legal proceedings in Spartanburg benefited most white defendants, it had the opposite effect for blacks accused of criminal activity. Between 1860 and 1865 the total number of guilty verdicts for black defendants was only seven less than the total for the entire decade of the 1850s, while cases resulting in severe punishments during the war period outnumbered the prior decade by six. As discussed in chapter 4, capital punishment for slaves was rare, occurring only six times in the entire history of the Magistrates and Freeholders Court. Two of these sentences were meted out in the desperate days of 1864, when lawlessness, destitution, and a general sense of defeat hung over much of the upcountry. The two unfortunate slaves were not convicted of murder or assault but of burglary, a crime that had never brought the death penalty in the antebellum era.[59]

As the war drew to a close and Confederate defeat became a foregone conclusion, some angry farmers took advantage of the weakened legal structure to exact their own justice on blacks suspected of criminal activity. While Spartanburg yeoman David Golightly Harris was with his Confederate unit near Charleston in January 1865, his slave Elifus and a neighbor's slave were whipped for a crime "without proof of their guilt." Harris's wife, Emily, had heard that the court would search for evidence against Elifus after the lashes had already been administered. "People used to be punished when found guilty," an exasperated Emily Harris recorded in her husband's journal. "Now they are punished and have the trial afterwards." She then commented on the source of this corruption in the legal system: "Elifus has cause to deplore the absence of his master as well as I. If he had been here it would not have been managed in this way." Thus, the absence of the master affected not only the internal operations of the household but also the balance between internal and external authority. Had Harris been home, he might have been able to use his role as the primary household authority to resist the informal trial of his slave. However, the master's absence left Elifus "unprotected," and Emily Harris did not possess the authority to object. This incident did teach Emily to adopt more authority, as she vowed to "never . . . allow another negro of mine punished when on suspicion."[60]

Beyond the irregularities in legal proceedings, the demands of war also affected the district's other major public institution, the common school. With state funding focused on the war effort, the number of common schools steadily declined from 114 in 1860 to 54 in 1862 to just 36 in 1864.[61] The poor white children likely to benefit most from these schools also found less and less opportunity to attend them as wartime destitution forced every available family member to focus on sustaining the household. Despite this decline in formal public education, St. John's College president Whiteford Smith viewed the war itself as an important learning experience for many farmers in the district. Smith thought that the war would bring "enlargement of mind to [the] very ignorant, contracted, country people" because families of soldiers would be compelled to learn to read newspapers so they could be informed of their relatives' whereabouts.[62]

Planters and some yeoman farmers were able to continue sending their children to one of Spartanburg's tuition-based schools. The Spartanburg Female College, St. John's College, and a number of classes taught out of private residences offered students an education in exchange for cash or its equivalent in provisions. Wofford College, initially slated to close as a result of the loss of young men and faculty, instead remained open as a high school for young women. In 1862 the *Carolina Spartan* pointed to these institutions as "a source of encouragement that while the war is upon us, we are still able to keep up our educational interests."[63] Some yeoman neighborhoods were able to continue providing their own schoolhouses and teachers to educate the community's children. David Golightly Harris was one of a number of farmers in the Fair Forest area who contributed to the building of a school in January 1862. Despite the financial and military demands of war, Harris spent a great deal of time and money to ensure steady schooling for his children.[64]

Spartanburg's social and institutional structure deteriorated further in the final months of the war. Some demoralized and defeated soldiers took to plundering the very communities they were supposed to defend. When store clerk Jim Harris refused to accept Confederate money for groceries from a group of soldiers, the men raided his storehouse and "robbed it of about five thousand dollars worth of goods." Local home guards, composed primarily of older men in the district, protected the community against bands of deserters who were raiding neighborhoods along the Spartanburg border. As Union general William Tecumseh Sherman's army swept across South Carolina on its way to the coast, Spartanburg residents nervously awaited the appearance of Yankee troops. Three weeks after Lee's surrender at Appomattox, a Pennsylvania and a Michigan regiment were the first Union troops to arrive at Spartanburg town. J. B. Grimball, a lowcountry planter refugeeing in Spartanburg, noted that all residents were "very apprehensive of [the Yankees'] usual outrages." Yet, aside from confiscation of horses and mules, Spartanburg residents found the troops to be generally respectful of property rights.[65] More than anything, the presence of Union forces announced the beginning of what would be a long and difficult process of Reconstruction.

With the dream of Confederate nationhood destroyed, most Spartanburg residents seemed only too willing to trade in their muskets for ploughshares and rebuild the district's economy. "I am now going to work insted of to the war," David Golightly Harris noted upon hearing of Robert E. Lee's surrender. "I think I will like it the best."[66] Hardly the most enthusiastic supporters of secession and Civil War, upcountry residents tended to express almost as much relief at the war's end as they did demoralization at Confederate defeat. Few were satisfied with the war's outcome, but most saw too much work ahead to spend their days bemoaning the Confederacy's failure. Devotion to the cult of the Lost Cause would only come later, when economic crisis and federally enforced equal rights for blacks led whites to seek refuge in a mythical southern past.

Spartanburg's political and economic leadership looked to resume their focus on progress through better market connections and more industrial development. Soon after Appomattox, these men embarked on an ambitious program of railroad construction designed both to create new markets for Spartanburg products and to entice more investment in the region. Of course, all development of the postwar economy would have to take place without the defining institution of the prewar South. Throughout the antebellum period, white progress, be it social, political, or economic, was largely based on the presence of a permanently enslaved lower class of

African Americans. White liberty's contrast with black slavery helped shape and define the meaning of freedom, equality, and prosperity for all whites. Emancipation threatened these very definitions and created the possibility of class conflict as the gulf separating poor whites and blacks narrowed. Spartanburg leaders responded by continuing to emphasize progress for whites while working to restrict the mobility and opportunities of ex-slaves.

CHAPTER SIX

"To Pay Our Debts and Build Up Our Fallen Fortunes"

Economic Recovery and Commercial Expansion in Postwar Spartanburg

GAZING OUT OVER his lands on Christmas Day, 1867, David Golightly Harris could only reflect on "a year of trouble and disappointment to all, both white and black." An unusually wet spring had resulted in poor crops at a time when debts ran high. "Much land was planted & high prices expected," Harris recalled, "and many debts contracted on the faith of the cotton crops to pay them, but the crops have turned out so bad & the prices so low that many have been unable to pay even the expence of making the crop." Harris found himself squeezed between his tenants' inability to pay rent and his own obligations to creditors.[1]

Harris's experience was repeated innumerable times in yeoman households throughout the postwar South. With no cash on hand, farmers had to rely on advances from local merchants or landlords to get a crop planted. The merchants and landlords, looking to ensure payment with interest, increasingly encouraged or required debtors to plant in the cash crop of cotton. A poor crop extended obligations to the next year's production, setting up a vicious vortex of debt compounded upon more debt.[2] These economic relations had the potential to cause real divisions within the white community between creditors and debtors. Yet despite some conflict over individual economic interests, there is little evidence of a conscious class of poor farmers who acted in concert to resist the policies of elites. Instead, race consciousness eclipsed class consciousness. During the transition from slavery to freedom, struggling whites directed much of their frustrations at ex-slaves. Town-based entrepreneurs often encouraged the racial divide by linking the federal and state Republican government's assistance to blacks with the hard economic times facing many whites.

The power and influence of Spartanburg town businessmen increased substantially over the course of Reconstruction. A desperate need for farm supplies created important opportunities for town merchants. Farmers' inabilities to repay advances issued by these merchants kept town lawyers busy with a host of debt collection cases. High prices for cotton through the early 1870s helped turn Spartanburg town into an important upcountry trading center and led to the rapid development of ancillary businesses. Yet for all of this accelerated expansion, the core of the postwar elites were those men who had supported economic change in the antebellum era. This context is important in considering the policies advanced by Spartanburg's postwar leadership. Although Reconstruction brought many unique economic problems, the end goals of elites remained essentially the same: achieving better access to credit to compete more fully in the market economy. Seen in this light, changes in fence laws, the adoption of the crop-lien system, and opposition to interest rate regulation were not simply designed to create an agricultural proletariat in the wake of slavery but were part of a wider trend toward economic efficiency and capitalist modernization. In practice, however, much of this postwar economic legislation only served to stagnate the economy and reduce many white farmers to tenants and laborers while preventing freedmen from acquiring land.

For the district as a whole, the Civil War and emancipation produced a substantial economic loss. In 1860 Spartanburg's combined real and personal wealth was valued at over $16 million. By 1870 this combined wealth had plummeted to $4 million. The most dramatic change occurred in the loss of personal property with the emancipation of the district's 8,240 slaves. Spartanburg's total property wealth declined from $10,375,887 in 1860 to just $1,365,021 in 1870.[3] Investments in Confederate bonds and currency served to compound this economic crash.

The strains of war, combined with early postwar taxation, left crops depleted and farmers with little money to restore their lands. The district's total farm value suffered a 74 percent decline between 1860 and 1870. Cotton production declined from 6,279 to 2,851 bales. The size of individual farms in Spartanburg, as in much of the rest of the South, also experienced a sharp reduction. Between 1860 and 1870 the number of farms under fifty acres exploded from 601 to 3,450, while those over one hundred acres declined from 539 to 65.[4]

These shrinking farms suffered additionally from the loss of farmers due to war-related deaths and injuries. Approximately 25 percent of Spartanburg's men were killed or wounded in the war, leaving many women to weather the harsh economic realities of the postwar period alone.[5] Without a man in the household, Ann Walker found her prospects for a successful farming season particularly bleak. Despite a neighbor's generosity in ploughing her land, Walker had yet to plant seed in late April because she had "no money and no prospect of getting [any]." A series of bad weather patterns of drought and poorly timed deluges further depressed the economic conditions in the late sixties and early seventies. By August 1871 lowcountry transplant Lewis Grimball had seen enough of Spartanburg and the entire upcountry. Having endured another disappointing crop year, Grimball informed his father that the "land of the upcountry is notoriously sterile and unprofitable and the result of the best crop & most prosperous seasons are mere existence."[6]

Although the war brought economic troubles to a large portion of the district's residents, Spartanburg's political and professional leaders who had diversified their investments in the antebellum period fared much better. Despite losing about half of his prewar wealth, politician, store owner, manufacturer, and farmer Gabriel Cannon was still worth thirty-one thousand dollars in 1870. Lawyer-industrialist Simpson Bobo continued to enjoy a combined wealth of fifty-three thousand dollars, including forty-eight thousand dollars in real estate. Bobo's loss was far more personal than economic; his son Howard was killed in battle. Antebellum merchant and hotel keeper Alfred Tolleson made a fortune during the war and, with the aid of his sons, opened a store in Charlotte, North Carolina, in 1865.[7]

Lawyers found abundant work following the war in the legal complexities over land, labor, and debt. Leading antebellum attorneys Bobo and John W. Carlisle handled at least sixty debt cases on behalf of creditors in the Court of Common Pleas in 1870. In the same year the firms of John H. Evins and John Earle Bomar and James Farrow and David R. Duncan each represented over thirty such cases. Every one of these lawyers either had served or would serve as a state legislator. Their political involvement represented a continuing trend from the antebellum era of town professionals increasing their influence over Spartanburg's economic development through the general assembly. Between 1866 and 1880 at least 50 percent of Spartanburg's representatives in the state government were professionals with occupations including four lawyers, two teachers, and three physicians. Total wealth among all the representatives averaged $7,390.[8]

In the immediate aftermath of the Civil War Spartanburg's politicians believed that the most practical course for economic resurgence and expansion was an amicable restoration of the Union. Among the last in South Carolina to support secession, these men were also among the first to urge reconciliation. An important symbolic gesture of reunion was the support of the 1866 National Union Convention, which met in Philadelphia to sustain Andrew Johnson's conservative, states'-rights-oriented Reconstruction policy versus Congress's more radical plan. James Farrow, then a representative-elect to Congress, served as a delegate to the Philadelphia convention and announced his determination "to cooperate in good faith . . . with any and all men who favored the restoration of the Union and the reestablishment of peaceful relations between the sections." Gabriel Cannon also came out in support of the national meeting and served as a vice president for South Carolina's delegation. Both men argued that such a course was necessary for a return to civilian government and subsequent prosperity. Some area farmers, however, were not ready for reconciliation. As one Spartanburg yeoman explained, traveling north in support of union would require proud southerners to "stoop to beg favor of those who laugh while we plead, who spit on us, while we bow." For these rank-and-file war veterans, personal honor and principle outweighed practical politics.[9]

Although looking for a quick restoration of the Union with minimal congressional intervention, Spartanburg leaders recognized that the dramatic social and economic changes sweeping through the postwar South would require a balance between community relief and emphasis on individual trade, private property, and the sanctity of contract. The key to both individual and community prosperity, they argued, was a policy of progressive development through capital investment, expanded trade networks, and an increase in mercantile and professional activity. However, during particularly difficult times, some of these men looked to provide at least a modicum of protection for citizens. There were important political and racial limitations to this protection, as white Republicans and blacks were subjected to standards of community welfare different from those applied to white Democrats.

The restoration of state and district government necessitated the restoration of systematic revenue collections. Noting an "indisposition to pay . . . taxes" among residents, the *Carolina Spartan* reminded readers that the civil government was once again in operation, and "to support that government is a duty." District assessor and collector R. C. Poole had the difficult task of convincing farmers who had resisted the imposing revenue policies of the

Confederacy to appear voluntarily before Poole and pay their taxes. Particularly challenging would be the unprecedented policy of assessing freedmen. Poole asked whites in the district to supply him with the names of all freedmen so that he could ensure they paid the poll tax.[10]

Through the spring and summer of 1866 Poole complained that a large number of both propertyless whites and freedmen were refusing to come forward to make their returns, leaving him little alternative but to double tax these individuals according to law. "I[t] is due to all," Poole announced, "both white men and freed men, that all should pay their Taxes, and all be on an equal footing—not for some to pay and others escape." The call for an equal tax burden is emblematic of the double standards inherent in the continuing race-conscious social ethos of the nineteenth-century South. Throughout the antebellum era Spartanburg leaders had justified government support for railroads and other improvements on grounds that the district was poorer than many others and thus should not be required to raise the same revenue as wealthier regions. However, local government officials did not apply that same logic to ex-slaves in the immediate postwar period. Although most freedmen emerged from the war with virtually no wealth, they were nevertheless required to contribute "on an equal footing" with whites.[11]

A main reason why both whites and blacks could not meet their public obligations had to do with the increased pressure to pay private debts and their inability to do so. In May 1866 the South Carolina Court of Errors pronounced the wartime stay law unconstitutional. Spartanburg sheriff J. H. Blassingame gave immediate notice to all district debtors that "unless settlement is made, or 'wait orders' marked thereon, I will be forced (at once) to collect as required by law." Commenting on the court's decision, the *Carolina Spartan* recognized the problems inherent in remaining true to the sanctity of contract while protecting the welfare of the entire white community. Although the paper acknowledged that "people should pay their debts, and any legislation protecting them in not doing so, if not unconstitutional, is unjust and unwise," the paper was also certain that the removal of the stay law would "be hurtful to those interests which form the substratum of our material prosperity." The editor feared that, without the restraint imposed by law, creditors would unleash a torrent of lawsuits that would rip at the social fabric and lead to the imprisonment of honest men. Creditors were urged to find other methods of ensuring the safety of their loans. "Depopulation, and transfer of property from one to another," the paper warned, "are inevitable results if unbridled avarice is permitted to indulge its voracious appetite. We must be indulgent to each other, or the entire community will be ruined."[12]

Unlike the *Carolina Spartan* editor, district representative John W. Carlisle had full faith that creditors would exercise restraint and found greater reason to fear government interference in contractual obligations. A successful lawyer in partnership with Simpson Bobo, Carlisle served as one of the region's leading economic boosters throughout the 1870s. When the state house of representatives considered a bill to postpone the fall 1866 courts to protect debtors, Carlisle rose in opposition. "Our aim should be to secure the greatest good to the greatest number," he argued, "not merely temporarily, not for the hour, the day or the year, but the permanent lasting good of the people." Carlisle believed that the only way to achieve this "lasting good" was for the government to stay out of private economic agreements. "I deny the right of any Legislature on this earth," he intoned, "to interfere with my private contract." The Spartanburg representative further explained that such a policy was not cruel to debtors because creditors knew that enforcing debt collection would be ruinous, and therefore they would exercise "forbearance and generosity."[13]

Carlisle's faith proved greater than the reality of conditions facing area farmers. Poor crop production resulting from successive droughts left many unable to pay their private and public debts. With money scarce and the stay law removed, farmer David Golightly Harris anticipated "a money panic with hard times ahead of us." In January 1867 Sheriff Blassingame advertised the intended sale of nineteen properties to settle lawsuits involving private debts. Two months later, twenty-four properties were set to be sold for nonpayment of taxes, and the Court of Common Pleas reported almost three hundred debt cases.[14] With farmers facing similar economic crises throughout the state, Governor James L. Orr successfully lobbied Gen. Daniel Sickles to issue a federal military stay law in April 1867 that abolished imprisonment for debt, suspended sheriffs' sales for twelve months, suspended debts for prewar slave purchases, and granted a homestead exemption of twenty acres, a house, furnishings, and necessary agricultural implements.[15]

Homestead protection was carried over into congressional Reconstruction. The 1868 South Carolina state constitution provided an exemption for buildings and lands owned by each household head to the value of one thousand dollars. During the consideration of the homestead bill during the constitutional convention, the *Carolina Spartan* urged adoption on grounds that it would invite immigration, increase land values, encourage capital investment, further the cause of education, and protect innocent women and children. Although the bill would cause some level of injustice to those looking to collect on debts, the *Carolina Spartan* argued that the question was one "between an individual right and that of a great public or national necessity."[16] By late 1868, however, Spartanburg's state legislators were part of a small minority in the general assembly who voted against a bill to perpetuate the exemption, and they opposed a law aimed at punishing sheriffs or other officers for violating the Homestead Act. These men did not deny the financial peril facing many farmers. For example, at a speech to the Democratic Club of Limestone Springs in 1868, future state representative J. Banks Lyle observed that the problem of indebtedness had to be solved because there could be "no progressive civilization without progressive wealth."[17] Yet Lyle and his colleagues saw no promise of progressive wealth through government interference in business transactions.

The conflicting notions of community protection from insolvency and the commitment to individual contractual obligations can be seen in the workings of the common pleas juries. In the late 1860s juries faced a dizzying array of debt cases, and the course of their deliberations was wholly unpredictable. Some juries found for the full amount and principal interest; others eliminated war interest; and yet others were unable to decide the case, which resulted in a mistrial. However, continuing to face over one hundred cases per year by 1870, Spartanburg juries had adopted the rule of scaling debts, which, the *Carolina Spartan* reported, "has become the 'common law' of the surrounding Districts." Prewar debts were generally reduced to half of the principal, and war debts were set at the value of money at the time of the contract. Aside from this case-based effort, however, Spartanburg lawmakers were reluctant to tamper with private exchange.[18]

Rather than provide protection for debtors and thus violate contractual agreements, Spartanburg leaders felt that the best way to achieve economic recovery was to provide easier access to credit for cash-poor farmers. As early as 1866 supporters for repeal of the state's usury law argued that the legislation was not only unfair regulation but also an impediment to securing investment in loans desperately needed by farmers throughout the state. "To restrict trade, or impose fetters upon those who have capital," the *Carolina Spartan*'s editor explained, "must necessarily be injurious to any people." The editor professed to know of instances where individuals with hundreds of thousands of dollars were interested in investing in loans for needy farmers but backed out when informed of the state's usury law. Proponents of the law's repeal argued that it was better for a person to borrow money at rates higher than the 7 percent allowed by law than to find no willing creditors and face immediate business failure and the prospect of a starving family. Besides, they contended, free enterprise would allow a healthy competition among loan agents, which would keep interest rates at reasonable levels.[19]

Spartanburg representatives were among the majority of legislators voting for repeal of the state's usury law in December 1866. The repeal appears to have had varying results throughout South Carolina.[20] While touring Columbia in 1870, Scottish journalist Robert Somers encountered complaints from farmers that banks and commercial lenders were charging interest rates as high as 25 and 30 percent. However, there is no evidence of such outrage in Spartanburg. In fact, the *Carolina Spartan* repeatedly commended merchants for lending on liberal terms. Although such a rosy picture is no doubt partially whitewashed boosterism, the lack of angry opposition in private and public sources suggests that, at least initially, local rates were not as high as in other regions. In practical terms, lenders preferred to collect on their loans rather than go through the process of foreclosure. Exorbitantly high rates of interest would only ensure the impossibility of collecting debts.[21]

Over the course of the 1870s, however, continued indebtedness led farmers to call for a return to interest rate regulation. Opponents of a usury law argued that interest rates were best left to natural market demands. *Spartanburg Herald* editor T. Stobo Farrow instructed supporters of rate regulation to "go to the bank and ask the president why he demands one per cent, for his money, then go to your grocer and ask him why he demands $110 for his corn. The answer in both cases would be the same, and should satisfy any reasonable man." The usury issue also led to division among Spartanburg lawmakers. In 1874 the state house of representatives considered a bill to repeal the act repealing the usury law. If the bill passed, it would initiate a return to rate regulation. Spartanburg's Gabriel Cannon, John Earle Bomar, and Andrew B. Woodruff supported a motion to kill the enacting clause of the bill, while fellow county representative Robert M. Smith voted against the proposal. Despite the bill's defeat, proponents of a usury law put forward another bill in January 1876 designed to restore interest rates to 7 percent. Smith supported the bill, while Cannon, Bomar, and Woodruff voted with the majority against the measure. Gabriel Cannon went so far as to call the move to regulate interest rates a "ridiculous proposition."[22]

A look at the backgrounds of these legislators makes clear the reasons for Smith's independent stand on the usury issue. Since the 1830s Cannon had worked as a store owner, manufacturer, and farmer and was an investor in railroad projects. John Earle Bomar served as a newspaper editor before becoming a lawyer in 1869. Having held a variety of local offices, Andrew B. Woodruff listed his occupation in 1870 as a carpenter. All three men resided in towns, Cannon and Bomar in Spartanburg and Woodruff in the town of Woodruff in the southeastern corner of the county. (The 1868 constitution changed the local government designation from district to county.) As townsmen, they were sensitive to mercantile interests and looked to promote outside investment in the county. Such investment was less likely, they feared, if interest rates were regulated. Robert M. Smith, on the other hand, represented the agricultural interests of Spartanburg. Although trained as a physician, Smith worked his father's land in Glenn Springs after the war; he grew two bales of cotton in 1868 and twenty-seven bales by 1880.[23] As a farmer interested in expanding his staple-crop production in the 1870s, Smith needed to be heavily involved with creditors. Although Smith no doubt supported new investment in the county, the bottom line for farmers was reducing debt.

The large debts facing farmers like Robert Smith in the mid-1870s were largely due to an earlier postwar law designed to provide more sources of credit. Since most farmers emerged from the war cash poor, creditors faced a high risk of default on their loans. In September 1866 South Carolina's legislature looked to allay creditors' fears by passing a crop-lien law that gave anyone who provided advances for farm supplies a lien on the debtor's crop. Most legislators supported the crop-lien law because they viewed it as a temporary way to provide farmers with the credit they so desperately needed. In practice, the law functioned very differently. Since the farmers' most immediate want was supplies for planting crops, merchants relied on the crop lien to protect advances they made to yeomen and tenants. Through 1874 this lien was superior to landlord-tenant contracts and thus gave merchants the power to bypass landlords and deal directly with tenants.[24] Recognizing the potential conflicts this law would produce between merchants and landlords, Spartanburg legislator Gabriel Cannon introduced a resolution that the judiciary committee consider "whether any additional legislation is necessary to secure to landlords their rents where

Table 9. Spartanburg State Legislators, 1870–1880

	Occupation in 1870	Wealth in 1870
State senators		
John C. Winsmith	Farmer	$36,000
Joel Foster	State senator	$5,000
State representatives		
John W. Carlisle	Lawyer	$2,560
Andrew B. Woodruff	Carpenter	$2,250
David R. Duncan	Lawyer	—
Gabriel Cannon	Farmer-entrepreneur	$31,000
Alexander Copeland	n.a.	n.a.
Samuel Littlejohn	Farmer	$4,500
Javan Bryant	Farmer	$1,600
Robert M. Smith	Physician-farmer	$3,600
Claudius C. Turner	Farmer	$2,000
J. Banks Lyle	Teacher	$900
Joseph L. Wofford	Physician	—
William P. Compton	Physician	$4,000
Thomas J. Moore	Farmer	$30,000
John Earle Bomar	Lawyer	$6,800
E. S. Allen	n.a.	n.a.
Charles Petty	Teacher	—
John W. Wofford	Farmer	$3,400
John C. Anderson	Farmer	—
John B. Cleveland	Lawyer	—
John Dewberry	County sheriff	$1,400
AVERAGE WEALTH		$7,390

Source: Manuscript Census Returns, Population Schedule, Spartanburg District and County, 1870, NA.

tenants are removing the crop before paying rents."[25] The desperate need for credit to secure farm implements, dry goods, and other necessities combined with the security of the crop-lien law to provide ripe opportunities for commercial ventures. Spartanburg merchants, like those throughout the South, most often advanced supplies on the condition that the farmer plant a certain percentage of his acreage in cotton, the most marketable crop of the late 1860s.[26] The merchants' preference for cotton was of central importance in explaining the explosion in cotton production and trade by the mid-1870s. Between 1860 and 1875 the county's cotton-to-corn ratio jumped from 3.5 to 10.4.[27] At the same time, the developing railroad network brought in cheap foodstuffs, which allowed farmers to devote more acreage to the staple crop.[28] Regions previously ill adapted to cotton in the antebellum period were transformed by the large-scale introduction of guano in 1873. Advertisements championed the miraculous results of Peruvian guano, and many farmers took their claims seriously. "The farmers are going pretty heavy for cotton this year," local farmer M. W. Goforth reported in early 1874, "and for the guano pretty extensively."[29]

Public campaigns throughout Spartanburg encouraged farmers to "make cotton" on all lands beyond those devoted to subsistence corn crops. With so many surrounding regions growing substantial corn and grain, staple-crop proponents argued, market competition in these crops would prove futile. Only by cultivating cotton could farmers pay their debts and reinvigorate the local economy. The *Carolina Spartan* suggested that profits from cotton maximization would provide capital necessary for factory expansion. "Does anybody think for a moment," editors Peter M. Wallace and Francis M. Trimmier queried, "that the people of the up-country can pay their debts, taxes, lawyers, physicians, merchants, and other demands, build factories &c., by raising corn, wheat, and peas to sell?" If these were the only crops, "there would never be another factory built by our people." Those preaching salvation through cotton chastised southerners who objected to cultivation on grounds that it would supply necessary goods to their northern enemies. "We don't care now, who gets the cotton or who wears it," one editorial noted, "so that we get its value in money—which money would go a great way in helping us out of the bad fix we are now in. The cotton and corn question is not a question of patriotism, but is one, how to pay our debts and build up our fallen fortunes." The *Carolina Spartan* issued these pleas for maximizing cotton production even as it reported on the anticipated arrival of four hundred bushels of corn from the Southern Relief Association of New York to help feed the district's destitute. Surplus provisions were discouraged as unmarketable at a time when many of the region's poor were in desperate need of sustenance.[30]

While poor farmers had trouble putting food on the table, a number of town merchants in Spartanburg found success unparalleled in the antebellum period. Despite findings that postwar mercantile opportunities gave rise to a new business class in some areas of the South, the most successful Reconstruction-era merchants in Spartanburg were those who had similar occupations in the antebellum era.[31] Considered Spartanburg's "best merchants" in the 1850s, the firm of Foster & Judd rebounded quickly from an initial wartime loss so that postwar credit reporters identified them as "one of the [area's] leading houses" in 1867 and "one of the strongest firms" in the county by 1876. The firm assured prospective clients that they made "liberal advances on cotton" and shipped to markets in Charleston and New York. David Cook Judd's prosperity helped garner him the presidency of the National Bank of Spartanburg in the mid-1870s. Lee & Twitty's John A. Lee, a successful merchant of small capital during the antebellum era, had emerged as one of the county's most substantial merchants by the late 1870s. Another antebellum merchant of small means, John H. Montgomery, suffered a more substantial wartime setback with the forced closure of his general store. Yet by the mid-1870s Montgomery operated another store and was "making money rapidly" through the buying and selling of cotton and fertilizer.[32]

Certainly, not all prewar merchants enjoyed continued success through Reconstruction. Prominent antebellum dry goods merchant R. A. Cates was insolvent through the 1870s, and one credit reporter noted that the "war ha[d] used him up." Hiram Mitchell had achieved enough prewar success to retire before the outbreak of the Civil War. By 1867, however, Mitchell had incurred such heavy losses that he went back into merchandising until his death in 1870. Likewise, B. F. Bates was a seemingly successful merchant worth about twenty thousand dollars in 1858. Yet by 1868 Bates was heavily in debt and declared insolvent by the early 1870s.[33]

Business success or failure would certainly affect a merchant's family as well. For some wives insolvency could mean a slide from middle-class culture to small farming or day labor. The change may not have been as drastic for other women, but a decline in wealth would still mean a difficult adjustment in social and economic behavior. The fortunate wives of continually successful merchants like John A. Lee and Joseph Foster saw little interruption in their middle-class cultural refinement. Just a year removed from the war, Spartanburg merchants were advertising the finest dress goods, hoop skirts, hats, fine china, and perfumes from the North and from Europe.[34] In addition to their activities as middle-class consumers, a few women became merchants in their own right over the course of the 1870s. Mrs. L. Kahn sold general merchandise from a store on Spartanburg's public square, and Mary Bird and Mary King each ran a grocery shop in town. Three women ran boardinghouses in Spartanburg, and another owned a millinery shop. Women also solidified their identity as members of the middle class through participation in associations like the Knights and Ladies of Honor and the Good Templars.[35] These organizations served as both a social gathering place and a means by which to promote middle-class commercial values throughout the community. As consumers, business owners, and participants in defining social norms, merchant women continued to play an important role in defining the region's commercial culture through the Reconstruction era.

An important determinant of which merchant families survived and succeeded through the war and Reconstruction and which failed was the degree to which a firm's finances were encumbered before secession. Antebellum credit reports of merchants who thrived from the 1850s through the 1880s most often listed these firms as "unencumbered," or devoted to the "cash system." In contrast, unsuccessful postwar firms had incurred significant prewar obligations. B. F. Bates, for example, had amassed substantial debts from slave purchases he made on credit in the 1850s.[36]

Mercantile firms begun for the first time in postwar Spartanburg generally struggled more than existing operations. This was due in large part to the capital required to weather the often unstable economic climate of the 1870s and, to a lesser extent, the lack of long-term community ties. In 1871 F. N. Walker opened a general store with little capital in Cross Anchor and moved to Spartanburg town two years later. By January 1875 he was doing very little trade, and after incurring substantial liens over the next six months, a credit agent declared Walker insolvent and "badly broken." M. F. Jordan arrived from Danville, Virginia, in 1879 to set up a general store, again with little capital. A year later Jordan's firm was considered "very weak" and likely to fail. Having failed at his business in Orangeburg, J. G. Shuck tried a new mercantile venture in Spartanburg. Less than one year later the business failed, and Shuck disappeared.[37]

The fact that the most prosperous postwar merchants had grounding in the prewar community helped discourage hostility from indebted farmers. In fact, the only instance of hostility toward a merchant noted by the credit agents at R. G. Dun and Company was due to economic dealings with freedmen, not unfair business practices.[38] By 1871 store owner E. F. Davis was "unpopular" with some local whites because he purchased cotton from blacks at night. This activity drew such opposition because it presented competition with white tenants and undermined the power of the freedmen's employers or landlords.[39] The hostile attitude of the community toward Davis's disregard for the economic and social mores highlights the importance of race in suppressing tendencies toward class conflict. In the antebellum period racial slavery was an essential compound in the glue that held Spartanburg white society together. Despite slavery's end in law, race continued to prevent economic division between creditors and debtors from developing into wider class antagonism.

By far the most significant postwar economic change was the introduction of former slaves into the free labor market economy.[40] Anxious to enjoy the fruits of their newly acquired liberation, Spartanburg freedmen, like emancipated slaves throughout the South, sought their own land. Starting with no collateral to purchase real estate, however, they pushed for rental arrangements with area farmers. In November 1865 farmer David Golightly Harris found "Negroes . . . anxious to rent land." Harris thought at least some freedmen would make good tenants and rented portions of his property to at least fifteen blacks between 1865 and 1870. His contract with a freedman named Julius was rather typical: "[Julius] promises to build two houses, clear one feild, work five hands, board his family, & give me half his crop." Harris was to furnish Julius with two mules, a harness, plows, and feed grain for the mules. However, less than two months later Harris upped his portion of the crop to two-thirds, explaining that he could not afford his expenses with any less.[41] Ex-slaves employed as domestic servants also entered into detailed contracts. Assuming the same paternalistic hierarchy in both black and white families, farmer John R. Jefferies contracted to pay Joseph Freedman for the employment of his wife, Amanda, and daughter Sophie as cooks. Amanda and Sophie were "entirely subject to the orders and requirements of [Jefferies'] family," and any refusal of these orders would result in the loss of one dollar for each offense. After three offenses the servant would be dismissed and forfeit half of any outstanding wages.[42]

Unlike many regions with black majorities, Spartanburg freedmen initially had little bargaining power in work arrangements. The large pool of white labor combined with a generally ineffective federal role in contract negotiations ensured that there would not be the serious labor shortage plaguing many other southern communities.[43] The Freedmen's Bureau official for Spartanburg, Laurens, and Union districts faced a continual shortage of agents and had to send officers out from his post at Unionville every time a complaint was made. Unionville's location in Union District, ten miles from Spartanburg's eastern border, also made it difficult for many freedmen to report labor disputes. Some did make the trek, however, and their complaints reveal the tendency of some white farmers to ignore their written agreements. In October 1866 subassistant commissioner A. P. Caraher sent a detail of officers to Spartanburg "to see why Mr. McAbee gives his Freedmen 1/4 crop when contract calls for 1/3." A freedman from Maurice A. Moore's farm complained that his contract was never fulfilled, to which Moore responded with an intention to settle the matter.[44]

The bureau at Unionville heard more than freedmen's complaints about contracts. White farmers also came forward with grievances about blacks refusing to work and stealing from their employers. When Spartanburg farmer A. G. Means complained that a freedwoman named Mary refused to labor in the fields, "the offendor was reprimanded and . . . sent back to work." The subassistant commissioner responded to John Fowler's charge that his black employee Jim Simms stole twenty-two dollars in gold by forcing Simms to work on the roads for three months and pay the amount stolen. White farmers may also have punished freedmen for seeking bureau assistance. When a freedwoman named Laura complained that her employer, Elias Fowler, turned her off the land without payment, Fowler initially agreed in the presence of a bureau officer to settle with Laura in three weeks' time. Just three days later, however, Fowler appeared at the bureau office, charging that Laura had stolen eggs from his farm. The theft may have occurred, but Fowler may also have invented the charge as a way to prolong or prevent payment.[45]

Finding little opportunity for rental arrangements on acceptable terms, many freedmen left the district in search of better opportunities. Lamenting the loss of cheap labor, local editors Peter M. Wallace and Francis M. Trimmier blamed the legislature for encouraging foreign immigration to the neglect of native freed blacks. The editors argued that blacks had "not yet had a fair trial" and that fair dealings with ex-slaves would ensure a productive and harmonious relationship in the district. Yet Wallace and Trimmier made it clear that "fair" labor agreements would be based on monthly hires for wages, not rental contracts.[46]

Early in the postwar period, white tenant farmers proved a disappointment to many landlords, a situation that provided some black tenants with opportunities for fairer treatment. Initially, white tenants were distinguished from freedmen in that their contracts permitted greater control over the crop and generally did not require additional noncrop work such as building houses, hauling wood, and clearing fields. However, landlords quickly grew disappointed in the production of their white renters, and editorials bemoaned their laziness. By April 1868 farmer and landlord David Golightly Harris was "disgusted" with his white tenant's laziness and found "negroes . . . more reliable as regards their working contracts than white men." Although Harris later grew unhappy with his black labor, he remained at least equally disappointed in the work of his white tenants.[47] Under these circumstances, with black labor at times preferable to white labor, freedmen were able to insist on share wages, which offered them a more vested interest in the crop and diminished the distinctions between black and white contracts.[48]

The similarities between black and white labor arrangements tore at the heart of antebellum notions of white independence. While the poorest prewar field laborer may have bemoaned his fate in working alongside black slaves, he was still free, maintaining control over his own household and selling his own labor. Now the line separating the poorest whites from the "mudsill" class of black slaves was eliminated. It was in large part the frustration at this change and an attempt to restore racial boundaries that motivated many poor whites to join the rank and file of the Ku Klux Klan.

Community leaders worked to utilize this racial divide along with the tenuous financial position of the area's small farmers in efforts to drive Republicans from power in the state. An early focus of blame for the farmers' economic plight was on radical corruption and incompetence in revenue policy. Following the imposition of congressional Reconstruction, local discussion no longer focused on the duty of each individual to pay taxes but rather on the corrupt behavior of Republican-appointed revenue collectors. In July 1869 Spartanburg's grand jury attacked tax collector Anson W. Cummings for substantial errors in his assessments, which were "almost invariably in favor of the Tax Collector." Although acknowledging that Cummings was correct in his reports that many taxes remained unpaid, jury foreman W. T. Miller blamed the situation on Cummings's refusal to keep reasonable hours so that working men could get to his office and perform their legal obligation. By keeping restricted hours Cummings was "disregarding the convenience and right of the people."[49]

A major grievance of the 1870s was the heavy burden of taxation imposed, conservatives argued, by Republican financial corruption and mismanagement. Clearly, South Carolina experienced its share of fraud and poor policy during Reconstruction, but Republican administrations also faced fundamental financial troubles. When the Reconstruction government took control in July 1868, the debt stood at over five million dollars, while emancipation removed the state's primary source of revenue through an ad valorem tax on slaves. With expanded services in the 1868 constitution requiring even more spending, the government borrowed on the securities of the state, driving the debt up to over fifteen million dollars by December 1871. Such a situation required increased rates of taxation and more careful collection of taxes.[50]

Conservatives throughout the state charged that the increased revenue was instituted by a collection of ignorant, propertyless whites and blacks serving in the legislature and that the money went to line the pockets of corrupt radicals rather than serve the public good. To address these grievances, the Charleston Chamber of Commerce organized the first statewide taxpayers' convention in May 1871. One of the primary goals of the convention was to obtain legislative representation for taxpaying voters proportionate to those who paid no tax. This, they argued, would restore the principle that those who paid taxes should be the ones to decide how much they paid. The main object, then, was to restore power to the propertied class and remove the unnatural rule of propertyless blacks and ignorant white scalawags. Only by returning government to the "hands of virtue, intelligence, and patriotism," the convention report explained, could the state "avert the impending calamity of barbarism."[51]

Although the taxes were said to hit small farmers hardest, Spartanburg's delegates to the convention were Gabriel Cannon, a merchant-manufacturer; Andrew B. Woodruff, a carpenter; and John H. Evins, a town lawyer. These were the same men who supported taxation for railroad development, more town taxes for services, and special government support or tax-exempt privileges for manufacturing. In addition, these delegates could not have been as unhappy as yeomen were with an 1868 Republican statute providing for a uniform assessment of all property to replace the antebellum system, which had taxed professional interests more heavily than land and slaves.[52] Although certain corruption was evident and tax rates were high, Cannon, Evins, and Woodruff were more interested in leading a coalition of rural farmers and town professionals against Republican government than launching a principled drive against taxation.

Despite the agitation of delegates at the first convention, state and county taxes continued to rise, and the blame continued to be laid at the door of nontaxpaying black politicians and corrupt white Republicans. Farmer Edward Lipscomb complained that "our negro legislat[ure] is ruin[in]g us with taxes." The *Carolina Spartan* agreed with the assessment of a Missouri newspaper that Republicans were "taxing white men to furnish spelling books, ballots, arms . . . to three millions of stench perspiring niggers."[53] Harnessing this agrarian hatred of Republican taxation policies and black politicians, conservative leaders called a second taxpayers' convention in 1874. This convention also reached out to moderate whites and discontented Republicans as part of a fusion strategy whereby conservatives would support state-level Independent Republicans in exchange for endorsements of local conservatives. As Michael Perman has observed, the taxpayers' convention allowed fusionists to present themselves as "reformers interested in good government rather than mere partisans seeking political gain."[54]

Woodruff again represented Spartanburg in the convention along with W. M. Foster. Cannon served as chairman of a committee charged with forming tax unions throughout the county. Both Woodruff and Cannon were skeptical of the success of the unions, and neither man was willing to embrace all of the convention's recommendations. Woodruff was particularly unsure of the convention's plan to redeem South Carolina through foreign immigration. This scheme included the creation of an immigration bureau to create a white majority sympathetic to conservative Democratic politics and willing to replace freed blacks in agricultural labor. While consenting to try the immigration scheme, Woodruff feared more harm than good. He did not think that a "crowd of paupers, of idle, untutored vagabonds thrown upon us without means, without aspirations, and having nothing in common with us but a desire to make money . . . [could] improve our society."⁵⁵

Apprehension over immigrant labor stemmed from a common perception that lower-class European immigrants were prone to drink and were undisciplined workers. When immigrant labor was first suggested in 1868, the *Carolina Spartan* bristled at the notion of giving the Sabbath over to "the low Dutch who select that holy day for exhibitions of merriment and low buffoonery" or allowing "the unscrupulous, intemperate and servile laborers from Ireland . . . [to] corrupt the moral principles of many of those for whom they are called to labor."⁵⁶ Although the *Carolina Spartan* later reversed its position to support the taxpayers' convention's recommendations for redemption through immigration, hostility toward foreigners did not disappear. The cultural habits of foreigners might hurt the county's image and thus jeopardize efforts to draw more capital to the region. There was also the potential for conflict between native white laborers and immigrants. Textile mills were already the domain of native whites, and it was uncertain how tenants and day laborers would react to new arrivals. Finally, while the freedpeople were seen as difficult and politically uncooperative, they were nevertheless part of the county's social fabric and a known quantity. Whites, particularly Spartanburg elites, had a lifetime of experience in controlling black labor.

These conflicts with the state taxpayers' convention plan limited the enthusiasm toward the movement. Despite the formation of local unions, the county tax union never enjoyed zealous support, and Spartanburg was one of seven South Carolina counties not represented at the state tax union in September 1874. Instead, the county's legislators looked to relieve farmers through the postponement of tax collection and the suspension of penalties for nonpayment. Between 1873 and 1875 legislators Robert M. Smith, Gabriel Cannon, and Andrew B. Woodruff all introduced bills (unsuccessfully) to extend the time for tax payment in the state. Prompt tax returns were a citizen's duty in a properly constituted representative government, these politicians believed, but the illegitimate and corrupt control exercised by the Republicans justified withholding this obligation.⁵⁷

However, rallying white conservatives against high taxation placed Spartanburg leaders in a delicate situation. Since one of their key developmental programs involved subscription taxes for railroads, they had to be careful not to generate too much anger toward taxation in general. In December 1874 the highest tax rate facing Spartanburg residents was levied by the county commissioners in the form of the Atlanta and Richmond Air-Line Railroad tax to pay interest on bonds. As a means of preventing local hostility toward railroad costs, boosters crafted a careful distinction between good and bad taxes. Bad taxes were unnecessarily heavy state levies that too often lined the pockets of corrupt officials. Railroad taxes served as a sound investment with the assurance of a good return. Besides, since the people had voluntarily agreed to a railroad tax by voting for subscriptions, it would be "idle and foolish for a sensible man to complain." While it was the duty of all citizens to fight the financial mismanagement of the state government, it was also their duty "to inaugurate enterprises which are intended to develop and enrich our country and not make it poorer."[58]

The rhetoric against Republican taxation served practical needs for political and economic leaders but did little beyond provide an outlet for the frustrations of indebted white small farmers. Similarly, agricultural reform organizations served as political and social bonds for planters and professionals without tackling problems of cash-poor farmers, tenants, and sharecroppers. Spartanburg chapters of the Patrons of Husbandry or the Grange offer an example.[59] Originally organized on the national level in response to the financial distress facing southern farmers as a result of war, crop failures, and overextended credit, local Grange chapters were often social gatherings for the "best planters," on the one hand, and political groups with the aim of reclaiming white conservative power, on the other. After the Tyger River Grange formed in 1873, the *Carolina Spartan* confessed that it looked "with great confidence to this new order as affording the most hopeful sign of our political regeneration and redemption." Leaders in the Spartanburg Grange were not always the simple, "uncorrupted yeomen" described in promotional articles. Town lawyer John H. Evins chaired an early meeting of the Tyger River Grange with planter Thomas John Moore as secretary and speeches by local professors John Adams Leland and Warren Dupre. Evins may have found benefits in securing contracts between local Granges and merchants, but his involvement in railroads diverged from the national Grange program to control shipping rates. Moore would also emerge as a leading railroad official, and his interest in the Grange was always more as a forum for agricultural experimentation than as a challenge to merchants and railroads.[60] Throughout the South the Grange never reached those most concerned with liens and high transportation costs because it charged rather high membership fees and sold cooperatively owned products only to those with cash. Ultimately, the Grange and most other agricultural reform organizations in the 1870s acted more as a means to maintain the social and political connections of wealthy community leaders than as a substantial economic reform organization.

After the initial wave of relief measures for farmers immediately following the war, local leaders increasingly moved away from encouraging government handouts and instead promoted the merits of self-help. "Small farms are becoming the order of the day," the *Carolina Spartan* noted, "and we say with confidence, that there is not an industrious, economical, small farmer in the county who is not making money. We have received no help from the outside world, but our progress is due to the activity and energy of our people, who are beginning to realize that hope and confidence and the determination to win is all that is necessary." Agricultural success stories were championed as proof positive that hard work would yield a land of plenty in Spartanburg. Charles Barry received praise as one of the "best and most intelligent farmers" in the county, since, equipped with only one mule, he was able to produce 23 bags of cotton, 135 bushels of corn, 30 bushels of peas, and 40 gallons of sorghum syrup. Barry's experience was held as an example to all farmers that if they remained in Spartanburg and placed their land "under [the] same skillful cultivation as that employed by our friend Capt. Barry [they] will produce just as fine crops." Glenn Springs farmer George Smith also received congratulations for growing wheat to an average height of three feet after experimenting with Peruvian guano. Pointing to Smith's success, the *Carolina Spartan* inquired, "Would it not be well for our farmers to try more frequently such experiments?"[61] Such examples were used to show farmers that they should not rely on outside help but instead double their individual efforts to bring about better financial circumstances. This notion of pulling oneself up by one's bootstraps tapped into a long tradition of hard work and self-reliance while fitting in nicely with an increased emphasis on private business transactions in an uninhibited liberal market.

In the quest for agricultural efficiency and the maximization of staple-crop production for the market, large landholders and town professionals led a drive to alter the county's fence law in the 1870s. The legislative change advocated was a shift from fencing crops to fencing stock. Supporters of the change argued that it would help both big and small farmers by protecting more acreage from animals, thus allowing for the expansion of marketable crops and a reduction in costs. Livestock owners were also told that, while the costs of enclosing stock might initially be more, in the long run fenced animals would bring a much higher value because they would be protected and cared for to a greater degree than those allowed to roam throughout the countryside. Drovers and tenant farmers who depended on stock for their livelihood were not easily swayed by such rhetoric and opposed a new fence law. When the law was changed in the late 1870s, it did bring greater efficiency to both crop and livestock production but at the cost of forcing many practitioners of animal husbandry out of business and into the ranks of dependent laborers.

Since long before the Civil War, South Carolina had permitted livestock grazing on all open pasturelands regardless of who owned the land. If an animal caused damage to a person's property, the stock owner was not liable, yet if the animal was killed on the property, the landowner would have to pay damages. Those landowners wishing to keep stock off their lands had to fence in their crops. Despite occasional grumblings about stock wasting good lands, most everyone accepted the fence law as both a traditional right and a sound economic policy. In 1850 Spartanburg's $657,000 worth of livestock ranked it first in the upper piedmont and eighth in the state. By 1860 livestock values had risen to over $865,000, and the county ranked second in the state in sheep values.[62] Under such prevailing economic factors it seemed only logical that owners of stock should enjoy open range rights.

The necessities and privations of the Civil War significantly reduced the numbers and values of livestock in Spartanburg. By 1870 the value of livestock had fallen to $612,000. Such declines were common throughout the state. Traveler Robert Somers noted with surprise the lack of good stock at the 1870 state fair in Columbia. "There is either no superior stock in this state," Somers observed, "or the stockowners have not sufficient interest in its extension to be at the trouble to show it." Yet with cotton production also suffering a severe decline, there were no immediate cries for changes in the county's fence law. Between 1870 and 1875, however, the numbers of sheep and swine continued to decline, while cotton production jumped from under three thousand to almost eleven thousand bales.[63] With cotton now the county's unrivaled economic power, it made sense to substantial farmers, merchants, and professionals connected to the crop to protect its value by requiring livestock owners to keep their animals penned. In his 1875 remarks to the grand jury in neighboring York County, Judge Thomas J.

Table 10. Farm Value and Agricultural Production, Spartanburg County, 1870–1880

	1870	1880	% change
Improved farm acres	97,675	153,087	+56.7
Value of farmland	$1,147,446	$3,515,466	+206.3
Value of livestock	$612,158	$521,269	−14.8
Wheat produced	73,783 bu.	79,991 bu.	+8.4
Corn produced	525,698 bu.	593,454 bu.	+12.9
Oats produced	36,106 bu.	74,572 bu.	+106.5
Cotton produced	2,851 bales	24,188 bales	+748.4
Wool produced	15,345 lb.	10,462 lb.	−31.8
Potatoes produced	38,689 bu.	25,078 bu.	−35.2

Sources: U.S. Bureau of the Census, *Ninth Census*, 238–40, and *Compendium*, pt. 1, 725–26.

Mackey highlighted the economic absurdity of landowners paying "$19 for the necessary fencing to keep out of their fields cattle the value of $1." The expenses arising out of the fence law were "peculiarly opresive to the small capitalists, whose money is consumed in building a fence." One Spartanburg farmer of two hundred acres complained that it cost him $445 a year to protect his farm, worth $800, from "little, worthless, slab-sided, perch-backed shoats." Although fencing land was causing economic hardship for small farmers, property owners argued that a stock law would not shift the burden to practitioners of animal husbandry. Enough fencing already existed, the *Carolina Spartan* contended, to fence most of the county's livestock. In addition, landowners would be encouraged to furnish small enclosed pastures for a nominal fee. Such a plan, proponents of the change argued, would reduce litigation over property rights, lower costs for the farmer, and provide for more improved, better-fed livestock.[64]

Despite arguments that a stock law would bring economic efficiency beneficial to all, herdsmen and tenants with stock recognized the new restrictions they would face. Much of the opposition to changes in the fence law was centered in the northern portion of the county, where herding had long been prevalent. In July 1875 a resident from northern Spartanburg objected to the proposed stock law on grounds that it would raise taxes, decrease livestock, and allow landholders to fleece their tenants. Since fence laws varied by county and state, the stock law would require fencing county boundaries and public roads. The additional taxation necessary for such a large project would likely hit the poorest residents hardest. Prohibiting owners from putting stock out to pasture in the fall, the argument continued, would cost an extra two months' feed. Higher taxes and extra costs would force poor people to get rid of their stock, the effect of which would be "to elevate many who are now rich, and to depress many who are already too poor to be comfortable."[65] A further decline in stock raising was also objected to on grounds that it meant more risky dependence on outside markets. Stock law opponents instead argued for a reduction in cotton and an increase in livestock to insure against economic downturns.

Carolina Spartan editor Hugh L. Farley countered objections to the stock law through appeals to economic interest and common sense. Since stock raising had become but a small part of the county's economy, it only made sense to make it "subservient to more important interests." People should not oppose changes in the fence law as class legislation, Farley explained, because anyone with enough energy and industry could become a landholder. Stock law proponents acknowledged that they had to work against a tide of tradition. In supporting changes to the fence law, the *Yorkville Enquirer* observed that the "man who undertakes to break an individual from a long formed habit, or to change the manners and customs of a people, engages in a difficult task. The world moves forward, but they stand still." Yet the paper urged traditionalists to accept this change as an inevitable and unstoppable event in the march of progress. For stock law supporters, part of this progress involved a strengthening of private property rights at the expense of common rights to insure greater individual profits for everyone. "[W]e want no agrarian or communistic doctrines," Farley announced. "The right of pasturage does not now belong to the tenant, and the landlord has now the right to object to his bringing stock on his lands." Farley softened this strong expression of economic liberalism by explaining that the security of a stock law would encourage landowners to work with tenants in providing areas for livestock. In fact, he contended, small areas of penned-in pasturage would force tenants to take better care of their livestock, which, in turn, would drive up values and increase profits on each animal.[66]

In the December session of the general assembly, Union County representative Benjamin Rice introduced a bill to authorize Chester, Anderson, Pickens, Greenville, Union, and Spartanburg counties to settle the fence question for themselves by voting for or against a change in the system. Although the bill passed the senate, local support for the measure was tempered by the potential for class conflict. Although certain that many propertyless whites and freedmen had come around to supporting a stock law, the *Carolina Spartan* acknowledged that portions of the county were likely to oppose the bill. By early 1876 such community divisions were particularly intolerable, since white conservative unity was being heralded as the Democrats' best hope of regaining the state in the fall elections. Even if Rice's bill passed and the fence question was permitted on the 1876 ballots, the *Carolina Spartan* proposed waiting until the following year to vote on the issue because there should be nothing "likely to divert the attention of our people, or to divide them."[67] The bill did not become law, and Spartanburg voters had no local option on changing the county's fence policy.

The situations and motives surrounding stock laws varied across time and space in the postwar South. In his study of central Georgia, Joseph Reidy finds that the stock law issue was launched by large planters in the early 1870s in an attempt to "reduce the freedpeople to an agricultural proletariat." In the process, planters unwittingly "re-created themselves as an agrarian bourgeoisie." Fence laws in the postbellum Georgia upcountry have been a source of heated historical debate. Steven Hahn has argued that the conflicts of the laws were representative of a fundamental cultural division between yeomen embracing a traditional notion of common rights in a commonwealth and an aggressive business class looking to affirm the predominance of private property in free-market capitalism. A counterargument, led by Shawn Kantor and J. Morgan Kousser, finds no such cultural gap but rather a simple clash of economic interests.[68] In the South Carolina upcountry such sharp divisions in the historiography are limited in their usefulness.

Spartanburg's stock law supporters recognized that they could not simply run roughshod over poorer residents who opposed the measure. When the introduction of the stock law in neighboring Union and Laurens counties in December 1878 produced angry protests and "indignation meetings" from stock owners, friends of the stock law in Spartanburg were encouraged to "act wisely and conservatively, and deal very tenderly towards those who oppose it." If and when the stock law was approved for the county, *Carolina Spartan* editor Charles Petty suggested that the law's supporters, many of whom were in the lower portion of the county, run a fence from around Pacolet Depot in the middle of the county up through Van Patten's Shoals rather than follow the county boundaries. The fence would be shorter and thus cost less, while stock owners in the northern portion of the county would remain relatively unaffected by the law. A bill to this effect was presented before the legislature in December but quickly drew the opposition of taxpayers in the northern part of Spartanburg town. These residents complained that they would have to pay the higher taxes necessary to complete the fence without deriving the benefits from the law. A Glenn Springs resident reported hearing that the law in Union resulted in arid pastures, leading to widespread death of livestock. He urged a significant amount of time for people to prepare for a change in the law and warned that if the law was immediately forced upon the people, "we can promise that legislator, or that set of legislators a *speedy* death (politically) and also a *long, protracted* funeral, in his or their hearing."[69]

On December 20 the legislature voted to amend the stock law to apply to Spartanburg effective January 1, 1881. County commissioners were directed to levy a tax to defray the expenses of erecting and maintaining the fences. "The agony about the Stock Law is over," local editor T. Stobo Farrow announced. "The deed is done, and Spartanburg has been emancipated from the domination of mischievous stock." In 1880 penalties for open stock extended to those who drove their cattle across state lines from North Carolina into Spartanburg, Greenville, and Pickens counties. Throughout the rest of the decade stock continued to dwindle, and hog meat was largely imported from markets north and west via the new rail connections.[70]

Spartanburg stock supporters noted no opposition to the law's adoption. Reports from the neighboring counties of Union and Laurens found initial opposition to the law falling away quickly and a general feeling of "peace and harmony." Furthermore, the change appeared to be proving its cost-effectiveness, with prices ranging from only $1.20 to $2.00 per hundred fence rails. State Senator Todd of Laurens reported that his constituents of "all classes and colors, landlords and tenants, town people and country people, are wonderfully pleased with their first year's experience" with the stock law and that cultivated land had already increased by one-tenth. Despite such positive rhetoric, however, it would become clear over the next decade that this encroachment of more crop acreage continued to reduce available pastureland for stock.[71] As a result, fewer people could make their livelihoods on animal husbandry and instead were increasingly brought under the control of landowners as tenants and day laborers. This was the irony resulting from town-based entrepreneurs allying with big landowners on the stock law. Modernizers certainly had their own self-interested goals and wanted to keep blacks from exercising political or economic power. However, their comprehensive plans for a modern commercial culture had always assumed the development of entrepreneurial values among the white masses. By working with large landowners to fence stock, Spartanburg's entrepreneurs blocked a significant part of the county's population from economic success and, in essence, retarded their own progressive goals for the upcountry.

In 1878 the restoration of white Democratic control statewide brought an official end to Republican Reconstruction, and with it came an attempt to return a greater share of economic power to rural landholders. Legislators identified the crop-lien system and unregulated interest rates as responsible for the large debts facing many landowners and blamed merchants for placing individual greed above community interest. Yet when confronted with the complex system of debt in the state, Democrats could offer no new programs of their own. Prosperity in the New South appeared to lie with town merchants, professionals, manufacturers, and entrepreneurs.

Since its inception in 1866, the crop-lien system had been viewed by farmers as little more than a temporary financial burden designed to get crops planted after the war. Over the course of Reconstruction, big and small farmers alike searched in vain for alternatives to a system that only seemed to generate further debt. In the mid-1870s Spartanburg residents found the credit system "doing injury to both merchants and farmers." A Cherokee resident viewed crop liens as "the deep and dangerous fountain of bankruptcy and general corruption." Shortly after the return of state Democratic control in 1877, the South Carolina legislature repealed the lien law, but by the time the repeal took effect on January 1, 1878, difficulties in obtaining agricultural credit forced the legislature to repeal the repeal. Initially a temporary restoration, the law was made permanent in December 1878. Significantly, however, the legislature did ensure that the new law gave landlords "a prior and preferred lien" for rent on at least one-third of the value of all crops raised on their land. There is little indication that the law, which was designed to give landholders claims superior to merchants, in practice had any significant impact on mercantile operations. Six years after the lien law was restored, a review of South Carolina's economy found the law in Spartanburg to have been abused and, in some instances, to have "worked great hardships" on some farmers.[72]

With farmers facing mounting debts and increased rates on credit, the first meeting of the Democratic state legislature pushed forward a bill to regulate interest rates at 7 percent. As early as January 1877 the *Spartanburg*

Herald reported that "one of the first reforms demanded by the people is the reenactment of a 'Usury law' that will put a wholesome check upon the avarice of the 'money changers.' As long as 18, 20, and 25 per cent interest is charged for the use of money no capital can be had for investment in legitimate enterprises."[73] Yet when the usury bill came up for a vote in the state house of representatives, Spartanburg's delegation showed their continued resistance to market restrictions.

By 1880 Spartanburg's small farmers found themselves snared in a complex system of debt. In his tour of eleven counties of the piedmont and upcountry, agriculturist Harry Hammond found that "the system of credits and advances prevails to a large extent, consuming from one-third to three-fifths of the crop before it is harvested." Hammond estimated that supplies purchased on credit went for 20 to 100 percent above market value, depending upon the level of competition among merchants, who, he noted, were "by far the most prosperous class of the community, in proportion to the skill and capital employed."[74] Liens were also reportedly on the increase, and rents were high. Share wages predominated among freedmen and were kept at a level that prevented blacks from entering the ranks of landowners. By 1880 only about 5 percent of the county's black population owned land. An 1884 promotional survey of the state compiled by the *Charleston News & Courier* admitted that the prospects for black farmers as landowners and tenants in Spartanburg were "only tolerably good."[75]

At the same time that many small farmers and freedmen faced financial peril, however, a burgeoning group of wealthy farmers, merchants, lawyers, and other professionals found prosperity. By 1880 the assessed valuation of Spartanburg's real estate and personal property ranked second only to Charleston. Spartanburg town's combined property valuation ranked it fourth among all cities in the state.[76] Again, diversification in farming, merchandising, and investing appeared to be a key element in financial success. For example, planter John C. Winsmith maintained real estate worth thirty thousand dollars and owned an additional six thousand dollars in personal property in 1870.[77] As early as 1867, however, credit agents seemed surprised that a man with Winsmith's wealth would be involved in no other business beyond planting and grew increasingly wary about his failure to diversify. By 1880 most of Winsmith's property had been sold off to pay his debts, leaving him just twenty-seven cultivated acres of farmland.[78]

The postwar advent of sharecropping, share wages, and the power of local merchants certainly inhibited freedmen's economic opportunities and drove many of the region's indebted white farmers into further insolvency. Yet the county's economy could hardly have worked out otherwise. Antebellum ideology held that the control of black labor was central to white progress. Poor whites, yeomen, and elites all participated in a racially divided political economy that would not disappear with Confederate surrender.

At the same time, massive debts resulting from war and emancipation forced farmers to take advances on purchases. Lacking collateral, creditors were unlikely to make loans without a legal right to collect on future production. Spartanburg's leaders contended that the initial obligations brought on by liens would be counteracted by new market opportunities. Central to the creation of these opportunities were a developing railroad network linking the county to trade centers and an expanding industrial sector producing home markets and jobs.

CHAPTER SEVEN

"A Great Commercial and Railroad Centre"
Textiles, Transportation, and Trade in the Postwar Era

AT AN 1873 MEETING in Asheville, North Carolina, Spartanburg lawyer John H. Evins rose to champion the long-awaited rail connection between Spartanburg and Asheville. Evins, who had supported railroads and manufacturing in the antebellum era, predicted that the completion of the line would make Spartanburg "a great commercial and railroad centre," following a path similar to Atlanta.[1] The economic engine driving Spartanburg town's success would be the cotton trade. The town's location on the expanding rail network would permit merchants to buy and sell cotton in every direction. In addition, railroads would provide greater incentive for factory expansion.

The defeat of the Confederacy and the resulting destruction of slavery caused, in historian Gavin Wright's words, "a basic change in the principles and directions of entrepreneurial energies."[2] Planters who had invested mostly in ownership of humans before the war now looked to develop natural resources and invest in infrastructural change. For Spartanburg entrepreneurs this meant a new opportunity to realize the level of economic diversity they had desired since the early antebellum era. The postwar period did not, therefore, require the birth of a new entrepreneurial spirit in the upcountry. Instead, a new political environment freed entrepreneurs from many of the obstacles to their plans in the antebellum era.

In the closing months of the Civil War, Union troops wreaked havoc on rail networks throughout the South. A large portion of South Carolina's roads fell victim to Gen. William Tecumseh Sherman's army during their march to the sea. As they swept through the state, they left a swath of twisted rails and burned freight yards in their wake. The Confederate army added to this destruction in an attempt to slow Sherman's advance. Of particular importance to the Spartanburg community, the Spartanburg and Union Railroad's bridge at Broad River near Columbia was destroyed along with depots heading into the state's hinterlands.[3] By comparison, most textile factories escaped wartime destruction, since they were generally located away from coastal areas and strategically important cities. It only made sense, then, that national, state, and local authorities directed their energies first to rebuilding southern railroads.

In August 1865 President Andrew Johnson authorized southern railroad companies to buy engines and cars that the federal government had brought down from the North. During presidential Reconstruction, conservative legislatures throughout the South passed substantial acts for railroad restoration and development.[4] South Carolina's legislature joined such efforts by supporting measures designed to provide emergency relief to the state's railroads. In 1865 the general assembly empowered the Spartanburg and Union to borrow or raise six hundred thousand dollars to rebuild the line's connection with Columbia. A year later the legislature authorized the company to issue four hundred thousand dollars in bonds for the same purpose.[5]

When Republicans took control of state houses throughout the South in 1868, they continued to support railroad operations with an eye toward creating a New South in the North's image. At least initially, southern white Democrats encouraged this state aid to promote rail lines but for reasons different from those of their Republican counterparts. As they had before the war, southern white leaders viewed modernization as a step toward independent prosperity and competition with the North, not as a South reborn to a New England mother.[6]

In late August 1868 the South Carolina House of Representatives considered and passed a bill permitting more liberal eminent domain rights when property was desired for railways and other works of internal improvement. The legislature also removed gauge restrictions in the charter of the Greenville and French Broad Railroad Company, thereby eliminating an important stumbling block to the route's connection with the Western North Carolina Railroad. This legislation set an important precedent for all charters with such restrictions, including the Spartanburg and Union.[7]

While government support of railroads gathered momentum, railroad officials searched for new ways to raise private revenue for their lines. In May 1868 Spartanburg and Union president Thomas Jeter reduced fares from five cents to three and a half cents per mile to encourage ridership. Following examples set by other lines in the state, supporters of the Spartanburg and Union's northwestward extension called on farmers to subscribe portions of their lands to the railroad, which would then be sold to immigrants and the proceeds from the sales invested in constructing the line. By utilizing this plan, boosters explained, the farmer would not be asked to invest his limited cash supply, and a new group of sturdy white workers would arrive to help rebuild the county's economy.[8]

Despite continued state interest in developing rail lines, however, stockholders and supporters of the Spartanburg and Union saw great inequities in government policy. At the center of the conflict was the state's involvement in the operations of the Spartanburg and Union's old archrivals, the Blue Ridge and the Greenville and Columbia railroads. Support for these two upcountry lines adhered to a general postwar policy of giving the lion's share of the state's attention to railroads that had received substantial assistance in the antebellum period. In September 1868 the South Carolina house passed a bill providing for state endorsement of bonds to one million dollars for the Blue Ridge, and the governor was authorized to advance the company twenty thousand dollars from the treasury to repair the road.[9] Spartanburg's representatives strongly opposed the measure. "Any unprejudiced mind will admit," the *Carolina Spartan* intoned, "that the claims of [the French Broad route advocated by the Spartanburg and Union] over those of any other are numerous and pressing." Spartanburg leaders contended that Charleston was ignoring its own interests by supporting the Blue Ridge, a road much costlier and longer than the route through Spartanburg.[10]

Spartanburg and Union supporters appeared to have justification in their charges of legislative favoritism toward the Blue Ridge and the Greenville and Columbia. Postwar South Carolina lawmakers essentially surrendered the state's security held against either company's failure. In 1871 the legislature gave up the first lien on the Greenville and Columbia and took a second so that the line's directors could negotiate a new bond issue. If the company went bankrupt, the state would stand to lose over one million dollars. The legislature also canceled its lien on the Blue Ridge and assumed responsibility for the state bonds that the company had pledged to pay. South Carolina's comptroller general and former Spartanburg resident Charles Leaphart assailed state support of the Blue Ridge as wasteful and deadly to the state's credit. In response, Blue Ridge supporters portrayed him as a spiteful upcountry man only interested in his own region's benefit.[11] Typically, groups interested in advancing their own schemes charged competitors with placing self-interest above the good of society as a whole.

Added to the inequitable distribution of state support was apparent corruption at the highest levels of government. In an effort to buy South Carolina's two major rail lines, the governor and his cronies induced the legislature to set up a sinking fund commission with the power to sell the state's interest in any corporation. The day after the bill passed, the commission sold the shares of the Greenville and Columbia to themselves at $2.75 per share despite the existing market price of around $4.00. In the 1870–71 session of the South Carolina house, Pennsylvania capitalist J. J. "Honest John" Patterson reportedly paid the speaker twenty-five thousand dollars to select a railroad committee favorable to the Blue Ridge line. By the end of the session, Patterson had bought the state's controlling interest in the Blue Ridge for a dollar a share, one-tenth of 1 percent of the state's original investment.[12]

In the midst of this political graft the Spartanburg and Union asked the legislature for two million dollars to be offered after the company had raised one hundred thousand dollars in additional stock and to be paid in installments as five-mile sections of the road were completed. The bill passed the house, but the legislature adjourned before consideration in the senate. Having grown impatient with legislative inaction, the *Carolina Spartan* turned away from legislative appropriation. Instead, the newspaper asked the state to release its preferred lien on the Spartanburg and Union so the company could raise six hundred thousand dollars by pledging the capital stock of its road for its payment. The legislature, however, was slow to consider the railroad's plight.[13]

Deeply in debt and having failed to secure enough state support, the Spartanburg and Union Railroad was put up for auction to pay its creditors in the spring of 1870. Angered by the favoritism and corruption surrounding other routes, Spartanburg railroad boosters expressed concern over which investors would purchase the line. "Our road ought not to fall into the hands of either those great interests which would be antagonistic to ours, or to those who would be likely . . . indifferent to our trade or business," wrote a Spartanburg resident. Those listed as most antagonistic to the county's interests were the Greenville and Columbia, the Blue Ridge, and the South Carolina railroads as well as groups representing the city of Charleston. The writer called for a link of the Spartanburg and Union with

North Carolina's Wilmington and Manchester Railroad, noting that the latter road had been approved for extension to Columbia. The distances from Columbia to Charleston and from Columbia to Wilmington were the same, "while Wilmington [was] much nearer Baltimore, Philadelphia, and New York—the great markets of the Continent!" The competition of a line through Wilmington, the letter argued, "would make Charleston think better of us."[14]

However, by early 1872 none other than Gabriel Cannon—the one-time president of the Spartanburg and Union and leading adversary of the Blue Ridge—supported the sale of the operation to the Blue Ridge.[15] Cannon's dramatic shift in position was the result of his new role as a board member with the Atlanta and Richmond Air-Line Railroad. Organized in 1869, the Atlanta and Richmond Air-Line Railroad was to link with the Richmond and Danville Railroad in Virginia and extend through the Carolinas to Atlanta. Most of the financing for the Air-Line was provided by the Richmond and Danville, with additional support from the Southern Railway Security Company, a combination controlled by northern financiers, including Thomas A. Scott of the Pennsylvania Railroad.[16]

Since the planned route would pass directly through Spartanburg town and bisect the entire county, longtime railroad boosters like Gabriel Cannon recognized the potential commercial revolution for the region if the Air-Line was completed. Cannon no doubt abandoned the Spartanburg and Union in favor of the Air-Line because his antebellum experience had shown that railroads solely dependent on local money had little chance of success. The Air-Line, by contrast, benefited from northeastern investors as well as those from Virginia, Maryland, North Carolina, South Carolina, and Georgia.[17]

Despite the substantial outside investment in the Air-Line, the company relied on financial contributions from the individual counties in the railroad's intended path. For their part, Spartanburg residents were asked to subscribe two hundred thousand dollars countywide and fifty thousand dollars in town. Spartanburg's subscription committee comprised a familiar cast of characters, including Gabriel Cannon, John H. Evins, and Dexter Edgar Converse. Cannon served on the Air-Line's board of directors. The subscription committee forwarded familiar arguments to secure support from rural farmers. The Air-Line, it was explained, would save agriculturists money by providing greater access to consumer goods while lowering the costs of transporting crops to larger markets. Farmers were warned that the railroad would be built somewhere else if local folks voted against the subscription, allowing some other region to surpass Spartanburg in economic progress. Such rhetoric appeared to have a basis in fact. When the upcountry's Anderson County failed to adopt a subscription tax, a railroad line was eventually built through neighboring Pickens, which had approved such a tax. As the voting neared, local newspapers printed a flurry of statements urging adoption of the subscription tax. "You who want your County to progress and improve," one typical editorial read, "see to it that the Railroad subscription on Thursday does not fail." Indeed, the subscription tax did not fail and was approved by voters the next week.[18]

Through the early 1870s Gabriel Cannon utilized his local power to ensure continued funding of the Air-Line. He convinced both the chairman of the county commissioners and the intendant (mayor) of Spartanburg town to prepare substantial railroad bonds. At the same time that he was orchestrating the sale of the Spartanburg and Union to the Blue Ridge in 1872, Cannon also served as director of the National Bank of Spartanburg. Having secured a down payment of twenty-five thousand dollars from the Blue Ridge men in February, Cannon turned around and authorized the bank to issue a low-interest loan of ten thousand dollars to the Air-Line Railroad.[19]

The Air-Line completed the connection from Spartanburg to Charlotte in March 1873.[20] A few days later the inaugural train ride from Charlotte was greeted with "the firing of guns, the ringing of bells, the waving of handkerchiefs and shouting of the multitude." A group of Spartanburg women showered wreaths and garlands upon the train "to tell our friends in Charlotte . . . how heartily and sincerely our Spartan women rejoice in the close relations already established and the tender ones which may yet grow out of this new Union with Old North State."[21] Although new trade outlets were the bottom line, the celebration was reserved for the soft affections of women rather than the hard economics of businessmen.

Spartanburg leaders began to tout the revolutionary effects of the Air-Line road on the region less than a month into operations. By mid-April the cost of flour had reportedly fallen $1.50 per barrel as a result of the improved access to grain crops farther north. Commenting on the continually arriving carloads of corn and freight from Charlotte, the *Carolina Spartan* proclaimed, "Wonders will never cease." This increased access to provision crops was also heralded for permitting farmers both large and small to focus more of their energies on cotton production.[22] Prior to the Civil War, local boosters had argued that railroad development would offer more flexibility in agriculture. Farmers could choose to grow and sell grains, corn, or cotton based on a crop's changing marketability. In the postwar period, however, railroad boosterism focused on making farmers consumers of grains and almost exclusive producers of cotton.

Despite the enthusiasm surrounding the Air-Line's arrival, the road quickly ran into financial troubles and passed into receivership in late 1874. Northern bondholders bought the railroad at public auction in December 1876 and renamed it the Atlanta and Charlotte Railroad. The sale changed the composition of the road's management entirely. Prior to the Air-Line's sale, the railroad's officers hailed from Virginia, Georgia, North Carolina, and South Carolina, including Gabriel Cannon of Spartanburg. After the sale, ten of the railroad's twelve officers were from New York, and the other two lived in Baltimore. In 1881 the line's northern directors leased the road to the Richmond and Danville, another line also controlled by northern interests.[23]

While outside control and investment drove the Air-Line from its origins, Spartanburg's push for a rail link to the northwestern regions of North Carolina was a more localized initiative. By early 1873 both of Spartanburg's main rivals for a western route, the Blue Ridge and the Greenville and Columbia, had declared bankruptcy due largely to corruption and mismanagement.[24] The demise of these two lines allowed upcountry interests to charter the Spartanburg and Asheville Railroad in February 1873. Following the same path laid out for the French Broad Railroad before the war, the Spartanburg and Asheville was to snake through the northwestern stretches of the county and link up with a North Carolina railroad to Asheville and points farther west. The railroad was chartered with a capital stock of $1 million in shares of $50 each. Work could begin on the line once subscriptions reached $100,000 and $1 was paid in on each share.[25]

In soliciting support for the road, Spartanburg businessmen and politicians faced a familiar set of obstacles. Influential Charlestonians continued to lobby for the resurrection of the Blue Ridge Railroad as the best route to serve lowcountry interests. Spartanburg boosters countered that the Blue Ridge had wasted hundreds of thousands of dollars, while the Spartanburg and Asheville would require one-twentieth of such an investment from Charleston. In an attempt to goad Charleston into supportive action, the *Carolina Spartan* held out both the carrot of cheap markets and the stick of isolation. The Spartanburg and Asheville was a "vital interest to business men and property holders of Charleston, who wish to continue their trade with this portion of the State, and in making Charleston an outlet for the productions of the West." Furthermore, the argument continued, the Spartanburg and Asheville was necessary to prevent Charleston from being overshadowed by Port Royal or another coastal area as a new link with South Carolina's western counties.[26]

These veiled threats to bypass Charleston, combined with substantial past investment in the Blue Ridge, led the *Charleston News & Courier* to support the Blue Ridge as the only "independent Western line that can be built, with the certainty that it can be controlled by, and worked in the interest of the City." The paper dismissed the Spartanburg and Asheville as looking only to connections with North Carolina railroads, "which roads are certainly not built for the benefit of Charleston." In response, the *Carolina Spartan* warned Charlestonians that, beyond the millions of dollars needed yet to finish the Blue Ridge, supporters of that line were more interested in connections with Athens, Georgia, than within their own state.[27]

After a railroad convention in Columbia in December 1873, Spartanburg delegate Thomas John Moore was pleased that everyone in attendance seemed impressed with the importance of the Spartanburg and Asheville. Moore informed his wife that books of subscription for the line were to be opened in Charleston, but he did not "look for much from them." Instead, he looked to North Carolina, where money and cooperation seemed abundant.[28] The previous August, voters in North Carolina's Henderson County approved a subscription of one hundred thousand dollars for the Greenville and French Broad Railroad to prepare for a connection with the Spartanburg and Asheville. In order to better coordinate completion of the lines, the two roads consolidated in July 1874 under the presidency of Charlestonian C. G. Memminger and directors, including Spartanburg's Gabriel Cannon and David R. Duncan.[29]

Facing grim prospects for reenergizing the Blue Ridge project, groups of Charleston and Columbia businessmen threw their endorsements to the Spartanburg and Asheville. The *Carolina Spartan* rejoiced that "we have at last succeeded in getting the ear of our fellow citizens in these two cities." Editor John H. Evins gloated on behalf of those Spartanburg leaders who, prior to the Civil War, had assured the legislature of the superiority of their western route to no avail. Yet Charlestonians were only interested in the Spartanburg and Asheville cause if they could be assured of the route's benefits to the lowcountry. In order to obtain such assurance, the *News &*

Courier noted, it was a "necessity that the majority of the capital stock be controlled by citizens of the State and City."[30] Burned by investments in the Blue Ridge railroad, many of the city's financial elite chose to beg off any further attachments to western rail projects.

At the September 1874 ceremony marking the breaking of ground for the Spartanburg and Asheville, ceremony chairman William Kennedy Blake proclaimed before a crowd of six thousand that the connection would "revolutionize the old channels of trade" and called for a county subscription of one hundred thousand dollars. Boosters appealed to individual subscribers' interests, noting that the connection to new markets would create new moneymaking opportunities for everyone. The *Rural Carolinian* asked people to subscribe to railroad stock "not upon the ground of patriotism simply, but as a matter of profit."[31] With little prospect of additional state support, a railroad subscription tax seemed the only way to guarantee continued construction of the railroad. Early in 1875 county commissioners obtained authorization to hold a special election in June to accept or reject a railroad tax.

Convincing voters throughout the county who had endured almost a decade of heavy revenue collection and increasing indebtedness that more taxes to support the railroad was in their best interest proved difficult. As in the antebellum period, farmers needed to feel that any costs shared equally would result in equally shared benefits. Therefore, an individual would have to be certain that a railroad would improve his life in some way before he could support a tax for that railroad. In May 1875 a Reidville resident reported that his village was "not ready . . . to vote for any more taxes to build railroads." Most of Reidville's inhabitants saw little benefit from paying for a road so far removed from their village, which was situated about thirteen miles southwest of Spartanburg town. Reidville's economic and intellectual philosophy also ran counter to further rail development. Reidville had fashioned itself as an educational community with prominent high schools for boys and girls, and its spokesmen had advocated against extensive cotton involvement and urged self-sufficiency throughout Reconstruction. Opposition was also reported in Cherokee, to the far northeast of the county. Even Millville, near David Golightly Harris's Fair Forest neighborhood, noted that only the area's largest taxpayers were in favor of the railroad tax.[32]

Although the railroad subscription tax won in the June special election, the results were hardly an overwhelming mandate. Overall, the tax garnered just 64 percent of the vote. Notably, ten of twenty-seven voting precincts voted against the tax. Location and self-interest seemed to drive the voting patterns. Grain-growing regions near the North Carolina border, which were several miles from the intended path of the Spartanburg and Asheville, voted against the subscription. These precincts included neighborhoods like Grassy Pond, a small farming community whose residents had complained in the antebellum period when Spartanburg town altered its taxation policy to earmark some revenue for town development only. Similarly, precincts in the southern half of the county that were far removed from rail lines, like Hebron and Walnut Grove, saw no significant benefits from a tax.

Precincts supporting the subscription tax were situated directly on a rail line, had important interests in manufacturing or cotton dealings, or were involved in tourism. Located on the Spartanburg and Union, Spartanburg town and Pacolet had already emerged as important cotton trading centers. Campobello, a rather isolated farming precinct in the county's northwestern corner, stood in the direct path of the proposed line and registered 94 percent of the vote for subscription in anticipation of an economic revolution. Prosubscription votes from the southern communities of Woodruff and Hobbysville reflected that area's interest in a future line from Spartanburg to Laurens that, together with the Spartanburg and Asheville, would provide access to cotton markets in the south, north, east, and west.[33]

This voting pattern was consistent with prewar attitudes toward infrastructural changes and taxation. Communities gauged first the benefits to their communities and then the effect on the entire county. Residents generally opposed a tax if the services from taxation clearly benefited another community more than their immediate neighborhood. Yet if a measure brought important local benefits, it was easier to argue that such a measure would bring improvement for all. These actions suggest no evidence of a principled objection to taxation for internal improvements but rather a consistent concern for neighborhood interest above countywide development.

Under the presidency of Spartanburg's David R. Duncan, the Spartanburg and Asheville finally opened for service between Spartanburg and Hendersonville, North Carolina, in 1879. However, like the Air-Line, the Spartanburg and Asheville quickly ran into serious financial difficulties and was sold in 1881 to a committee of bondholders led by Spartanburg merchant Joseph Walker. The next year, the Richmond and Danville gained majority control of the Spartanburg and Asheville.[34]

Spartanburg's other railroads had met similar fates by the end of 1881. After its purchase by the Air-Line in 1873, the Spartanburg and Union—

reorganized as the Spartanburg, Union and Columbia—continued to face financial trouble. The railroad was foreclosed on in June 1880 and quickly purchased by the Richmond and West Point Terminal Company, the parent company of the northern-controlled Richmond and Danville Railroad. By 1881 no Spartanburg men served on the Spartanburg, Union and Columbia's board of directors, while a number of the officials represented interests in New York.

By the early 1880s, then, northern-led corporations owned or controlled all the rail routes through Spartanburg County. It is important to recognize, however, that it was through the initiative and effort of local entrepreneurs like Gabriel Cannon that rail development continued through the tumultuous period of Reconstruction. Drawing largely on their antebellum experience with local lines, these men lent their regional expertise to larger rail projects and helped assure their completion. The triumph of largely northern-controlled corporate railroads ended the problems of local competition and ensured a more coordinated approach to rail service in the South.[35]

For smaller farmers and some politicians the growing remoteness of consolidated railroad enterprises throughout the South led them to take an increasing interest in regulating railroad expansion and financial behavior. Through the mid-1870s Spartanburg farmer J. B. Davis retained an interest in railroad development, at one point serving as a delegate to a Spartanburg and Asheville promotional meeting in Hendersonville, North Carolina. After a string of railroad subscription taxes and consolidation of area lines by the northern-controlled Richmond and Danville, however, Davis complained that "the present power of railroad corporations to tax the public [produced] a monied aristocracy in this country such as the world has never seen." Davis was not alone in his thinking. In 1878 the state Grange petitioned the legislature to create a railroad commission to supervise and regulate the lines.[36]

Since 1873 the specter of economic panic and a conservative approach toward state aid resulting from corruption had left many roads throughout the state in dire financial condition. As a result, railroad directors raised rates, particularly on short-haul freight. These rates drew little political attention through 1877 due to preoccupation with ousting the Republicans and controlling black labor. However, the increasing northern involvement in South Carolina's roads along with the return of conservative Democratic control in the state legislature brought more attention to the issue of regulation. The legislature created a one-man railroad commission with advisory and supervisory powers. If the commissioner found violations or exorbitant rates, he could ask the railroads to make changes. If a road refused to cooperate, the commissioner could then request a restraining order from a state circuit court.[37]

Charleston interests led the cause of railroad regulation in the late 1870s and early 1880s. The old port city watched its position as a major commercial center slip away as north–south routes like the Air-Line road through Spartanburg channeled goods to Atlanta. Charleston had good reason to be fearful of the new lines. In an effort to control cutthroat competition, these routes formed a pool, the Associated Railroads of the Carolinas. The association discriminated against nonmember routes, particularly the South Carolina railroad connecting the upcountry to Charleston. In 1882 it cost 46 cents per mile to ship a five-hundred-pound bale of cotton from the upcountry town of Abbeville to New York, while the trip from Abbeville to Charleston cost $1.50 per mile. In December 1882 the Charleston interests helped push through a law increasing the size of the railroad commission and granting it the power to set rates.[38] Between 1870 and 1880 the legislature and, indeed, local farmers steadily moved from supporting government assistance to railroads to advocating government regulation.

The postwar boom in railroads also produced new tensions between town and rural interests. Wherever depots were located, towns rapidly expanded as centers for cotton trade and other mercantile exchange. By October 1873 nine businesses in Spartanburg town were engaged in the cotton trade. The increasingly common sight of streets crowded with cotton wagons prompted the *Carolina Spartan* to "rejoice in our 'manifest destiny.'" Between September 1, 1873, and June 1, 1874, Spartanburg town had shipped almost 6,500 bales of cotton via the Spartanburg and Union with an additional 415 bales coming out of Pacolet village. Among the "men of great enterprise and capital" who traded in cotton was prominent businessman Joseph Walker. Walker began his career as a clerk in John B. Cleveland's store and formed a partnership with Cleveland in 1866. Three years later Walker was running his own mercantile business and was already actively trading in cotton. By the mid-1870s Walker had formed a new partnership with local druggist C. E. Fleming and merchant John H. Montgomery. In

1876 creditors considered Walker's store worth at least thirty thousand dollars, and the firm continued to be one of the strongest in the state through the end of the century.[39]

Spartanburg town's boom as a cotton trading center further energized merchants and professionals to modernize the physical space around them to create a safer, more attractive, and more accessible community. As early as 1871 the legislature had authorized the town council to expand its powers to include establishing a market house; requiring all persons owning lots to "make and keep in good repair sidewalks" of a specific width; granting or refusing tavern licenses; and imposing a tax of up to twenty cents on every one hundred dollars of value of all real and personal property lying within the town. Five years later, Spartanburg's charter was again amended. This time the act granted the town council new powers to open, close, or widen streets, prevent wooden construction on the public square, appoint a board of health, organize a fire department, and establish public scales for certifying cotton weights. These expanding powers meant more bureaucracy and more intrusions into what had previously been private concerns. For example, the board of health consisted of twelve members with authority to enter any homes omitting foul odors in order to remove the offensive substances. These increased services would naturally lead to increased taxation, as evidenced by the proposal for a two-mill tax for the organization of a fire department in December 1876.[40]

Spartanburg was not the only town in the county to experience significant economic change. The Air-Line Railroad also proved a boon to Limestone Springs, a once-sleepy village in the northeastern section of the county. William Curtis, one of the town's most influential residents, labored hard to convince Air-Line Railroad officials of Limestone Springs' importance as a crossroads. Curtis hoped that the location of the Air-Line near the village would enable him and his business partners "to establish a new County with its seat [in Limestone Springs]." In 1875 the town was renamed Gaffney, and a newspaper correspondent reported nine stores and "cotton buyers in abundance."[41]

The general enthusiasm surrounding town development was tempered by an awareness of new problems associated with commercial expansion. With town property now in demand, complaints surfaced that landowners were refusing to sell lots at reasonable rates. By demanding high prices while not improving their property, an editorial noted, these men were impeding the progress of the community. Other residents found discouraging a "dispo-

Table 11. Rural and Town Property Values in Spartanburg County, 1873–1878

Year	Value of rural real estate	Value of town real estate
1873	$2,329,637	$386,730
1874	$2,114,169	$364,485
1875	$2,254,360	$419,360
1877	$2,312,170	$516,587
1878	$2,404,940	$573,140
% CHANGE, 1873–78	+3.2	+53.4

Source: Compiled from data in "Reports of the Comptroller General," in *Reports and Resolutions of the General Assembly of the State of South Carolina*, 1873–78.

sition of every other man to put up a whisky saloon" and complained that the town had recently been "infested with tramps" who were absorbing the town's resources. In May 1876 Orphelia Dawkins felt that only a religious revival could restore the community from the depravity brought by the railroads. "If there is another little town this side of bad that needs [a revival] worse," Dawkins wrote her sister Mary, "I pitty it indeed. I do not think I ever heard of another place that has gone back in point of morals as this has since the Air Line Road has passed here."[42]

Despite concerns over some of the social costs of economic change, town development accelerated after the end of Reconstruction. Between 1878 and 1882 approximately thirty new stores were erected in Spartanburg. Yet reports complained that finding stores or homes available for rent was nearly impossible. By 1880 the town's population stood at thirty-two hundred, representing a 200 percent increase over the previous decade. Businesses and many homes in town were furnished with gas from a newly erected gasworks, and the fire department operated with a new steam fire engine. By 1882 most townspeople felt they had successfully overcome the seedier side of development by electing a dry ticket to all town offices. As Lacy Ford has noted, this quick pace of development in upcountry towns strengthened a sense among businessmen that they were part of a progressive community working together for the economic success of the town as a whole.[43]

This focus on town development, however, inevitably weakened the sense of countywide community progress championed in the antebellum era. Because struggling rural farmers could not help but notice the financial boon to town residents resulting from the railroads and increased mercantile activity, their uncertainty over the equality of benefits from railroad construction meant a continued need to diffuse distrust between town and country.

Spartanburg and Asheville engineer Thomas H. Bomar had pointed out in 1873 the erroneous thought of some farmers that "because they live in a remote part of the country or because the line is not in front of their barns that they are not interested" in railroad development. Instead, he argued, the line would help every man, woman, and child who had a pound of produce to sell in the town of Spartanburg. Anticipating the increased flow of money to the town as a result of the railroad, Bomar joined other boosters in assuring that this cash would circulate "into the most remote and obscure corners, and every one, even the humblest laborer [would feel] its vivifying and warming influence."[44] Instead of receiving the "warming influence" of cash, however, many struggling farmers slipped further into indebtedness, tenantry, and landless labor over the course of the decade. Towns offered some opportunities for the growing population of unemployed and underemployed farmers, while others turned to the mill villages growing up in Spartanburg and neighboring counties.

Since the antebellum era Spartanburg's town-based entrepreneurs had argued that rail links were essential for the establishment of a vital industrial sector. These boosters continued to view railroad and industrial expansion as intertwined throughout the Reconstruction era.[45] As was the case with railroads, the difference in the postwar period was a change in political economy that resulted in greater state support for industry and an increased awareness of the exigencies of a diversified economy. For many, the material shortages of the war had made clear the importance of developing local industry in order to maintain a healthy, independent economy. *"We have got to go to manufacturing to save ourselves,"* long-time southern industrial proponent James D. B. DeBow pleaded in 1867. South Carolina's governor James L. Orr concurred with DeBow and noted the many benefits northerners enjoyed as a result of their industrial development. "I am tired of South Carolina as she was," Orr explained. "I covet for her the material prosperity of New England. I would have her acres teem with life and vigor and industry and intelligence, as do those of Massachussetts."[46]

A host of Spartanburg's town residents exhibited a sizable curiosity in postwar industrial innovations. One of the premier showcases for new technological developments in the United States, Philadelphia's Centennial Exposition of 1876, aroused considerable interest in the county. Mary Dawkins informed her sister that "almost everybody in Spartanburg" had been to the exposition. She further reported that only two-thirds as many students were enrolled in Wofford College as the previous year because people were "begging or borrowing" to go to the exposition and that some were willing to "cut down the children's education to accomplish that end."[47]

Industrial development within Spartanburg varied according to the size and type of business. Small industries experienced only moderate growth after the Civil War. This had much to do with the fact that these industries had advanced further than most other counties in the antebellum period and thus had less room for expansion in the postwar era. The county's flour mills and gristmills, for example, grew only slightly, from thirty-four in 1860 to thirty-eight ten years later. Yet for South Carolina as a whole the number of flour mills and gristmills in South Carolina more than doubled, from 270 to 624. This statewide increase has been attributed to the breakup of plantations into smaller farm units, which resulted in a shift from the centralized plantation mill to the smaller localized operations. With fewer plantations and smaller farms than the lowcountry or midlands in the antebellum period, Spartanburg already led the state in flour mills and gristmills by 1860. Although the county experienced some reduction in farm sizes after the war, there were already enough neighborhood mills to handle demands. By 1880 Spartanburg's mills had actually declined by one over the previous decade. An important factor in this leveling off of production was the arrival of cheap grains via the Air-Line and Spartanburg and Asheville railroads.[48]

Population increase and town development in the county were key factors in the expansion of carriage factories and other small manufactures. The arrival of railroads and subsequent town growth as a trading center meant more people needed to transport goods to and from commercial markets and rail depots. Although a twenty-year growth from two carriage factories in 1860 to five in 1880 may seem small, the entire state reported only ten such operations in the latter year. Even more carriage factories may have taken root in Spartanburg were it not for the domination of James A. Fowler's firm, which began before the war as Fowler, Foster & Company. Principal owner James A. Fowler quickly gained a reputation for quality work and a keen business mind. Fowler's company was one of the first postwar town businesses to employ steam power in its factory. When the arrival of the Air-Line railroad threatened to bring in competition, Fowler imported skilled workers, further updated his machinery, and stocked his yard with local timber to ensure uninterrupted production. In 1879 Fowler turned the factory over to his son, who, along with partner R. A. Robison, continued to improve the operation. By 1880 Fowler & Robison's capital investment of twenty thousand dollars was more than six times that of its nearest competitor.[49]

The expansion in business activity and population around Spartanburg town also fueled the demand for more sawmills in the county. As early as January 1873 the *Carolina Spartan* was "confident that fifty new and comfortable dwelling houses could be at once rented to good tenants if they were now ready to be occupied." Warehouses were also in short supply, and "men of capital" were urged to "go to work at once in erecting new buildings." To meet the demand for lumber, the number of sawmills tripled between 1870 and 1880. The 1876 town law banning wooden construction on the public square, however, gave rise to yet another industry. By 1880 four new brickyards were in operation employing a total of sixty-one people.[50]

In contrast to these burgeoning businesses, Spartanburg's iron industry expired in the 1870s. Despite a boost from Confederate demands for war materials, the poor condition of the immediate postwar economy followed by improved rail connections to Pennsylvania's anthracite region doomed the upcountry's ability to compete. At the close of the war Simpson Bobo's South Carolina Manufacturing Company, long the exception to the general diminution in iron production, remained strong.

In 1868 Bobo owned more than half of the company's stock, valued at one hundred thousand dollars. However, just two years later Bobo, perhaps sensing an inevitable declivity associated with northern competition, looked to sell his company. With the subsequent arrival of the Air-Line Railroad bringing cheaper iron products from the North, Bobo chose to close his doors in 1873. By the end of the decade Bobo had sold off all of his land around the Hurricane Shoals foundry to representatives of the fastest-growing industry in postwar Spartanburg: textiles.[51]

In the immediate postwar period upcountry South Carolina experienced a boom in textile factory expansion that was only halted by the economic depression of 1873. Since most of the state's cotton mills were in portions of the upcountry untouched by invading armies, eleven of eighteen prewar factories remained intact at the close of hostilities. Despite the economic disruptions and labor shortages resulting from the war, Spartanburg County reported eight textile factories operating in 1867. The Bivingsville and Crawfordsville mills installed new machinery as early as 1866, and a year later Bivingsville remained one of only two upcountry mills operating over a thousand spindles. As they had before the war, Spartanburg's economic boosters continued to court industry by noting the superior geographical and commercial advantages of the region. Reflecting on both the county's reputation as an educational center and its industrial promise, an 1871 editorial queried, "If Spartanburg is the Athens why should it not be the Manchester of the State[?]"[52]

Between 1860 and 1870 capital investment in South Carolina's cotton mills increased 33 percent, while the value of manufactured cotton products experienced over 70 percent growth. These percentages rose despite a reduction in the number of factories in the state from seventeen to twelve. Over the same ten-year period Spartanburg operated one less textile mill, while its overall capital investment remained steady. However, between 1860 and 1870 the county's value of manufactured products more than doubled, from 87,817 to 190,430. The inverse relationship of fewer mills and higher product value suggests that those factories still remaining expanded their operations and increased their influence in the community. The Bivingsville factory, for example, operated with a capital of eighty thousand dollars in 1870, representing a 62 percent increase over the previous decade along with a 56 percent rise in the value of its manufactured products. Bivingsville also continued to expand the ancillary operations in and around the textile mill; these included a sawmill, shoe shop, gristmill and wheat mill, blacksmith shop, and wool-carding operation. Samuel Morgan's factory, the other large textile operation in the county, experienced a 46 percent increase in the value of its manufactured goods.[53]

Spartanburg's representatives and entrepreneurs hung their hopes for future industrial development on legislation exempting manufacturers from taxation. The Republican Reconstruction legislature, led by northern whites and native blacks, generally supported these measures. In 1870 the state passed an act providing that the tax on property or capital employed in the manufacture of cotton or wool should be returned to investors annually. Since the act was scheduled to remain in force for just four years, however, industrial proponents urged more substantive inducements. In early 1873 a bill came before the legislature to exempt manufacturers of wool and cotton from taxation for ten years. Spartanburg lawyer John H. Evins regarded the bill as the most important issue before the legislature because it offered opportunities for both poor laborers and men of substantial capital. When the bill failed to pass, Spartanburg representative David R. Duncan angrily condemned "the hard hand of the taxgatherer, [who] under the heavy laws of the state, has shut the door against the coming of those who would, by capital invested here, contribute to our growth and prosperity." Duncan purported to have a telegram from a large capitalist ready to invest three hundred thousand dollars upon the bill's passage, which represented just one example "out of hundreds." Industrial proponents complained that those arguing against the tax exemption as class legislation were mistaken. Tax exemptions, supporters contended, would bring factories, factories would provide good jobs for the destitute, more jobs would reduce the poor tax for all taxpayers. In addition, the wealthy capitalists who would move to the region would bring substantial taxable property with them.[54]

In December 1873 the legislature passed another version of the act offering ten-year tax exemptions for all capital invested in the manufacture of cotton, woolen, and paper fabrics, iron, lime, and agricultural implements. These industries were only subject to a two-mill tax for schools. The act appeared to stimulate development, for despite an economic depression in the mid-1870s, South Carolina's textile industry experienced substantial growth between 1870 and the early 1880s. By 1880 the number of spindles, capital investment, and value of products in South Carolina's textile operations all more than doubled, while the number of factories made only a meager increase, from twelve to fourteen. Between 1870 and 1882 capital investment and the value of products in Spartanburg's textile mills both increased almost six times.[55]

The men responsible for Spartanburg's textile development were not antebellum plantation owners who refashioned themselves as industrial entrepreneurs. Instead, these men either had been involved in prewar factories or had worked in commercial business.[56] Samuel Morgan's Cedar Hill factory did well through the war and continued strong after the mid-1870s, when control was transferred to Morgan's three sons, all of whom had had prewar experience in the mill. The Morgans brought in new partners John L. Green and John Wheeler to help expand operations. The Morgans, Green, and Wheeler moved to corner the market on textile production in the Tyger River region of western Spartanburg County with the purchase of the Crawfordsville factory, which they proposed to "put . . . in thorough order and repair." Looking to control distribution as well as production, the Morgan group also ran a store at Welford—the nearest railroad depot to the factory.[57]

Table 12. Textile Mills in Spartanburg County, 1870

Mill	Capital	Machinery		Operatives	Value of products
		Spindles	Looms		
Cedar Hill Factory	$30,000	1,400	60	40	$40,000
Fingerville	$3,500	400	0	13	$11,550
Bivingsville/Glendale	$80,000	2,600	62	105	$129,000
Valley Falls	$8,000	412	0	19	$2,800
Crawfordsville	$8,500	n.a.	n.a.	28	$7,080
TOTAL	$130,000	4,812	134	205	$190,430
% OF STATE TOTAL	10	n.a.	n.a.	18	12

Source: Manuscript Census Returns, Schedule 4: Products of Industry, 1870, Spartanburg District and County, SCDAH.

One of the first entirely new textile factories erected in postbellum Spartanburg, the Pacolet Manufacturing Company, was developed at the initiative of merchant John H. Montgomery. His involvement in textiles was indicative of a rising generation of manufacturers who had first made their money as postwar merchants and then turned their skill in commercial operations toward the production of textiles. Born in Spartanburg in 1833, Montgomery worked initially as a clerk before entering into a general merchandising business with his father-in-law in 1858. Montgomery recovered from wartime losses and joined the prosperous firm of Walker, Fleming & Company in the mid-1870s. At his urging, the company purchased 350 acres of land around Trough Shoals on the Pacolet River in March 1881. A year later the Pacolet Manufacturing Company was organized. By the turn of the century Montgomery was recognized as one of the largest industrialists in the South.[58]

Near the Pacolet operation, the Bivingsville Manufacturing Company offered the most impressive example of Reconstruction-era growth among Spartanburg textile mills. Following principal owner John Bomar's death in 1868, Dexter Edgar Converse took over direction of the mill. In September 1870 Converse bought out the Bomar firm and established a copartnership with A. H. Twichell and Jon C. Zimmerman. Under Converse's skillful management the factory underwent a substantial plan of remodeling and expansion. Converse also added more structure to long-distance sales when he contracted with the New York commission house of E. W. Holbrook. By 1875 the mill's 5,000 spindles and 120 looms were producing 500 pounds of bunched yarn and 6,000 yards of cloth per day and paying out 10 percent

Table 13. Textile Mills in Spartanburg County, 1882

Mill	Capital	Machinery Spindles	Looms	Operatives	Value of products
Cedar Hill Factory	$50,000	804	16	35	$29,241
Fingerville	$15,000	504	9	18	$17,200
Bivingsville/Glendale	$150,000	5,000	120	150	$187,000
Valley Falls	$22,000	566	0	14	$16,900
Crawfordsville	$30,000	1,055	0	35	$22,775
Clifton Manufacturing Co.	$500,000	19,000	0	600	$806,000
TOTAL	$767,000	26,929	145	852	$1,079,116
% OF STATE TOTAL	19	n.a.	n.a.	19	13

Source: South Carolina Department of Agriculture, *South Carolina*, 582.

yearly dividends to investors. South Carolina's third largest factory, Bivingsville was a well-organized and efficient operation with individual floors for carding, spinning, reeling, spooling, warping and weaving, baling, and folding. "Every department here," the *Carolina Spartan* reported, "is conducted with the regularity of clock-work."[59]

Most striking, however, was Bivingsville's operation as a factory village. Aside from textile production, the company ran a flour mill, machine shops, a brass foundry, a blacksmith, a carpenter shop, a sawmill, two cotton gins, and a large store, and it oversaw 250 acres of cultivated land. These operations were patronized by the village's four hundred inhabitants. After visiting Bivingsville in April 1875, the *Carolina Spartan* issued an encomium reflective of the area's faith in industrial expansion. The factory had brought together the best of all worlds. It had improved the community's welfare by providing jobs and homes for the county's helpless people, particularly widows and poor children. Village schools and temperance lodges provided a "civilizing influence" upon these people, which was evidenced by the "remarkably respectable appearance of the operatives." Bivingsville offered the perfect mix of modernity and tranquility, with its "neat and comfortable houses, . . . the factory, the mills, the store, workshops, and last but not least the tasteful residences of the proprietors, to which add the blended harmony of falling waters and the busy hum of machinery . . . a scene where art and nature have combined to make life pleasant and profitable."[60]

In 1879 Converse further expanded his industrial power in Spartanburg through the purchase of property at Hurricane Shoals on the Pacolet River as a site for a new textile operation. The following January, Converse orga-

Table 14. Textile Mills in South Carolina, 1884

| County | No. of mills | Capital | Machinery | | Operatives | Value of products |
			Spindles	Looms		
Aiken	3	$1,000,000	44,180	1,212	1,092	$2,010,000
Anderson	2	$527,000	15,000	412	385	$345,000
Charleston	1	$500,000	15,000	312	400	$820,000
Chester	2	$98,000	3,724	0	52	$64,398
Greenville	8	$929,000	48,360	773	1,165	$2,420,000
Lexington	2	$326,000	12,448	0	200	$180,000
Orangeburg	1	$125,000	4,200	0	106	$185,000
Spartanburg	7	$1,048,000	37,680	945	1,100	$1,670,000
Sumter	1	$60,000	1,984	0	38	$88,800
York	2	$193,000	11,936	0	146	$180,000
TOTAL	29	$4,795,900	195,112	3,652	4,714	$7,963,198

Source: South Carolina in 1884.

nized the Clifton Manufacturing Company and received subscriptions for the entire $100,000 of original stock within the first two weeks. Stockholders quickly increased capital stock, first to $200,000 and then to $500,000, to meet subscription demands. In addition to upcountry interest, $50,000 of stock was taken out in Charleston and another $41,000 in Boston. The Boston subscriptions suggest the growing recognition among northerners of the advantages of cheap, nonunionized labor and a cheap source of motive power in the South. This investment also reflects the changing political and social climate in the North as the political focus shifted away from social conditions to the opportunities of industrial capitalism. Many northern businessmen welcomed the end of Reconstruction and looked to capitalize on promising southern enterprises. By 1882 Converse's two mills accounted for 85 percent of the county's capital investment in textiles, 89 percent of textile machinery, 88 percent of factory operatives, and 92 percent of finished product values. Converse's corporate skill would serve as a model for the county's explosion in textile factories through the 1880s and 1890s.[61]

Although northern money could provide an important boost to a factory's expansion, native interest and involvement appeared essential to success. Postwar Spartanburg's largest nonnative industrial endeavor offers a case in point. In 1875 a group of British investors formed the English Manufacturing Company and purchased three thousand acres from Simpson Bobo's defunct ironworks. The company had the authority to raise three hundred thousand dollars in capital for its planned factory complex, which was to include a cotton mill of ten thousand spindles, a shoe factory, and a hosiery mill. All capital subscribed to the company was tax exempt until 1885. Part of the plan for raising funds involved subdividing the land into six-acre plots that would be sold to settlers who took stock in the operation. Company representative Alfred Peete toured both England and New England soliciting subscriptions and recruiting mechanics for the planned operation. Early in 1876 Peete secured sixteen thousand dollars in subscriptions from a group in Holyoke, Massachusetts, under the condition that the shoe factory would be staffed entirely by Massachusetts workers. Locally, Peete lectured to Spartanburg's mercantile and professional community on the important link between prosperity and the division of labor through industrial diversification. Farmers were encouraged to support manufacturing because it created both internal and external markets for agricultural products. "By encouraging the building of factories," *Carolina Spartan* editor Hugh L. Farley was convinced, "we make them the handmaid of agriculture."[62]

Through 1876 creditors expressed great confidence that the English Manufacturing Company was moving along with "every indication of success." Yet less than half of the capital stock had been paid in by the fall of 1877, and work on the proposed operation ceased completely in December. A host of financial difficulties may explain the company's failure, but it seems clear that local investment for the endeavor was lacking.[63] Spartanburg's growing mercantile community appeared much more inclined to invest in established firms or to start their own operations, which they could control.

Local concern with manufacturing was not restricted to wealthy merchants and professionals. Some people who lost all of their old agrarian lives saw the potential for ground-floor opportunities in the new industrial developments. Lalla Pelot, a Newberry resident who had lost both her husband and her financial stability by the mid-1870s, reported that she was "literally living day to day not knowing where a meal is coming from tomorrow." Prior to the failure of the English Manufacturing Company, Pelot had placed great hopes for future stability in selling her home for four thousand to five thousand dollars and investing the money in the English Manufacturing Company. In addition to the investment, Pelot wanted her family to live on the company's land, where life would be "comforting." She also urged her son to find employment at the cotton factory, which, when completed, would be a "great work."[64]

Although Lalla Pelot no doubt envisioned her son working for the textile factory in an administrative capacity, most mill employees worked as operatives and were generally poor landless whites and tenants in need of supplemental income or seasonal work. At a time when racial divisions in agricultural labor were becoming less certain, the cotton mill was offered as a solely white domain. David Golightly Harris's cousin Gwin and a man named David Miller looked for work at the Bivingsville factory to supplement their employment as hired hands on Harris's farm. Having worked alongside freedmen while digging ditches, hauling wood, and performing field labor, Gwin Harris and David Miller could find additional work during slow periods in an exclusively white atmosphere.[65] Thus, textile factories offered a possible avenue to additional economic security not open to freedmen. Factory owners and supporters emphasized these opportunities and the mill's important role as a safety net offering both social and economic benefits to employees. Managers saw mills operating as a form of "working welfare" for families who had lost fathers and husbands and had poor prospects for managing profitable crops. In 1870 83 percent of Spartanburg's mill operatives were women or children. By 1880 the mills had drawn the attention of underemployed northern workers. Massachusetts resident John F. Dyar wrote to Converse for information on wages paid for a "good woman" and a man who was a "green hand." Equally important to Dyar was whether Spartanburg's mills employed black weavers or "respectible white women."[66]

The rhetoric of factory boosters thinly masked the often tedious and unsafe conditions in the cotton mills. Although the mills offered another means of income, entrance into the world of factory employment meant surrendering one's control over work hours and work rhythms. In isolated cases South Carolina operatives had shown themselves willing to challenge mill managers when work speed-ups or low wages prompted united action. In 1875, for example, workers at Graniteville engaged in a four-week strike over wage cuts and received minor concessions from management.[67] Although Spartanburg mills experienced no such labor unrest, both factory operatives and farmers saw reason to question the community benefits derived from manufacturing. Workers complained of long hours and low wages, while farmers cited unfair tax exemptions for factories. By the mid-1880s young politicians in Spartanburg found these issues prevalent enough to push for legislative reform in the general assembly. Two men in particular, Edwin H. Bobo and John Stanyarne Wilson, led a campaign in the state house to overturn the 1873 tax exemption for manufacturing. Both men attacked the law as "class legislation" and succeeded in securing the act's repeal in 1885. Later, in 1890, Wilson introduced a bill to ban the employment of children under sixteen in cotton mills.[68]

This seeming turn in Spartanburg's political leadership toward limiting the power of the region's factories was more apparent than real. Bobo and Wilson did not represent a traditional rural animosity to modernization. Edwin Bobo was the son of lawyer-industrialist Simpson Bobo, one of the wealthiest men in the county. After serving as a lieutenant during the Civil War, Edwin Bobo returned to his law practice in Spartanburg and became editor of the *Carolina Spartan* in 1870. Losing his bid for the state senate in 1880, Bobo was elected to the house in 1882. Some of Bobo's most vocal attacks on the tax-exemption law occurred while he was once again running for the state senate in 1883. By then over a thousand people were employed in the mills, and farmers had suffered from drought, high interest rates, and high taxation. Repeal of the tax-exemption law, then, would resound with many voters. Also in 1883 Bobo served as director of the Spartanburg and Rutherfordton Railroad.[69] Rail companies had long relied on special taxes to build, expand, and develop their lines. Therefore, his position against the tax-exemption law served the dual purpose of appealing to voters while garnering more tax money for railroads.

Like Bobo, John Stanyarne Wilson had studied law in his father's office and settled as a town lawyer in the postwar period. He was elected to the state house of representatives in 1884 and again in 1890. Wilson's fight against the tax-exemption law and child labor was hardly an attack on manufacturing itself. In fact, he called for repeal of the tax-exemption legislation even though he owned significant stock in several Spartanburg mills. Once he had secured election to the U.S. Congress in 1894, Wilson focused little attention on manufacturing reforms and instead became director of a mining company and an incorporator of a local ironworks.[70] Postwar Spartanburg leaders looked to soften some of the rougher edges of factory life, but, like their antebellum predecessors, they did not engage in any studied resistance to manufacturing. Factory operatives, despite occasional rallies for reform, remained hamstrung by appeals to Anglo-Saxon unity and by the lack of immigrant influence so crucial to labor resistance in the late-nineteenth-century North.[71]

By 1880 Spartanburg's wealthiest and most influential residents were closely connected to railroads, textile mills, and town development. These men included the likes of Gabriel Cannon, Dexter Edgar Converse, and John Montgomery. Many of the core proponents of infrastructural diversification and change in the antebellum period remained prominent throughout Spartanburg's postbellum era. Most of those representing the new economic leadership had begun their careers in the antebellum era as merchants, lawyers, manufacturers, and other professionals; they were men for whom the movement toward greater economic expansion and diversification would have been a logical step regardless of the effects of Civil War and Reconstruction. However, the Civil War and Reconstruction did permit these entrepreneurs unprecedented economic opportunities that accelerated infrastructural change in the community.

By the mid-1880s railroads criss-crossed the county, increasing access to new markets and creating new possibilities for those near a depot. The railroads' effect on town prosperity fell in sharp contrast with the plight of farmers in the countryside. A debt-ridden yeoman farmer in northern Cherokee township, ten miles from the nearest railroad, would find little common ground with an enterprising town professional. Textile factory expansion provided jobs for some but at the expense of men's control over their households and both men's and women's control over their work hours. Tax exemptions for factories created a special interest at odds with farmers, who labored under heavy tax burdens throughout the 1870s.

Despite these potentially divisive issues, Spartanburg's leaders expected to preserve the cohesion of the white community in much the same way they had prior to the Civil War. By espousing continued schooling opportunities and strong legal protection for the white community, local leaders argued that they would ensure a better life for their race. Yet emancipation created new challenges to those looking to promote white progress while maintaining restrictions on the social and economic opportunities available for freedmen.

CHAPTER EIGHT

"Educate Your Sons, They Will Build Reservoirs and Railroads"
Race, Class, and Postwar Public Education

WHETHER VIEWING RECONSTRUCTION as a success, a failure, or an unfinished revolution, southern historians have generally concurred that the creation of a state-supported system of public schooling for both whites and blacks was one of the most visible and lasting achievements of the period.[1] Over the past thirty-five years, studies have focused on the efforts of Freedmen's Bureau agents, Yankee "schoolmarms," and missionary societies to establish schools for ex-slaves in black majority areas. These scholars have carefully delineated areas of success along with the challenges of northern white cultural biases, the freedmen's own educational expectations, and southern white opposition.[2]

Postwar public education in white majority areas of the southern upcountry has not received equal attention. In the case of Spartanburg, an antebellum ideology that supported public education as an important element in widening the gap between white independence and black slavery ensured substantial resistance to Republican Reconstruction schooling initiatives for freedmen. Leading whites denounced taxation for black schools even as they looked to expand educational opportunities for their own race. Redemption in South Carolina brought retrenchment in education spending, which most heavily affected black institutions. By the late 1870s and 1880s town boosters supported public education for whites to further their goals of economic diversification and industrialization. Although this focus on schooling for town prosperity increasingly discriminated against rural areas, the continued reliance on racial distinction in educational policy reduced conflict within the white community.

The problems of debt and desolation facing South Carolina in the immediate postwar period left little time or money for public education. In 1865 provisional governor James L. Orr recommended that the appropriation for free schools be discontinued, and the state constitution made no provision for a public school system.[3] Over the next two years those concerned with educating Spartanburg's youth relied solely on charity, fund-raising, and loans to support schools. Principal W. B. Carson of Reidville High School, a private, tuition-based institution, offered a plan entitled "How to Educate Our Poor Young Men." Carson called on area planters to pledge an annual contribution to the school of wheat, corn, beef, or pork "to be applied to the boarding of indigent young men." The Reidville principal insisted that this food would not be a donation but a loan rated at ten dollars in specie per month to be refunded "as soon as the student shall be able." In March 1866 the *Carolina Spartan* urged county residents to "retrench in everything until we are able to spend money upon the improvement and advancement of the children of the country." Floral festivals and theatrical productions were held to raise funds for local schools.[4] The *Carolina Spartan* expressed certainty that, with this "energy" and "high-toned public sentiment" directed at education, the county's "schools will continue to number among the best and most useful institutions of learning in the State."[5]

These schools would also continue to exclude blacks from enrollment. In fact, aside from the very limited operations of the Freedmen's Bureau in the upcountry, no provisions were made for schooling former slaves during presidential Reconstruction. As a result, much of the initiative for freedmen's education came from within the black community. In the summer of 1866 E. J. Snetter, one of only a handful of black educators in Spartanburg, received verbal support from South Carolina Freedmen's Bureau Superintendent of Schools Reuben H. Tomlinson to start a black school. Four months after commencing classes, however, Snetter had no formal authorization for the school, and he and an assistant had yet to receive any pay.[6] As in the antebellum period, local white leaders continued to look to education as an important distinction between the races and thus did little to assist in the schooling of ex-slaves. By early 1867, however, the very nature of the relationship between public schooling and the community at large had undergone a profound change.

Following the imposition of congressional Reconstruction in March 1867, Republican-led state constitutional conventions throughout the South addressed a host of important questions concerning the integration of blacks into the political and institutional mainstream. At the South Carolina convention, delegates engaged in particularly rancorous debate over the issue of free schools.[7] A combination of northern and native whites and native blacks challenged a clause making education in the state compulsory for all children between the ages of six and sixteen. R. C. DeLarge, a black Republican from Charleston, and C. P. Leslie, a northern white Republican representing Barnwell, argued that forced schooling was "contrary to the spirit and principles of republicanism" because it interfered with a man's household decisions. Another black delegate, Benjamin Byas of Berkeley District, also opposed compulsory education, maintaining that "a man should not be compelled to educate his children, any more than he should be forced to direct them to heaven or hell." Leading black Republicans like A. J. Ransier reminded colleagues that the Civil War had altered the meaning of southern republicanism. "To be free," Ransier replied to DeLarge, "is not to enjoy unlimited license, or my friend [DeLarge] himself might desire to enslave again his fellow men." Delegate John A. Chestnut argued that government "cannot by any persuasive and reasonable means establish civilization among an ignorant and degraded community.... Force is necessary, and, for one, I say let force be used." Although a provision for compulsory attendance was included in the South Carolina Constitution of 1868, Charleston black Republican delegate Francis L. Cardozo secured a compromise amendment providing that no mandatory schooling law would be passed "until a system of public schools has been completely organized."[8]

Lengthy debate also surrounded a proposed section of the constitution requiring all schools receiving state funding to be open to all students regardless of race. B. O. Duncan, a native white Republican from Newberry, warned that existing prejudices would make mixed-race schools a failure. Whites, he argued, would keep their children at home, resulting in a public school program that only benefited blacks. Duncan predicted that "in attempting to enforce mixed schools, you [will] bring trouble, quarreling and wrangling, into every neighborhood." Most Republican delegates felt different, however, arguing that the section merely permitted integration and that separate schools would be used in practice. The section passed by a vote of ninety-eight to four with nineteen absent. Spartanburg's two black delegates, Rice Foster and Coy Wingo, voted with the majority, while the county's white delegates, John S. Gentry and J. P. F. Camp, were absent from voting.[9]

The South Carolina Constitution of 1868, the first such document submitted before the people for ratification, introduced a uniform system of education open to all children with provisions for a state superintendent and a state board of education that consisted of the superintendent and the school commissioners from each county in the state. The schools would be funded by an annual property tax and a poll tax. In addition, the state was to provide institutions for the blind, deaf, and mentally ill as well as support the elderly and infirm.[10] Although many of these reforms were similar to those advocated by Spartanburg leaders in the antebellum era, the provision for biracial access to public schools led most county whites to reject these education initiatives.

In the weeks prior to the vote on ratification of the 1868 constitution, county conservatives blasted the section permitting integration of the public schools. A committee of whites led by T. Stobo Farrow, John H. Evins, S. T. Poinier, and J. J. Boyd asked the registered voters of Spartanburg if they were willing to "force whites and blacks to send their children to the same school." Neither race, they argued, wanted integration, but Radicals forced the issue "to produce discord between the races." Beyond the inevitable racial tensions, the committee also warned that the costs of such a compulsory school program would break the small white farmer. "[B]y the time we pay taxes sufficient to keep up public schools enough to afford facilities of education to all the ignorant and uneducated negroes in the State," the committee predicted, "we will all be poor men, and unable to send our children to any but public schools."[11]

In the months following ratification of the constitution, it became increasingly apparent that conservative fears of integrated schooling were unwarranted. Robert K. Scott, the new Radical Republican governor, made clear his preference for separate schools in South Carolina. Scott, former head of the South Carolina Freedmen's Bureau, worried that integration would lead whites to keep their children away from schools, leaving only blacks to benefit from the new universal system of education. The governor argued that, over time, the "elevating influence of popular education" would permit the two races to accept integration.[12]

Tracing the course of education for both blacks and whites in South Carolina's local communities can prove a difficult task. Educational statistics for the 1860s and 1870s are incomplete, and, to make matters worse, county school commissioners engaged in a confusing policy of labeling all schools as public institutions. These officials continued an antebellum practice of permitting private schools to use free school appropriations for the purpose of reducing tuition charges. For example, of the twenty-nine "public" schools reported by the Spartanburg school commissioner in 1869, sixteen charged tuition and included institutions such as Wofford College, the Spartanburg Seminary for women, and Limestone Springs Male Academy. Despite these deficiencies in the sources, however, certain trends in the postwar educational life of the county and the state are quite clear. Early Reconstruction attempts to organize schools, hire teachers, and develop curriculum were hampered by the failure of the general assembly to pass a permanent common school law for two years after the ratification of the Republican constitution. In January 1870 the state superintendent of education, Justus K. Jillson, complained that his department had been "in a state of comparative inactivity for nearly a year, whereby much precious time has been lost." Financial support was also slow in coming. The money expended by the state for school support in 1869 amounted to just over half of the 1860 appropriation despite the added postwar responsibility of educating about one hundred thousand black children. In Spartanburg the collection of over twenty-four hundred dollars in poll taxes, added to the state appropriation of sixteen hundred dollars, was still only enough to open half of the county's fifty-eight schools.[13]

Those charged with organizing black schools in Reconstruction Spartanburg faced the dual problems of inadequate state support and white hostility. In 1867 teacher Eva Poole opened a school for black children in Spartanburg town. By spring 1869 she taught over one hundred students at a building owned by the estate of industrialist John Bomar and controlled by attorney Simpson Bobo. Shortly after the school session began, the county school commissioner, R. H. Reid, visited Poole's classes and, having "heard some of her pupils *read* and *spell*," informed Superintendent Jillson that he was "pleased with their progress." When asked to report on white public sentiment toward the school, however, Poole responded simply, "Hostile, Hostile."[14] Beyond white animosity, she also faced problems of overcrowding, poor material conditions, and overdue pay. By September 1869 Poole and two black women assistants faced a peak enrollment of 150 students. At the end of the month the school had to close for necessary repairs. Securing payment for such taxing work proved to be a challenge in and of itself. In early 1869 Poole was still petitioning the legislature to compensate her for her 1867 teaching duties. The frustrated teacher wrote Jillson in November to settle her account, informing him that she had "resumed again my school duties after many disadvantages and in a place that I do not admire. But it was the best I could do for the present."[15]

The following spring Poole obtained some relief with the opening of two more black schools near town. Enrollments at these schools, both taught by southern black women, averaged forty pupils and helped bring Poole's students down to around sixty-five. These numbers were still high, however, when compared to an average enrollment of twenty-four students at the fourteen non-tuition-based white schools located throughout the county. Despite these less-than-comfortable conditions, black interest in education is revealed by the fact that, on average, 92 percent of those enrolled attended school versus just 58 percent for whites.[16]

Although many freedmen had an unquenchable thirst for schooling, black educational advancement in the upcountry was circumscribed by a white ideology that had long identified access to learning as an important indication of white independence and superiority. Most whites acknowledged that the end of slavery would bring some system for educating blacks, but few were willing to pay the taxes necessary to support such a system, and virtually no one would tolerate integration. Even those southern whites who were seemingly sympathetic to black schooling inadvertently acknowledged the obstacles to success. In his 1869 report to the state superintendent, Spartanburg commissioner R. H. Reid determined that "no plan will succeed in this County, which contemplates mixing the two races in the same schools under the same teachers. . . . Its effects will be to array the wealth and intelligence of the County against the system." The demand for separate schools, Reid continued, "grows out of no prejudice or unkindness in the bosom of the whites toward the blacks" but was simply a recognition that the people were not yet ready for social equality. After providing dubious assurances to Jillson that whites were "willing to aid [blacks] in every reasonable way, and will cheerfully pay the school taxes, if they can see that they are wisely, economically and judicially applied," the commissioner nevertheless admitted that creating separate schools for blacks would be difficult in most areas of the county because the number of black children in any given neighborhood was often too small to warrant a school. Having identified this troubling problem, Reid just as quickly dismissed it, suggesting to Jillson that "such cases will soon heal themselves; the blacks will congregate in the neighborhood of their schools."[17]

This attitude that problems in black education would "heal themselves" in large part accounts for the limited success of Reconstruction-era schooling. Although both races struggled to improve educational opportunities in the early postwar period, far fewer black children in the county were able to attend the handful of schools clustered around Spartanburg town. In 1870 just under 30 percent of the county's white student population of 4,709 actually attended school. The county nevertheless bested the statewide white school attendance rate of under 20 percent. By contrast, just 259, or under 11 percent, of Spartanburg's black student population of 2,414 attended school in 1870.[18]

White resistance to black schooling and most social services enacted by the Republican government not only ensured a hostile environment for freedmen's education but also limited local funding for educational purposes. Whites complained that propertyless, penniless blacks were able to take advantage of government services while white farmers struggled to pay oppressive state and local taxes. "We doubt if one in twenty of the colored persons in the State ever pay their capitation tax," the *Carolina Spartan* opined. "These delinquents contribute nothing to the school fund of the State, while they come in for a full share of the benefits of the new system." The editor proposed harsher penalties for nonpayment of taxes, including disability as jurors and exclusion from schools.[19] White hostility to perceived black "freeloading" was the major reason why not a single school district in the county voted for a special tax for education in 1874.

Freedmen became scapegoats for educational deficiencies in the early 1870s due, in large part, to a renewed attempt by superintendent Jillson to promote integration. Fearing that statements made by both Jillson and Governor Franklin Moses foreshadowed social equality in the common schools, an 1873 Spartanburg teachers' convention produced a resolution stating that such a change would be "injurious to the educational interests of both white and black. That while we will give encouragement to the education of both races in *separate schools*, we deprecate the agitation of *mixed* schools, as they are desired by neither race and will defeat the end in view in this county." Jillson first experimented with forced integration at the State Institution for the Education of the Deaf, Dumb, and Blind in Cedar Springs, Spartanburg County. In September 1873 he insisted not only that the institution admit black pupils but that "an earnest and faithful effort must be made to induce such pupils to apply for admission." Once admitted, blacks were to be housed, fed, and taught in the same dormitories and classrooms as whites. In response, the administrators and faculty resigned, and the school was forced to close for three years. The institution reopened only when Governor Daniel Chamberlain's administration rescinded the demand for integration in 1876.[20]

Although not a single common school was integrated in South Carolina during Reconstruction, whites continually warned of a Republican conspiracy to "mix" the races. Spartanburg resident W. Waddy Thomson warned his fellow whites that "the satanic artificers of our subjugation have fully in mind their object; it is to mingle the blood which flowed in the veins of Jenkins and Gregg and Jackson and Lee, and made sacred the battlefields of the Confederacy, with an alien race that the bastard stream may forever go on with sordid taint." Particular concern surrounded a federal attempt to force integration through Massachusetts senator Charles Sumner's civil rights bill, which called for equal rights in public conveyances, hotels, places of public entertainment, churches, and common schools. First introduced in 1870, the bill met a series of defeats over the next few years. When it was reintroduced in December 1873, the *Carolina Spartan* identified the proposal for integrated schooling as the "most atrocious feature" of the bill. Whites throughout the South complained that federally mandated integration would destroy the public school system. Following Sumner's death in March 1874, a series of amendments were made to the civil rights bill to ensure its passage. One of these amendments, introduced by Connecticut congressman Stephen W. Kellogg, struck all reference to schools. As a result, the Civil Rights Act of 1875 did nothing to alter separate schooling in the South or, for that matter, much of the North.[21]

Spartanburg freedmen struggled to control their own education in the face of opposition from both native whites and northern Republicans. In the late 1860s northern white minister Anson W. Cummings came to Spartanburg, opened a mercantile business, and quickly became involved in local Republican politics. Under contract with the U.S. government, he built a schoolhouse for "Freedmen & Refugees" in 1870 at a cost of eight hundred dollars. Shortly thereafter, Gabriel Cannon, working on behalf of the Air-Line Railroad, gave notice that the school lot was desired for the erection of track and a depot. Cannon hoped to condemn the property, but he feared that the nearby presence of U.S. troops would embolden the school's black trustees to resist. When they challenged the legality of Cannon's efforts to demolish the school, he complained that "the trustees were all ignorant colored men."[22] The response of this local white entrepreneur to blacks resisting his economic interests is not surprising. However, Republican Anson Cummings also blasted the school's black trustees.

Cummings had proposed to the school's trustees that he serve as their agent in negotiations with the railroad company "to erect another and a larger & better [school]house." What happened next is not entirely clear, but Cummings contended that the trustees were persuaded into giving all control to a black Zion Methodist preacher and that during Cummings's absence a jury assessed the railroad's damages to the school at $499.25. Cummings told Superintendent Jillson that he could have received at least $1,000 for the schoolhouse and lot. The trustees, Cummings charged, were "wholly irresponsible," and the preacher was "a very bad man." Cummings also argued that the black trustees had lied when they maintained that they had been deeded the schoolhouse by Freedmen's Bureau head O. O. Howard. After looking into the matter, state attorney general (later governor) Daniel Chamberlain agreed with Cummings that the poor compensation had "arisen from the neglect or, more probably, incompetency of the trustees of this property or their agents." With the railroad excavation almost at the schoolhouse steps and nowhere for the full classes to go, Cummings urged Jillson to intervene and take control away from the preacher and trustees.[23]

This dispute over negotiations for a schoolhouse reveals some of the wider divisions between Republican whites and blacks concerning the control over freedmen's education. White Republicans argued that they could best educate freedmen in the rights and responsibilities of citizenship and prepare them for the competitive free labor economy. For blacks, however, self-determination was a crucial element of freedom, and they wanted black trustees to chart the course of freedmen's education.[24] Blacks also wanted control over their children's schooling to ensure positive lessons in equal rights. James Anderson finds that black schools in the South adopted the classical liberal curriculum of white schooling not in imitation but to convey the inherent rights to equality for all races in the Western world. For freedmen and freedwomen, free public schools were foremost among these inherent rights.[25]

While Spartanburg blacks struggled to realize the promise of new educational opportunities, leading whites in the county looked to expand public schooling for their own race despite financial and social obstacles. In 1869 Commissioner Reid complained that many uneducated parents were allowing their children to grow up in ignorance, while others "make slaves of their children." Arguing that this indifference to learning was no longer tolerable in the changed economic conditions facing the South, Reid expressed his support for a law "*compelling* people to educate their children." The Spartanburg commissioner cited three obstacles to the education of the masses: the apathy of the people, the lack of qualified teachers, and insufficient funds. School officials and supporters of public education expressed frustration at portions of the white community for failing to connect improved schooling with a healthier, more diversified economy. P. J. Oeland, a member of the executive committee for the county teachers' convention, warned Spartanburg citizens that if they withheld the means of education from their children, they could not "expect much material or political progress in the coming decades. Our country boasts of many natural advantages; but of what avail are all her varied resources of mineral, manufacturing and agricultural wealth without cultivated intellect to control and develop nature, and render her inert forces the allies and servitors of man." Newspaper articles maintained that "a good PUBLIC SCHOOL" open to all—at least all whites—was the county's greatest need. "Educate your sons," the *Spartanburg Herald* advised, "they will build reservoirs and railroads."[26]

Farming communities responded that the problem was not so much apathy as agricultural necessity that kept children away from the schoolhouse. A correspondent to the *Carolina Spartan* from Cherokee township near the North Carolina border lamented that in "the education of the masses, there is truly a serious and an alarming neglect. The most of us are poor, and our children are compelled by stern necessity to labor upon our farms." School absences were made worse, the correspondent argued, by the yeoman's insistence on planting a portion of his lands in cotton. The cotton crop required hard labor and much of the year to cultivate, forcing the farmer's children to miss "half the time the public schools are in session." More focus on the less labor-intensive grain crop would allow farmers to send their children to school for three to five months out of the year. The correspondent warned poor farmers who looked to make immediate profits from cotton that "the future welfare, greatness, grandeur, and glory of all well-regulated governments" depended upon "the intellectual condition of the masses."[27] By thinking only of current economic returns, educators warned, farmers were jeopardizing the future prosperity of the community.

Teachers were assigned a large share of the blame for early postwar educational problems. Superintendent Jillson attributed the "unsatisfactory condition of our school system . . . to the employment of so many incompetent, inefficient, and worthless teachers." Jillson found that many instructors did little preparation for the classroom and that they only took the job "from a consciousness of being unfit for everything else." Unqualified teachers were hired, he maintained, because ignorant people on the local boards of county examiners gave certificates to anyone who applied. Commissioner Reid confirmed that incompetent teachers were a problem in his county and offered solutions in the form of state normal schools and an elevation in both pay and respect for instructors.[28]

Inadequate and inefficient funding was indeed a major obstacle to luring skilled individuals to the teaching profession in South Carolina. Many instructors found they had to wait months and even years for their services to be fully compensated. Between 1872 and 1874 the state had unpaid balances on the free school appropriation totaling $158,568, which, Jillson warned, had been "the cause of great distress and privation to teachers, and its effects upon our schools have been of the most grave and unfortunate nature." Spartanburg's unpaid school claims for the period between October 1870 and October 1872 amounted to $17,536.75, the fourth highest in the state. These unpaid debts not only distressed local teachers but provided white farmers with yet another reason to oppose Republican taxation policies.[29]

The Reconstruction free school fund initially consisted of a local poll tax and a state appropriation that was apportioned according to each county's representation in the lower house of the general assembly. Between 1868 and 1870 the state appropriation rose steadily from $25,000 to $300,000. Over the same period Spartanburg's share of this fund jumped from just over $800 to just under $11,000, while county poll tax revenues averaged $2,420 annually. By an act of March 1871 each local school district was required to levy an additional tax for educational purposes in order to continue receiving its share of the state appropriation. This law produced widespread resentment among whites who felt that the Republican-controlled legislature, already overtaxing state residents, was now holding each district's right to a portion of the state fund hostage in order to exact more money from already overburdened farmers.

In 1872 county resident Sebal Conner petitioned the state legislature "to allow school districts which fail to levy a tax in accordance with the Act of March 1871 to receive their share of the appropriation made for common schools." Residents of Spartanburg County's Reidville school district directed their anger at Commissioner Reid for withholding the state appropriation after the district's refusal to levy a local school tax. Reid insisted on following the law, arguing that "few if any of the Districts in this county will vote a tax" if the state appropriation were not withheld.[30]

Reid's assessment that only penalties would compel school districts to levy a local tax proved accurate when the act withholding the state appropriation was repealed in early 1875. The following year a group of citizens of the Poole's Mill school district held a meeting to discuss local taxes. Washington Poole, clerk of the school board of trustees, made a speech "condemnatory of the manner in which our special tax money had been managed." Those present passed a set of resolutions stating that the school district would not vote for any more taxes because they were already too high for farmers to pay and because a considerable portion of "a liberal special tax for the purpose of building school houses . . . has never been realized by us." Trustees at Reidville school district adopted a similar fiscal conservatism. They reduced the number of white schools from five to four, thereby eliminating the need for two teachers. The district's two black schools, each with one black instructor, remained in operation. The trustees further expressed their resolve to "only pay $30 for any teacher if in our power."[31]

Despite financial retrenchment in common school funding, many still viewed the county's educational advancement as a priority and looked for creative ways to support schooling. In 1872 Spartanburg representative Robert M. Smith amended a bill for the relief of widows and orphans of persons killed by the Ku Klux Klan to include a section providing that "if in any County said levy of one-half mill shall be more than sufficient for the support of the widows and orphans aforesaid in said County, then said excess shall be applied to the School Fund." Since Smith's amendment made no mention of who would determine that the tax was more than sufficient, the decision was likely left to the county commissioners. In the case of Spartanburg, this meant local white Democrats who, if not sympathetic to some of the Klan's activities, were at least opposed to any special taxes designed to compensate blacks and Republican whites who were victims of violence. When school districts throughout the county refused to levy a local tax in 1875, local officials diverted over thirteen hundred dollars of the Klan fund to the support of schooling. Less than a year before Reconstruction's end in South Carolina, county resident Waddy Thomson looked to solve the problem of high taxation by returning to elements of the antebellum school system, where a state appropriation was supplemented by charitable contributions. "This State pays a burdensome tax for the support of our public free schools," Thomson instructed county residents, "and a false pride should not prevent our wealthier citizens from patronizing these schools because it is not only their just right but it is useful in the encouragement it affords to the poorer farmer to send his child." Antebellum schooling, Thomson maintained, had reared "virtuous men," and a return to elements of that system would cost taxpayers less than the Radical Republican policy.[32]

Although racism and fiscal irregularities hampered educational development in South Carolina, the provision for common schooling in the 1868 constitution and the subsequent actions of the Republican legislature, state superintendent, local officials, and individual teachers introduced structured learning to far more children, both black and white, than at any time in the state's prior history. Between 1870 and 1875 the percentage of South Carolina's white children between the ages of six and sixteen attending school more than doubled, from 19.6 to 54.9 percent. Spartanburg County's growth in white school attendance was even more impressive, jumping from 29.7 percent in 1870 to a state high of 83.4 percent in 1875. Most blacks in South Carolina and throughout the South were introduced to formal education for the first time with the assistance of the Freedmen's Bureau in the immediate postwar period and the provisions for universal schooling in the Reconstruction constitutions. By 1870 just under 22 percent of the state's black student population attended school. Five years later attendance rates had increased to over 41 percent of black children. Over the same time period Spartanburg's black student attendance rate climbed from 10.7 to 49 percent.[33]

Clearly, learning opportunities for black and white children of the South experienced fundamental growth over the course of Reconstruction. One historian of southern schooling argues that the "reorganization and general improvement of [the] systems of education of both races on a tuition-free basis undoubtedly proved to be the most outstanding and durable achievement of the Radical state governments between 1868 and 1877." Yet the numbers also reveal limitations to this educational advancement in the racially divided South. Although Spartanburg's increase in black student attendance outpaced white growth during Reconstruction, over half of the county's black children did not attend school when white Democrats regained control of the state government in 1877.[34] General resistance among most whites to Republican taxation aimed at securing black social and political rights restricted educational opportunities. The distribution of Spartanburg's black population also worked against widespread schooling. Most freedmen in the county lived on land owned by yeoman farmers who employed a small number of black families for share wages. As a result, few neighborhoods sustained a black student population high enough for white school officials to feel justified in building a schoolhouse with revenue collected primarily from white farmers. Commissioner Reid's suggestion that blacks should cluster in areas near schools was impractical, since household heads were tied to farming contracts that prevented easy mobility.

Throughout Reconstruction whites benefited from schooling opportunities not open to freedmen. Yeomen and professionals with enough cash could send their children to the numerous tuition-based schools in the county. For example, Spartanburg High School offered instruction from elementary through high school levels, with tuition ranging from $17.50 to $20.00 per twenty-week term. Reidville High School for boys offered white children schooling at a tuition of between $10 and $20 per session and board at $10 to $12 per month. Some school administrators, like W. B. Carson of Reidville High School, extended credit to white students who were low on cash with the agreement that they would pay the tuition once they graduated and found employment. Sunday schools connected to local churches also provided basic instruction for whites.[35]

Some middling farmers chose to hire their own teachers and schoolhouses for their children. Having struggled through the 1850s to secure personalized instruction for his children, David Golightly Harris continued to locate instructors and makeshift schoolrooms despite financial constraints in the postwar period. In June 1866 Harris hired Emma Ramsour to teach his four boys. Before lessons could commence, however, the boys and "black Dave" had to whitewash an old house on Harris's property for Ramsour's classes. The Fair Forest farmer recorded his hope that "Miss Emma will prove a good teacher to my little folks and be satisfied with her situation." Two years later Harris employed relative Julia Ray Harris to instruct his boys "part of the time." Although happy at the prospect of having his children continue their education, he admitted that he could "hardly see how I can pay her." Harris's financial worries aside, there is no indication that any blacks in Spartanburg shared his ability to hire a personal teacher. Poor white children attended school less frequently than their wealthier neighbors, but the availability of tuition-free white schoolhouses throughout the districts in the county provided much greater opportunities for learning than were afforded black families.[36]

At times, Spartanburg's leading white citizens voiced their support for black education, but even on these infrequent occasions it was clear that expectations and interests were limited. Following the removal of all mention of schooling in the 1875 Civil Rights Bill, the *Carolina Spartan* looked to highlight the "success" of separate schooling in the county. A correspondent to the paper reported on a celebration for the black common and Sunday schools held at Foster's chapel seven miles outside of Spartanburg town. The writer applauded the competent presentations by many of the students despite noting that the "love of fun and burlesque, so characteristic of their race, would constantly show itself." Having deemed the celebration a success, the correspondent pointed to the student performances at this affair as evidence of the "good will and perfect understanding between the two races, which we hope will continue to increase." An observer of a similar occasion for a black school in Rich Hill noted that the good conduct of the "colored teachers, their patrons and pupils . . . proved to all by acts that there was no natural animosity or ill feeling between the races."[37] Such rhetoric was employed more to counteract Republican charges of discrimination than to promote any significant advancement in the cause of black schooling. The correspondent's reference to the students' "love of fun and burlesque" reveals the limited expectations that black children would develop any substantial cognitive skills. Most whites expected black schooling to promote positive attitudes toward agricultural labor and proper social behavior (i.e., deference). As noted earlier, although discipline and manners were part of the white public school curriculum, leading educators also stressed the importance of developing the creative energy necessary for economic diversification and innovation.

Shortly after statewide Republican defeat was affirmed in 1877, a group of black educators and residents of Spartanburg town looked to enlist the support of white Democrats, arguing that there was no longer need for animosity between the races. In July 1877 two young black teachers, Walter I. Lewis, a graduate of North Carolina's Biddle University, and J. L. Dart, a member of the Georgia State Institution for colored students, organized a meeting to highlight the necessity of a regular graded school for blacks in Spartanburg town. A circular from the meeting asserted that the "best educational interests of the colored population of our town have been, for a long time, sadly neglected by themselves and others. While children of other towns of the State have enjoyed the blessings of Graded and High Schools during nine months of the year, ours have received little more than the two or three months' public teaching given every summer." Dart was joined by Spartanburg black religious leaders J. E. McKnight and Thomas Pickenpack in a committee charged with enlisting support for the school. The committee's main goal was to raise the several hundred dollars necessary to qualify for the Peabody Education Fund.[38] Established in 1867 by northern banker, financier, and philanthropist George Peabody, this fund was distributed to segregated public schools throughout the South that raised enough local money to hire a teacher and build a schoolhouse. In 1877 Spartanburg apparently received a few thousand dollars from the Peabody fund to be used by both black and white schools in the county.[39]

Speakers at the July education meeting included the new state superintendent of education, Hugh S. Thompson, who pledged that black schools would receive some support from the state while he also endeavored to "impress them with the importance of going to work themselves." Longtime county leader Simpson Bobo addressed the crowd by providing "the colored people a good old fashioned talk about their duties and responsibilities as citizens, [and] showing a kindly feeling towards and a willingness to contribute to the furtherance of the object in view." The *Carolina Spartan* agreed with Bobo that whites had an obligation to assist in the schooling of disadvantaged blacks. "Now that the government of the State is in the hands of the white people," the paper stated, "and the colored people dependent upon them for all educational advantages, (being poor and unable to help themselves to any great degree)—we hope that a liberal policy will prevail. The colored man is dependent upon the white for education, moral and mental—in short, for civilization, and we hope it will not be denied him."[40]

The *Carolina Spartan*'s repeated reference to black dependence upon whites for schooling and "civilization" reflects an attempt on the part of white Democrats to reintroduce paternalistic race relations along with the restoration of political control. As long as Republicans controlled taxation for and organization of black education, white Democrats withheld support, whether verbal or material, fearing social equality and undue benefits to freedmen. Following the political victory of the "conservative regime" in South Carolina, local Democrats stressed racial harmony based on white "guidance" of black social and intellectual advancement. Much as antebellum apologists for slavery argued that the institution provided practical education and introduced Africans to civilization, so too did Redeemer Democrats maintain that their control over black learning ensured a civilized community without the threat of social equality.

Despite rhetoric supportive of expanding county school services for blacks, however, Spartanburg achieved little in this regard through the early 1880s. In 1879 black schools in Spartanburg town were consolidated into one building with 130 pupils taught by Walter Lewis, while black families throughout the rest of the county continued to suffer from too few neighborhood schoolhouses.

Democratic officials distributed a disproportionate share of funds to white schools, further impeding educational opportunities for blacks. In Reidville school district the combined education funds rose consistently from a low of $384.20 in 1877 to a high of $1,234.66 in 1881. In the latter year the seven white schools each received $142, while the two black schools received just $90 each. Between 1877 and 1880 the distribution disparity averaged around $20 less for each black institution.[41] With just two schools, the number of black children per class was undoubtedly higher than in the white schools, which only served to magnify the gap in funding. From the antebellum period through the Civil War and Reconstruction and on into the New South, access to education remained an important racial boundary in Spartanburg County.

White education in immediate post-Reconstruction Spartanburg and South Carolina underwent two important changes, one financial, the other pedagogical. Inheriting the financial troubles of their Republican predecessors, Redeemer Democrats adopted a policy of retrenchment and fiscal reform in all areas of government spending, including public education.[42] In 1877 the legislature reduced the state free school appropriation to $100,000, its lowest amount since 1870. Much of this limited fund was not applied to the immediate educational needs of counties because of unpaid school claims dating back several years. Prior to Reconstruction's end, fiscally conservative legislators challenged an 1874 state law providing for the payment out of the poll tax of school claims due prior to November 1, 1873. The state supreme court reversed the earlier decision by a circuit judge that the law was unconstitutional and found it constitutional in August 1877. Having already expended much of the year's poll tax on 1876 school debts, the state was forced to tap into the general school appropriation. Spartanburg's share of the state funds for 1877 was $4,694.50, just one-third of the county's apportionment in 1874. Much of this state loss was counterbalanced by a greater collection of the poll tax and an apparent infusion of money from the Peabody Education Fund. These sources added over $10,000 to the state appropriation.[43] However, with the problems of past indebtedness facing every county in the state, it is uncertain just how much of these funds was applied to the needs of the current school year.

With fiscal conservatism a major policy of the state Democratic Party and white hostility to the Republican method of school taxation prevalent, new superintendent Thompson appointed a committee of four to suggest changes to the school law in 1877. Heading the committee were two of Spartanburg's leading educators, Charles Petty and James H. Carlisle. Citing the incompetence of many county school commissioners in appointing teachers, the committee recommended changing the composition of the state board of school examiners from the superintendent and all county school commissioners to the superintendent and four persons appointed by the governor. In this way, they argued, teacher appointments would be made more skillfully and efficiently than under the old system. In 1878 the legislature accepted the committee's recommendations and gave the new board of examiners broad powers to interpret school law and enforce its decisions. Although the law was promoted in the name of efficiency and better instruction, white Democrats also recognized that it worked to prevent local districts with black majorities from having control over curriculum and employees.[44]

An important source of popular discontent among white South Carolinians, particularly property owners, was the Reconstruction law that granted school districts the authority to levy local taxes. Opponents of the law were especially angered because nontaxpayers (here, Democrats were thinking almost exclusively of freedmen) could vote on questions of local revenue. Such a policy, they argued, would permit the propertyless to enact oppressive taxation aimed at redistributing land. Not surprisingly, then, one of the first acts of the Democratic legislature was to repeal the law authorizing school districts to levy local taxes. Shortly after the elimination of this source of school funding, Superintendent Thompson and Governor Wade Hampton both urged ratification of a constitutional amendment requiring each county to levy an annual tax on all taxable property to replace the yearly legislative appropriation. Supporters of the two-mill tax amendment argued that it would remove the uncertainty of the legislative appropriation and allow county school commissioners to accurately estimate their funds for the coming year. The amendment passed in January 1878.[45] Despite this new source of revenue, the elimination of both the state appropriation and the local school district tax had a telling effect on the availability of free school funds. In 1878 the new two-mill tax yielded just $2,778.12 in Spartanburg County, and the local revenue officer collected an incredibly low $552.50 in poll taxes. The combined $3,330.62 in school funds marked the county's lowest available budget since the beginning of Reconstruction. Financial shortfalls continued to vex local school district administrators and teachers for the next few years. In March 1879 Reidville trustees had to stop school operations "for the present" because the school fund was "shorter than expected." The following year lack of funds forced trustees to deny a petition from citizens of Liberty Church to organize a school there.[46]

Recognizing that the two-mill tax combined with the poll tax proved insufficient for schools statewide and that South Carolina continued to have the highest illiteracy rate among eligible voters of any state in the Union, Superintendent Thompson suggested granting incorporated towns the right to levy taxes voluntarily for public schools. In an attempt to allay the fears of white landowners, Thompson proposed restricting the right to vote for or against a tax to property holders so that "it will not be within the power of those who own nothing to impose a tax upon their more fortunate neighbors."[47]

Some proponents of common schooling viewed South Carolina's educational deficiencies as a crisis threatening the state's economic and political stability in the New South. In 1878 Samuel Dibble returned to his Spartanburg alma mater, Wofford College, for delivery of an address entitled "The Duty of the State in Regard to Education." Born in Charleston in 1837, Dibble received a private school education in his native city and in Bethel, Connecticut, before he entered the College of Charleston in 1853 and graduated from Wofford three years later. After a brief stint as a teacher he was admitted to the bar in 1859 and opened a practice at Orangeburg. Dibble continued his practice after the Civil War and was elected to the state house of representatives in 1877. Maintaining a lifelong interest in education, he served as an elected trustee of the University of South Carolina and chairman of the executive committee of the state's agricultural college and mechanics institute for colored students in the post-Reconstruction period. Dibble opened his Wofford address by noting the persistent problem of widespread ignorance throughout South Carolina. The only answer to this educational "emergency," Dibble concluded, was state involvement. The Wofford graduate opined that government-sponsored education was responsible for the great ancient civilizations where the "individuality of the citizen was swallowed up in the State."[48]

At the heart of Dibble's argument for state-supported education were the responsibilities of the people in a republic. The sovereign power of any land must exercise intelligent judgments, he observed, and in a republic the masses were the sovereign power. This left only two options: qualified suffrage based on education and universal schooling. "But qualified suffrage is probably impracticable," Dibble reasoned, "for revolutions do not go backward. And I very much doubt whether it is consistent with the spirit of republican institutions to create a privileged order in the community which would be more accessible to the rich than the poor." The need for intelligent masses also meant that "no parent ha[d] any right to rear a child in ignorance." Thus, education had to be state supported, universal, and compulsory.[49]

Beyond ensuring the civic health of the state, Dibble explained that education was also morally and materially necessary. He reminded his audience that proper education "cultivates not only the mind, but also the moral nature of man, elevates his motives, increases his self-respect, and makes him hold in higher esteem his reputation among his fellow men." With the self-respect and opportunity that accompanied education, men would be less likely to commit crimes. The increased opportunities resulting from education also meant that universal schooling would lead "inevitably to the advancement of . . . material prosperity."[50]

Dibble's last two points—that proper schooling would produce a more law-abiding and economically prosperous society—reflect an increased emphasis on the practicality of education in the New South. Previous concentration on southern schooling as a training ground to ensure proper social behavior in the community had limited applicability to the increasingly competitive market economy brought by railroads, heavy investment in cotton, and manufacturing. In 1879 a contributor to the *Carolina Spartan* urged more focus on marketable skills in school curriculum, arguing that a "teacher [who] does his work has little time for moralizing." An instructor concerned primarily with morals and manners, the writer maintained, will "talk by the hour about a delicate sense of propriety when he ought to be showing his pupils how to make m's and n's."[51] To the practical skills of writing and arithmetic, education officials added a learning atmosphere based around competitive individualism. Responding to an article opposed to the use of competitive rewards in schools, Principal W. M. Jones of Spartanburg's New Prospect High School reminded the public that the world was far from a Utopia where everyone looked out for each other's needs and interests. Instead, Jones observed, "life is one long struggle to appropriate from the general as much of nature's goods as possible. The artisan, the merchant, the lawyer, physician, or the college, that, by exertion, builds up a reputation and a patronage, does it at the expense of rivals. All business is a rivalry of rival competitors. What one man gains another loses." To ignore competition in the training of the county's youth, Jones maintained, would be to leave them wholly unprepared for life.[52]

Spartanburg town took an important step in acknowledging the importance of preparing children for the world of market competition with the adoption in 1884 of the graded school system. In his study of North Carolina schools in the New South, James Leloudis finds that the graded school, with its emphasis on assigning students to different levels based on their skills in relation to other pupils, represented a shift in southern education from a concentration on civic virtue to competitive individualism.[53] In the case of Spartanburg, educational leaders had long made the connection between common schooling and greater opportunities for economic prosperity. During the antebellum period, however, the emphasis was as much on promoting southern values as it was on adopting some of the preparation for economic success found in northern schools. By the early 1880s this emphasis was reversed as increased economic diversification in Spartanburg town led business leaders to look for a more skilled labor force to assume bookkeeping duties and fill the increasing demand for store clerks, stenographers, and other positions important to the professional class.[54] Rural areas would wait much longer to see graded schools, although even here some public education proponents recognized the need to prepare farmers for more complex business transactions. For example, Robert Scruggs, a wealthy landowner near the predominantly farming community of Cherokee, recognized "the great necessity and importance of educating the rising generation" in his school district. In 1881 Scruggs donated one acre of his land to the trustees of the common schools for the erection of a new schoolhouse. To a large extent, however, pedagogical changes were self-serving for the professional and business classes in the towns. As David Carlton finds, public education was part of leading townsmen's organized efforts to ensure the cooperation necessary for successful economic development independent of agricultural conditions in the countryside. "Organization was to the townspeople the great lever of Progress," Carlton argues, "the tool with which men could shape their own lives rather than have them shaped by implacable external forces."[55] This tightening of cooperation and organization for town growth would produce greater suspicion and distrust from the countryside over the course of the 1880s and 1890s.

The role of economic class interest in the course of public education was most clearly exhibited in the factory schools of post-Reconstruction Spartanburg. In both antebellum and postbellum South Carolina, textile mills were expected to provide some arrangements for primary schooling of children whose parents were employed in the factory or who were employees themselves. Graniteville factory owner William Gregg championed compulsory education at his establishment as essential to good workers and good citizens. During Reconstruction, however, the compulsory requirement at Graniteville was removed, and schools at mills throughout the state received little attention.[56]

Factory expansion in the late 1870s led management to publicize schooling in large part to assure southerners that they had nothing to fear from a wage-earning white industrial class. Mill owners stressed their selection of quality teachers and a curriculum that emphasized responsible citizenship in the community and the value of hard work, that is, factory work. Despite the contention of mill managers and Spartanburg industrial boosters like Charles Petty that factory schools were a cornerstone of the mill community, the twelve-hour workdays endured by men, women, and children left time for little else. In 1882 a local writer complained that the "people of Clifton [textile factory] are poor and must of necessity work hard and to this general rule, the children who ought to be at school most of the time, are no exception." Two years later, a "Factory Girl" revealed that actual mill conditions differed markedly from management's professions of interest in the education of employees. "Now can you give one who has to work ten to fourteen hours a day," the young woman inquired, "some hint as to the best plan for improving the mind. Sometimes I feel low-spirited and see nothing but work and drudgery ahead of me. I do not dislike the work, but I would like to improve my mind a little, and know something of what is going on in the world." When children did have the opportunity to attend school, overcrowding made for a difficult learning environment. One observer estimated that there were about 350 school-age children at Clifton, necessitating seven or eight teachers, yet factory officials hired no more than four instructors through 1890. The buildings used for instruction were often in poor condition or served multiple purposes. As late as 1920 the schoolhouse at Fingerville was described as an "old shack."[57]

Despite variations in the quality and consistency of schooling, educational advancement in post-Reconstruction Spartanburg outpaced every other county in the state. By 1880 the county's 160 public schools ranked first in South Carolina. The following year the *Carolina Spartan* reported that the "outlook for the schools of the present year is more favorable than that of any previous year." This positive outlook was attributed to a significant rise in property valuation owing to railroad improvements and increases in mercantile business and manufacturing operations. By 1885 Spartanburg's free school funds totaled over nineteen thousand dollars, seventh highest out of thirty-four counties.[58]

The county also developed a reputation as a forerunner in teacher training and curriculum development. In 1878 Spartanburg was one of only five counties in the state to hold a teachers' convention. Hugh Thompson noted that the Spartanburg convention was "attended not only by those engaged in teaching, but by many citizens interested in the cause of education." In his annual report, Thompson found that the "conventions held in Spartanburg County have done much to raise the standard of education in that County and it is hoped that more Counties will follow this example."[59]

In August 1880 Wofford College hosted the first state teachers' institute for public schoolteachers. Aided by a grant from the Peabody fund, the institute brought together professors with school instructors to discuss educational content, philosophy, and discipline. In his review of the institute Thompson commended the "proverbial hospitality of the people of Spartanburg, and the public spirit which always moves them to aid in any enterprise that will promote the general welfare." Wofford professor and longtime Spartanburg advocate of public education James H. Carlisle felt the institute provided an intellectual atmosphere beneficial to the county. "In estimating the gross results of the Institute," Carlisle informed Thompson, "the general educating influence on visitors and on the local community must not be overlooked. For this perquisite alone, if no other benefits follow, Spartanburg will gladly welcome at any time another session under the same management."⁶⁰

From Old South to New South, Spartanburg's entrepreneurs had placed improvement in public education alongside infrastructural development and legal reform as essential elements for the region's progress. Reconstruction did produce some alterations in the county's approach to schooling as Republican taxation and concern over integration made white leaders resist government involvement in education. Statewide Democratic victory in 1877 brought further retrenchment in government support of social services, but Spartanburg's growing wealth permitted relatively successful support of public schooling. As with infrastructural development, the shift in educational focus toward mill and town brought increased tensions between town and country, management and workers, and rich and poor. Yet the central issue of race continued to prevent serious divisions in the white community from forming. By focusing on the prospect of mixed-race schools, suggesting low expectations for black education, and resisting local taxation, whites were able to prevent widespread schooling opportunities for freedmen while continuing to work for better white instruction. Following Reconstruction, white Democrats controlled black schooling and urged instruction as a form of paternalistic protection. Despite guarantees of citizenship offered by the Fourteenth Amendment, white leaders in Spartanburg and throughout the South continued to view black schooling as preparation for civilization and white schooling as preparation for citizenship and economic success.

CHAPTER NINE

"The Timely and Judicious Administration of the Laws"
Law, Vigilantism, and the Business Community of Postwar Spartanburg

THE CONVENING OF THE Spartanburg Court of Common Pleas and the Court of General Sessions in April 1866 occasioned local editor F. W. Trimmier to rejoice that "the wild and reckless dominion of lawlessness and riot is at an end" and that "society will be improved . . . by the timely and judicious administration of the laws."[1] Most residents concurred with Trimmier that moral and material improvement would surely flourish in a community committed to the rule of law. After four long years of carnage on distant battlefields and chaos on the home front, families looked forward to a peaceful society where weapons were few, temperance prevailed, and economic opportunities were abundant. Yet many believed this ideal community could exist only if political control remained in the hands of conservative whites and if the traditional racial hierarchy was upheld. When the Reconstruction Acts of 1867 introduced Republican control and black political rights in Spartanburg and the rest of the South, area leaders found it necessary to adjust their approach to the law and to extralegal authority.

Most southern whites argued that the imposition of "illegitimate" radical government effectively legitimized the use of vigilante resistance.[2] In the interests of regaining "legitimate" political control and maintaining white unity, Spartanburg's entrepreneurs made temporary alliances with extralegal groups and relaxed their assault on the perceived sources of crime. The return of "legitimate" Democratic government in 1877, however, also meant a return to the rule of law in the interests of economic development.

In the year following Appomattox, small groups of ex-Confederates, many of whom had been deserters, resisted the return of law and order by Union soldiers and local white authorities alike. David Golightly Harris reported "much meischeif done by the home raiders or thieves" who promised to return to Spartanburg town "& help themselves to the public property on a more extensive scale." Fearing violence, town residents organized a local guard to protect the community. The U.S. military headquarters for the Spartanburg area received reports of individuals "commiting the grossest outrages upon whites and blacks," including firing on U.S. soldiers. District commander B. B. Murray ordered the arrest and prosecution before military courts of all those found to be aiding and harboring such lawless individuals. An additional order prohibited citizens from carrying concealed firearms or any deadly weapons.[3] These actions initially found support in the district, particularly in Spartanburg town. The *Carolina Spartan* observed that white residents were abiding by the law and that only freedmen continued to carry guns.[4]

Leading town residents like lawyer George Legg worried that violence in general would continue as long as liquor remained readily available. Before the municipal election in the fall of 1866, a group of five town merchants organized a dry ticket with the promise of outlawing liquor sales in the town. The ticket was victorious and prohibited alcohol retailing in January 1867. The prohibition remained unenforceable, however, until popular approval through an 1868 referendum. The referendum was defeated, and dry ticket men blamed the newly enfranchised blacks, who, they argued, had an extraordinary fondness for strong drink. Prior to the Reconstruction Acts, the town council also worked to maintain a disciplined community by empowering the marshal to arrest people for tumultuous or riotous conduct, including such seemingly trivial offenses as swearing in the public streets. As one might expect, rural areas of the district were more difficult to police, but it seems clear that Spartanburg leaders were poised to resume their antebellum focus on a well-ordered, progressive society and encourage economic development.[5]

Central to this return to a well-ordered society was the readmission of the state under a republican constitution that restored power to white men in local communities throughout the state. Provisional governor Benjamin F. Perry set in motion the plans for a constitutional convention in September 1865. Spartanburg's delegates were planter-physician John C. Winsmith, farmer M. C. Barnett, and lawyers John W. Carlisle and James Farrow.

Aside from the required abolition of slavery and the removal of property qualifications for holding legislative office, the 1865 state constitution provided for a restoration of most of the laws in force prior to secession, including the restriction of voting to white males. At its special session in September, the legislature worked out the terms of the relationship between freedmen and the law. These infamous "black codes" provided limited rights for blacks while restricting employment options, outlawing interracial relationships, and establishing apprenticeship laws that created a master-servant relationship and confirmed the continuation of a racial caste in South Carolina.[6]

The constitution also restructured the courts to reflect emancipation while retaining as much of the legal racial hierarchy as possible. A system of district courts was given exclusive jurisdiction in all civil and criminal cases involving blacks. Although these courts also had the power to try cases involving white litigants, their focus on vagrancy and tenancy disputes was clearly aimed at controlling black labor and mobility. In effect, the district courts acted as a replacement for the antebellum Magistrates and Freeholders Courts. At the insistence of military commander Daniel Sickles, the legislature revised the constitution so that no specific reference was made to color in regard to these courts. In their actual operation throughout the state, however, they most often handled cases against freedpeople for larceny, trespassing, and other property crimes.[7]

Despite the intended focus of these courts on controlling black mobility, many conservatives opposed their operation because of the added bureaucracy and cost to government. John C. Winsmith, who would soon adopt the banner of Republicanism, called on the legislature to investigate the utility of the courts with an eye toward abolishing them. Spartanburg judge T. O. P. Vernon was one of a small number of legalists in the upcountry who defended the district court as a necessary means of teaching freedmen—whom he referred to as an "extemporaneous, semi-citizenship"—their rights and responsibilities in government. The district court in Spartanburg only operated between late 1867 and early 1868, when all the district courts were abolished by the Republican constitution.[8]

In between the military courts of the immediate postwar period and the later opening of the district courts, cases involving both blacks and whites were heard in the Court of Common Pleas and the Court of General Sessions. Commenting on the proceedings of the Spartanburg court in November 1866, a local editor argued that blacks "received the utmost leniency of the laws." This kind treatment, it was argued, stemmed from feelings of pity for the freedmen's utter helplessness. The *Carolina Spartan* issued assurances that "the poor unfortunate negro will never suffer wrong when arraigned before a *Southern* Court of Justice." Early actions of the courts belied such congenial rhetoric. At the spring 1867 term of the court, all those on criminal trial were black. The charges included rape, burglary, grand larceny, and petty larceny. This focus on property crime reflected the changed nature of southern labor relations. Before emancipation some slaves engaged in the practice of "taking"; that is, they appropriated extra food or clothing from their master as part of their compensation. These cases of theft were often handled on the farm or plantation, and small incidents were not seriously investigated. Under the new postwar landlord-tenant arrangements, however, property crimes were more strictly prosecuted in large part to keep freedmen under their employer's control. Sentences for the convicted were stiff. Following his conviction for burglary, freedman William Dawkins was sentenced to be hanged in June. Two other blacks were convicted of larceny and sentenced to small fines and ten months in the new penitentiary. Despite this focus on black prosecution, however, some juries showed a willingness to weigh evidence with some care. Freedman Granville Smith, for example, was acquitted on charges of rape after a spirited defense by white lawyer I. G. McKissick.[9]

During presidential Reconstruction, Spartanburg freedmen had more to worry about than increased criminal prosecution. Extralegal violence was a menacing statement of the continued power of white conservatives in the region. As word of emancipation slowly reached Spartanburg slaves, whites wasted little time in reminding blacks that their freedoms were circumscribed by community tradition. Attempts to exercise anything resembling equality could and did result in deadly consequences. In November 1865 farmer David Golightly Harris noted that several black men in the district had been severely whipped and a few had been hanged. Harris nonchalantly observed that this extralegal violence had the "tendency to keep them in their proper bounds & make them more humble."[10]

Racial violence of this nature was supposed to be addressed and, ideally, prevented by agents of the Bureau of Refugees, Freedmen, and Abandoned Lands.[11] In addition to handling general relief efforts and contract negotiations, the bureau also operated its own courts, with the authority to hear minor civil and criminal cases involving blacks. The Freedmen's Bureau, however, faced insurmountable problems in the South Carolina upcountry. Throughout the agency's existence, the bureau's assistant commissioner for South Carolina, Rufus Saxton, and his successor (and later governor), Robert K. Scott, reported a serious shortage of bureau officers, particularly in the upcountry. Overworked agents were left to rely on civilian magistrates to help administer the courts. Although many magistrates identified themselves as Republican, few were enthusiastic about black equality, and even fewer were willing to risk retribution from the community for finding in favor of freedmen and against whites. A. P. Caraher, the subassistant commissioner responsible for the bureau's work in Spartanburg, Union, and Laurens districts, was stationed in Unionville and rarely ventured from his office. Instead, Caraher warned Scott of the desperate need for officers or agents in both Spartanburg and Laurens. In Spartanburg, like so many regions of the upcountry South, the limited presence of the Freedmen's Bureau was no match for local violence.[12]

Discrimination in the courts, extralegal violence, and a general refusal on the part of whites throughout the South to accept the basic rights of blacks embodied in the pending Fourteenth Amendment led to the imposition of congressional Reconstruction in March 1867. Under the Reconstruction Acts the southern states were divided into five military districts, and existing civilian government was declared provisional. North Carolina and South Carolina composed the Second Military District, first under the command of Gen. Daniel Sickles, then Maj. Gen. E. S. R. Canby. The military's primary job was ensuring proper voter registration for an election to decide for or against a constitutional convention in the state. Voters were to consist of all adult males in South Carolina without regard to race or previous condition of servitude. Election provisions stipulated that a statewide majority of those registered had to vote in favor of the convention for the results to be valid. With this in mind, Spartanburg's white Democrats joined their compatriots throughout the state in encouraging registration but discouraging voting on election day. In this way they hoped to invalidate the election and look for better terms while continuing under military control. When the polls closed, just 26 percent of Spartanburg's 2,710 registered voters had cast ballots, and over 70 percent of these votes were against the convention. In contrast, over 90 percent of the county's blacks voted in the election, and almost all of these ballots were in favor of the convention. Despite Spartanburg's minority showing, high black turnout statewide ensured the convention's approval.[13]

At the same election for or against the constitutional convention voters were asked to choose delegates in case the measure passed. The abstention of most Spartanburg whites thus ensured that the county's delegates would be Republican. These delegates were two whites, J. P. F. Camp and John S. Gentry, and two freedmen, Rice Foster and Coy Wingo. Farmer Edward Lipscomb spoke for many conservative whites in the county when he expressed his disgust at being represented by "too white negroes & two black ones." Lipscomb tried to take heart in his faith that "a good god will not suffer the low down whites and fool negroes [to] be in power." Although freedmen and Republican whites made initial gains under the new constitution, Lipscomb no doubt saw his "faith" justified when, on the local level, white Democrats quickly regained political control due both to the county's white majority and to a campaign of violence and intimidation.[14]

Spartanburg's 70 percent white majority virtually ensured that the county would remain Democratic even if it were faced with a strongly organized Republican Party. County conservatives, led by prominent individuals like Gabriel Cannon and lawyer John H. Evins, formed Constitutional Clubs aimed at defeating the Republican constitution. A majority of voters in Spartanburg rejected the 1868 constitution, but black support across the state ensured its ratification. Unable to prevent the imposition of an "alien" government in South Carolina, white Democrats looked to the legislative elections as a means of restoring Democratic politics, if not to the entire state, then at least to the county. In an effort to develop broad appeal, Spartanburg Democrats nominated two moderates and two conservatives to the state house of representatives in 1868. Moderate Claudius C. Turner, the son of a well-to-do farmer, had worked as a journalist prior to the war. Following his service in the Confederacy, Turner opened a rather lucrative real estate business in Spartanburg town. Fellow moderate Javan Bryant was a middle-class town merchant. Both Turner and Bryant would switch to the Republican Party in 1870. The two more conservative candidates were Dr. Robert M. Smith and Samuel Littlejohn. Raised on his father's plantation in Glenn Springs, Smith received a degree in medicine from Atlanta Medical College in 1858. During the Civil War he served as a lieutenant in the Confederacy before losing his right arm at the battle of John's Island in 1864. Smith inherited most of his father's land after the war and possessed a total estate worth $3,600 in 1870. Farmer Samuel Littlejohn also inherited his father's property and was worth an estimated $4,500. For the county's senate seat Democrats nominated Joel Foster. An antebellum planter with $6,000 worth of real estate and personal property including twenty slaves valued at $60,000, Foster suffered heavy losses during the war, retaining a total estate of just $5,000 in 1870. He worked to rebuild his fortune in politics and later served as cashier of the National Bank of Spartanburg and director of the South Carolina Manufacturing Company.[15]

During the summer Democratic clubs worked throughout the county to guarantee victory for the party. Although the Democratic candidates won the fall election, a rather meager five-hundred-vote margin suggested the need for continued vigilance in keeping the Republican threat at bay. The 1868 elections, however, were a harbinger of things to come as Spartanburg became one of only six counties in South Carolina to remain Democratic throughout the entire course of Reconstruction.[16] As a result, the county's white conservatives worked to subvert many of the Republican-led constitutional changes through both legislative and nonlegislative means.

The 1868 state constitution, drawn up to a large extent by newly enfranchised blacks, did bring important legal changes to the state. Few of these changes drew stronger reaction and comment than the introduction of freedmen into the courts as equal participants. For white Democrats this innovation was a violation of the central judicial ideal that only educated citizens should sit in judgment of their peers. Indeed, one of the primary justifications for an improved public school system in the antebellum era was that it would create an intelligent citizenry well equipped to perform their civic duties. Most southern whites, both before and after the Civil War, maintained that blacks did not have the capacity to make intelligent judgments in matters of law even if they had access to schooling. On his visit to Spartanburg's court in December 1868, David Golightly Harris noted the presence of a black man on the grand jury. "That was the first time that I have seen that humbling & disgusting site," Harris reported. "Ignorant negroes to decide important cases between white men. How intolerable!" The sight of freedmen in the jury box made Edward Lipscomb "glad that I am so near the end of my race to sit on a jury with them[.] I don't intend to do it[,] and we have a law that exemps a man at 65 & I take the advantage of it." Leading Spartanburg lawyer and entrepreneur Simpson Bobo observed that "negroes are very stupid in the jury-box." Southern newspapers created tales of hopelessly incompetent juries to drive home the point. One such tale focused on the inability of black jurors to find verdicts. The paper fictitiously reported that when a judge demanded to know why the jury could not reach a verdict, the foreman responded in exaggerated black dialect, "de ossifer didn't take us out into de grounds but he took us into a room and locked us in, an' tole us when we found de verdict he would leff us out. So we began to find the verdict, and search ebery nook, coner, crevis, an, ebery ting dere was in dat room, but we found no verdict—no noffin ob de kine dar."[17]

Democrats lashed out at a proposed amendment to the state's jury law that called for jury membership to reflect the racial proportion of legal voters in the town where the trial was held. The *Carolina Spartan* editor attacked the law, arguing that wherever there now existed a "preponderance of debased and ignorant voters in any section of the State there we are bound to have jurors of a like character." The all-white juries of the antebellum era, it was explained, always ensured a basic level of intelligence in dealing with legal matters. Although acknowledging that antebellum juries sometimes contained uneducated whites, Simpson Bobo maintained that they were generally composed of "substantial men."[18]

Republican control over local judicial offices also brought the wrath of white Democrats. Despite a constitutional provision that magistrates were to be chosen by qualified electors, the governor was given power to appoint these officials for each county until the courts were "properly organized." As before the war, magistrates had original jurisdiction in matters of assault, contract, and recovery of small fines and forfeitures.[19] The magistrate's powers in matters of contract took on special importance in the contests over labor arrangements between ex-slaves and ex-masters. During the first term of the Republican legislature these magistrates were replaced in name by trial justices who had the same powers, but the law allowed the continuation of executive appointment indefinitely. For Democrats this represented a clear violation of constitutional law and a stark example of the Republican spoils system.[20] Local whites worked to counteract this spoils system by raising doubts about the loyalty of judicial candidates. In October 1868 Democratic office seeker R. C. Poole wrote Governor Robert K. Scott that there was "not a single man who belongs to the Leag[u]e or Radical Party in Spartanburg County that could fill the office of even a Constable." Poole asserted that prominent county Republicans like J. P. F. Camp were only interested in securing an office and had no principled attachment to the Republican Party. Another citizen found it necessary to warn Governor Scott that a certain James Perry would be requesting appointment as a magistrate and that he would only "pretend to be a Republican [and] a good loyal man." Having failed to secure the appointment of county treasurer a year later, Poole bitterly condemned Spartanburg Republicans as corrupt swindlers and urged Scott "for gods sake & your own sake & the sake of Spartanburg County & the sake of South Carolina—and the U. S.—put in honest men and men that will do their duty."[21]

Democrats complained that, with few exceptions, judicial offices were "conferred upon men who are totally unfit for them, and who use them simply to fill their own pockets at the public expense." This lust for money, it was argued, extended to jurors and witnesses, which resulted in unnecessary litigation, high taxes, and a mockery of justice. In December 1872 Gabriel Cannon introduced a resolution to the South Carolina House of Representatives calling on the legislature to consider repealing or modifying the law authorizing pay for jurors and witnesses.[22] During the same legislative session Spartanburg state senator David R. Duncan introduced a bill requiring trial justices to give bond before being commissioned and to provide full reports of all criminal cases before the opening of the Court of General Sessions. If the justice failed to make a report, he would not receive pay; if no report were made for two consecutive terms, he would be subject to indictment and possible fines and imprisonment. The move to force trial justices to pay a bond was one way to restrict poorer whites and freedmen from securing the office. Republican control of the legislature ensured the bill's defeat.[23]

If for white Democrats two of Reconstruction's primary affronts to southern order were the executive appointment of radicals to local offices and attempts to enforce social and political equality for blacks, then the governor's selection of black officeholders was the most grievous violation of southern principles. When Governor Scott appointed freedman Anthony Johnson trial justice in October 1869, the *Carolina Spartan* sarcastically announced Johnson's promotion from "his stool in the chimney corner, to the magisterial bench." Although confessing ignorance of Johnson's qualifications, the paper reminded readers that Scott tended to appoint radicals even if they were "unjust, partial, ignorant, and stupid." Johnson's elevation from slave to lawman was too much for some in the white community to endure. Only months after his appointment, Anthony Johnson was brutally murdered by a band of white men while his terrorized mother watched in horror.[24]

Johnson's murder occurred within the context of a growing extralegal movement designed to restore Democratic control of politics and the traditional racial hierarchy through intimidation and violence. Almost as soon as congressional Reconstruction began, accounts surfaced of whites banding together to address perceived threats to the social and political order. At a Spartanburg church gathering in August 1868 a black man made what was deemed an insulting remark to a white woman. A group of men saw fit to hang the offender right at the church "until he was almost dead."[25] The first recorded appearance of the Ku Klux Klan in the upcountry occurred in neighboring York County in March 1868. Over the next two years bands of white men were reported terrorizing freedmen and Republican whites in and around the Spartanburg area. During this period organizational connections between these various groups were hard to detect, and few seemed to use the nomenclature of the "official" Ku Klux Klan. As the fall 1870 elections approached, however, reports of extralegal activity increased, and Klan organization began to take shape.[26]

Historians have argued effectively that the Klan was a postemancipation version of traditional extralegality in the South.[27] Slave patrols, plantation control, and even the Magistrates and Freeholders Courts acted as a separate system of justice for slaves and free blacks in the antebellum period. When fears arose in the 1850s that abolitionists were infiltrating the community, extralegal Committees of Safety organized to fend off the alien threat. Disputes between whites were also often settled through a combination of legal redress and extralegal revenge. Even local officials and businessmen, those most often interested in maintaining the rule of law, at times turned to this tradition when community order was threatened. It is important, then, to place the Klan within a larger framework of southern ideals about legitimate vigilante resistance rather than view it as an innovative response to emancipation and Confederate defeat.

Both contemporary investigations of the Klan and later historical examinations have also debated the demographics of its membership. Some accounts portray a more elite-sponsored organization designed to suppress Republican voters and officeholders and control black labor, while others view the Klan primarily as a reaction from poorer white farmers to the social and economic upheaval unleashed by emancipation.[28] In the case of Spartanburg, these interpretations present a false dichotomy. Although the Klan groups were secret organizations, the words of Spartanburg's own politicians strongly suggest early elite control. Conservative trial justice William Irwin found that "the organization and system with which some acts of violence and lawlessness were carried on, would indicate . . . that they were done by men of more than ordinary intelligence." Carriage-maker Isaac

Cantrell concurred that the *genuine* Ku Klux Klan was composed of "better men than many others." Despite personal denials of involvement, Gabriel Cannon acknowledged the possibility that "better men" played a role in early Klan groups.[29]

Some testimonies went beyond such generalities and identified prominent individuals connected with the Klan. In April 1871 a Klan group terrorized white Republican John Genobles and threatened his life if he did not agree to go to the courthouse on the next sales day and publicly renounce all connection to the radicals. Genobles testified that when sales day rolled around it was none other than Simpson Bobo who interrupted the sheriff's sale so that Genobles could enunciate his forced rejection of Republicanism. Bobo denied the charge as "utterly false" and expressed his belief that the Klan was composed "generally of the lower class of men."[30] In 1871, however, Bobo informed northern congressional investigators that blacks were "great thieves" who only obeyed the law under the threat of the lash. Following a rash of cotton thefts in a neighborhood along the Enoree River, Bobo explained that the Klan made examples of a few freedmen and thereby "cured the neighborhood of stealing."[31]

Although few accounts place community elites in actual Klan raids, Democratic leaders nevertheless relied on threats of physical violence to secure political aims. H. H. Foster, a black Republican in the county, testified that Gabriel Cannon had threatened freedmen at a Republican meeting. "We own the lands; you live on them," Foster recalled Cannon stating. "You eat our bread and meat, and if you vote for our enemies, the radicals, you will get your earth, two by six; you will go like the Indians, and your bones will whiten our hill-sides." Cannon denied the accuracy of this quote and stated that he was only trying to inform blacks that they were being deceived by the radicals and that Republican policies would destroy the freedmen's chances in life.[32] Town entrepreneurs like Bobo and Cannon recognized that utilizing racism to remove local Republicans would help them achieve their political and economic goals. Rank-and-file Klan members, who were often from the poorer elements of the white community, would heed the advice of local leaders known for their allegiance to white superiority and their opposition to Republican Party principles.[33] Historian Scott Nelson has found that the Southern Railway Security Company employed similar tactics in hiring known Klansmen as local railroad officials to outmaneuver its competitors.[34]

Since town entrepreneurs controlled much of local Democratic politics, some members of the older planter aristocracy may have seen the switch to

Republicanism as a way to regain power both politically and economically. By 1870 prominent antebellum planter John C. Winsmith had switched to the Republican Party. Local rumors linked Winsmith to a group of Republicans well positioned to acquire valuable land near the intended path of the Atlanta and Richmond Air-Line Railroad. Perhaps most troubling to white farmers were rumors that he was arming colored militia and granting freedmen weekends off to attend school.[35] As a result, Winsmith was no longer viewed as a champion of Spartanburg's white farmers and instead was accused of supporting Republican corruption, elitism, and black equality. Winsmith's new allegiance resulted in a violent confrontation with the Ku Klux Klan that left him suffering from multiple bullet wounds. Although the elderly Winsmith recovered, he rather quickly faded from local prominence.[36]

Despite apparent early involvement in the Klan, local leaders began distancing themselves from extralegal violence by the spring of 1871. This shift occurred for three basic reasons. In the first place, extralegal violence had accomplished the leadership's main objectives of preserving the 1870 election of local Democrats and preventing any serious attempt to alter race relations in the county. Second, Klan groups had gotten beyond the control of the elites, and violence had escalated for reasons beyond the purely political. Finally, and perhaps most important, was the fear of the threatened imposition of martial law in Spartanburg.

Locally, the Klan's policies were successful. As mentioned earlier, Klan groups broke up Union League meetings and threatened potential Republican voters throughout the county. Farmer Edward Lipscomb reported that the Klan's strong showing in the upcountry forced Governor Scott to appoint "such men as the whites want."[37] Initially, Republican election manager William Magill Fleming reported victory for his party in the 1870 election. However, election assistant William Irwin forwarded a separate report to the legislature indicating that Fleming had tampered with ballot boxes and thrown the election for the Republicans. Local precinct manager and white Republican John Genobles seemed to confirm the corruption when he testified that Fleming had reported a Republican majority in his district despite a margin of over one hundred votes for Democrats.[38] The state canvassers of elections sustained Irwin's report, and the Democratic representatives were admitted. Republicans immediately contested the election and called for an investigation. This move most assuredly prolonged the intensity of Klan violence and kept leading Democrats from speaking out against the outrages. Once the Republicans withdrew their contest, however, Democratic representatives J. Banks Lyle and Joel Foster held a meeting at which they pledged to suppress the violence and uphold the civil law. In his opening remarks former Klan chief Lyle said he "regretted the condition of the country and advised all classes of citizens to yield in obedience to the civil law and assist in enforcing the same against all acts of outrage." At a similar meeting Gabriel Cannon also urged support of the laws and condemned the violence.[39]

By the summer of 1871 it was clear that any prior connections between the Klan and Democratic leaders had evaporated. In testimonies before the congressional committee investigating Klan violence, both Republicans and Democrats concurred with William Irwin's assessment that the Klan had "deteriorated into a set of low vagabonds . . . who have no regard for person or property, but probably are influenced in a great many instances by personal malice." Indeed, the testimony of Klan victims makes clear that while political issues remained significant in the extralegal night rides, personal frustrations arising out of the social and economic changes sweeping the region could play an equally important role. The murder of Wallace Fowler is instructive in this regard. In 1871 a group of whites terrorized freedmen on land owned by a Dr. Jones. When it was all over, Fowler—a black man—had been killed and several others had been severely whipped. Fowler's widow and another freedman both testified that the white men were upset because Jones had recently turned a group of poor whites off his land and replaced them with freedmen.[40] The lawless band did not attack the person directly responsible for the eviction, Dr. Jones, a respected and successful member of the white community. Instead, violent anger was directed at the symbolic representation of white economic troubles, the freedmen.

The widespread violence also had the effect of forcing many blacks and some white Republicans off their lands and into the woods for security. Every time this happened landlords and employers lost work time from their laborers. Concerned that his black workers would flee in the midst of planting season, prominent Democrat and wealthy planter Elihu Penquite Smith looked to strike a deal whereby his laborers would refrain from political activity and, in exchange, the Klan would stop its raids.[41] Additionally, reports of outrages from local Republicans drew the attention of the federal government and the possibility of martial law. By March 1871 Republican leader Anson W. Cummings had reported to Governor Scott that there were Klan groups in nearly every township of the county. He maintained that only the presence of soldiers prevented bands of outlaws from controlling Spartanburg town. "The condition of the colored people in this county is most deplorable," Cummings observed, "incomparably worse than at any time before during or since the war." For Spartanburg's leadership extralegal violence had succumbed to the law of diminishing returns. The longer the night rides continued, the more they interfered with the business of the community and the greater the chance of federal intervention.[42]

Most troubling for Spartanburg's entrepreneurs were the increasing attacks on freedmen who were grading the railroad line between Charlotte and Atlanta. Klan rhetoric focused on the corruption of greedy capitalists in Republican government. Northern-sponsored railroad lines that utilized cheap black labor represented a base violation of southern white principles. As the violence in areas undergoing rail construction increased, railroad investors like Gabriel Cannon lamented that the Klan activity "operates very seriously on all business."[43]

When the U.S. congressional committee arrived in Spartanburg in July 1871 to take testimony regarding the condition of law and order, leading county Democrats adopted a three-pronged strategy of playing down the violence, placing the blame for any problems on corrupt Republicans, and vowing to clamp down on any future lawlessness. State representatives Joel Foster and Robert M. Smith maintained that the laws were being executed with minimal trouble. Lawyer Simpson Bobo went further to express astonishment at as "little disturbance as there has been" when he considered the county's treatment at the hands of radical corruption. "If the Government had given us a good government," Bobo argued, "none of these troubles would have been in this country." Gabriel Cannon also centered responsibility for lawlessness squarely upon Republican officeholders. The actions of incompetent and corrupt officials, he explained, led people to feel as though all law was suspended.[44]

Local juries had also pledged to suppress the Klan while focusing blame for these illegal bands on the abusive power exhibited by Republican trial justices. An 1870 jury noted one particular instance in which an elderly man suspected of Klan ties was handed over to a group of black men "who in their rage and excitement, caused the old man to be double-quicked until he was completely exhausted." The civil officers involved in the affair, jury foreman Elias Lipscomb argued, "should be made to know that inhuman treatment is not to be tolerated under the garb of legal proceedings."[45]

Despite this seeming rationalization of extralegal violence, most leading Democrats responded to the congressional investigating committee by condemning violence and pledging to do all that was necessary to enforce the laws.[46] Spartanburg's leadership worked hard to avoid the imposition of martial law in the months following the committee's departure. The county's representatives joined leading citizens Gabriel Cannon, Dexter Edgar Converse, John H. Evins, Robert Cleveland, Simpson Bobo, and a number of others in authoring a letter to committee chairman Senator John Scott attesting that reports of violence since the committee had left were untrue. Additional letters from local Republican Anson W. Cummings and the commanding officer stationed in Spartanburg, a Major Reno, confirmed the peace in the county. Reno added that the property holders were "willing & anxious" to prevent any recurrence of violence.[47] Gabriel Cannon implored Congress to recognize that under martial law the "innocent must suffer with the guilty." Not only would this suffering take the form of restrictions on constitutional rights, but it would also strike a blow to efforts to attract outside investments.[48]

These struggles to keep federal interference at bay proved of no account. On October 17, 1871, after prolonged consultations with the congressional investigating committee and U.S. Attorney General Amos Akerman, President Grant suspended the writ of habeas corpus in nine counties of the South Carolina upcountry, including Spartanburg.[49] The presence of troops may have quelled the worst of the terrorism, but the prosecution of Klan activity proved difficult. Although over two hundred arrests were made in Spartanburg by April 1872, county Republicans complained that few Klan members had been brought to justice for their crimes against innocent citizens. Local conservative officials rarely offered assistance to the work of federal soldiers during the period of martial law in the region. Spartanburg mayor John Earle Bomar concentrated his efforts more on convincing federal officers to release suspected Klan members on bond and arresting disorderly soldiers than on mounting any campaign against conservative vigilante groups.[50] Local Republican leader W. F. Parker charged both fellow Republican trial justice William Magill Fleming and the U.S. commissioner in charge of investigating Klan violence in Spartanburg with accepting bribes in exchange for not bringing known members to justice. Such corruption, Republicans argued, meant that only poor Klansmen were arrested while the wealthier leaders escaped.[51] Over the entire South, prosecution of Klansmen was seriously curtailed by a growing desire for sectional rapprochement in the nation and a split in the Republican Party. By late 1872 the U.S. attorney general reported that only 96 of 1,303 Klan cases in South Carolina had been tried since the start of prosecutions in 1870. Many of those who were convicted and imprisoned secured pardons from the governor within a short time. Spartanburg's experience with martial law came to a close when Congress allowed the suspension of habeas corpus to expire in June 1872.[52]

Although the federal government was generally ineffective at prosecuting prominent Klan leaders, officials did manage to drive J. Banks Lyle from his position of power in Spartanburg. In 1871 Lyle was removed from the legislature for alleged Klan activities, and he fled to Texas to avoid prosecution. He resumed teaching in Paris, Texas, where, according to at least one account, Lyle remained an "unreconstructed Rebel, whose clothes were Confederate gray until his death."[53]

Following the Klan-related violence of the early 1870s, county boosters looked to restore Spartanburg's reputation as a peaceful, law-abiding community. "There is not a prisoner in our county jail," the *Carolina Spartan* reported in June 1873. "This has been the case for several weeks. . . . Sheriff Dewberry talks about discharging the cook and all hands, locking the door and throwing the key away."[54] Yet despite the seeming end to widespread Klan activity in Spartanburg, freedmen still had reason to fear violent outbreaks in the county. In May 1873, for example, a group of white bridge workers on the Air-Line Railroad concluded an evening of drinking by arming themselves with pistols, rocks, and sticks and swearing they would "run every (d——) negro and white radical out of the county." Apparently, some black men were whipped, and several others spent a few nights camping out in the woods for fear of their lives.[55] The potential for such incidents to occur intimidated many Republicans from voting throughout the remaining years of Reconstruction and kept many blacks from asserting their social and economic rights.

The evolution of the county leadership's position on alcohol production in many ways mirrored their dealings with the Klan. Since before the war, local leaders had worked to limit distilling operations as part of a general crackdown on alcohol consumption and its connections to immorality, laziness, and crime. The war only heightened the restrictions on distilleries as grain became dear. However, when the U.S. Revenue Department took over this crusade against illicit distilling and required legal alcohol producers to pay for licenses in the postwar period, town leaders softened their stance against distillers.[56]

In early 1867 the first federal revenue collector for Spartanburg, A. S. Wallace, warned distillers that they would be vigorously prosecuted if they did not conform to the law. An individual or firm needed a license from both the state and the federal governments to operate a distillery. Those in violation would have their distilling operations destroyed, be imprisoned up to a year, and pay a fine of five hundred dollars. When the civil courts failed to convict violators of the revenue laws, the military ordered all distillation of whiskey from grain illegal and all distillers to be tried in military courts. Most residents of Spartanburg town initially supported this policy, and the *Carolina Spartan* proclaimed that the "order w[ould] be hailed by every lover of virtue and good order in our community."[57]

Not surprisingly, the town's view of the liquor law differed from the attitudes of regions where distilleries proliferated. The small farms and wooded acres in the northern stretches of the county played host to a substantial number of moonshining operations. Some of these distilleries dated to the antebellum era, while others had opened during the financial chaos of the Civil War. Many more, however, had emerged since the war's end in response to new economic troubles. A combination of poor crops, high prices, and rising taxes crippled small farmers' ability to sustain themselves and pushed some into the ranks of the landless laborer. As a result, both small farmers and laborers needed to sell their products for cash to buy necessary provisions. Yet northern areas of the county like Limestone Springs and Cowpens remained relatively isolated from market centers, at least until the arrival of the Air-Line Railroad in the mid-1870s. Before then, a farmer from Cowpens had to take his mule wagon ten miles to Spartanburg depot, and the Limestone Springs farmer had to cover twice that distance. Whiskey production seemed to offer economic salvation for these farmers. The same mule that could carry four bushels of corn could pack the equivalent of twenty-four bushels in the form of whiskey. Wilbur Miller has calculated that in the late nineteenth century a wagon loaded with 20 bushels of corn would yield $10, while the same wagon could haul 120 gallons of whiskey worth at least $150.[58]

Whether or not Spartanburg moonshiners realized great profits is unclear, but the point is that they viewed the practice as an important means of securing cash and thus securing their independence. This accounts for their fierce, often violent defense of the business against federal taxation. In regions where illicit distilling was widespread, entire communities worked to thwart revenue officers and local law enforcement. It is hardly a coincidence that many of these areas also experienced heavy Ku Klux Klan activity. Klan groups in places like Limestone Springs, Cowpens, and Pacolet viewed driving out revenue officers as an important part of their work. Black tenant farmer and Pacolet resident Julius Cantrell recalled that on one of their terrifying visits to his home Klan members informed him that they were "to protect the stills, and keep the revenue officers from getting them." In trying to enforce the revenue laws in these areas, sheriffs and constables were fired upon by suspected distillers, and Republican trial justice William Magill Fleming found whole neighborhoods "leagued against law and order."[59]

The experience of local revenue officer Adolphus P. Turner sheds important light on the actions of moonshiners and the priorities of county leaders. Turner's attempts to crack down on distilling in the Cowpens area were particularly complicated because he was a native of the region. Local residents resented him as a traitor to his community and reacted to his authority with contempt. Between July and December 1869 a band of local whites terrorized Turner by riding out to his home and taking shots at the official while his wife and children cowered inside. At other times they burned down his smokehouse, and one individual physically assaulted Turner on the street.[60]

In January 1870 a squad of soldiers arrived in Spartanburg to protect Turner from further attacks. This military presence, combined with the changed political atmosphere since 1867, led to a temporary shift in the local leadership's position toward illicit distilling. Prior to radical control of the state, many of the county's political and economic leaders—particularly those in Spartanburg town—supported the crackdown on the illegal manufacture of alcohol. Congressional Reconstruction and the resulting appointments of local Republican officials, however, led county leaders to look for opportunities to erode radical power. County Democrats cited the resort to military protection for Turner as an indication of the incompetence of local Republican court officials. The *Carolina Spartan* argued:

> There never has been a time before in the history of our District when the meanest and lowest citizen thereof could not find ample protection for person and property in the civil courts of the land, and it certainly augurs a desperate state of affairs, if every man who may suffer from the violence of the lawless . . .

is to find protection and safety only in the bayonets of a military guard. . . . [I]s it possible that the present select corps of magistrates and constables, the appointees of Executive wisdom and discrimination, are unable to protect a single citizen from the brutal persecutions of a few lawless ruffians?[61]

While Republican appointees struggled to control violence, conservative white juries assured that many of the lawless went unpunished. By 1870 white conservatives had gained control over the grand and petit juries through a consistent program of intimidation. In the July 1870 term of court, for example, six men were brought before the grand jury for having committed violent acts against Adolphus P. Turner ranging from attempted murder to assault to arson. In all but one of these cases the grand jury found no bill, and they were dismissed. The one exception was John L. McCall, who pled guilty to assaulting Turner and received a five-dollar fine.[62]

Turner, however, suffered for his betrayal of the community. His enemies charged him with setting fire to fences belonging to farmer Benson Martin and for perjuring himself by testifying that Martin's brother Othello was a whiskey retailer. The jury found Turner guilty on both counts and sentenced him to a fifty-dollar fine and six months in jail.[63] Turner's case reveals how the commitment to the rule of law remained proscribed by the community ethos in Spartanburg. In a bit of a role reversal, the jury acted as an extension of extralegal violence in that it approved of the actions against Turner through the acquittal of those involved while continuing to harass the officer through legal means. County Republican leaders appealed to the governor for Turner's pardon, arguing that conservatives had testified falsely against him. "The Democrats can make any proof that they wis[h] against a Republican here," the leadership noted, "and this court Both Judge and the most of the Jury will Hang a Radical on suspicion. . . . [I]t is impossible for a Republican to get justice before the juries of this County." Governor Robert Scott pardoned Turner in January 1871.[64]

Throughout Reconstruction the local Democratic press continued a softened stance toward distillers while attacking federal revenue collection. The *Carolina Spartan* pointed out that those engaged in the distilling business regarded it as "an honest and legitimate way of making a living." As such, the taxes and restrictions imposed by the revenue law produced understandable anger from this segment of the community. The revenue soldiers were also condemned for overstepping their authority when raiding distilling operations. Some accounts held that soldiers not only burned still houses but confiscated bacon, sugar, coffee, horses, and other necessary provisions.[65]

Local Democrats saw a blatant example of this excessive authority in the murder of Henry B. Hall. In February 1876 federal soldiers arrived at Hall's home with the purpose of arresting him for illegal distilling. Accounts differ on how Hall reacted to the troops, but it is clear that he was shot and killed by a Corporal Davis. Hall's murder produced shock and outrage throughout the community. Although not defending Hall's illicit distilling, the *Carolina Spartan* professed that "human life is more valuable than whisky, and . . . the men who are employed in the revenue department, to hunt up distilleries, are generally grand scoundrels and deserve punishment more than those whom they are sent to hunt down."[66] This altered attitude toward unlicensed distilling was a temporary response brought on by a recognition that during Reconstruction the external threats to the community exceeded the internal threats. That is, county leaders who ordinarily attacked the *internal* threat from illegal whiskey making and the resulting increase in alcohol consumption as disruptive to law, order, and progress in the community instead temporarily allied with distillers and others evading revenue collectors in an attempt to drive out the *external* threat of Republicanism.

This point becomes clearer in the behavior of Spartanburg's elite in the post-Reconstruction era. With South Carolina back in the hands of Democrats just a year after Hall's murder, leading conservatives seemed more willing to work with revenue officials in prosecuting lawbreakers. In late 1877 federal revenue officers captured a wagon of unlicensed and therefore illegal tobacco near the Spartanburg/Union County border. On the way back to their headquarters in Spartanburg the officers were surrounded by a group of men on horseback, who commandeered the wagon by force and further demanded any confiscated whiskey. Gabriel Cannon labeled the attack "an outrage against the laws of the land" and quickly met with a revenue agent from Washington to assist in the investigation. Cannon assured the agent that the "great body of citizens would willingly aid in enforcing the laws." Spartanburg's elder statesman also wrote to the new Democratic governor, Wade Hampton, of the need to make an example of the lawbreakers, explaining that it was of "great importance that we prove to the world that such unlawful acts are discountenanced by the State authorities and the citizens generally."[67]

Following Reconstruction, not only did the county leadership's focus return to enforcing revenue laws and cracking down on illicit distilling, but commentaries on the evil of drink also appeared more frequently. In 1879, for example, the *Carolina Spartan* cited the need for more temperance revivals, observing that "too many of our good citizens are drinking too much whiskey, and bad citizens ought not to be allowed to drink a drop." On a visit to Spartanburg sales day in 1879 H. P. Griffith encountered men he had "long known and honored as sober men, who were considerably intoxicated."[68] Wherever whiskey flowed freely, men like Griffith warned, violence was likely. The press popularized the fear that drink turned law-abiding men into murderous brutes. Thomas White's case seemed to confirm such fears. In April 1880 a jury convicted White, who was in fact a white man, of shooting a black man named Pet Hawkins outside a Spartanburg bar. While White awaited the hangman's noose, he maintained his innocence but could not substantiate his claim due to his inebriation on the night Hawkins was killed. White wished his fate to be a tragic lesson for all. "Whiskey is the leading thing that brought me to this," White proclaimed. "My last words to all men, and especially to young men, is to let whiskey alone." A month later, Circuit Judge Thomas J. Mackey blamed a recent rise in the region's death rate on the volatile mixture of whiskey and pistols. By 1882 enough Spartanburg town residents feared the effects of drink on the community and its business to elect a slate of dry candidates. Two years later a promotional review of the state reported that the lack of crime resulting from the dry ticket had made the Spartanburg police "rather useless."[69]

Judge Mackey's warning about the lethal combination of liquor and pistols marked the revival of another policy originally pursued prior to Reconstruction: gun control. Town boosters made a clear link between handgun violence and the region's attractiveness to outsiders with cash. Simply put, street violence involving firearms gave the town a bad name. Although most of those involved in shootouts tended to be undesirables, *Carolina Spartan* editor Charles Petty argued that the damage from these violent episodes extended far beyond those immediately involved. "There is scarcely a day but there is a score, or more, of strangers in our town," Petty observed. When visitors witnessed these gun battles, "they set all down to the credit of Spartanburg, and most certainly all the citizens must suffer for the lawlessness of the few." Petty urged the courts to adopt stricter measures in dealing with violence and asked all citizens to take a stand against such cowardly acts. "Twelve months of lawlessness and street riots and bar-room rows," the *Carolina Spartan* warned, "will do more to clog the wheels of progress in our midst than a financial panic." The June 1880 grand jury condemned the "unseeming, unmanly and lawless practice of carrying about the person deadly weapons *concealed*." Jury foreman A. G. Means labeled those who engaged in such activity as "the enemies both of the public peace and purse." One local plan encouraged the state to require a license for the sale of pistols and cartridges, arguing that a costly license together with a law prohibiting the carrying of guns would make it "almost impossible to buy a pistol in the State."[70]

Coinciding with the attack on concealed weapons was a concentrated effort to eliminate dueling in the state. In 1880 South Carolina amended the law against dueling so that persons who challenged or accepted a duel or assisted in arranging a duel would be disqualified from voting or holding office. Any person responsible for killing someone in a duel would be sentenced to death, and all peace officers had to take an oath that they would enforce the laws against dueling.[71] Local Circuit Judge Kershaw was certain that the vast majority of Spartanburg citizens condemned the duel as an obstruction to the region's material prosperity and moral advancement. Kershaw suggested that officeholders be required to take an oath to prosecute cases of dueling to their fullest extent. In the state senate Thomas John Moore supported a tougher bill against dueling and fought a motion to strike a section requiring an oath that legislators had not engaged in a duel after January 1, 1881.[72]

Despite these efforts to reduce crime and restrict the right of force to constituted governmental authority, the tradition of extralegality within accepted community norms continued into post-Reconstruction Spartanburg. The case of John J. Moore offers an example. Moore had developed a reputation as a ne'er-do-well ever since he was drummed out of the Confederate army for stealing early in the war. During Reconstruction Moore was suspected of having poisoned a local man and was charged with malicious trespass in 1874.[73] On June 5, 1879, a young woman named Fanny Heaton arrived at Moore's door asking for directions and a glass of water. Moore's wife invited Heaton to dine with her family and suggested that her thirteen-year-old son accompany the young woman part of the way to her destination. When the son grumbled at the idea, John Moore volunteered his services and left with Fanny Heaton. A few days later, Heaton's body was discovered half a mile from Moore's house. An autopsy revealed that the woman had been sexually assaulted and shot and that her head had nearly been severed by two sharp blows.

A grand jury quickly ordered the arrest of Moore on suspicion of Fanny

Heaton's murder. Outraged at the nature of the crime and aware of Moore's criminal history, the community saw little reason to wait for a trial. At about eleven o'clock in the evening after his arrest, a party of about 150 men arrived at the jail looking for Moore. Sensing trouble, the sheriff had moved the prisoner to a depot along the Air-Line Railroad with designs of taking him to safety in Columbia. Before the train arrived, however, the mob found Moore, seized him from the sheriff, and marched him out to the scene of Fanny Heaton's rape and murder. Along the way, groups of men joined the march until one report estimated about a thousand spectators were present. The crowd was described as "cool and determined," with "not a drop of whiskey carried along." The vigilantes urged Moore to confess his many crimes over the past ten years, but he did not comply. As the noose was prepared, a Colonel Woodward of Fairfield County pleaded with the crowd to avoid such an illegal course, but he reportedly "made no more impression on the calm, determined multitude than a light rain on a mass of granite." As if lending an air of dignity to the proceedings, Moore was permitted to visit with his family for a final farewell. At 3:30 in the morning Moore was hanged from the limb of a post oak.[74]

The district court held its regular session the week following Moore's lynching. In his charge to the grand jury, presiding Judge Pressley lashed out at the lawless act. Pressley suggested that a lynch mob may have been more understandable under the Reconstruction governments, "when juries could be packed and public officials induced to compromise cases or pardon the convicted," but with the courts now securely in the hands of Democrats, such a course was inexcusable. Pressley particularly feared a witch hunt, when the simple suspicions of neighbors could lead to lawless executions. "The only safety is in good government," the judge explained, "when the laws are fairly administered." For its part, the grand jury pointed out that Moore was clearly guilty and that the citizens acted unanimously to deal with a known criminal. The jury also noted that crimes were on the increase, suggesting that lynch law was a natural response to keep control in the community.[75]

Although the number of cases brought before the Court of General Sessions actually declined slightly between 1870 and 1880, the jury's contention that criminal activity was on the rise held true for violent crimes. In 1870 thefts constituted the highest number of cases (35 percent) in criminal prosecutions, with assaults running a close second (30 percent). Following the Civil War, economic depression and emancipation left many poor whites and ex-slaves in a desperate state, and some turned to theft for survival. By 1880, however, assaults outdistanced thefts by 14 percent, and assault and murder cases together accounted for 51 percent of cases brought before the court. Overall, the number of cases declined from fifty-seven to forty-three, but violence clearly remained a part of Spartanburg society into the post-Reconstruction period.[76] Despite public pronouncements against crime, county leaders were unable to rid their society of illegal activity. In part this was because these very leaders had earlier supported extralegality and had devoted most of their postwar legal attention to the punishment of alleged black crimes.

Throughout Reconstruction Spartanburg's leaders worked to protect the political and racial order while encouraging economic development whenever possible. Nowhere did these issues more clearly converge than in the evolution of the state penitentiary.[77] Not long after the war's conclusion, antebellum calls for the institution were renewed. Yet the political, social, and economic changes wrought by the Civil War had altered the justifications for a state prison. The *Carolina Spartan*, for example, engaged in a bit of revisionist history. Forgetting the continuous discussions in support of a penitentiary throughout the 1850s, the paper declared that it was only recently that such an institution became necessary due to the "dissolution of our ancient laws and usages, by the impertinent and concious intermeddling of Northern legislators." Prior to the war, the argument continued, crimes were too few to warrant a central institution. However, the postwar period brought lower classes from the North who were associating with "bad negroes." The removal of plantation discipline and the abolition of the Magistrates and Freeholders Courts were offered as further reasons necessitating a penitentiary.[78] Noticeably absent from this discussion was the need for a better correlation of crimes and punishments and a more rationalized, systematic organization of criminal justice championed by many leaders in prewar Spartanburg.

Following its completion in 1867, the state penitentiary essentially acted as a repository for the state's black convicts. Even after the advent of congressional Reconstruction the racial composition of the institution continued to be overwhelmingly African American. In April 1869, 230 of 262, or 88

Table 15. Cases before the Spartanburg Court of General Sessions, 1870 and 1880

Type of crime	1870		1880	
	No. of cases	% of total cases	No. of cases	% of total cases
Personal				
Murder	4	7	6	14
Assault	17	30	16	37
TOTAL	21	37	22	51
Property				
Theft	20	35	10	23
Malicious trespass/breaking and entering	1	2	1	2
Receiving stolen goods	2	4	—	—
Arson	1	2	—	—
Contract violation	—	—	1	2
Shooting cattle	—	—	1	2
TOTAL	24	43	13	29
Order/morals				
Bastardy	2	4	2	5
Liquor violations	2	4	—	—
Riot	3	5	—	—
Keeping a bawdyhouse	—	—	2	5
Bigamy	—	—	1	2
TOTAL	7	13	5	12
Miscellaneous				
Oppression in office	—	—	1	2
Perjury	5	9	—	—
Forgery	—	—	1	2
Obstructing a railroad	—	—	1	2
TOTAL	5	9	3	6

Source: Sessions Rolls, 1870 and 1880, Spartanburg Court of General Sessions, SCDAH.

percent, of the total inmates in the penitentiary were black.[79] The conservative white majority in Spartanburg conformed to this general pattern of sending convicted blacks, particularly black Republicans, to the state prison. The case of a freedman named John Myers offers an example. Myers ran a small store and eatery in Spartanburg. A witness explained that sometime in 1869 Myers received sixteen pounds of pork from another freedman who, unbeknownst to Myers, had stolen the hog. A jury found Myers guilty of receiving stolen goods, and he was sentenced to serve time in the state penitentiary. Spartanburg resident and Republican Anson W. Cummings pleaded to Governor Scott on Myers's behalf, arguing that he had no knowledge that the meat was stolen and that, even if he had, the charge should have been petty larceny, since the stolen merchandise was only worth $1.60. Petty larceny should have resulted in one to three months in jail, not a trip to the penitentiary. "Had he been a white man, or even a Black Democrat," Cummings argued, "no bill would have been found."[80] Another Spartanburg black resident, George Garrett, was convicted at Greenville of stealing clothes and received the stiff sentence of five years in the penitentiary. A group of leading Spartanburg Republicans petitioned for his pardon, citing the poverty of his dependent wife and three children.[81] Prior to 1868 many Spartanburg whites had advocated the creation of a penitentiary to ensure greater justice and reduce capital punishment. When the institution was created in the defeated and emancipated South, however, it was often used as a means of ridding society of "troublesome" blacks.

The actions of local politicians regarding the push for a penitentiary also reveal the important link made between the institution and economic progress in the county. From early in the postwar period, the promise of cheap convict labor was an important consideration for Spartanburg's leading supporters of the prison.[82] In the general assembly Gabriel Cannon defeated an effort to confine consideration of the institution's location to Columbia. Cannon, along with local newspaper editors Peter M. Wallace and Francis M. Trimmier, objected to one proposed location in the state capital, charging that the area was unhealthy and would result in a hospital for rogues rather than "obtaining the labor of Penitentiary convicts." Wallace and Trimmier instead proposed a location convenient to railroads and to water power. Such places were more available in the upcountry. Plainly, these men looked to utilize cheap convict labor in laying the rails and roads they saw as so crucial to their further economic development. Although the Spartanburg contingent lost its argument when the penitentiary was located on the banks of the Congaree River near Columbia, they continued to promote the use of prison labor for economic expansion.[83]

In 1872 the Republican-dominated legislature inaugurated a convict-lease system to fund the prison's upkeep but quickly had second thoughts. Before many companies could take advantage of the law, the legislature limited the use of convict labor to state government projects only.[84] Over the course of the following year Gabriel Cannon worked against this restriction through resolutions urging the legislature to consider the "expediency of farming out the Penitentiary," and he eventually introduced his own bill to repeal the act. Spartanburg's three other representatives lent their support to the measure.[85] Despite Cannon's efforts, the state general assembly went in the opposite direction when it passed an 1875 act prohibiting any hiring out of convicts from the state penitentiary. Citing the need to reduce the expenses of the institution and prevent the state from "keeping a gang of rogues and thieves in idleness," Cannon urged the law's repeal. The Spartanburg representative attempted to widen the appeal of convict leasing by adding humanitarian rhetoric to his argument. By January 1876 Cannon reported that of the 336 convicts in the penitentiary, only about 25 were white, thus "showing great demoralization of the negro." These black criminals could be reformed, he explained, through a renewed appreciation of hard labor on public works projects throughout South Carolina that would simultaneously add to the state's material progress.[86] While the state's convict labor issue remained unresolved, Spartanburg's economic leaders continued to prove a resourceful group. In late 1875 Spartanburg and Asheville Railroad president—and former Spartanburg representative—David R. Duncan skirted around the whole problem by reaching an agreement with North Carolina authorities to use their convicts to work on the road. The following May Governor Daniel Chamberlain and the Spartanburg and Union Railroad's board of directors reached a special agreement whereby the company could hire about two hundred convicts.[87]

The end of Republican Reconstruction in South Carolina resulted in an about-face in the state's convict labor law. In June 1877 the new Democratic legislature replaced the Act to *Regulate* the Convict Labor of This State with the Act to *Utilize* the Convict Labor of This State. The new law established a board of directors with the power to hire out convicts for nonagricultural work "as they may think most advantageous to the State."

Once again, Spartanburg representatives played a key role in shaping the law. Later in the year, county lawmaker E. S. Allen introduced a bill to amend the convict labor law so that railroad companies "or other institutions of a public character" could pay for convict labor with certificates of company stock. Allen's bill became law, thereby allowing cash-deficient internal improvement companies to utilize cheap labor. By late 1878 the legislature had removed the last significant restriction on convict labor by permitting the hiring out of prisoners for agricultural work.[88]

The debate over convict labor and the purposes of the penitentiary itself did not end with the return of Democratic control to the state. Earlier supporters of convict leasing grew disheartened by reports that corporations were abusing prisoners through overwork and insufficient food. The corporations, the *Carolina Spartan* argued, "care nothing for the moral improvement of the convicts so long as they can make money." This shift in attitude was in large part a reaction to the notoriously brutal treatment of convicts leased to the Greenwood and Augusta Railroad in Edgefield. Out of 285 convicts sent to the company, 128, or 45 percent, died while in the company's care. These horrifying statistics moved the legislature to require monthly inspections of convicts and gave the governor authorization to recall them from companies engaging in maltreatment of prisoners.[89] In contrast, Spartanburg residents were urged to take pride in the fact that the thirty-eight convicts working in the county along the Air-Line Railroad in July 1880 were "a healthy, well fed set of laborers, [with] a cheerful and contented appearance." Despite the county's seeming success with prison labor, outrage over the Greenwood and Augusta's cruelty led to a more general questioning of the penitentiary's effectiveness. There were reports of poor conditions at the institution itself, with some instances of prisoners shot to death by guards. "The State has no shadow of a right to kill a convict," the *Carolina Spartan* intoned, "by a process of ill treatment and torture that breaks down the health and spirits and produces certain death." Instead, the penitentiary should bring reform to prisoners so that they might return to society as productive members. Calls went out for a study of how many convicts were truly reformed and whether or not the example of the penitentiary reduced criminal activity in the state. If this was not the case, *Carolina Spartan* editor Charles Petty opined that it would be better for the "integrity and honor and reputation" of South Carolina to close the prison and revert all criminals back to county jails. An 1879 Spartanburg grand jury called for the repeal of the convict-lease law, explaining that not only were convicts mistreated but they were improperly guarded, and their escapes threatened society at large.[90]

More general concerns were raised in post-Reconstruction Spartanburg over the racial component of the penitentiary. Observers noted that blacks were hardened in their belief that their race was not receiving anything near equal treatment before the courts, and thus they were sent to the penitentiary at rates substantially higher than whites convicted of similar crimes. With the legislature firmly in Democratic hands, judges and juries were encouraged to show fairness and magnanimity so that "all friction be removed from our criminal laws and courts and modes of punishment, so far as the races are concerned."[91]

Spartanburg's experience with the penitentiary and convict-lease system provides a useful example of what happened when the issues of emancipation, economic development, criminal justice, and racism all converged in the postwar South. The end of slavery forced Spartanburg white leaders, and white leaders throughout the South, to find new ways of exerting control over black labor and maintaining racial dominance in laws. The penitentiary, initially supported for its rationalization of criminal law, was used in Reconstruction as a means of removing threats to the racial order while providing a source of cheap labor for the harbingers of economic expansion, the railroads. Historian Edward Ayers has described the postbellum South's convict-lease system as "the most visible product of a society caught between the worst of the past and the worst of the future."[92] The combined focus on racial discrimination and economic efficiency presented modernizers with the same irony that resulted from the alteration of fence laws. Using cheap black convict labor, Spartanburg entrepreneurs accepted violence and exploitation within the legal system and killed wage-earning opportunities for whites. Statewide victory for the conservative regime in 1877 brought about some alterations in local attitudes toward prison labor. With the racial order in law and society seemingly secure, community leaders looked to avoid fomenting tensions that might result from excessively inhumane treatment of black prison labor. The attacks on the "corporate" abuse of convict labor also reflects the growing detachment of the local community from the county's expanding railroad projects. By the early 1880s most of the railroad operations in Spartanburg were controlled by northern interests, not prominent individuals from the upcountry.

When viewed in the wider context of the nineteenth century, Spartanburg's postwar experience in law and violence was hardly an aberration. Local leaders had long sought a more disciplined, restrained community as one of the hallmarks of a modern, progressive age. Such restraint would be attractive to outsiders while making county residents secure enough in their persons and property to meaningfully pursue the main chance. Yet coinciding with this focus on juridical modernization was a community tradition of extralegality. This tradition was particularly employed when individuals or groups perceived genuine threats to the racial order of society. The Ku Klux Klan initially drew support from a wide cross-section of whites because Reconstruction and black political activity so clearly violated accepted notions of legitimate republican order. Progress for whites in the South was inconceivable in a world of racial equality. By 1880, with the "proper" government restored, county leaders renewed their focus on eliminating the sources of disorder. However, as John Moore's execution so vividly demonstrates, extralegality continued for both races as a ritualized defense of the county's honor and moral code. The coexistence of law and violence would continue to define Spartanburg and most of southern society throughout the lynch mobs of the 1890s and beyond.

Conclusion

IN JULY 1890 writer Edward McKissick surveyed Spartanburg's progress for the *Charleston News & Courier* and highlighted the county's "magnificent railway facilities, its superb educational advantages, and greatest of all, its manufacturing enterprises," which, he maintained, had earned the region a reputation as the "Greatest Cotton Manufacturing Centre in the South." McKissick also found unrivaled success in Spartanburg city, where the population had more than quintupled since 1870 and the streets were lined with attractive brick homes and prosperous shops. Even racial tensions appeared resolved, as McKissick noted with pride the election to the city council of Thomas Bomar, "one of the representative colored men of this place."[1]

McKissick's article is typical of New South promotional literature and suggests the power of post-Reconstruction town business elites, railroad officials, and industrialists that historian C. Vann Woodward so clearly identified half a century ago. A study of Spartanburg's business leadership from the antebellum period through the Civil War and Reconstruction, however, reveals that an ideology of modernization was not born out of the wrenching changes of war and its aftermath. Instead, the first half of the nineteenth century witnessed the rise of a town-oriented leadership with a plan for agricultural diversification, railroad development, factory expansion, and legal and educational reforms. Despite a general resistance in the Old South to government support for economic development, Spartanburg's leaders urged the South Carolina state legislature to assist their program liberally. These findings challenge persistent generalizations that the antebellum South as a whole produced few viable plans for modernization of the slave economy. Although recent scholarship has significantly challenged these generalizations, the predominant historical image of the Old South remains that of either powerful planters discouraging diversification and investment in human capital or yeomen and poor whites looking to avoid the web of the market economy.

The activity of Spartanburg's town-oriented entrepreneurial leadership brought the potential for division within the white community between rich and poor and town and rural residents. However, this leadership worked to preserve white unity by presenting plans for modernization as a means of strengthening both white independence and black slavery. Economic diversification was touted as offering struggling farmers new market opportunities and, by implication, providing those who did not own slaves with better hope of entering the ranks of slave owners. Legal reform would protect slave property, guarantee punishment of "dangerous" blacks, and preserve basic harmony within the white community. Better schools would prepare whites for emerging economic opportunities while excluding blacks, thereby making the racial definition of educated citizenship all the more clear.

The Civil War and Reconstruction brought massive economic and social upheaval to Spartanburg and the rest of the South. Farmers faced depleted resources and heavy debts, while emancipation meant the transition of Spartanburg's eight thousand slaves into free laborers. Despite these important changes, however, the essential plans of the county's progressive economic leaders remained the same. Town merchants and professionals continued to push for increased market opportunities through better access to credit, the development of internal improvements to open new markets, and reforms in law and education both to make Spartanburg an attractive market center and to prepare white residents for an increasingly competitive world.

Over the course of Reconstruction, the gap between the rhetoric of progress and the reality facing many farmers expanded further and further. Lawyers and merchants in Spartanburg town grew wealthy for many of the same reasons that rural farmers faced financial crisis. The crop-lien system drew farmers into a spiraling cycle of debt at the same time that it offered opportunities for merchants. Those unable to pay their debts provided business for town lawyers representing creditors. Divisions between rich and poor and rural and town populations also developed over railroad and factory expansion. Residents throughout the county were asked to pay taxes in support of railroads, which most clearly benefited those living in towns along the lines. At the same time, Spartanburg's economic leaders were supporting tax exemptions for new factories while farmers struggled to meet their public and private obligations. New fence laws and convict labor further reduced white economic opportunity and, ironically, hindered some of the modernizers' goals by stunting the growth of entrepreneurial values among the masses.

Despite these widening gaps between rural farmers and town elites, however, no overt class conflict developed in Spartanburg before 1880. Race consciousness continued to define the region and stall the formation of class consciousness. Following emancipation, whites looked to retain as much of the political, economic, and social controls of slavery as possible. Defeated and debt-ridden farmers directed much of their frustration at freedmen. Many whites turned to the tradition of extralegality in preventing blacks from exercising their new rights. Spartanburg leaders, fearing Republican political control and looking to preserve harmony within the white community, supported early efforts to limit black opportunities. Changes in law and education continued to emphasize the distinctions between white freedoms and black restrictions.

In the case of Spartanburg, racism did serve the goals of modernizers who were looking to avoid white class tension, but racial injustice was not the New South expression of class domination that historian Woodward suggested it was in his seminal work. Since the antebellum era, modernizers had equated progress with racial division. Yeomen and poor whites found far greater similarities between themselves and white elites than themselves and black slaves. This tradition helps explain why, when populist farmers and factory workers in Spartanburg and throughout South Carolina resisted early twentieth-century progressive reforms that would further depress wages and economic opportunities, they offered no real alternative to existing social and economic conditions. In 1910 Spartanburg farmers and mill workers joined the groundswell of popular support that propelled Cole Blease to the governorship. Blease gave voice to the frustrations of many poor whites but offered no concrete reform program of his own. Instead, as Bryant Simon notes, he "produced a misogynist, racist, nonradical, and antireform version of class politics."[2] Economic and institutional change disrupted white society, but persistent racism prevented a new definition of society from rising in its place. In this sense, the story of Spartanburg is very much the story of the American South.

Notes

ABBREVIATIONS

DU   Perkins Library, Duke University, Durham, North Carolina
HBS   Baker Library, Harvard University Business School, Cambridge, Massachusetts
LC   Manuscripts Division, Library of Congress, Washington, D.C.
NA   National Archives and Records Administration, Washington, D.C.
SCDAH   South Carolina Division of Archives and History, Columbia
SCL   South Caroliniana Library, University of South Carolina, Columbia
SHC   Southern Historical Collection, Wilson Library, University of North Carolina, Chapel Hill

INTRODUCTION

1. For good discussions of structural weaknesses and the relative lack of industry in the southern economy see Gavin Wright, *Political Economy*, 107–20; Coclanis, *Shadow of a Dream*, 144–54; Fogel and Engerman, *Time on the Cross*, 254–57; and Goldfarb, "Note," 545–58. On attitudes toward industry in South Carolina see Boucher, "Antebellum Attitude," 243–70.

2. See Genovese, *Political Economy of Slavery*, 157–220.

3. See Bateman and Weiss, *Deplorable Scarcity*; Chaplin, *Anxious Pursuit*; Lakwete, *Inventing the Cotton Gin*; and Coclanis, "Paths before Us/U.S.," 12–23.

4. An excellent collection of essays by leading southern historians who use comparative approaches is Delfino and Gillespie, eds., *Global Perspectives*.

5. Chad Morgan, *Planter's Progress*, 4.

6. Wells, *Origins*, 68.

7. Downey, *Planting a Capitalist South*, 8.

8. Frank Byrne's study *Becoming Bourgeois* spans the antebellum era through the end of the Civil War. The course of economic change is explored in Jonathan M. Bryant, *How Curious a Land*.

9. A few examples of works that do explore cultural and institutional reform efforts in the South are Wells, *Origins*; Byrne, *Becoming Bourgeois*; Bellows, *Benevolence among Slaveholders*; and Quist, *Restless Visionaries*.

10. See Weiman, "Petty Commodity Production," esp. chap. 2; Allman, "Yeoman Regions," esp. chap. 2.

11. See Genovese, "Yeoman Farmers," 331–42; and Hahn, *Roots of Southern Populism*.

12. Ford, *Origins of Southern Radicalism*.

13. An excellent recent study of intrastate political and economic tension in the South is Link, *Roots of Secession*. Tom Downey (*Planting a Capitalist South*) also finds evidence of intrastate tension in South Carolina.

14. Towers, *Urban South*, 35.

15. Carolyn Hoffman ("Development") found similar divisions emerging between town and countryside just to the north of Spartanburg in Mecklenberg County, North Carolina.

16. Wells, *Origins*, 7–12.

17. Byrne, *Becoming Bourgeois*, 7.

18. Long, "Meaning of Entrepreneurship," 47–59. Also see Brouwer, "Weber, Schumpeter and Knight," 83–105.

19. Peter Coclanis, for example, suggests the entrepreneurial activity of lowcountry South Carolina planters when he states that their efforts "to diversify the lowcountry economy to a degree are indicative of considerable enterprise rather than entrepreneurial lethargy" (*Shadow of a Dream*, 139).

20. Richard D. Brown, *Modernization*, 19.

21. In his study of merchant families Frank Byrne (*Becoming Bourgeois*) finds that women played an important role in southern commercial culture.

22. See, for example, Fredrickson, *Black Image*; Edmund S. Morgan, *American Slavery, American Freedom*; and Cooper, *Liberty and Slavery*.

23. Gillespie, *Free Labor*, 146.

1. "THE RISING GENERATION"

1. Zelotus Holmes to Mrs. Marshall, May 10, 1847, Zelotus Holmes Papers, SCL.

2. On the duality of the southern frontier see Dupre, *Transforming the Cotton Frontier*, 11–13.

3. Simms, *Geography of South Carolina*, 128; Rosser H. Taylor, *Ante-Bellum South Carolina*, 105; Mills, *Statistics*, 727; Mathew, ed., *Agriculture, Geology, and Society*, 285.

4. Mathew, ed., *Agriculture, Geology, and Society*, 285, 287; Simms, *Geography of South Carolina*, 128–29.

5. On the nature of early lowcountry settlement see Peter H. Wood, *Black Majority*, 3–62.

6. See Genovese, *Political Economy of Slavery*, *World the Slaveholders Made*, and *Roll, Jordan, Roll*.

7. Landrum, *History of Spartanburg County*, 7–10; Simms, *Geography of South Carolina*, 128; Weir, *Colonial South Carolina*, 209–12.

8. An influential article highlighting the primary importance of caring for the household and preserving social relationships in preindustrial communities is Henretta, "Families and Farms," 12–19.

9. Bond, *Political Culture*; Chaplin, *Anxious Pursuit*, 278, 287.

10. Information drawn from a sampling of Spartanburg households by Steven West ("From Yeoman to Redneck," 74, 78).

11. Manuscript Census Returns, 1860, Agricultural Schedule, Spartanburg District, SCDAH; Manuscript Census Returns, Population and Slave Schedules, Spartanburg District and County, 1860, NA.

12. West, "From Yeoman to Redneck," 95.

13. Since they provide a rare insight into the world of the antebellum yeoman farmer, Sloan's papers and journals have been used effectively by other scholars. See Rumble, "Carolina Country Squire," 323–37; Ford, *Origins of Southern Radicalism*, 78–80; McCurry, *Masters of Small Worlds*, 81–85; and James F. Sloan Papers and Diaries, SCL.

14. Racine, ed., *Piedmont Farmer*, 1, 3, 4, 9.

15. Ibid., 30, 35, 40, 47–49, 109.

16. U.S. Bureau of the Census, *Agriculture*, 128–29; "Memoirs of John Earle Bomar," 7–8, SCL; McCord, *Statutes at Large of South Carolina*, 6:331–32; Inscoe, *Mountain Masters*, 45–46.

17. U.S. Bureau of the Census, *Population*, 448–52; Racine, ed., *Piedmont Farmer*, 2.

18. Landrum, *History of Spartanburg County*, 156–60; Manuscript Census Returns, Population and Slave Schedules, Spartanburg District and County, 1860, NA; Manuscript Census Returns, 1860, Agricultural Schedule, Spartanburg District, SCDAH.

19. Landrum, *History of Spartanburg County*, 213–20, 333–35; Manuscript Census Returns, Population and Slave Schedules, Spartanburg District and County, 1860, NA; Manuscript Census Returns, 1860, Agricultural Schedule, Spartanburg District, SCDAH.

20. Wells argues that professional and commercial people were growing in influence throughout the antebellum South as part of "an evolving social order" (*Origins*, 10). Downey (*Planting a Capitalist South*) also traces the development of merchants and industrialists in Edgefield and Barnwell districts in South Carolina.

21. Landrum, *History of Spartanburg County*, 167–68.

22. Bailey, Morgan, and Taylor, *Biographical Directory*, 265–66; Manuscript Census Returns, Population and Slave Schedules, Spartanburg District and County, 1860, NA.

23. Landrum, *History of Spartanburg County*, 274, 338–39, 353–54; South Carolina Credit Report Ledger no. 13, 8–9, HBS.

24. *Carolina Spartan*, October 10, 1850, June 23, 1853.

25. Byrne finds that there was a high level of consumerism among merchant families in the antebellum South and that wives were left in charge when merchants left home on northern buying trips (*Becoming Bourgeois*, 36, 94–97).

26. South Carolina Credit Report Ledger no. 1, 562, HBS; Landrum, *History of Spartanburg County*, 254–57; Manuscript Census Returns, Population and Slave Schedules, Spartanburg District and County, 1850, NA.

27. Schaper, "Sectionalism," 367–83.

28. Chaplin, *Anxious Pursuit*, 234, 132.

29. Ford, *Origins of Southern Radicalism*, 106–7; Schaper, "Sectionalism," 419–37.

30. Freehling, *Road to Disunion*, 220.

31. U.S. Bureau of the Census, *Compendium of the Ninth Census*, 88–89.

32. Byrne, *Becoming Bourgeois*, 26.

33. Ford, *Origins of Southern Radicalism*, 91–92, 320–22; "Memoirs of John Earle Bomar," 14, SCL.

34. On the operations of the BSSC in the antebellum period see Lesesne, *Bank*, 35–152.

35. Ibid., 148–51; Ford, *Origins of Southern Radicalism*, 178–79.

36. Ford, *Origins of Southern Radicalism*, 177–82, 324–26; Lesesne, *Bank*, 71–88; James Edward Henry to Samuel F. Patterson, January 28, 1848, Samuel Finley Patterson Papers, DU.

37. *Carolina Spartan*, August 29, 1850, September 12, 1850, September 19, 1850, September 26, 1850, October 3, 1850, October 10, 1850, October 17, 1850.

38. Ibid., November 5, 1857; Grand Jury Presentments, Spartanburg District Court of General Sessions, SCDAH; *Carolina Spartan*, November 11, 1858, September 26, 1850.

39. MacArthur, "Antebellum Politics," 8–11.

40. For an extensive look at the Wilmot Proviso and the southern response see Morrison, *Democratic Politics and Sectionalism*. For an overview of the sectional politics concerning the western territories see Potter, *Impending Crisis*, 18–62.

41. Boucher, "Secession and Cooperation Movements," 67–138.

42. *Carolina Spartan*, March 13, 1849; MacArthur, "Antebellum Politics," 19–20.

43. *Carolina Spartan*, April 24, 1849; MacArthur, "Antebellum Politics," 22–26.

44. See Barnwell, *Love of Order*.

45. *Journal of the House of Representatives of the State of South Carolina, Being the Annual Session of 1850*, 165–68, 192–94.

46. MacArthur, "Antebellum Politics," 29–30; Manuscript Census Returns, Population and Slave Schedules, Spartanburg District and County, 1850, NA.

47. *Carolina Spartan*, October 20, 1853.

48. MacArthur, "Antebellum Politics," 34–35; Manuscript Census Returns, Agriculture and Industrial Schedules, 1850, Spartanburg District, SCDAH.

49. Manuscript Census Returns, Population and Slave Schedules, Spartanburg District and County, 1860, NA.

50. MacArthur, "Antebellum Politics," 37–40; H. H. Thomson Folder, August 24, 1851, SCL.

51. *Carolina Spartan*, September 4, 1851.

52. MacArthur, "Antebellum Politics," 42–47.

53. Oakes, *Ruling Race*, esp. 37–95. Oakes's notion of aggressively acquisitive, market-oriented southerners contrasts with an earlier historical interpretation of a precapitalist South advanced by Genovese in a number of works, most notably *Political Economy of Slavery* and *Roll, Jordan, Roll*. On the westward migration of South Carolinians see Alfred Glaze Smith Jr., *Economic Readjustment*, 19–44.

54. The conflict over development through time versus expansion over space had deep roots in the American political economy. In the early republic Thomas Jefferson led a group of agrarians who argued that the development of manufacturing and trade in small areas of the Old World had led to political corruption and social decay. Jefferson maintained that only by continuing to expand over space could white men retain their virtue and independence. Of course, Spartanburg professionals understood the importance of farming, and many were involved in agriculture to some extent. The point here is that they were more interested in developing community infrastructure than westward migration. On these conflicting views of development see McCoy, *Elusive Republic*.

55. The late antebellum period witnessed the expansion of urban centers in a number of areas in the South. See Towers, *Urban South*, and Goldfield, *Region, Race, and Cities*, 189–246.

56. The 1840 number was taken from a chart listing pounds of cotton gathered in Simms, *Geography of South Carolina*, 155. I assume that 1840 merchants used the 1850 definition of a bale as 400 pounds and thus arrived at a figure of 3,988 bales. Since in practice bale weights could vary significantly, 4,000 bales seems a good approximation for 1840. The 1850 figure was taken from U.S. Bureau of the Census, *Seventh Census*, 346.

57. U.S. Bureau of the Census, *Agriculture*, 128–31.

58. U.S. Bureau of the Census, *Seventh Census*; Manuscript Census Returns, 1850, Population Schedule, Spartanburg District, SCDAH; U.S. Bureau of the Census, *Ninth Census*, 260.

59. South Carolina Credit Report Ledger no. 13, 5, 14D, 20, 27, HBS.

60. *Reports and Resolutions of the South Carolina General Assembly, 1850*, 10; *Reports and Resolutions of the South Carolina General Assembly, 1855*, 35–36.

61. *Carolina Spartan*, April 10, 1851, June 29, 1854.

62. Ibid., October 20, 1853.

63. Wells, *Origins*, 19–65.

64. *Carolina Spartan*, September 1, 1853.

65. "Petition from the Citizens of Spartanburgh to Amend the Charter of the Town," 1853, and Committee on Incorporation Report, 1853, General Assembly Papers, SCDAH.

66. Landrum, *History of Spartanburg County*, 483–84.

67. *Carolina Spartan*, February 1, 1855.

68. Ibid., August 2, 1855.

69. Ibid., January 22, 1857.

70. Ibid., January 29, 1857.

71. Ibid., June 14, 1855.

2. "WE MUST MANUFACTURE"

1. *Carolina Spartan*, May 15, 1849.

2. On the importance of independence in antebellum southern ideology see Thornton, *Politics and Power*, 54–58; Hahn, *Roots of Southern Populism*, 86–133; Ford, *Origins of Southern Radicalism*, 49–51; and McCurry, *Masters of Small Worlds*.

3. *Carolina Spartan*, October 27, 1849.

4. South Carolina Department of Agriculture, *South Carolina*, 127–44; Simms, *Geography of South Carolina*, 11–13.

5. Landrum, *History of Spartanburg County*, 117. For overviews of the iron industry in antebellum South Carolina's upcountry see Lander, "Iron Industry," 337–55, and Ferguson and Cowan, "Iron Plantations," 113–44.

6. Ferguson and Cowan, "Iron Plantations," 113, 122; Manuscript Census Returns, 1860, Manufacturing Schedule, Spartanburg District, SCDAH; South Carolina Credit Report Ledger no. 13, 7, 9, HBS.

7. Mathew, ed., *Agriculture, Geology, and Society*, 289.

8. James S. M. Davis to Marion, March 22, 1845, James S. M. Davis Papers, SCL.

9. Ferguson and Cowan, "Iron Plantations," 136; Ford, *Origins of Southern Radicalism*, 268.

10. *Carolina Spartan*, August 1, 1850, January 9, 1851.

11. Lander, "Iron Industry," 354.

12. Tucker, *Samuel Slater*, 99–111.

13. Lander, *Textile Industry*, 13–15.

14. For another example of the influence of northern middle-class immigrants on commercial culture in the South see Wells, *Origins*, 19–65.

15. Ibid., 14–16. For an example of the argument that manufacturing was ancillary to agricultural production see Alfred Glaze Smith Jr., *Economic Readjustment*, 112.

16. Lander, *Textile Industry*, 16–18; Landrum, *History of Spartanburg County*, 254–57.

17. Alfred Glaze Smith Jr., *Economic Readjustment*, 115–16; Ford, *Origins of Southern Radicalism*, 37–42.

18. Tucker, *Samuel Slater*, 110–24.

19. On Gregg see Broadus Mitchell, *William Gregg*, and Downey, "Riparian Rights," 77–108.

20. Broadus Mitchell, *William Gregg*, 11–14, 29; Downey, "Riparian Rights," 92–93.

21. Broadus Mitchell, *William Gregg*, 16.

22. Downey, "Riparian Rights," 94. See also Martin, "Advent," 389–423, and Gregg, *Enquiry*, 3–14.

23. Downey, "Riparian Rights," 95.

24. *Carolina Spartan*, May 10, 1855.

25. South Carolina Credit Report Ledger no. 13, 11, 17, HBS.

26. Ibid., 19, 37.

27. Landrum, *History of Spartanburg County*, 156.

28. South Carolina Credit Report Ledger no. 13, 12, 32, HBS; Bailey, Morgan, and Taylor, *Biographical Directory*, 265–66.

29. South Carolina Credit Report Ledger no. 13, 41, HBS; *Cyclopedia*, 465; Lander, *Textile Industry*, 13–15; U.S. Bureau of the Census, *Manufactures*, 552–57.

30. J. Bomar & Co. to P. Whitin & Sons, February 24, 1859; Wm. Bates & Co. to P. Whitin & Sons, April 23, 1853; Wm. Gregg to P. Whitin & Sons, March 31, 1848, all in P. Whitin and Sons Papers, SCL.

31. Gavin Wright, "Cheap Labor," 655–80; Ford, *Origins of Southern Radicalism*, 273–74.

32. On the use of white labor in textile mills see Stokes, "Black and White Labor"; Griffin, "Poor White Laborers," 26–40; and Terrill, "Eager Hands," 84–99.

33. U.S. Bureau of the Census, *Manufactures*, 556; *Carolina Spartan*, October 10, 1850.

34. Manuscript Census Returns, Population and Slave Schedules, Spartanburg District and County, 1860, NA.

35. On antebellum northern free labor ideology see Foner, *Free Soil*, and Glickstein, *Concepts of Free Labor*.

36. Thomas John Moore to his mother, June 15, 1860, Thomas John Moore Papers, SCL.

37. See Walters, *Antislavery Appeal*.

38. On similar efforts to promote manual labor in other parts of the South see Shore, *Southern Capitalists*, 8–35, and Gillespie, *Free Labor*, 144–48.

39. *Carolina Spartan*, July 14, 1853.

40. Ibid., August 11, 1853.

41. Ibid., October 27, 1853.

42. Gillespie, *Free Labor*, esp. 144–48.

43. *Carolina Spartan*, November 9, 1854, June 23, 1853, May 8, 1849.

44. See Olmsted, *Journey*, 542–43; William Cullen Bryant, *Letters of a Traveller*, 348–49; Stokes, "Black and White Labor," 87.

45. *Carolina Spartan*, July 15, 1857.

46. Ibid., March 27, 1851. On the idea that factory work would elevate the moral character of the upcountry see Stokes, "Black and White Labor," 84, 98, 118.

47. Receipts and promissory notes from Andrew Feaster for 1841–42 can be found in folders 1–2, box 1, Coleman, Feaster, and Faucette Family Papers, SCL.

48. Stokes, "Black and White Labor," 26. See various debt slips and accounts for Bivingsville in the antebellum portion of the James F. Sloan Papers and Diaries, SCL. On the nature of local exchange in the nineteenth-century United States see Merrill, "Cash," 42–71.

49. Downey, *Planting a Capitalist South*, 90.

50. Hosea J. Dean to Elihu Smith, March 23, 1847; Hosea J. Dean to Elihu Smith, May 4, 1848; Gabriel Cannon to Elihu Smith, June 5, 1849; promissory note from Elihu Smith to Cannon and Finger for $283.90, January 13, 1858, all in Elihu P. Smith Papers, SCL.

51. Magistrate summonses for debts owed by Catherine Stone to Jacob Zimmerman, J. B. Morgan, Morgan and Woods, February 23, 1852; debts to Bivingsville Company, February 4, 1852, November 22, 1855; Hiram Mitchell to Catherine Stone, December 2, 1852, Stone Family Papers, SHC.

52. Ford, *Origins of Southern Radicalism*, 269–71; U.S. Bureau of the Census, *Manufactures*, 556.

53. *Carolina Spartan*, October 27, 1853.

54. Alfred Glaze Smith Jr., *Economic Readjustment*, 5–6; Ford, *Origins of Southern Radicalism*, 16–19; Chaplin, *Anxious Pursuit*, 295–96.

55. Petition of the Citizens of Spartanburg, York, and Union Districts for Improved Navigation of the Broad River above King's Creek, ca. 1845; Petition of Sundry Citizens of Union, York, and Spartanburgh Districts for Improved Navigation of the Broad River, ca. 1845, both in General Assembly Papers, SCDAH.

56. Petition of the Citizens of Spartanburg, York, and Union Districts for Improved Navigation of the Broad River above King's Creek, ca. 1845, General Assembly Papers, SCDAH.

57. Petition of Sundry Citizens of the Districts of Union and Spartanburg for Navigation of the Pacolet River to Easterwoods Shoals or River to Be Closed, October 1846, General Assembly Papers, SCDAH; Charles, *Narrative History*, 141.

58. Petition of Sundry Citizens of Union and Spartanburg Districts that Pacolet River Remain Navigable to Grindal Shoals, ca. 1846, General Assembly Papers, SCDAH. The exclusive owner of the mill at Grindal Shoals was most likely John Littlejohn, who had five thousand dollars invested in five mill runs at the shoals in 1850. See Charles, *Narrative History*, 141.

59. *Journal of the South Carolina Senate for the Year 1847*, 160. Although there is little evidence of state activity regarding Spartanburg's petitions, Downey finds a different story in Edgefield and Barnwell, South Carolina. Downey argues that a

state exemption allowing William Gregg to dam a creek for powering his factory signaled a shift toward support of manufacturers over the rights of small sawmill operators (*Planting a Capitalist South*, 221).

60. Charles, *Narrative History*, 145; also see Derrick, *Centennial History*.

61. Alfred Glaze Smith Jr., *Economic Readjustment*, 173.

62. Simpson Bobo to James H. Saye, November 22, 1848, James H. Saye Papers, DU.

63. *Statutes at Large of South Carolina*, 11:481–89.

64. *Carolina Spartan*, April 10, 1849, April 17, 1849.

65. Ibid., May 31, 1849. For an overview of the factorage system, in which farmers contracted with merchants to sell their goods in distant markets, see Woodman, *King Cotton*.

66. *Carolina Spartan*, November 14, 1850, November 21, 1850.

67. Ibid., November 21, 1850.

68. Ibid.

69. Ibid., December 12, 1850.

70. *Charleston Mercury*, November 21, 1850.

71. Charles, *Narrative History*, 146.

72. On developing urban-rural tensions in the Old South see Towers, *Urban South*. In his study of Virginia Goldfield argues that urban and rural tensions were largely offset by a "basic mutuality of interest" (*Region, Race, and Cities*, 67–86).

73. *Carolina Spartan*, May 15, 1849.

74. Ibid.

75. Ibid., August 24, 1854, February 15, 1855.

76. Ibid., August 21, 1856.

77. Quoted in Racine, ed., *Piedmont Farmer*, 117–18.

78. Ibid., 120.

79. November 25, 1859, James F. Sloan Papers and Diaries, SCL.

80. *Carolina Spartan*, August 4, 1853; *Statutes at Large of South Carolina*, 12:252.

81. *Carolina Spartan*, May 19, 1855, June 21, 1855.

82. Memorial of Sundry Citizens of Union, Spartanburgh, and Greenville on the Subject of the French Broad Rail Road, 1854, General Assembly Papers, SCDAH.

83. Ibid.

84. Ibid.

85. *Carolina Spartan*, August 3, 1854, August 15, 1854. For more information on the Blue Ridge Railroad see George Dewitt Brown, "History."

86. *Carolina Spartan*, August 3, 1854, August 15, 1854.

87. Ibid., August 24, 1854, September 7, 1854, September 14, 1854, September 21, 1854.

88. Ibid., August 7, 1856, August 14, 1856, August 21, 1856, August 28, 1856.

89. Ibid., December 23, 1858, January 6, 1859.

90. Ibid., August 23, 1855.
91. Ibid., January 4, 1860.
92. Ibid., March 8, 1860.
93. Ibid., April 12, 1860.
94. Ibid., April 19, 1860.
95. Ibid., May 17, 1860.
96. MacArthur, "Antebellum Politics," 60–61.
97. *Carolina Spartan*, May 17, 1860, September 13, 1860, October 18, 1860.

98. Some choice examples of those historians emphasizing postwar change in economic ideas and practices of white leaders are Woodward, *Origins*, 107–41; Carlton, *Mill and Town*, 1–39; Bond, *Political Culture*, esp. 184–87. John Ashworth's (*Slavery*) central argument is that the Civil War represented a "bourgeois revolution" in America.

3. "AN EDUCATED AND INTELLIGENT PEOPLE CANNOT BE ENSLAVED"

1. *Carolina Spartan*, June 28, 1849.

2. For an important assessment of the historiography of southern education see Best, "Education," 3–18. A thorough synthesis of postrevisionist history of common schooling can be found in Kaestle, *Pillars of the Republic*.

3. Best, "Education," 12. Among the few studies addressing public education in the antebellum South are Pippin, "Common School Movement"; Knight, *Public Education* and *Influence*; Dabney, *Universal Education*; William R. Taylor, "Toward a Definition," 412–26; and Plank and Ginsberg, eds., *Southern Cities, Southern Schools*, 17–35. On public education in antebellum South Carolina see Meriwether, *History*; Stoddard, "Backgrounds"; Thompson, *Establishment*; and Lewis P. Jones, "History," 1–29.

4. On planter reluctance to invest in human capital see Gavin Wright, *Old South, New South*, 17–24.

5. Jefferson and Marion are quoted in Knight, *Public Education*, 114–15.

6. Ibid., 118.

7. See Bellows, *Benevolence among Slaveholders*; Quist, *Restless Visionaries*; Varon, *We Mean to Be Counted*.

8. Wells, *Origins*, 135.

9. Knight, *Public Education*, 154.

10. Ibid., 133–38.

11. Ibid., 160–304.

12. *Statutes at Large of South Carolina*, 5:639. On the mingling of public and private efforts in education see Jorgensen, *State*, 5.

13. *Statutes at Large of South Carolina*, 5:639.

14. Lewis P. Jones, "History," 9.

15. Ibid. Four excellent works that highlight the importance of independence and individual autonomy to antebellum white Southerners are Thornton, *Politics and Power*; Hahn, *Roots of Southern Populism*, 15–85; Ford, *Origins of Southern Radicalism*; and McCurry, *Masters of Small Worlds*.

16. Knight, *Public Education*, 169–70, 216–28; Stoddard, "Backgrounds," 57.

17. Knight, *Public Education*, 215–27. Barbara Bellows argues that the upcountry resisted changes in the school law because poorer farmers felt that any educational program would likely benefit larger towns in the state (*Benevolence among Slaveholders*, 157).

18. Schaper, "Sectionalism," 367–83, 419–37; Ford, *Origins of Southern Radicalism*, 106–7.

19. Burton, *In My Father's House*, 80. Charleston is an important exception to the pattern of lowcountry resistance to structured public education. In the 1850s growing concerns about class tensions in the city led to discussions about a new educational system that would encourage the integration of both rich and poor children in common schools. Christopher Memminger led a sustained effort to create a common school system supported by city taxes. In 1858 Charleston's first coeducational model school opened. These worries about class tensions were not as acute in rural areas and small towns where there were far fewer mechanics and white day laborers. For a discussion of Charleston's common school initiatives see Bellows, *Benevolence among Slaveholders*, 157–59, and Edgar, *South Carolina*, 298–99. Urban areas in the South experienced more activity in public education overall. See Newman, "Antebellum School Reform," 17–35.

20. James Edward Henry to S. F. Patterson, January 8, 1839, and January 14, 1840, Samuel Finley Patterson Papers, DU.

21. *Carolina Spartan*, October 10, 1849.

22. Manuscript Census Returns, Population and Slave Schedules, Spartanburg District and County, 1850, NA.

23. In his study of southern poor whites Charles C. Bolton finds that "advocates of public education in North Carolina during the early 1840s claimed that it would . . . socialize the poor to the reality of political leadership by a wealthy elite" (*Poor Whites*, 54).

24. Magistrate J. Wofford Tucker won election to the state house of representatives, and G. W. H. Legg became intendant of Spartanburg (Landrum, *History of Spartanburg County*, 173, 411).

25. Walters, *Antislavery Appeal*, 72–78. Drew Faust (*Sacred Circle*) points out that southern intellectuals were marginalized in the antebellum South and turned to reforms that would strengthen the proslavery argument as an acceptable form of creative outlet. Similarly, common schools offered a way for educated leaders to support reform while negating abolitionist attacks.

26. *Carolina Spartan*, September 13, 1849; James Edward Henry to S. F. Patterson, August 8, 1849, Samuel Finley Patterson Papers, DU.

27. Michael Stephen Hindus argues that South Carolina magistrates were greedy and incompetent (*Prison and Plantation*, 29).

28. Grand Jury Presentments, Spartanburg District Court of General Sessions, fall term, 1850, spring term, 1854, SCDAH.

29. Ibid., fall term, 1855, spring term, 1857.

30. Hindus, *Prison and Plantation*, 97; Grand Jury Presentments, Spartanburg District Court of General Sessions, 1849–60, SCDAH; Manuscript Census Returns, Population and Slave Schedules, Spartanburg District and County, 1850, 1860, NA.

31. U.S. Bureau of the Census, *Seventh Census*, 342; Report of the Commissioner of Free Schools, Spartanburg District, 1855, 1856, 1858, 1859, 1860, 1861, Department of Education Files, SCDAH.

32. Ford, *Origins of Southern Radicalism*, 106.

33. U.S. Bureau of the Census, *Seventh Census*, 342.

34. *Carolina Spartan*, October 11, 1849.

35. Porcher, "Free School System," 32–33.

36. *Memoir of Professor F. A. Porcher*, 1–4.

37. Porcher, "Free School System," 46–48.

38. Petition of Spartanburg Citizens to the General Assembly, September 10, 1853, General Assembly Papers, SCDAH.

39. Manuscript Census Returns, Population and Slave Schedules, Spartanburg District and County, 1850, NA.

40. I based my categories of wealth on three sources. In his classic study, Ulrich B. Phillips classified planters as those owning twenty or more slaves, while owners of five to nineteen slaves were considered middle class (*Life and Labor*, 339). J. Mills Thornton adds that holders of fewer than five slaves and non–slave owners were presumably lower middle to lower class (*Politics and Power*, 63). The problem with basing wealth on slaves alone is that a rich town physician might not own a single slave. As such, I have followed Jonathan Bryant's example of including real estate values in the equation (*How Curious a Land*, 188).

My wealth distribution chart for the signers of the 1853 petition is as follows:

CATEGORY	WEALTH	NUMBER
Lower-middle yeomen	0 slaves, $0 real estate	10
Middling yeomen	Fewer than 10 slaves and/or $200–$2,500 real estate	10
Substantial farmers/professionals	10 or more slaves and/or $2,501–$10,000 real estate	10

Manuscript Census Returns, Population and Slave Schedules, Spartanburg District and County, 1850, NA. For a discussion of the literature and difficulties involved in determining wealth in the nineteenth-century South see Campbell, "Planters and Plain Folk: The Social Structure of the Antebellum South," 63–70.

41. Manuscript Census Returns, Population and Slave Schedules, Spartanburg District and County, 1850, NA.

42. *Carolina Spartan,* October 25, 1849.

43. Manuscript Census Returns, Population and Slave Schedules, Spartanburg District and County, 1850, NA.

44. Bolton contends that "even in areas where adequate public schools did emerge, the greater economic necessity of child labor in landless families insured that poor white children would attend school less frequently than the children of yeomen families" (*Poor Whites,* 55).

45. Abernethy, *From Frontier to Plantation,* 309–18.

46. Committee on Education Report on Petition of Spartanburg Citizens Concerning Free Schools, General Assembly Papers, SCDAH.

47. Landrum, *History of Spartanburg County,* 173.

48. *Carolina Spartan,* March 2, 1854.

49. Wells, *Origins,* 142–46.

50. Adeline Harlow to her mother, August 20, 1847, Adeline Harlow Correspondence, DU; Karen Mitchell, "Phoebe Paine, Educator," 6–7; *Catalogue of Instructors and Pupils,* 5–15.

51. Manuscript Census Returns, Population Schedule, Spartanburg District and County, 1850, NA; *Catalogue of Instructors and Pupils,* 22–23.

52. *Carolina Spartan,* March 2, 1854.

53. Some of the many interpretations stressing the role of race in muting class tensions in the South are Fredrickson, *Black Image*; Edmund S. Morgan, *American Slavery, American Freedom*; and Harris, *Plain Folk.*

54. The classic work on the promotion of an orthodoxy in southern education in the antebellum era is Ezell, "Southern Education for Southrons," 303–27. John McCardell argues that there were two distinct groups promoting higher education in the South: those with the primary goal of academic excellence, and those with the goal of southern educational orthodoxy (*Idea,* 177–226). For a further discussion of southern educational orthodoxy see William R. Taylor, "Toward a Definition," 412–26.

55. Green quoted in Ezell, "Southern Education for Southrons," 306.

56. Ibid., 309–12.

57. The *Carolina Spartan* (March 23, 1854) reprinted excerpts on Tucker's speech from the *Laurensville Herald, Anderson Gazette, Newberrian, Newberry Sentinel,* and *Due West Telescope.*

58. *Carolina Spartan,* December 22, 1853.

59. Ibid., March 9, 1854.

60. Ibid., October 27, 1853.

61. Ibid., November 24, 1853, November 17, 1853.

62. *Carolina Spartan*, May 17, 1855.

63. On Gregg's advocacy of education for factory operatives see Alfred Glaze Smith Jr., *Economic Readjustment*, 119, and Broadus Mitchell, *William Gregg*, 144–45.

64. *Carolina Spartan*, May 17, 1855.

65. Carlton, *Mill and Town*, 36.

66. In addition to Sullivan, legislators J. J. Middleton and Thomas Thomson were quite vocal about their concerns over state centralization. See debates in the *Carolina Spartan*, December 22, 1853.

67. *Carolina Spartan*, December 21, 1854, January 4, 1855. The final vote in the house was fifty-one yeas and fifty-five nays (ibid., December 20, 1855).

68. Ibid., May 1, 1856.

69. Louis B. Wright, *South Carolina*, 156–57; Rosser H. Taylor, *Ante-Bellum South Carolina*, 120–21. See also Hollis, *University of South Carolina*.

70. *Carolina Spartan*, May 1, 1856.

71. Ibid., July 31, 1856, August 7, 1856, August 14, 1856, August 21, 1856, August 28, 1856.

72. Ibid., August 21, 1856.

73. Ibid., March 18, 1858.

4. "MORAL AND INDUSTRIAL REFORM MAY BE UNITED IN ONE SYSTEM"

1. Jack K. Williams, *Vogues in Villainy*, 13–14.

2. Two excellent discussions of the interaction of legal and extralegal authority in the South are Hindus, *Prison and Plantation*, 1–56, and Grimsted, *American Mobbing*, 85–113.

3. Pocock, *Machiavellian Moment*, 12–13.

4. Wyatt-Brown, "Community," 174–77.

5. A number of works have examined the role of honor in southern society. Foremost among these is Bertram Wyatt-Brown's masterful *Southern Honor*. See also Greenberg, *Honor and Slavery*; Ayers, *Vengeance and Justice*, esp. 9–33; Hindus, *Prison and Plantation*, xxi–xxv, 35–36, 56–57.

6. Bruce, *Violence and Culture*, esp. 7–16.

7. On dueling in the Antebellum South see Jack K. Williams, *Dueling*; Stevens, *Pistols at Ten Paces*; Greenberg, "Nose," 57–74.

8. See, for example, Gorn, "Gouge and Bite," 18–43; Bruce, *Violence and Culture*, 89–113.

9. Jack K. Williams, *Vogues in Villainy*, 33, 13–14.

10. See Hindus, *Prison and Plantation*; Sydnor, "Southerner and the Laws," 3–24.

11. Wooster, *People in Power*, 4–9; Ayers, *Vengeance and Justice*, 58–59; Hindus, *Prison and Plantation*, 33–35.

12. Wyatt-Brown, "Community," 178; Sessions Rolls, spring and fall terms, 1850, Spartanburg District Court of General Sessions, SCDAH.

13. Hindus, *Prison and Plantation*, 90; Sessions Rolls, spring and fall terms, 1850, Spartanburg District Court of General Sessions, SCDAH; *Carolina Spartan*, October 4, 1849; *State v. Calvin Cantrell*, *State v. Hudson Vickers*, and *State v. Patsey O'Shields*, all in Sessions Rolls, spring term, 1850, Spartanburg District Court of General Sessions, SCDAH.

14. Racine, "Spartanburg District Magistrates and Freeholders Court," 198.

15. Hindus, *Prison and Plantation*, 155.

16. *Carolina Spartan*, February 1, 1855. On O'Neall's career see Nash, "Negro Rights," 141–90.

17. Racine, "Spartanburg District Magistrates and Freeholders Court," 200; Thomas D. Morris, *Southern Slavery*, 226–28.

18. *Carolina Spartan*, March 18, 1858.

19. Survey of Spartanburg District Magistrates and Freeholders Court, 1849–60, SCDAH; Racine, "Spartanburg District Magistrates and Freeholders Court," 203, 207–8.

20. The sentences for the two attempted rape cases were twenty-five lashes and fifty lashes. Racine points to these relatively "light" sentences as evidence that the court did not believe the testimony of the women involved. If this was true, the decision to permit a person's flesh to be ripped apart twenty-five or more times despite doubts about the case seems all the more monstrous. Harry, the slave convicted of rape, received a sentence of five hundred lashes and was required to leave the state. See Racine, "Spartanburg District Magistrates and Freeholders Court," 209–10; Hindus, *Prison and Plantation*, 151–53; *State v. Tom*, 1846, *State v. Redman*, August 2, 1850, *State v. Harry*, November 5, 1851, *State v. Daniel*, January 15, 1857, all in Spartanburg District Magistrates and Freeholders Court, SCDAH.

21. *Carolina Spartan*, March 18, 1858; Hindus, *Prison and Plantation*, 161. On the historical connection between white independence and black slavery see Edmund S. Morgan, *American Slavery, American Freedom*, and Cooper, *Liberty and Slavery*.

22. Racine, "Trial," 30, 33; *Carolina Spartan*, October 18, 1849.

23. Racine, "Trial," 36–37.

24. *Carolina Spartan*, September 17, 1857, March 5, 1857, July 14, 1853.

25. *Carolina Spartan*, March 5, 1857; *Statutes at Large of South Carolina*, 12:680; *Carolina Spartan*, February 9, 1860; fall term, 1860, Grand Jury Presentments, SCDAH.

26. *Carolina Spartan*, August 18, 1849.

27. Ibid., June 14, 1849, August 30, 1849; James Edward Henry to S. F. Patterson,

August 8, 1849, Samuel Finley Patterson Papers, DU; *Carolina Spartan*, August 16, 1849; MacArthur, "Antebellum Politics," 23.

28. *Carolina Spartan*, September 13, 1849. The lawyers were Joseph Wofford Tucker, James Edward Henry, and Hugh H. Thomson, and the two manufacturers were Peter M. Wallace and Gabriel Cannon (ibid., September 6, 1849).

29. Ibid., April 20, 1854, April 10, 1851, April 6, 1854, April 5, 1855.

30. Abstract of Judgements, 1850 and 1860, Spartanburg District Court of Common Pleas, and Session Rolls, 1850 and 1860, Spartanburg District Court of General Sessions, SCDAH.

31. *Greenville Southern Patriot*, May 4, 1854.

32. South Carolina Credit Report Ledger no. 1, 562–63, HBS; Landrum, *History of Spartanburg County*, 484.

33. *Greenville Southern Patriot*, May 4, 1854; *Carolina Spartan*, April 20, 1854.

34. Petition of Citizens of Spartanburg District, 1846; fall term, 1846, Grand Jury Presentments; Report of the Judiciary Committee on Expanding the Jurisdiction of Magistrates, December 14, 1846, all in General Assembly Papers, SCDAH; *Journal of the Senate of South Carolina, 1846*, 22, 220.

35. Fall term, 1858, Grand Jury Presentments, SCDAH.

36. Hindus, *Prison and Plantation*, 29; fall term, 1855, Grand Jury Presentments, SCDAH.

37. This interpretation differs somewhat from that of Hindus, who portrays South Carolina magistrates as generally greedy and incompetent (*Prison and Plantation*, 28–31). Yet Spartanburg magistrates displayed seriousness of purpose in their conventions and a willingness to forgo some of their fees in the interests of the community. See the magistrate's proposal concerning education in ibid., 189.

38. On court structure in other southern states see Wooster, *Politicians* and *People in Power*.

39. Wooster, *People in Power*, 64–66; *Carolina Spartan*, April 2, 1857, November 12, 1857.

40. Hindus, *Prison and Plantation*, 23–25.

41. Fall term, 1849, Grand Jury Presentments, Spartanburg District Court of General Sessions, SCDAH; Grimsted, *American Mobbing*, 97.

42. *Carolina Spartan*, November 16, 1854, April 2, 1857; *Statutes at Large of South Carolina*, 12:634–35.

43. On the rise of the penitentiary in the South see Ayers, *Vengeance and Justice*, 34–72; Hindus, *Prison and Plantation*, 210–13. On the evolution of the penitentiary in the early American republic see Hirsch, *Rise of the Penitentiary*; Rothman, *Discovery of the Asylum*; Friedman, *Crime and Punishment*, 77–82. For comparisons with European prisons see Ignatieff, *Just Measure of Pain*; Foucault, *Discipline and Punish*.

44. See Ignatieff, *Just Measure of Pain*; Melossi and Pavarini, *Prison and the Factory*.

45. Ayers, *Vengeance and Justice*, 37–40.
46. Ibid., 41–59.
47. Hindus, *Prison and Plantation*, 210–13.
48. Ibid., 213; fall term, 1849, Grand Jury Presentments, SCDAH.
49. Fall term, 1855, Grand Jury Presentments, SCDAH; Hindus, *Prison and Plantation*, 101.
50. *Carolina Spartan*, April 30, 1857.
51. Ibid., November 12, 1857.
52. See especially Heyrman, *Southern Cross*, 24–27; Boles, "Evangelical Protestantism," 32.
53. Wells, *Origins*, 69–75.
54. Landrum, *History of Spartanburg County*, 102–3.
55. Ford, *Origins of Southern Radicalism*, 26, 32–33; Boles, *Great Revival*, 1–3; Dupre, *Transforming the Cotton Frontier*, 154–56; *Carolina Spartan*, October 18, 1849, June 1, 1854.
56. Landrum, *History of Spartanburg County*, 88–90, 466–69; Griffith, *Life and Times*, 72.
57. Landrum, *History of Spartanburg County*, 91–95; entries of July 23, 1857, and May 13, 1858, Mary Davis Brown Papers, SCL; Sumter Tarrant to Robert Benson Tarrant, February 16, 1860, Robert Benson Tarrant Papers, SCL.
58. *Carolina Spartan*, September 15, 1853, March 30, 1854; Sessions Rolls, spring term, 1850, spring and fall terms, 1860, Spartanburg District Court of General Sessions, SCDAH.
59. *Carolina Spartan*, June 1, 1854.
60. South Carolina Credit Report Ledger no. 1, 563, and South Carolina Credit Report Ledger no. 13, 37, HBS; *Carolina Spartan*, September 15, 1853.
61. *Carolina Spartan*, August 3, 1854.
62. Ibid., September 21, 1854.
63. Ibid., October 12, 1854; Ayers, *Vengeance and Justice*, 58.

5. "WE HAVE NO UNION NOW"

1. On the wartime experiences of other upcountry areas of the South see Hahn, *Roots of Southern Populism*, 116–33; Harris, *Plain Folk*, 140–66; Escott, *After Secession*, 94–167.
2. Ford, *Origins of Southern Radicalism*, 341.
3. Schultz, *Nationalism*, 21–23.
4. *Carolina Spartan*, January 10, 1856; MacArthur, "Antebellum Politics," 64–66.
5. *Carolina Spartan*, August 13, 1857, August 27, 1857.
6. For an overview of the Kansas crisis see Potter, *Impending Crisis*, 199–224.
7. MacArthur, "Antebellum Politics," 67; *Carolina Spartan*, September 11, 1856.

8. Ford, *Origins of Southern Radicalism*, 348; *Carolina Spartan*, July 24, 1856.

9. *Carolina Spartan*, January 4, 1860; MacArthur, "Antebellum Politics," 70–71. It is my contention that Steven Channing (*Crisis of Fear*) overstates his case that all areas of South Carolina suffered from a "crisis of fear."

10. Schultz, *Nationalism*, 210–14; MacArthur, "Antebellum Politics," 71–72.

11. Schultz, *Nationalism*, 215–19; Cauthen, *South Carolina*, 20–24; *Carolina Spartan*, June 21, 1860, June 28, 1860.

12. On the secession crisis in the Upper South see Crofts, *Reluctant Confederates*.

13. Ford, *Origins of Southern Radicalism*, 338–73; McCurry, *Masters of Small Worlds*, 277–304; Channing, *Crisis of Fear*.

14. Sinha, *Counter-Revolution of Slavery*.

15. For examples see the *Carolina Spartan*, August 23, 1860, August 30, 1860, October 18, 1860; *Spartanburg Express*, August 29, 1860, September 12, 1860, October 3, 1860.

16. The other two legislators were Samuel McAliley of Chester and Andrew Wallace Thomson of Union (Moore, *Southern Homefront*, 202).

17. *Carolina Spartan*, November 22, 1860.

18. West, "From Yeoman to Redneck," 233–38; Cauthen, *South Carolina*, 45–47; MacArthur, "Antebellum Politics," 76.

19. West, "From Yeoman to Redneck," 237; *Carolina Spartan*, September 27, 1860.

20. *Carolina Spartan*, October 18, 1860; *Spartanburg Express*, December 12, 1860; MacArthur, "Antebellum Politics," 79.

21. *Carolina Spartan*, November 29, 1860; Cauthen, *South Carolina*, 70; Racine, ed., *Piedmont Farmer*, 168.

22. Byrne, *Becoming Bourgeois*, 123, 129–31.

23. William Gregg to P. Whitin & Sons, April 18, 1861, May 17, 1861, P. Whitin and Sons Papers, SCL.

24. Barney, *Road to Secession*, 205.

25. Racine, ed., *Piedmont Farmer*, 173–74, 179.

26. Landrum, *History of Spartanburg County*, 524, 528. Jonathan M. Bryant finds the same affirmation of power in the military companies of Greene County, Georgia (*How Curious a Land*, 84).

27. Diary entry of August 24, 1861, James F. Sloan Papers and Diaries, SCL; John Carson to father, March 25, 1862, Carson Family Papers, SCL.

28. See Minutes of the Spartanburg, South Carolina, Methodist Sunday School Relief Society, Thomas Dillard Johnston Papers, SHC; Towles, ed., *World Turned Upside Down*, 309, 320; *Carolina Spartan*, October 10, 1861.

29. September 23, 1861, Ladies Relief Association, Spartanburg, SCL. Byrne also finds that many women in merchant families formed institutions in support of the Confederacy (*Becoming Bourgeois*, 132–33).

30. Racine, ed., *Piedmont Farmer*, 213.

31. Cauthen, *South Carolina*, 193.

32. Diary entries of July 23, July 28, July 30, 1862, and January 3, 1863, William C. Anderson Papers, SCL.

33. *Charleston Daily Courier*, December 6, 1862.

34. *Statutes at Large of South Carolina*, 13:16–17; Racine, ed., *Piedmont Farmer*, 225.

35. On speculation in the Confederacy see Escott, *After Secession*, 122–25; Massey, *Ersatz*, 17–20.

36. Eliphus Smith to his mother, October 9, 1861, Elihu P. Smith Papers, SCL.

37. Andrew Charles Moore to his mother, February 15, 1862, Thomas John Moore Papers, SCL.

38. Thomas John Moore to Thomas Hill, April 9, 1863, Thomas John Moore Papers, SCL; S. C. Means to George Larsen, August 16, 1863, George Larsen Papers, SCL.

39. Captain J. J. Legare to Brigadier General Thomas Jordan, October 30, 1862, J. J. Legare Folder, SCL; *Carolina Spartan*, January 23, 1863; South Carolina Credit Report Ledger no. 13, 12, HBS.

40. *Carolina Spartan*, November 24, 1864; Elizabeth Lipscomb to her sister, October 23, 1863, Lipscomb Family Papers, SHC; Racine, ed., *Piedmont Farmer*, 224–25.

41. Captain J. J. Legare to Brigadier General Thomas Jordan, October 30, 1862, J. J. Legare Folder, SCL; Petition of Greenville Citizens to Governor Pickens, February 10, 1863, Pickens-Bonham Papers, LC.

42. Escott, *After Secession*, 59–61.

43. Chad Morgan, *Planter's Progress*, 47; DeCredico, *Patriotism for Profit*, 70.

44. *Carolina Spartan*, January 23, 1863.

45. John Bomar to "Dear Sir," April 12, 1865, SCL.

46. Black, *Railroads of the Confederacy*, 84.

47. Nelson, *Iron Confederacies*, 37–45.

48. Escott, *After Secession*, 68–69; Tax-in-Kind Account Books of A. H. Kirby, 1863–65, Kirby Family Papers, DU.

49. Racine, ed., *Piedmont Farmer*, 308, 326.

50. *Acts of the General Assembly of the State of South Carolina Passed in December, 1862 and February and April, 1863*, 109. On planter preference to pay the fine see Governor Bonham's message to the general assembly in *Journal of the House of Representatives of South Carolina Being the Sessions of 1863*, 7–10.

51. *Charleston Daily Courier*, December 6, 1862.

52. Racine, ed., *Piedmont Farmer*, 252; James F. Sloan to his wife, June 22, 1862, James F. Sloan Papers and Diaries, SCL.

53. In August 1863 conscription officer C. D. Melton informed his superior that "letters are written from home giving deplorable pictures of the destitution of families." See U.S. Department of War, *War of the Rebellion*, ser. 4, 2:770.

54. Moore, *Southern Homefront*, 123, 125–26; U.S. Department of War, *War of the Rebellion*, ser. 4, 2:741, 769–74.

55. Racine, ed., *Piedmont Farmer*, 269; Captain James F. Sloan to Major Joel Ballenger, March 1865, James F. Sloan Papers and Diaries, SCL.

56. Thomas John Moore to Mrs. Ann Means, November 19, 1862, and Thomas John Moore to Thomas Hill, April 29, 1863, Thomas John Moore Papers, SCL.

57. Moore, *Southern Homefront*, 218.

58. Racine, ed., *Piedmont Farmer*, 240, 248, 326.

59. Racine, "Spartanburg District Magistrates and Freeholders Court," 203–4; Index of Cases, 1861–65, Magistrates and Freeholders Court, SCDAH.

60. Racine, ed., *Piedmont Farmer*, 360.

61. Reports of Free School Commissioners, Spartanburg District, 1860, 1862, 1864, Department of Education Files, SCDAH.

62. Entry of September 5, 1862, Margaret Ann (Meta) Morris Grimball Diary, SHC.

63. *Carolina Spartan*, October 20, 1864, January 9, 1862; William Kennedy Blake Reminiscences, 76, typescript, SHC.

64. Racine, ed., *Piedmont Farmer*, 223, 225, 251.

65. Ibid., 369; entry of April 30, 1865, J. B. Grimball Diary, Grimball Family Papers, SHC; diary entry of April 30, 1865, William C. Anderson Papers, SCL; William Kennedy Blake Reminiscences, 86, SHC.

66. Racine, ed., *Piedmont Farmer*, 371.

6. "TO PAY OUR DEBTS AND BUILD UP OUR FALLEN FORTUNES"

1. Racine, ed., *Piedmont Farmer*, 452.

2. An important overview of the operations of the postbellum credit system in the South Carolina upcountry is Ford, "Rednecks and Merchants," 294–318. For an examination of credit throughout the postwar South see Woodman, *King Cotton*, 254–333, *New South—New Law*, and "Post–Civil War Agriculture," 319–37.

3. U.S. Bureau of the Census, *Statistics*, 312; U.S. Bureau of the Census, *Ninth Census*, 56.

4. U.S. Bureau of the Census, *Agriculture*, 128–31; U.S. Bureau of the Census, *Ninth Census*, 238–41, 362.

5. Grigsby, "Breaking the Bonds," 16; U.S. Bureau of the Census, *Population*, 448–49.

6. Ann E. Walker to Beck, April 24, 1869, Rebecca Easterling Papers, SCL; Lewis Grimball to his father, August 23, 1871, Grimball Family Papers, SHC.

7. Manuscript Census Returns, Population Schedules, Spartanburg District and County, 1860 and 1870, NA; *Carolina Spartan*, May 19, 1867; South Carolina Credit Report Ledger no. 13, 5, HBS.

8. Abstracts of Judgements, Court of Common Pleas, SCDAH; Manuscript Cen-

sus Returns, Population Schedule, Spartanburg District and County, 1870, NA; Landrum, *History of Spartanburg County*, 177, 483–84.

9. *Carolina Spartan*, August 9, 1866. On the National Union movement and convention see Carter, *When the War Was Over*, 237–53.

10. *Carolina Spartan*, June 7, 1866.

11. Ibid., July 5, 1866, May 31, 1866.

12. *State v. Carew*, 47 S.C.L. (13 Rich.) 498–99 (1866); *Carolina Spartan*, May 31, 1866, June 14, 1866.

13. *Carolina Spartan*, September 27, 1866.

14. Racine, ed., *Piedmont Farmer*, 414; *Carolina Spartan*, January 17, 1867, March 14, 1867, April 11, 1867; Abstracts of Judgements, Court of Common Pleas, SCDAH.

15. Simkins and Woody, *South Carolina during Reconstruction*, 46–47; *Carolina Spartan*, April 25, 1867.

16. *Statutes at Large of South Carolina*, art. 2, sec. 32, 14:11; *Proceedings of the Constitutional Convention of South Carolina*, 1:888–89; *Carolina Spartan*, August 20, 1868.

17. Speech to the Democratic Club of Limestone Springs on the Current State of Government, August 1, 1868, J. Banks Lyle Papers, SCL.

18. *Carolina Spartan*, December 2, 1869, April 7, 1870; Abstract of Judgements, Court of Common Pleas, SCDAH.

19. *Carolina Spartan*, November 29, 1866.

20. *Statutes at Large of South Carolina*, 13:462.

21. Somers, *Southern States*, 57; Simkins and Woody, *South Carolina during Reconstruction*, 272.

22. *Spartanburg Herald*, May 12, 1875. The house vote on the motion to strike the enacting words of the first usury bill was sixty yeas to thirty-four nays (*Journal of the House of Representatives of South Carolina, 1874–1875*, 377–78). The vote on the 1876 usury bill was thirty-nine yeas to forty-eight nays (*Journal of the House of Representatives of South Carolina, 1875–1876*, 641; *Carolina Spartan*, February 2, 1876).

23. Landrum, *History of Spartanburg County*, 270, 327; Manuscript Census Returns, Population Schedule, Spartanburg District and County, 1870, NA; South Carolina State Agricultural Census for 1868 and Manuscript Census Returns, 1880, Agricultural Schedule, Spartanburg County, SCDAH.

24. For a discussion of the crop-lien law's operation in the South Carolina upcountry see Ford, "Rednecks and Merchants," 307–11; West, "From Yeoman to Redneck," 271–72. An overview of the crop-lien system throughout the South is contained in Woodman, "Post–Civil War Agriculture," 319–37.

25. *Carolina Spartan*, December 13, 1866.

26. On the role of the postbellum southern merchant see Ronald L. F. Davis, "Southern Merchant," 131–41; Woodman, *King Cotton*, 295–314; Hahn, *Roots of Southern Populism*, 170–203; Clark, *Pills, Petticoats, and Plows*.

27. The cotton-to-corn ratio, a standard method used by historians to indicate self-sufficiency and the importance of the staple crop in a given region, is calculated by dividing pounds of cotton by bushels of corn. See Ford, *Origins of Southern Radicalism*, 251; "Exhibit G—Aggregate of Crops Produced, and Other Statistics—Census of 1875," in *Reports and Resolutions of the General Assembly of the State of South Carolina at the Regular Session of 1876*.

28. See chapter 7 for an extended discussion of railroad development in postwar Spartanburg.

29. M. W. Goforth to Edward Lipscomb, March 15, 1874, Lipscomb Family Papers, SHC.

30. *Carolina Spartan*, February 21, 1867, March 14, 1867, April 18, 1867, March 28, 1867.

31. The best exposition of the argument for a new business class in the postbellum South is Woodward, *Origins*. Ford suggests the persistence of many antebellum merchants in "Labor and Ideology," 33.

32. South Carolina Credit Report Ledger no. 13, 8–9, 6, 59, HBS; *Carolina Spartan*, November 26, 1868.

33. South Carolina Credit Report Ledger no. 13, 6, 28, 28k, 32, HBS.

34. Examples can be found in the *Carolina Spartan*, July 12, 1866, September 13, 1866, January 17, 1867, March 4, 1869.

35. Spartanburg Business Directory for 1880 in *Spartanburg and Greenville Directories, 1880–1881*, 68, 97–98.

36. South Carolina Credit Report Ledger no. 13, 32, HBS.

37. Ibid., 28v, 51.

38. Ibid., 5.

39. On hostility to trading arrangements between merchants and freedmen see Joel Williamson, *After Slavery*, 174.

40. Some examples of the now-voluminous literature on the postwar transition from slavery to free labor include Saville, *Work of Reconstruction*; Reidy, *From Slavery to Agrarian Capitalism*; Foner, *Nothing but Freedom*; Berlin et al., *Slaves No More*.

41. Racine, ed., *Piedmont Farmer*, 396, 401. In 1866 traveler Sidney Andrews found many freedmen in the upcountry who were "anxious to become landholders" (*South since the War*, 221–22).

42. "Terms of Agreement between John R. Jefferies and Joseph Freedman and Amanda, his Wife," Jefferies Family Papers, SCL.

43. In his study of black majority Greene County, Georgia, for example, Jonathan M. Bryant finds that black workers created a labor shortage by "holding out for sharecropping and tenancy arrangements" (*How Curious a Land*, 151).

44. Entries of October 17, 1866, and December 4, 1866, Register of Complaints, Subassistant Commissioner at Unionville, South Carolina, BRFAL, NA.

45. Entries of July 10, 1866, July 24, 1866, November 16, 1866, and November

19, 1866, Register of Complaints, Subassistant Commissioner at Unionville, South Carolina, BRFAL, NA.

46. *Carolina Spartan*, January 24, 1867.

47. Saville, *Work of Reconstruction*, 126; Racine, ed., *Piedmont Farmer*, 452, 462, 483; "Terms of Agreement between Permilia A. Duncan on one part and Thomas Cornelius and his family Harriet, Allison & Sally," Jefferies Family Papers, SCL.

48. Ford, "Labor and Ideology," 31.

49. Fall term, 1869, Grand Jury Presentment, Court of General Sessions, SCDAH; *Carolina Spartan*, August 26, 1869.

50. Simkins and Woody, *South Carolina during Reconstruction*, 152–55. For a concise example of revenue problems in the postbellum South see Wallenstein, *From Slave South*, 183–95.

51. On the taxpayers' convention see Norton, "South Carolina Taxpayers' Convention"; Grigsby, "Breaking the Bonds," 68; Simkins and Woody, *South Carolina during Reconstruction*, 179; Reynolds, *Reconstruction in South Carolina in South Carolina*, 162–70. Quote from the convention report is in Ford, "One Southern Profile," 125.

52. Simkins and Woody, *South Carolina during Reconstruction*, 177–79.

53. Edward Lipscomb to Smith and Sallie Lipscomb, April 11, 1871, Lipscomb Family Papers, SHC; *Carolina Spartan*, October 30, 1873.

54. Reynolds, *Reconstruction in South Carolina*, 245; Perman, *Road to Redemption*, 166.

55. Reynolds, *Reconstruction in South Carolina*, 246; *Carolina Spartan*, February 26, 1874, April 9, 1874.

56. *Carolina Spartan*, November 8, 1866, September 20, 1866; Grigsby, "Breaking the Bonds," 19–20.

57. See *Journal of the House of Representatives of South Carolina, 1873–1874*, 139, and *Journal of the House of Representatives of South Carolina, 1874–1875*, 170, 238.

58. *Carolina Spartan*, January 6, 1875, January 27, 1875, April 7, 1875.

59. On the Grange movement see Easterby, "Granger Movement," 21–32; Chapman, "Historical Development."

60. *Carolina Spartan*, March 13, 1873, May 15, 1873, August 28, 1873; Thomas John Moore to Mary, November 13, 1873, Thomas John Moore Papers, SCL. In his study of upcountry Georgia Hahn points out that the planters and wealthier farmers in the Grange cooperated with town professionals and merchants rather than offering a challenge to commercial modernization (*Roots of Southern Populism*, 222–24).

61. *Carolina Spartan*, January 30, 1873, April 24, 1873.

62. U.S. Bureau of the Census, *Seventh Census*, 346–47; U.S. Bureau of the Census, *Agriculture*, 128–31.

63. U.S. Bureau of the Census, *Ninth Census*, 239; Somers, *Southern States*, 57; "Exhibit G—Aggregate of Crops Produced."

64. *Carolina Spartan*, February 17, 1875, July 23, 1879, April 14, 1875.
65. Ibid., September 29, 1875.
66. Ibid., September 1, 1875, August 4, 1875; *Yorkville Enquirer*, May 26, 1875.
67. *Carolina Spartan*, February 16, 1876, February 23, 1876.
68. Reidy, *From Slavery to Agrarian Capitalism*, 181; Hahn, "Common Right and Commonwealth," 51–88, "Hunting, Fishing, and Foraging," 37–64, and *Roots of Southern Populism*, 239–68; Kantor and Kousser, "Common Sense or Commonwealth?" 201–42; Hahn, "Response," 243–58; Kantor and Kousser, "Rejoinder," 259–66; Kantor, *Politics and Property Rights*.
69. *Carolina Spartan*, February 5, 1879, December 17, 1879, June 25, 1879; *Spartanburg Herald*, December 17, 1879.
70. *Statutes at Large of South Carolina*, 17:100–101; *Spartanburg Herald*, December 24, 1879; *Statutes at Large of South Carolina*, 17:335–36; South Carolina Department of Agriculture, *South Carolina*, 153.
71. *Carolina Spartan*, February 19, 1879; Kantor, *Politics and Property Rights*, 2–3; South Carolina Department of Agriculture, *South Carolina*, 150; *South Carolina in 1884*, n.p.
72. *Carolina Spartan*, February 3, 1875, June 9, 1875; Cooper, *Conservative Regime*, 136–39; *South Carolina in 1884*, n.p.
73. *Spartanburg Herald*, January 10, 1877.
74. South Carolina Department of Agriculture, *South Carolina*, 153; Writers' Program, *History*, 185.
75. Tindall, *South Carolina Negroes*, 104; *South Carolina in 1884*, n.p.
76. U.S. Bureau of the Census, *Tenth Census*, 126–27.
77. Manuscript Census Returns, Population Schedule, Spartanburg District and County, 1870, NA.
78. South Carolina Credit Report Ledger no. 13, 22, HBS.

7. "A GREAT COMMERCIAL AND RAILROAD CENTRE"

1. *Carolina Spartan*, September 11, 1873.
2. Gavin Wright, *Old South, New South*, 17.
3. Stover, *Railroads of the South*, 40–43; Trowbridge, *Desolate South*, 295–96; *Carolina Spartan*, September 9, 1866.
4. Summers, *Railroads*, 5, 9.
5. *Statutes at Large of South Carolina*, 13:292; *Carolina Spartan*, September 20, 1866.
6. Summers, *Railroads*, 7.
7. *Carolina Spartan*, September 3, 1868.
8. Ibid., June 4, 1868, June 11, 1868.
9. Summers, *Railroads*, 9; Simkins and Woody, *South Carolina during Reconstruction*, 211.

10. *Carolina Spartan*, September 2, 1869; see also Representative Randolph Turner's address in ibid., October 22, 1868.
11. Summers, *Railroads*, 44, 89.
12. Ibid., 45, 103, 179.
13. *Carolina Spartan*, September 2, 1869, December 2, 1869.
14. Ibid., May 19, 1870.
15. Alfred Austell to A. S. Buford, February 7, 1872, Atlanta and Richmond Air-Line Railway Company Letterbook, DU.
16. Stover, *Railroads of the South*, 99–121; Poor, *Railroad Manual of the United States, 1875–1876*, 435–36.
17. Poor, *Railroad Manual of the United States, 1873–1874*, 374.
18. *Carolina Spartan*, June 2, 1870, June 9, 1870, June 23, 1870, June 30, 1870.
19. Gabriel Cannon to A. S. Buford, October 27, 1871, Alfred Austell to A. S. Buford, February 7, 1872, Atlanta and Richmond Air-Line Railway Company Letterbook, DU.
20. *Carolina Spartan*, February 6, 1873, March 27, 1873, April 3, 1873.
21. Ibid.
22. Ibid., April 17, 1873.
23. Poor, *Railroad Manual of the United States, 1873–1874*, 374–74; Poor, *Railroad Manual of the United States, 1875–1876*, 435–36; Poor, *Railroad Manual of the United States, 1877–1878*, 580–81; Poor, *Railroad Manual of the United States, 1882*, 420–21.
24. In 1872 the Greenville and Columbia, under foreclosure and bankruptcy proceedings, was sold to the South Carolina Railroad. In the same year Blue Ridge officials bribed the legislature to pass an act allowing the state to replace its bond guarantee with $1.8 million in certificates of indebtedness known as revenue bond scrip. Reformers in the government lashed out at the act as corrupt and unconstitutional, since neither the state nor the federal government was permitted to issue bills of credit. With the state supreme court behind him, the state auditor sued to keep Blue Ridge scrip out of circulation, and the scrip was ruled illegal in April 1873. That same month the Blue Ridge declared bankruptcy. See Summers, *Railroads*, 242–44; Simkins and Woody, *South Carolina during Reconstruction*, 216–21, 261.
25. *Statutes at Large of South Carolina*, 15:346–49.
26. *Carolina Spartan*, June 26, 1873.
27. *Charleston News & Courier*, July 3, 1873; *Carolina Spartan*, July 17, 1873.
28. Thomas John Moore to his wife, December 14, 1873, Thomas John Moore Papers, SCL.
29. *Charters*, 13–14, 16.
30. *Charleston News & Courier*, March 5, 1874.
31. *Carolina Spartan*, September 17, 1874, July 3, 1873.
32. Ibid., May 12, 1875.
33. Voting results taken from ibid., June 9, 1875.

34. Poor, *Railroad Manual of the United States, 1875–1876*, 337; Poor, *Railroad Manual of the United States, 1877–1878*, 580–81; Poor, *Railroad Manual of the United States, 1881*, 393–94; Poor, *Railroad Manual of the United States, 1882*, 420–21.

35. Summers makes a similar point about the shift from community-based to consolidated railroad enterprises in *Railroads*, 179–80.

36. *Carolina Spartan*, August 6, 1874; J. B. Davis quoted in Ford, "Rednecks and Merchants," 314.

37. Cooper, *Conservative Regime*, 127.

38. Ibid., 128–29.

39. *Carolina Spartan*, October 16, 1873, October 22, 1873, November 18, 1873, August 13, 1874; Carlton, *Mill and Town*, 53–54; South Carolina Credit Report Ledger no. 13, 28b6, HBS.

40. *Statutes at Large of South Carolina*, 14:539–43; *Carolina Spartan*, March 8, 1876, June 28, 1876, November 29, 1876.

41. *Charleston News & Courier*, July 28, 1890; *Historical and Descriptive Review of the State of South Carolina*, 2:149–50; William Curtis to A. S. Buford, December 21, 1871, William Curtis to A. S. Buford, May 22, 1872, Atlanta and Richmond Air-Line Railway Company Letterbook, DU; *Carolina Spartan*, April 7, 1875. For excellent discussions of postbellum town development in upcountry South Carolina see Carlton, *Mill and Town*, 13–39, and Ford, "Rednecks and Merchants," 311–12.

42. *Carolina Spartan*, May 17, 1876; Orphelia Dawkins to sister Mary, May 9, 1876, Dawkins and Henry Family Papers, DU.

43. McKissick, "The Story of Spartan Push," SCL; *Historical and Descriptive Review of the State of South Carolina*, 2:149–50; Ford, "Rednecks and Merchants," 311–12. For an excellent discussion of postbellum town development in upcountry South Carolina see Carlton, *Mill and Town*, 13–39.

44. *Carolina Spartan*, July 31, 1873.

45. Gustauvus Galloway Williamson Jr., "Cotton Manufacturing," i, 51; Simkins and Woody, *South Carolina during Reconstruction*, 21, 300–301; *Carolina Spartan*, February 2, 1871.

46. For a good overview of the rhetoric supporting industrialization in the postwar South see Gaston, *New South Creed*, esp. 15–42; *DeBow's Review*, March 3, 1867, 174–76; Summers, *Railroads*, 5–6.

47. *Carolina Spartan*, February 2, 1871; Mary Dawkins to sister, October 7, 1876, Dawkins and Henry Family Papers, DU.

48. Manuscript Census Returns, 1870, Manufacturing Schedule, Spartanburg County, SCDAH; Simkins and Woody, *South Carolina during Reconstruction*, 292–93; Manuscript Census Returns, 1880, Manufacturing Schedule, Spartanburg County, SCDAH.

49. *Historical and Descriptive Review of the State of South Carolina*, 2:187; Manuscript Census Returns, 1880, Manufacturing Schedule, Spartanburg County, SCDAH.

50. *Carolina Spartan*, January 9, 1873, April 24, 1873; Manuscript Census Returns, 1880, Manufacturing Schedule, Spartanburg County, SCDAH.

51. South Carolina Credit Report Ledger no. 13, 7, 9, 18, HBS. Competition from northern iron foundries so undermined South Carolina's firms that not a single foundry was in operation statewide by 1880.

52. Gustauvus Galloway Williamson Jr., "Cotton Manufacturing," i, 51; Simkins and Woody, *South Carolina during Reconstruction*, 21, 300–301; *Carolina Spartan*, February 2, 1871.

53. Simkins and Woody, *South Carolina during Reconstruction*, 299; Manuscript Census Returns, 1870, Manufacturing Schedule, Spartanburg County, SCDAH.

54. *Carolina Spartan*, February 20, 1873, March 6, 1873, March 13, 1873; Stokes, "Black and White Labor," 151.

55. Simkins and Woody, *South Carolina during Reconstruction*, 291–92, 299; Manuscript Census Returns, 1870, Manufacturing Schedule, Spartanburg County, SCDAH; South Carolina Department of Agriculture, *South Carolina*, 582.

56. Carlton finds similar backgrounds for New South industrialists in his work (*Mill and Town*, 49–57).

57. *Carolina Spartan*, April 19, 1876; South Carolina Credit Report Ledger no. 13, 68, HBS.

58. Stokes, "John H. Montgomery," 15–20, 35–38.

59. Gustauvus Galloway Williamson Jr., "Cotton Manufacturing," 52–53; *Carolina Spartan*, June 30, 1875.

60. *Carolina Spartan*, April 28, 1875. Throughout the 1870s William Gregg's Graniteville factory had continued to set the example of the perfect manufacturing community and most likely influenced Converse's plans at Bivingsville. See an account of Graniteville's operations in the *Augusta Constitutionalist*, May 10, 1876.

61. Gustauvus Galloway Williamson Jr., "Cotton Manufacturing," 73; South Carolina Credit Report Ledger no. 13, 116, HBS; South Carolina Department of Agriculture, *South Carolina*, 582. By 1890 there were sixteen factories in Spartanburg, and the county reached its zenith in textile production, with thirty mills in the mid-1920s. See *Charleston News & Courier*, July 28, 1890; Waldrep, "Politics," 9.

62. *Carolina Spartan*, September 8, 1875; Lalla Pelot to Robert, July 18, 1876, Lalla Pelot Papers, DU; *Carolina Spartan*, April 12, 1876.

63. South Carolina Credit Report Ledger no. 13, 58, HBS.

64. Lalla Pelot to Robert, July 18, 1876, Lalla Pelot Papers, DU.

65. Racine, ed., *Piedmont Farmer*, 411, 413; Saville, *Work of Reconstruction*, 126. The importance of the textile factory as a white domain continued through the end of the nineteenth century and well into the twentieth century. In 1899, for example, Spartanburg industrialist John Montgomery was forced to abandon a proposal to revive a Charleston cotton mill with black labor when he got wind of a potential

uprising from white operatives in the upcountry (Gustauvus Galloway Williamson Jr., "Cotton Manufacturing," 178).

66. Stokes, "Black and White Labor," 9–10, 158; U.S. Bureau of the Census, *Compendium of the Ninth Census*, 839; John F. Dyar to Dexter Converse, January 17, 1880, Clifton Manufacturing Company Records, SCL.

67. Gustauvus Galloway Williamson Jr., "Cotton Manufacturing," 187.

68. Ford, "Rednecks and Merchants," 314; Gustauvus Galloway Williamson Jr., "Cotton Manufacturing," 200–202.

69. Bailey, Morgan, and Taylor, *Biographical Directory*, 1:154–55; *South Carolina in 1884*, n.p.

70. Gustauvus Galloway Williamson Jr., "Cotton Manufacturing," 202; Bailey, Morgan, and Taylor, *Biographical Directory*, 3:1758–59.

71. On the central role of immigrants in late-nineteenth-century working-class resistance see Gutman, *Work*, 3–78.

8. "EDUCATE YOUR SONS, THEY WILL BUILD RESERVOIRS AND RAILROADS"

1. See, for example, Stampp, *Era of Reconstruction*, 183; Foner, *Reconstruction*, 602.

2. See Rose, *Rehearsal for Reconstruction*, 85–89, 229–35; Vaughn, *Schools for All*; Small, "Yankee Schoolmarm"; Butchart, *Northern Schools*; Robert C. Morris, *Reading, 'Riting, and Reconstruction*; Jacqueline Jones, *Soldiers of Light*; Wyatt-Brown, "Black Schooling during Reconstruction," 146–65; James D. Anderson, *Education*.

3. Lewis P. Jones, "History," 19.

4. *Carolina Spartan*, December 20, 1866, March 1, 1866, April 26, 1866.

5. Ibid., April 26, 1866.

6. Assistant Superintendent F. G. Wright to Superintendent Reuben H. Tomlinson, October 17, 1866, Correspondence of Reuben H. Tomlinson, Department of Education Files, SCDAH.

7. Bullock, *History of Negro Education*, 47–49.

8. *Proceedings of the Constitutional Convention of South Carolina*, 683–709.

9. Ibid., 890–94, 901–2. Foner notes that the issue of school integration caused highly charged debates in all of the state conventions of 1868 (*Reconstruction*, 139).

10. Underwood, *Constitution of South Carolina*, 47.

11. *Carolina Spartan*, April 9, 1868.

12. Vaughn, *Schools for All*, 67–68.

13. Knight, *Influence*, 86; Second Annual Report of the State Superintendent of Education, in *Reports and Resolutions of the General Assembly of the State of South Carolina for 1869*, 403–4; Knight, *Influence*, 75–76; Second Annual Report of the State Superintendent of Education, in *Reports and Resolutions of the General Assembly of the State of South Carolina 1869*, 457–61; Eighth Annual Report of the State

Superintendent of Education, in *Reports and Resolutions of the General Assembly of the State of South Carolina for 1875*, 435.

14. *Journal of the Senate of South Carolina, 1869*, 132; Report of Free Schools in Spartanburg County, June 1869, Department of Education Files, SCDAH; R. H. Reid to Justus K. Jillson, June 12, 1869, Correspondence of Justus K. Jillson, Department of Education Files, SCDAH.

15. Report of Free Schools in Spartanburg County, September 1869, Department of Education Files, SCDAH; *Journal of the Senate of South Carolina, 1869*, 132; Eva Poole to Justus K. Jillson, November 6, 1869, Correspondence of Justus K. Jillson, Department of Education Files, SCDAH. Black students may not have found the school overcrowding as difficult as the teachers did. From a pedagogical standpoint, Wyatt-Brown notes that freedmen preferred group learning because it was more amenable to oral tradition than individualistic learning ("Black Schooling during Reconstruction," 147, 152–54).

16. Report of Free Schools for Spartanburg County, January–December, 1870, Department of Education Files, SCDAH.

17. Spartanburg County Commissioner's Report in the Annual Report of the State Superintendent of Education, in *Reports and Resolutions of the General Assembly of the State of South Carolina, 1869*, 482–85.

18. *Reports and Resolutions of the General Assembly of the State of South Carolina for the Year 1870*, 370–73.

19. *Carolina Spartan*, February 2, 1871.

20. Ibid., September 4, 1873; Vaughn, *Schools for All*, 68–69. The quote from Jillson's letter to the governing board of the Cedar Springs institution is in Thompson, *Establishment*, 14.

21. *Carolina Spartan*, June 7, 1876, June 18, 1874; Vaughn, *Schools for All*, 124–38.

22. Nelson, *Iron Confederacies*, 137.

23. A. W. Cummings to Superintendent Justus K. Jillson, August 30, 1871, Correspondence of Justus K. Jillson, Department of Education Files, SCDAH; Daniel H. Chamberlain to Governor Robert K. Scott, October 24, 1871, Governor Robert K. Scott Papers, SCDAH.

24. James D. Anderson, *Education*, 12.

25. Ibid., 30, 4.

26. *Carolina Spartan*, July 30, 1874; *Spartanburg Herald*, May 12, 1875.

27. *Carolina Spartan*, February 2, 1876.

28. *Reports and Resolutions of the General Assembly of the State of South Carolina for the Year 1874*, 388; *Reports and Resolutions of the General Assembly of the State of South Carolina for the Year 1869*, 482–85.

29. *Reports and Resolutions of the General Assembly of the State of South Carolina for the Year 1875*, 424; *Journal of the House of Representatives of the State of South Carolina Being the Session 1873–1874*, 382–83.

30. *Reports and Resolutions of the General Assembly of the State of South Carolina for the Year 1875*, 434–41; *Journal of the House of Representatives of the State of South Carolina Being the Session 1872–1873*, 63–64; R. H. Reid to Superintendent Jillson, July 4, 1872, Correspondence of Justus K. Jillson, Department of Education Files, SCDAH.

31. *Carolina Spartan*, March 17, 1875, June 28, 1876; Board of Trustees of School District No. 1 Record Books, June 17, 1876, SCDAH.

32. *Journal of the House of Representatives of the State of South Carolina Being the Session 1871–1872*, 471; *Reports and Resolutions of the General Assembly of the State of South Carolina for the Year 1875*, 441; *Carolina Spartan*, June 7, 1876, June 28, 1876.

33. *Reports and Resolutions of the General Assembly of the State of South Carolina for the Year 1870*, 370–73; *Reports and Resolutions of the General Assembly of the State of South Carolina for the Year 1875*, 454–57.

34. Vaughn, *Schools for All*, 158. Although there are no accurate measures for attendance in 1877, fewer than half of blacks between six and sixteen did not attend school in 1875, and finances were only constrained further over the next two years. Thus, it is reasonable to conclude that fewer than half of school-age blacks attended school.

35. *Carolina Spartan*, September 8, 1875, September 23, 1873, January 9, 1873.

36. Racine, ed., *Piedmont Farmer*, 412–13, 458.

37. *Carolina Spartan*, September 29, 1875, October 13, 1875.

38. "Address of the Educational Mass Meeting of the Colored Citizens of Spartanburg to the Friends of Popular Education" and undated clipping from the *Carolina Spartan* in box 5, folder 11, Governor Wade Hampton Papers, SCDAH.

39. Vaughn, *Schools for All*, 141–59.

40. Ibid.

41. Board of Trustees of School District No. 1 Record Books, 1877–81, SCDAH.

42. For a general overview of the Democratic policy of retrenchment in the South see Woodward, *Origins*, esp. 58–61.

43. *Reports and Resolutions of the General Assembly of the State of South Carolina for the Year 1877*, 375–76, 427.

44. Ibid., 385–86; *Reports and Resolutions of the General Assembly of the State of South Carolina for the Year 1878*, 320; Thompson, *Establishment*, 22–23.

45. Thompson, *Establishment*, 21–22.

46. "Table No. 1—Free School Funds, Fiscal Year Ending October 31, 1878," in Tenth Annual Report of the State Superintendent of Education, *Reports and Resolutions of the General Assembly of the State of South Carolina for the Year 1878*; Board of Trustees of School District No. 1 Record Books, March 3, 1879, July 10, 1880, SCDAH.

47. *Reports and Resolutions of the General Assembly of the State of South Carolina for the Year 1878*, 334.

48. *Cyclopedia*, 677–78; Dibble, *Duty of the State*, 3–4.
49. Dibble, *Duty of the State*, 4, 9.
50. Ibid., 5.
51. *Carolina Spartan*, January 29, 1879.
52. Ibid., September 29, 1880.
53. *Historical and Descriptive Review*, 2:150; Leloudis, *Schooling the New South*, 20–22.
54. Carlton, *Mill and Town*, 36–37.
55. Deed of February 10, 1881, Richard Scruggs Papers, DU; Carlton, *Mill and Town*, 38.
56. For an extended discussion of schooling at post-Reconstruction mills in South Carolina see Carlton, *Mill and Town*, 91–103.
57. *Carolina Spartan*, June 28, 1882, March 12, 1884; Carlton, *Mill and Town*, 97.
58. *Reports and Resolutions of the General Assembly of the State of South Carolina for the Year 1880*, 371; *Carolina Spartan*, January 12, 1881; *Reports and Resolutions of the State of South Carolina at Regular Session Commencing November 24, 1885*, 1:810–11.
59. *Reports and Resolutions of the General Assembly of the State of South Carolina for the Year 1878*, 323.
60. *Reports and Resolutions of the General Assembly of the State of South Carolina for the Year 1880*, 303–32, 339.

9. "THE TIMELY AND JUDICIOUS ADMINISTRATION OF THE LAWS"

1. *Carolina Spartan*, April 12, 1866.
2. See chapter 4 on antebellum traditions of vigilantism and Ayers, *Vengeance and Justice*, 155.
3. Racine, ed., *Piedmont Farmer*, 374; William Kennedy Blake Reminiscences, typescript copy, 80, SHC; Herd, *South Carolina Upcountry*, 387–443; Croushore and Potter, eds., *Union Officer*, 14. Lawlessness was prevalent throughout the South during the summer of 1865. See Carter, *When the War Was Over*, 10–13; *Carolina Spartan*, March 1, 1866.
4. *Carolina Spartan*, March 1, 1866.
5. Lewis Grimball to his father, September 14, 1866, Grimball Family Papers, SHC; Grigsby, "Breaking the Bonds," 24–25; *Carolina Spartan*, January 17, 1867.
6. Reynolds, *Reconstruction in South Carolina*, 16; Simkins and Woody, *South Carolina during Reconstruction*, 37–43.
7. *Statutes at Large of South Carolina*, 13:254–85; Joel Williamson, *After Slavery*, 327–28.
8. *Carolina Spartan*, February 7, 1867.
9. Ibid., November 8, 1866, April 4, 1867, April 11, 1867. On the operation of

the military provost courts in South Carolina see Thomas D. Morris, "Equality," 15–33.

10. Racine, ed., *Piedmont Farmer*, 397.

11. On the Freedmen's Bureau's activities in South Carolina see Abbott, *Freedman's Bureau*.

12. A. P. Caraher, Subassistant Commissioner at Unionville, to Assistant Commissioner Robert K. Scott, April 16, 1867, M869, reel 5, Register of Letters Received, Records of the South Carolina Assistant Commissioner, BRFAL, NA; Ayers, *Vengeance and Justice*, 155.

13. Simkins and Woody, *South Carolina during Reconstruction*, 64–89; Grigsby, "Breaking the Bonds," 28–29.

14. Reynolds, *Reconstruction in South Carolina*, 78; Edward Lipscomb to Smith Lipscomb, June 5, 1868, Lipscomb Family Papers, SHC.

15. Grigsby, "Breaking the Bonds," 32–34; Landrum, *History of Spartanburg County*, 210; Manuscript Census Returns, Population Schedule, Spartanburg District and County, 1870, NA; Bailey, Morgan, and Taylor, *Biographical Directory*, 1:522–23.

16. Grigsby, "Breaking the Bonds," 38–39; Reynolds, *Reconstruction in South Carolina*, 107.

17. Racine, ed., *Piedmont Farmer*, 475; Edward Lipscomb to his brother, June 30, 1869, Lipscomb Family Papers, SHC; U.S. Congress, Joint Select Committee, *Testimony*, 4:808; *Carolina Spartan*, January 27, 1870.

18. *Carolina Spartan*, April 29, 1869; U.S. Congress, Joint Select Committee, *Testimony*, 4:809.

19. *Statutes at Large of South Carolina*, 14:16, 99–101.

20. Zuczek, *State of Rebellion*, 73.

21. Spartanburg Citizen to Governor Robert K. Scott, January 1, 1869; R. C. Poole to Governor Robert K. Scott, October 16, 1869; Poole to Scott, December 10, 1869, Letters Received, Governor Robert K. Scott Papers, SCDAH.

22. *Journal of the South Carolina House of Representatives, 1872–1873*, 114.

23. *Carolina Spartan*, January 23, 1873, February 27, 1873. Legislator A. B. Woodruff tried to resurrect the bill in another form in 1875 but was unsuccessful. See *Journal of the South Carolina House of Representatives, 1875–1876*, 242.

24. *Carolina Spartan*, October 10, 1869; Wm. Magill Fleming to Governor Robert K. Scott, January 1, 1871, Letters Received, Governor Robert K. Scott Papers, SCDAH.

25. Racine, ed., *Piedmont Farmer*, 470.

26. On the Klan in York County see Ford, "One Southern Profile"; Trelease, *White Terror*, 70–73.

27. See, for example, Ayers, *Vengeance and Justice*, 161–64, and Wyatt-Brown, *Southern Honor*, 369–84.

28. Those arguing for the primarily political nature of the Klan include Trelease, *White Terror*; Shapiro, "Ku Klux Klan," 34–55; and Olsen, "Ku Klux Klan," 340–62. Historians emphasizing social and economic change as motivating factors in Klan activity include Stagg, "Problem of Klan Violence," 303–18; and Ford, "One Southern Profile." Although he does not take a clear position in this debate, George C. Rable (*But There Was No Peace*) finds that the Klan was composed of unorganized local groups that were generally ineffective at eliminating Republican challenges. For an excellent historiographical overview of the Klan see Perman, "Counter Reconstruction," 121–40.

29. U.S. Congress, Joint Select Committee, *Testimony*, 4:624, 844, 762.

30. Ibid., 800–804.

31. Ibid., 797.

32. Ibid., 765–66.

33. On the Klan and Klan leadership see Trelease, *White Terror*; Shapiro, "Ku Klux Klan," 34–55; Olsen, "Ku Klux Klan," 340–62; Stagg, "Problem of Klan Violence," 303–18; and Rable, *But There Was No Peace*.

34. Nelson, *Iron Confederacies*, 9.

35. U.S. Congress, Joint Select Committee, *Testimony*, 3:29, 99, 186–87, 4:625–32.

36. Ibid., 4:620–32. By late 1871 Cannon and other leading town entrepreneurs were condemning Klan activities both because of the threat of martial law and because the violence had escalated beyond the control of early leaders and increasingly targeted railroad depots and black rail workers. See Gabriel Cannon to Hon. John Scott, U.S. Senator, September 4, 1871; Spartanburg Citizens to Hon. John Scott, U.S. Senator, September 4, 1871; M. A. Reno to Hon. John Scott, U.S. Senator, September 6, 1871; Gabriel Cannon to Governor Robert K. Scott, September 9, 1871, Letters Received, Governor Robert K. Scott Papers, SCDAH. Scott Nelson argues that Grant's administration declared martial law in the South Carolina upcountry largely to protect the important rail lines (*Iron Confederacies*, 5).

37. Edward and Elizabeth Lipscomb to Smith and Sallie Lipscomb, April 11, 1871, Lipscomb Family Papers, SHC.

38. U.S. Congress, Joint Select Committee, *Testimony*, 3:359.

39. Ibid., 4:876; *Carolina Spartan*, February 2, 1871.

40. U.S. Congress, Joint Select Committee, *Testimony*, 3:386–91, 4:844.

41. Trelease, *White Terror*, 361; *Carolina Spartan*, May 11, 1871.

42. Anson Cummings to Governor Robert K. Scott, March 25, 1871, Letters Received, Governor Robert K. Scott Papers, SCDAH.

43. Nelson, *Iron Confederacies*, 136.

44. U.S. Congress, Joint Select Committee, *Testimony*, 4:810, 725, 796; *Carolina Spartan*, February 2, 1871.

45. November term, 1870, Grand Jury Presentments, Spartanburg District Court of General Sessions, SCDAH.

46. U.S. Congress, Joint Select Committee, *Testimony*, 4:791.

47. Gabriel Cannon to Hon. John Scott, U.S. Senator, September 4, 1871; Spartanburg Citizens to Hon. John Scott, U.S. Senator, September 4, 1871; M. A. Reno to Hon. John Scott, U.S. Senator, September 6, 1871; Gabriel Cannon to Governor Robert K. Scott, September 9, 1871, Letters Received, Governor Robert K. Scott Papers, SCDAH.

48. U.S. Congress, Joint Select Committee, *Testimony*, 4:792.

49. Zuczek, *State of Rebellion*, 98–99. Nelson suggests that one of the reasons Grant may have moved to suspend habeas corpus was to protect railroad construction in the upcountry (*Iron Confederacies*, 136).

50. "Memoirs of John Earle Bomar," 23–24, SCL. In a letter to his son, Edward Lipscomb confirmed that the "Yanks have been arresting several [suspected Klan members through the fall of 1872] but they all were bonded" (November 25, 1872, Lipscomb Family Papers, SHC).

51. Republicans of Spartanburg County to Governor Robert K. Scott, June 28, 1872, Governor Robert K. Scott Papers, SCDAH.

52. Zuczek, *State of Rebellion*, 120–22, 128–29. For an excellent constitutional study of the Klan trials see Lou Faulkner Williams, *Great South Carolina Ku Klux Klan Trials*.

53. *Journal of the South Carolina House of Representatives, 1871–1872*, 159; reprint of reminiscences of A. W. Neville, *Paris (Texas) News*, July 6, 1952, J. Banks Lyle Papers, SCL; *New York Herald* quoted in Writers' Program, *History*, 154; Neville, *Paris (Texas) News*, July 6, 1952, J. Banks Lyle Papers, SCL.

54. *Carolina Spartan*, June 26, 1873.

55. W. F. Parker to Governor Daniel Chamberlain, February 24, 1875, Letters Received, Governor Daniel Chamberlain Papers, SCDAH.

56. The best single source on the prosecution of illicit distilling in the postwar southern upcountry is Miller, *Revenuers and Moonshiners*.

57. *Carolina Spartan*, January 3, 1867, May 30, 1867, June 6, 1867.

58. Miller, *Revenuers and Moonshiners*, 26–28.

59. U.S. Congress, Joint Select Committee, *Testimony*, 3:422; William Magill Fleming to Governor Robert K. Scott, December 26, 1869, Letters Received, Governor Robert K. Scott Papers, SCDAH.

60. *Carolina Spartan*, January 20, 1870; November 1870, Session Rolls, Court of General Sessions, SCDAH.

61. *Carolina Spartan*, January 6, 1870.

62. July term, 1870, Sessions Rolls, Court of General Sessions, SCDAH.

63. July and November terms, 1870, Sessions Rolls, Court of General Sessions, SCDAH.

64. Spartanburg Republicans to Governor Robert K. Scott, December 20, 1870; Pardon of A. P. Turner, November 15, 1871, Letters Received, Governor Robert K. Scott Papers, SCDAH.

65. *Carolina Spartan*, March 3, 1870.
66. Ibid., March 1, 1876.
67. Statement of U.S. Revenue Officers to Charles W. Cummings, January 12, 1878; Gabriel Cannon to Governor Wade Hampton, December 31, 1877; Cannon to Hampton, January 9, 1878, Letters Received, Governor Wade Hampton Papers, SCDAH.
68. *Carolina Spartan*, December 3, 1879; Griffith, *Variosa*, 110–11.
69. *Carolina Spartan*, May 19, 1880, June 30, 1880; *Historical and Descriptive Review*, 2:150.
70. *Carolina Spartan*, October 10, 1879, July 7, 1880, April 21, 1880, April 28, 1880.
71. *Statutes at Large of South Carolina*, 17:501–2.
72. *Carolina Spartan*, October 20, 1880, December 22, 1880.
73. Ibid., June 25, 1874; W. F. Parker to Governor Franklin B. Moses, June 26, 1874, Letters Received, Governor Franklin B. Moses Papers, SCDAH.
74. *Carolina Spartan*, June 18, 1879.
75. Ibid., June 25, 1879.
76. 1870 and 1880, Sessions Rolls, Court of General Sessions, SCDAH.
77. For an overview of the penitentiary system in the postwar South see Zimmerman, "Penal Systems," and Ayers, *Vengeance and Justice*, 186–89. On the penitentiary in postwar South Carolina see Oliphant, *Evolution*.
78. *Carolina Spartan*, September 27, 1866.
79. Ibid., April 22, 1869.
80. A. W. Cummings to Governor Robert K. Scott, February 6, 1870, Letters Received, Governor Robert K. Scott Papers, SCDAH.
81. Spartanburg Citizens to Governor Robert K. Scott, August 29, 1871, Letters Received, Governor Robert K. Scott Papers, SCDAH.
82. On the convict-lease system in the postwar South see Ayers, *Vengeance and Justice*, 185–222; Mancini, *One Dies, Get Another*, esp. 198–212; and Carter, "Prisons, Politics, and Business."
83. *Carolina Spartan*, November 15, 1866.
84. *Statutes at Large of South Carolina*, 14:601; Holt, *Black over White*, 169.
85. *Journal of the South Carolina House of Representatives, 1874–1875*, 134, 267, 625–27.
86. *Carolina Spartan*, February 10, 1875, January 26, 1876.
87. *Columbia Register*, December 1, 1875; *Carolina Spartan*, May 31, 1876. In 1876 Governor Chamberlain sought to reinstate convict leasing as part of his plan for government financial reform (Mancini, *One Dies, Get Another*, 203).
88. *Statutes at Large of South Carolina*, 16:263–64; *Journal of the South Carolina House of Representatives, 1877–1878*, 234, 436; *Statutes at Large of South Carolina*, 16:393–94, 721.
89. *Carolina Spartan*, November 29, 1879; *Statutes at Large of South Carolina*, 17:469–70. In 1880 94 of the state's 590 convicts died (Mancini, *One Dies, Get Another*, 198).

90. *Carolina Spartan*, July 14, 1880, November 26, 1879, October 22, 1879, November 5, 1879.
91. Ibid., November 26, 1879.
92. Ayers, *Vengeance and Justice*, 184.

CONCLUSION

1. *Charleston News & Courier*, July 28, 1890.
2. Simon, "Appeal," 86.

Bibliography

PRIMARY SOURCES

Manuscripts

Perkins Library, Duke University, Durham, North Carolina (DU)
Atlanta and Richmond Air-Line Railway Company Letterbook; Edward Earle Bomar Papers; Dawkins and Henry Family Papers; J. D. Epps Diary; John Joseph Gentry Papers; Adeline Harlow Correspondence; Kirby Family Papers; Samuel Finley Patterson Papers; Lalla Pelot Papers; James H. Saye Papers; Richard Scruggs Papers

*Baker Library, Harvard University Business
School, Cambridge, Massachusetts (HBS)*
South Carolina Credit Report Ledgers, R. G. Dun and Company Collection

Manuscripts Division, Library of Congress, Washington, D.C. (LC)
Pickens-Bonham Papers

*Southern Historical Collection, Wilson Library, University of
North Carolina, Chapel Hill (SHC)*
William Kennedy Blake Reminiscences; Grimball Family Papers; Margaret Ann (Meta) Morris Grimball Diary; Thomas Dillard Johnston Papers; Lipscomb Family Papers; Benjamin F. Perry Diaries; William D. Simpson Papers; Stone Family Papers

*South Caroliniana Library, University of
South Carolina, Columbia (SCL)*
William C. Anderson Papers; "Memoirs of John Earle Bomar" by Edward Earle Bomar (typescript); John Bomar to "Dear Sir," April 12, 1865; Mary Davis Brown Papers; Carson Family Papers; Clifton Manufacturing Company Records; Coleman, Feaster, and Faucette Family Papers; James S. M. Davis Papers; Rebecca Easterling Papers; John Christopher Faber Papers; Zelotus Holmes Papers; Jefferies Family Papers; Ladies Relief Association, Spartanburg; George Larsen Papers; J. J. Legare Folder; J. Banks Lyle Papers; Thomas John Moore Papers; Benjamin F. Perry Papers; James F. Sloan Papers and Diaries; Elihu P. Smith Papers; Robert

Benson Tarrant Papers; H. H. Thomson Folder; P. Whitin and Sons Papers; John Winsmith Papers

Government Documents

National Archives and Records Administration, Washington, D.C. (NA)
Manuscript Census Returns, Population and Slave Schedules, Spartanburg District and County, 1850–80; Records of the Bureau of Refugees, Freedmen, and Abandoned Lands (BRFAL), RG 105; Records of U.S. Army Continental Commands, 1821–1920, RG 393; War Department Collection of Confederate Records, RG 109

South Carolina Division of Archives and History, Columbia (SCDAH)
Spartanburg District and County Records (Board of Trustees of School District No. 1 Record Books; Court of Common Pleas; Grand Jury Presentments; Grand Jury Presentments, Spartanburg District Court of General Sessions; Magistrates and Freeholders Court); State Records (Governor Daniel Chamberlain Papers; Department of Education Files; General Assembly Papers; Governor Wade Hampton Papers; Manuscript Census Returns, Agricultural and Industrial Schedules, 1850–1880, Spartanburg District and County; Governor Franklin B. Moses Papers; Governor Robert K. Scott Papers)

Newspapers and Contemporary Journals

Augusta Constitutionalist
Charleston Mercury
Charleston News & Courier
DeBow's Review
Edgefield Advertiser
Greenville Mountaineer

Greenville Southern Patriot
Southern Quarterly Review
Spartanburg Carolina Spartan
Spartanburg Express
Spartanburg Herald
Yorkville Enquirer

Published Government Documents

South Carolina

Acts of the General Assembly of the State of South Carolina.
Department of Agriculture. *South Carolina: Resources and Population, Institutions and Industries.* Charleston, 1883.
Journals of the House of Representatives of the State of South Carolina.
Journals of the Senate of South Carolina.
Proceedings of the Constitutional Convention of South Carolina. Vol. 1. New York, 1968.

Reports and Resolutions of the General Assembly of the State of South Carolina.
Statutes at Large of South Carolina.

United States

U.S. Bureau of the Census. *Agriculture of the United States in 1860: Compiled from the Original Returns of the Eighth Census.* Washington, D.C.: Government Printing Office, 1864.

———. *Compendium of the Ninth Census.* Washington, D.C.: Government Printing Office, 1872.

———. *Compendium of the Tenth Census.* Washington, D.C.: Government Printing Office, 1883.

———. *Manufactures of the United States in 1860.* Washington, D.C.: Government Printing Office, 1865.

———. *Ninth Census.* Vol. 3, *Statistics of Wealth and Industry.* Washington, D.C.: Government Printing Office, 1872.

———. *Population of the United States in 1860.* Washington, D.C.: Government Printing Office, 1864.

———. *Seventh Census of the United States: 1850.* Washington, D.C.: Armstrong, 1853.

———. *Statistics of the United States in 1860.* Washington, D.C.: Government Printing Office, 1864.

———. *Tenth Census: Report on Valuation, Taxation, and Public Indebtedness.* Washington, D.C.: Government Printing Office, 1884.

U.S. Congress. Joint Select Committee to Inquire into the Conditions of Affairs in the Late Insurrectionary States. *Testimony Taken by the Joint Select Committee to Inquire into the Conditions of Affairs in the Late Insurrectionary States.* 42nd Cong., 2nd sess., no. 22. Vols. 3, 4. Washington, D.C.: Government Printing Office, 1872.

U.S. Department of War. *The War of the Rebellion: A Compilation of the Official Records of the Union and Confederate Armies.* Washington, D.C.: Government Printing Office, 1882.

Published Primary Sources

Andrews, Sidney. *The South since the War.* Boston, 1866. Reprint, New York: Arno Press and New York Times, 1969.

Bryant, William Cullen. *Letters of a Traveller; or Notes of Things Seen in Europe and America.* New York, 1856.

Catalogue of Instructors and Pupils in the Limestone Springs Female High School, Spartanburg, South Carolina. Columbia, S.C.: A. W. Gibbes, 1859.

The Charters of the S. & A. R.R. and the G. & F. R.R. Together with the Articles of

Consolidation of the Two Companies and the Report of the County Board of Commissioners. Spartanburg, S.C.: Model Job and Book Printing Office, 1876.

Colton, Henry E. *Mountain Scenery: The Scenery of the Mountains of Western North Carolina and Northwestern South Carolina.* Philadelphia, 1859.

Croushore, James F., and David M. Potter, eds. *A Union Officer in the Reconstruction.* New Haven, Conn.: Yale University Press, 1948.

Cyclopedia of Eminent and Representative Men of the Carolinas of the Nineteenth Century. Vol. 1. Madison, Wis.: Brant & Fuller, 1892.

Dibble, Samuel. *The Duty of the State in Regard to Education: An Address Delivered before the Calhoun and Preston Literary Societies of Wofford College, Spartanburg, S.C., June 11, 1878.* Charleston, S.C., 1878.

Glenn Springs, South Carolina: Its Location, Discovery, History, etc. Spartanburg, S.C.: Trimmer's Book Store and Printing House, 1892.

Gregg, William. *An Enquiry into the Propriety of Granting Charters of Incorporation for Manufacturing and Other Purposes, in South Carolina.* Charleston, S.C., 1845.

Historical and Descriptive Review of the State of South Carolina. Charleston, S.C.: Empire Publishing, 1884.

Howe, George. *The Scotch-Irish, and Their First Settlements on the Tyger River and Other Neighboring Precincts in South Carolina. A Centennial Discourse, Delivered at Nazareth Church, Spartanburg District, S.C., September 14, 1861 by George Howe.* Columbia, S.C.: Southern Guardian Steam Power Press, 1861.

Mathew, William M., ed. *Agriculture, Geology, and Society in Antebellum South Carolina: The Private Diary of Edmund Ruffin, 1843.* Athens: University of Georgia Press, 1992.

Mills, Robert. *Statistics of South Carolina, Including a View of Its Natural, Civil, and Military History, General and Particular.* Charleston, S.C.: Hurlbut and Lloyd, 1826.

Olmsted, Frederick Law. *A Journey in the Seaboard Slave States.* New York, 1850.

Poor, Henry V. *Railroad Manual of the United States.* Volume years 1873–82.

Racine, Philip N., ed. *Piedmont Farmer: The Journals of David Golightly Harris, 1855–1870.* Knoxville: University of Tennessee Press, 1990.

Simms, William Gilmore. *The Geography of South Carolina.* Charleston, S.C.: Babcock & Company, 1843.

Somers, Robert. *The Southern States since the War, 1870–1871.* London, 1871. Reprint, University: University of Alabama Press, 1965.

South Carolina in 1884: A View of the Industrial Life of the State. Charleston, S.C.: News and Courier Book Presses, 1884.

Spartanburg and Greenville Directories, 1880–1881. Atlanta: H. H. Dickson, 1880.

Towles, Laura, ed. *A World Turned Upside Down: The Palmers of South Santee, 1818–1881.* Columbia: University of South Carolina Press, 1996.

Trowbridge, John T. *The Desolate South: 1865–1866*. Ed. Gordon Carroll. Boston: Little, Brown and Company.

SECONDARY SOURCES

Abbott, Martin. *The Freedmen's Bureau in South Carolina, 1865–1872*. Chapel Hill: University of North Carolina Press, 1967.
Abernethy, Thomas Perkins. *From Frontier to Plantation in Tennessee: A Study in Frontier Democracy*. University: University of Alabama Press, 1967.
Adams, Sean Patrick. "Old Dominions and Industrial Commonwealths: The Political Economy of Coal in Virginia and Pennsylvania, 1810–1875." *Enterprise & Society* 1 (December 2000): 675–82.
———. "Old Dominions and Industrial Commonwealths: The Political Economy of Coal in Virginia and Pennsylvania, 1810–1875." Ph.D. diss., University of Wisconsin at Madison, 1999.
Allman, John Mitchell. "Yeomen Regions in the Antebellum Deep South: Settlement and Economy in Northern Alabama, 1815–1860." Ph.D. diss., University of Maryland, 1979.
Anderson, James D. *The Education of Blacks in the South, 1865–1935*. Chapel Hill: University of North Carolina Press, 1988.
Andrews, Columbus. *Administrative County Government in South Carolina*. Chapel Hill: University of North Carolina Press, 1983.
Appleby, Joyce O. *Capitalism and a New Social Order: The Republican Vision of the 1790s*. New York: New York University Press, 1984.
Ashworth, John. *Slavery, Capitalism, and Politics in the Antebellum Republic*. New York: Cambridge University Press, 1995.
Ayers, Edward L. *Vengeance and Justice: Crime and Punishment in the Nineteenth Century American South*. New York: Oxford University Press, 1984.
Bailey, N. Louise, Mary L. Morgan, and Carolyn R. Taylor. *Biographical Directory of the South Carolina Senate, 1776–1985*. Columbia: University of South Carolina Press, 1985.
Bailyn, Bernard. *Education and the Forming of American Society*. Chapel Hill: University of North Carolina Press, 1960.
Barney, William L. *The Road to Secession: A New Perspective on the Old South*. New York: Praeger Publishers, 1972.
———. *The Secessionist Impulse: Alabama and Mississippi in 1860*. Princeton, N.J.: Princeton University Press, 1974.
Barnwell, John. *Love of Order: South Carolina's First Secession Crisis*. Chapel Hill: University of North Carolina Press, 1982.
Bateman, Fred, and Thomas Weiss. *A Deplorable Scarcity: The Failure of Industri-

alization in the Slave Economy. Chapel Hill: University of North Carolina Press, 1981.

Bellows, Barbara L. *Benevolence among Slaveholders: Assisting the Poor in Charleston, 1670–1860.* Baton Rouge: Louisiana State University Press, 1993.

Berlin, Ira. *Slaves without Masters: The Free Negro in the Antebellum South.* New York: Pantheon, 1974.

Berlin, Ira, Barbara Fields, Steven F. Miller, Joseph P. Reidy, and Leslie S. Rowland. *Slaves No More: Three Essays on Emancipation and the Civil War.* New York: Cambridge University Press, 1992.

Best, John Hardin. "Education in the Forming of the American South." In *Essays in Twentieth-Century Southern Education: Exceptionalism and Its Limits,* edited by Wayne J. Urban, 3–18. New York: Garland Publishing, 1999.

Binder, Frederick M. *The Age of the Common School, 1830–1865.* New York: John Wiley and Sons, 1974.

Black, Robert C., III. *The Railroads of the Confederacy.* Chapel Hill: University of North Carolina Press, 1952.

Boles, John B. "Evangelical Protestantism in the Old South: From Religious Dissent to Cultural Dominance." In *Religion in the South,* edited by Charles Reagan Wilson, 13–34. Oxford: University Press of Mississippi, 1985.

———. *The Great Revival, 1787–1805.* Lexington: University Press of Kentucky, 1972.

Boles, John B., and Evelyn Thomas Nolen, eds. *Interpreting Southern History: Historiographical Essays in Honor of Sanford W. Higginbotham.* Baton Rouge: Louisiana State University Press, 1987.

Bolton, Charles C. *Poor Whites of the Antebellum South: Tenants and Laborers in Central North Carolina and Northeast Mississippi.* Durham, N.C.: Duke University Press, 1994.

Bond, Bradley G. *Political Culture in the Nineteenth-Century South: Mississippi, 1830–1900.* Baton Rouge: Louisiana State University Press, 1995.

Boucher, Chauncey S. "The Antebellum Attitude of South Carolina towards Manufacturing and Agriculture." *Washington University Studies* 3 (April 1916): 243–70.

———. "The Secession and Cooperation Movements in South Carolina, 1848–1852." *Washington University Studies* 5 (April 1918): 67–138.

———. "Sectionalism, Representation, and the Electoral Question in Antebellum South Carolina." *Washington University Studies* 4 (October 1916): 3–62.

Bradley, John Calvin. "The Political Reconstruction of Spartanburg County, 1865–1868." B.A. thesis, University of South Carolina, 1983.

Brouwer, Maria T. "Weber, Schumpeter and Knight on Entrepreneurship and Economic Development." *Journal of Evolutionary Economics* 12 (2002): 83–105.

Brown, George Dewitt. "A History of the Blue Ridge Railroad, 1852–1874." M.A. thesis, University of South Carolina, 1967.

Brown, Richard D. *Modernization: The Transformation of American Life, 1600–1865.* New York: Hill and Wang, 1976.

Bruce, Dickson D., Jr. *Violence and Culture in the Antebellum South.* Austin: University of Texas Press, 1979.

Bryant, Jonathan M. *How Curious a Land: Conflict and Change in Greene County, Georgia, 1850–1885.* Chapel Hill: University of North Carolina Press, 1996.

Bullock, Henry Allen. *A History of Negro Education from 1619 to the Present.* Cambridge, Mass.: Harvard University Press, 1967.

Burton, Orville Vernon. *In My Father's House Are Many Mansions: Family and Community in Edgefield, South Carolina.* Chapel Hill: University of North Carolina Press, 1985.

Burton, Orville V., and Robert C. McMath, eds. *Class, Conflict, and Consensus: Antebellum Southern Community Studies.* Westport, Conn.: Greenwood Press, 1982.

Butchart, Ronald E. *Northern Schools, Southern Blacks, and Reconstruction: Freedmen's Education.* Westport, Conn.: Greenwood Press, 1980.

Byrne, Frank J. *Becoming Bourgeois: Merchant Culture in the South, 1820–1865.* Lexington: University Press of Kentucky, 2006.

Campbell, Randolph B. "Planters and Plain Folk: Harrison County, Texas, as a Test Case, 1850–1860." *Journal of Southern History* 40 (August 1974): 369–98.

———. "Planters and Plain Folk: The Social Structure of the Antebellum South." In *Interpreting Southern History: Historiographical Essays in Honor of Sanford W. Higginbotham*, edited by John B. Boles and Evelyn Thomas Nolen, 63–70. Baton Rouge: Louisiana State University Press, 1987.

———. *A Southern Community in Crisis: Harrison County, Texas, 1850–1880.* Austin: Texas State Historical Association, 1983.

Carlton, David L. *Mill and Town in South Carolina, 1880–1920.* Baton Rouge: Louisiana State University Press, 1982.

Carter, Dan T. "Prisons, Politics, and Business: The Convict Lease System in the Post–Civil War South." M.A. thesis, University of Wisconsin, 1964.

———. *When the War Was Over: The Failure of Self-Reconstruction in the South, 1865–1867.* Baton Rouge: Louisiana State University Press, 1985.

Cauthen, Charles Edward. *South Carolina Goes to War, 1860–1865.* Chapel Hill: University of North Carolina Press, 1950.

Censer, Jane Turner. "'Smiling through Her Tears': Ante-Bellum Southern Women and Divorce." *American Journal of Legal History* 25 (1981): 24–47.

Channing, Steven A. *Crisis of Fear: Secession in South Carolina.* New York: W. W. Norton, 1970.

Chaplin, Joyce E. *An Anxious Pursuit: Agricultural Innovation and Modernity in the Lower South, 1730–1815.* Chapel Hill: University of North Carolina Press, 1993.

Chapman, Harry A. "The Historical Development of the Grange in South Carolina." M.A. thesis, Furman University, 1951.

Charles, Allan D. *The Narrative History of Union County, South Carolina.* 2nd ed. Greenville, S.C.: A Press Printing Company, 1990.

Clark, Thomas D. *Pills, Petticoats, and Plows: The Southern Country Store, 1865–1900.* Norman: University of Oklahoma Press, 1944.

Coclanis, Peter A. "The Paths before Us/U.S.: Tracking the Economic Divergence of the North and the South." In *The South, the Nation, and the World: Perspectives on Southern Economic Development,* edited by David L. Carlton and Peter A. Coclanis, 12–23. Charlottesville: University of Virginia Press, 2003.

———. *The Shadow of a Dream: Economic Life and Death in the South Carolina Low Country, 1670–1920.* New York: Oxford University Press, 1989.

Cooper, William J., Jr. *The Conservative Regime: South Carolina, 1877–1890.* Baltimore, Md.: Johns Hopkins University Press, 1968.

———. *Liberty and Slavery: Southern Politics to 1860.* New York: Alfred A. Knopf, 1983.

———. *The South and the Politics of Slavery, 1828–1856.* Baton Rouge: Louisiana State University Press, 1978.

Crofts, Daniel W. *Old Southampton: Politics and Society in a Virginia County, 1834–1869.* Charlottesville: University of Virginia Press, 1992.

———. *Reluctant Confederates: Upper South Unionists in the Secession Crisis.* Chapel Hill: University of North Carolina Press, 1989.

Dabney, Charles William. *Universal Education in the South.* Vol. 1. Chapel Hill: University of North Carolina Press, 1936.

Davis, David Brion. *Slave Power Conspiracy and the Paranoid Style.* Baton Rouge: Louisiana State University Press, 1961.

Davis, Ronald L. F. "The Southern Merchant: A Perennial Source of Discontent." In *The Southern Enigma: Essays on Race, Class, and Folk Culture,* edited by Walter J. Fraser, Jr., and Winifred B. Moore, Jr., 131–41. Westport, Conn.: Greenwood Press, 1983.

DeCredico, Mary A. *Patriotism for Profit: Georgia's Urban Entrepreneurs and the Confederate War Effort.* Chapel Hill: University of North Carolina Press, 1990.

Delfino, Susanna, and Michele Gillespie, eds. *Global Perspectives on Industrial Transformation in the American South.* Columbia: University of Missouri Press, 2005.

DeLorme, Charles DuBose. "The Development of the Textile Industry in Spartanburg County, 1816–1900." M.A. thesis, University of South Carolina, 1963.

Derrick, Samuel M. *Centennial History of the South Carolina Railroad.* Columbia: University of South Carolina Press, 1930.

Downey, Tom. *Planting a Capitalist South: Masters, Merchants, and Manufacturers in the Southern Interior, 1790–1861.* Baton Rouge: Louisiana State University Press, 2006.

———. "Riparian Rights and Manufacturing in Antebellum South Carolina: William Gregg and the Origins of the 'Industrial Mind.'" *Journal of Southern History* 65 (February 1999): 77–108.

Dupre, Daniel S. *Transforming the Cotton Frontier: Madison County, Alabama, 1800–1840.* Baton Rouge: Louisiana State University Press, 1997.

Easterby, J. H. "The Granger Movement in South Carolina." *Proceedings of the South Carolina Historical Association* (1931): 21–32.

Eaton, Clement. *Freedom of Thought in the Old South.* Durham, N.C.: Duke University Press, 1940.

Edgar, Walter B. *South Carolina: A History.* Columbia: University of South Carolina Press, 1998.

Escott, Paul D. *After Secession: Jefferson Davis and the Failure of Confederate Nationalism.* Baton Rouge: Louisiana State University Press, 1978.

———. *Many Excellent People: Power and Privilege in North Carolina, 1850–1900.* Chapel Hill: University of North Carolina Press, 1985.

Ezell, John S. "A Southern Education for Southrons." *Journal of Southern History* 17 (August 1951): 303–27.

Faust, Drew Gilpin. *A Sacred Circle: The Dilemma of the Intellectual in the Old South, 1840–1860.* Baltimore, Md.: Johns Hopkins University Press, 1977.

Ferguson, Terry A., and Thomas A. Cowan. "Iron Plantations and the Eighteenth- and Nineteenth-Century Landscape of the Northwestern South Carolina Piedmont." In *Carolina's Historical Landscapes: Archaeological Perspectives,* edited by Linda F. Stine, Martha Zierden, Lesley M. Drucker, and Christopher Judge, 113–44. Knoxville: University of Tennessee Press, 1997.

Fogel, Robert William, and Stanley L. Engerman. *Time on the Cross: The Economics of American Negro Slavery.* Boston: Little, Brown and Company, 1974.

Foner, Eric. *Free Soil, Free Labor, Free Men: The Ideology of the Republican Party before the Civil War.* New York: Oxford University Press, 1971.

———. *Nothing but Freedom: Emancipation and Its Legacy.* Baton Rouge: Louisiana State University Press, 1983.

———. *Reconstruction: America's Unfinished Revolution, 1863–1877.* New York: Harper & Row, 1988.

———. "Reconstruction Revisited." *Reviews in American History* 10 (December 1982): 82–100.

Ford, Lacy K. "Labor and Ideology in the South Carolina Upcountry: The Transition to Free-Labor Agriculture." In *The Southern Enigma: Essays on Race, Class, and Folk Culture,* edited by Walter J. Fraser, Jr., and Winfred B. Moore, Jr., 25–41. Westport, Conn.: Greenwood Press, 1983.

———. "One Southern Profile: Modernization and the Development of White Terror in York County, 1856–1876." M.A. thesis, University of South Carolina, 1976.

———. *Origins of Southern Radicalism: The South Carolina Upcountry, 1800–1860.* New York: Oxford University Press, 1988.

———. "Rednecks and Merchants: Economic Development and Social Tensions in the South Carolina Upcountry, 1865–1900." *Journal of American History* 71 (September 1984): 294–318.

———. "Self-Sufficiency, Cotton, and Economic Development in the South Carolina Upcountry, 1800–1860." *Journal of Economic History* 45 (June 1985): 261–67.

———. "The Tale of Two Entrepreneurs in the Old South: John Springs III and Hiram Hutchinson of the South Carolina Upcountry." *South Carolina Historical Magazine* 95 (July 1994): 198–224.

———. "Yeomen Farmers in the South Carolina Upcountry: Changing Production Patterns in the Late Antebellum Period." *Agricultural History* 60 (Fall 1986): 17–37.

Foucault, Michel. *Discipline and Punish: The Birth of the Prison.* Translated by Alan Sheridan. New York: Pantheon, 1977.

Fredrickson, George M. *The Black Image in the White Mind: The Debate on Afro-American Character and Destiny, 1817–1914.* New York: Harper & Row, 1971.

Freehling, William W. *Road to Disunion.* Vol. 1, *Secessionists at Bay, 1776–1854.* New York: Oxford University Press, 1990.

Friedman, Lawrence M. *Crime and Punishment in American History.* New York: Basic Books, 1993.

Gaston, Paul M. *The New South Creed: A Study in Southern Mythmaking.* New York: Alfred A. Knopf, 1970.

Genovese, Eugene D. *The Political Economy of Slavery: Studies in the Economy and Society of the Slave South.* New York: Pantheon, 1965.

———. *Roll, Jordan, Roll: The World the Slaves Made.* New York: Pantheon, 1974.

———. *The World the Slaveholders Made: Two Essays in Interpretation.* New York: Pantheon, 1969.

———. "Yeomen Farmers in a Slaveholders' Democracy." *Agricultural History* 49 (April 1975): 331–42.

Gillespie, Michele. *Free Labor in an Unfree World: White Artisans in Slaveholding Georgia, 1789–1860.* Athens: University of Georgia Press, 2000.

Glickstein, Jonathan. *Concepts of Free Labor in Antebellum America.* New Haven, Conn.: Yale University Press, 1991.

Goldfarb, Stephen J. "A Note on the Limits to Growth of the Cotton-Textile Industry in the Old South." *Journal of Southern History* 48 (November 1982): 545–58.

Goldfield, David. *Region, Race, and Cities: Interpreting the Urban South.* Baton Rouge: Louisiana State University Press, 1997.

Gorn, Elliott J. "'Gouge and Bite, Pull Hair and Scratch': The Social Significance of Fighting in the Southern Backcountry." *American Historical Review* 90 (February 1985): 18–43.

Gray, Lewis C. *History of Agriculture in the Southern United States to 1860*. Gloucester, Mass.: Peter Smith, 1933.

Green, Andy. *Education and State Formation: The Rise of Education Systems in England, France, and the USA*. New York: St. Martin's Press, 1990.

Greenberg, Kenneth S. *Honor and Slavery: Lies, Duels, Noses, Masks, Dressing as a Woman, Gifts, Strangers, Humanitarianism, Death, Slave Rebellions, the Proslavery Argument, Baseball, Hunting, and Gambling in the Old South*. Princeton, N.J.: Princeton University Press, 1996.

———. *Masters and Statesmen: The Political Culture of American Slavery*. Baltimore, Md.: Johns Hopkins University Press, 1985.

———. "The Nose, the Lie, and the Duel in the Antebellum South." *American Historical Review* 95 (February 1990): 57–74.

Griffin, Richard W. "Poor White Laborers in Southern Cotton Factories, 1789–1865." *South Carolina Historical Magazine* 41 (January 1960): 26–40.

Griffith, H. P. *Life and Times of Rev. John G. Landrum*. Philadelphia: H. B. Garner, 1885.

———. *Variosa: A Collection of Sketches, Essays and Verses*. 1911.

Grigsby, David. "Breaking the Bonds: Spartanburg County during Reconstruction." M.A. thesis, University of North Carolina at Chapel Hill, 1991.

Grimsted, David. *American Mobbing, 1828–1861: Toward Civil War*. New York: Oxford University Press, 1998.

Gutman, Herbert G. *Work, Culture, and Society in Industrializing America: Essays in American Working-Class and Social History*. New York: Alfred A. Knopf, 1976.

Hahn, Steven. "Common Right and Commonwealth: The Stock-Law Struggle and the Roots of Southern Populism." In *Region, Race, and Reconstruction: Essays in Honor of C. Vann Woodward*, edited by J. Morgan Kousser and James M. McPherson, 51–88. New York: Oxford University Press, 1982.

———. "Hunting, Fishing, and Foraging: Common Rights and Class Relations in the Postbellum South." *Radical History Review* 26 (1982): 37–64.

———. "A Response: Common Cents or Historical Sense?" *Journal of Southern History* 59 (May 1993): 201–42.

———. *The Roots of Southern Populism: Yeomen Farmers and the Transformation of the Georgia Upcountry, 1850–1890*. New York: Oxford University Press, 1983.

Harris, J. William. *Plain Folk and Gentry in a Slave Society: White Liberty and Black Slavery in Augusta's Hinterlands*. Middletown, Conn.: Wesleyan University Press, 1985.

Harrold, Stanley. *The Abolitionists and the South, 1831–1861*. Lexington: University Press of Kentucky, 1995.

Henretta, James A. "Families and Farms: *Mentalité* in Pre-Industrial America." *William and Mary Quarterly* 35 (1978): 3–33.

Herd, E. Don, Jr. *The South Carolina Upcountry, 1540–1980: Historical and Biographical Sketches.* Vol. 2. Greenwood, S.C.: Attic Press, 1982.
Heyrman, Christine Leigh. *Southern Cross: The Beginnings of the Bible Belt.* New York: Alfred A. Knopf, 1997.
Hindus, Michael Stephen. *Prison and Plantation: Crime, Justice, and Authority in Massachusetts and South Carolina, 1767–1878.* Chapel Hill: University of North Carolina Press, 1980.
Hirsch, Adam J. *The Rise of the Penitentiary: Prisons and Punishment in Early America.* New Haven, Conn.: Yale University Press, 1992.
Hoffman, Carolyn Frances. "The Development of Town and Country: Charlotte and Mecklenberg County, North Carolina, 1850–1800." Ph.D. diss., University of Maryland, 1988.
Hollis, Daniel Walker. *University of South Carolina.* Columbia: University of South Carolina Press, 1951.
Holt, Thomas. *Black over White: Negro Political Leadership in South Carolina during Reconstruction.* Urbana: University of Illinois Press, 1977.
Ignatieff, Michael. *A Just Measure of Pain: The Penitentiary in the Industrial Revolution, 1750–1850.* New York: Pantheon, 1978.
Inscoe, John C. *Mountain Masters, Slavery, and the Sectional Crisis in Western North Carolina.* Knoxville: University of Tennessee Press, 1989.
Jeffrey, Thomas E. *State Parties and National Politics: North Carolina, 1815–1861.* Athens: University of Georgia Press, 1989.
Johnson, Michael P. *Toward a Patriarchal Republic: The Secession of Georgia.* Baton Rouge: Louisiana State University Press, 1977.
Jones, Jacqueline. *Soldiers of Light and Love: Northern Teachers and Georgia Blacks.* Chapel Hill: University of North Carolina Press, 1980.
Jones, Lewis P. "History of Public Education in South Carolina." In *Public Education in South Carolina: Historical, Political, and Legal Perspectives*, edited by Thomas R. McDaniel, 1–29. Spartanburg, S.C.: Converse College, 1984.
Jorgensen, Lloyd P. *The State and the Non-Public School, 1825–1925.* Columbia: University of Missouri Press, 1987.
Kaestle, Carl F. *Pillars of the Republic: Common Schools and American Society, 1780–1860.* New York: Hill and Wang, 1983.
Kantor, Shawn Everett. *Politics and Property Rights: The Closing of the Open Range in the Postbellum South.* Chicago: University of Chicago Press, 1998.
Kantor, Shawn Everett, and J. Morgan Kousser. "Common Sense or Commonwealth? The Fence Law and Institutional Change in the Postbellum South." *Journal of Southern History* 59 (May 1993): 201–42.
———. "A Rejoinder: Two Visions of History." *Journal of Southern History* 59 (May 1993): 259–66.

Karier, Clarence J. *The Individual, Society, and Education: A History of American Educational Ideas.* 2nd ed. Urbana: University of Illinois Press, 1986.

Kenzer, Robert C. *Kinship and Neighborhood in a Southern Community: Orange County, North Carolina, 1849–1881.* Knoxville: University of Tennessee Press, 1988.

Kibler, Lillian A. *Benjamin F. Perry: South Carolina Unionist.* Durham, N.C.: Duke University Press, 1946.

Knight, Edgar Wallace. *The Influence of Reconstruction on Education in the South.* New York: Teachers College, Columbia University, 1913.

———. *Public Education in the South.* Boston: Ginn and Co., 1922.

Lakwete, Angela. *Inventing the Cotton Gin: Machine and Myth in Antebellum America.* Baltimore, Md.: Johns Hopkins University Press, 2003.

Lander, Ernest M., Jr. "The Iron Industry in Antebellum South Carolina." *Journal of Southern History* 20 (August 1954): 337–55.

———. *The Textile Industry in Antebellum South Carolina.* Baton Rouge: Louisiana State University Press, 1969.

Landrum, J. B. O. *A History of Spartanburg County.* Atlanta, Ga.: Franklin Printing, 1900.

Leloudis, James L. *Schooling the New South: Pedagogy, Self, and Society in North Carolina, 1880–1920.* Chapel Hill: University of North Carolina Press, 1996.

Lesesne, J. Mauldin. *The Bank of the State of South Carolina: A General and Political History.* Columbia: University of South Carolina Press, 1970.

Link, William A. *The Roots of Secession: Slavery and Politics in Antebellum Virginia.* Chapel Hill: University of North Carolina Press, 2003.

Long, Wayne. "The Meaning of Entrepreneurship." *American Journal of Small Business* 8, no. 2 (1983): 47–59.

MacArthur, William Joseph. "Antebellum Politics in an Upcountry County: National, State, and Local Issues in Spartanburg County, South Carolina, 1850–1860." M.A. thesis, University of South Carolina, 1966.

Majewski, John. *A House Dividing: Economic Development in Pennsylvania and Virginia before the Civil War.* New York: Cambridge University Press, 2000.

———. "Who Financed the Transportation Revolution? Regional Divergence and Internal Improvements in Antebellum Pennsylvania and Virginia." *Journal of Economic History* 56 (December 1996): 763–88.

Mancini, Matthew J. *One Dies, Get Another: Convict Leasing in the American South, 1866–1928.* Columbia: University of South Carolina Press, 1996.

Martin, Thomas P. "The Advent of William Gregg and the Graniteville Company." *Journal of Southern History* 11 (August 1945): 389–423.

Massey, Mary Elizabeth. *Ersatz in the Confederacy.* Columbia: University of South Carolina Press, 1952.

———. *Refugee Life in the Confederacy.* Baton Rouge: Louisiana State University Press, 1964.

Mathews, Donald G. *Religion in the Old South.* Chicago: University of Chicago Press, 1977.

McCardell, John. *The Idea of a Southern Nation: Southern Nationalists and Southern Nationalism, 1830–1860.* New York: W. W. Norton, 1979.

McCoy, Drew R. *The Elusive Republic: Political Economy in Jeffersonian America.* New York: W. W. Norton, 1980.

McCurry, Stephanie. *Masters of Small Worlds: Yeomen Households, Gender Relations, and the Political Culture of the Antebellum South Carolina Low Country.* New York: Oxford University Press, 1995.

Melossi, Dario, and Massimo Pavarini. *The Prison and the Factory: Origins of the Penitentiary System.* Translated by Glynic Cousin. London: Macmillan, 1981.

Memoir of Professor F. A. Porcher. Charleston, S.C.: Walker, Evans and Cogswell, 1889. Historical Society of South Carolina.

Meriweather, Colyer. *History of Higher Education in South Carolina with a Sketch of the Free School System.* Washington, D.C.: Government Printing Office, 1889.

Merrill, Michael. "Cash Is Good to Eat: Self-Sufficiency and Exchange in the Rural Economy of the United States." *Radical History Review* 3 (Winter 1977): 42–71.

Miller, Wilbur R. *Revenuers and Moonshiners: Enforcing Federal Liquor Law in the Mountain South, 1865–1900.* Chapel Hill: University of North Carolina Press, 1991.

Mitchell, Broadus. *William Gregg: Factory Master of the Old South.* Chapel Hill: University of North Carolina Press, 1928.

Mitchell, Karen. "Phoebe Paine, Educator (1802–1872)." In *The Lives They Lived: A Look at Women in the History of Spartanburg,* edited by Linda Powers Bilanchone, 6–7. Spartanburg, S.C., 1981.

Moore, John Hammond. *Southern Homefront, 1861–1865.* Columbia, S.C.: Summerhouse Press, 1998.

Morgan, Chad. *Planter's Progress: Modernizing Confederate Georgia.* Gainesville: University Press of Florida, 2005.

Morgan, Edmund S. *American Slavery, American Freedom: The Ordeal of Colonial Virginia.* New York: W. W. Norton, 1975.

Morris, Robert C. *Reading, 'Riting, and Reconstruction: The Education of the Freedmen in the South, 1861–1870.* Chicago: University of Chicago Press, 1981.

Morris, Thomas D. "Equality, 'Extraordinary Law,' and Criminal Justice: The South Carolina Experience, 1865–1866." *South Carolina Historical Magazine* 83 (January 1982): 15–33.

———. *Southern Slavery and the Law, 1619–1860.* Chapel Hill: University of North Carolina Press, 1996.

Morrison, Chaplain W. *Democratic Politics and Sectionalism: The Wilmot Proviso Controversy*. Chapel Hill: University of North Carolina Press, 1967.

Nash, A. E. Keir. "Negro Rights, Unionism, and Greatness on the South Carolina Court of Appeals: The Extraordinary Chief Justice John Belton O'Neall." *South Carolina Law Review* 21 (1969): 141–90.

Nelson, Scott Reynolds. *Iron Confederacies: Southern Railways, Klan Violence, and Reconstruction*. Chapel Hill: University of North Carolina Press, 1999.

Newman, Joseph W. "Antebellum School Reform in the Port Cities of the Deep South." In *Southern Cities, Southern Schools: Public Education in the Urban South*, edited by David N. Plank and Rick Ginsberg, 17–35. Westport, Conn.: Greenwood Press, 1990.

Norton, Jerry William. "South Carolina Taxpayers' Convention of 1871." M.A. thesis, University of South Carolina, 1971.

Oakes, James. *The Ruling Race: A History of American Slaveholders*. New York: Alfred A. Knopf, 1982.

O'Brien, Gail Williams. *The Legal Fraternity and the Making of a New South Community, 1848–1882*. Athens: University of Georgia Press, 1986.

Oliphant, Albert D. *The Evolution of the Penal System of South Carolina from 1866 to 1916*. Columbia, S.C.: State Company, 1916.

Olsen, Otto H. "The Ku Klux Klan: A Study in Reconstruction Politics and Propaganda." *North Carolina Historical Review* 39 (1962): 340–62.

Owsley, Frank L. *Plain Folk of the Old South*. Baton Rouge: Louisiana State University Press, 1949.

Perman, Michael. "Counter Reconstruction: The Role of Violence in Southern Redemption." In *The Facts of Reconstruction: Essays in Honor of John Hope Franklin*, edited by Eric Anderson and Alfred A. Moss, Jr., 121–40. Baton Rouge: Louisiana State University Press, 1991.

———. *The Road to Redemption: Southern Politics, 1869–1879*. Chapel Hill: University of North Carolina Press, 1984.

Phillips, U. B. *Life and Labor in the Old South*. 1929. Reprint, Boston: Little, Brown and Company, 1963.

Pippin, Kathryn A. "The Common School Movement in the South, 1840–1860." Ph.D. diss., University of North Carolina at Chapel Hill, 1977.

Plank, David N., and Rick Ginsberg, eds. *Southern Cities, Southern Schools: Public Education in the Urban South*. Westport, Conn.: Greenwood Press, 1990.

Pocock, J. G. A. *The Machiavellian Moment: Florentine Political Thought and the Atlantic Republican Tradition*. Princeton, N.J.: Princeton University Press, 1975.

Porcher, Frederick. "Free School System in South Carolina." *Southern Quarterly Review* 31 (1849): 32–33.

Potter, David M. *The Impending Crisis, 1848–1861*. Completed and edited by Don E. Fehrenbacher. New York: Harper & Row, 1976.

Quist, John W. *Restless Visionaries: The Social Roots of Antebellum Reform in Alabama and Michigan.* Baton Rouge: Louisiana State University Press, 1998.

Rable, George C. *But There Was No Peace: The Role of Violence in the Politics of Reconstruction.* Athens: University of Georgia Press, 1984.

Racine, Philip N. "The Spartanburg District Magistrates and Freeholders Court, 1824–1865." *South Carolina Historical Magazine* 87 (October 1986): 197–212.

———. "The Trial and Tribulations of Jesse Hughey, Free Negro." *Proceedings of the South Carolina Historical Association* (1985): 29–39.

Ransom, Roger L., and Richard Sutch. *One Kind of Freedom: The Economic Consequences of Emancipation.* New York: Cambridge University Press, 1977.

Reidy, Joseph P. *From Slavery to Agrarian Capitalism in the Cotton Plantation South: Central Georgia, 1800–1880.* Chapel Hill: University of North Carolina Press, 1992.

Reynolds, John S. *Reconstruction in South Carolina, 1865–1877.* Columbia: University of South Carolina Press, 1905.

Ridgway, Whitman H. *Community Leadership in Maryland, 1790–1840: A Comparative Analysis of Power in Society.* Chapel Hill: University of North Carolina Press, 1979.

Rogers, Daniel T. "Republicanism: The Career of a Concept." *Journal of American History* 79 (1992): 11–38.

Rose, Willie Lee. *Rehearsal for Reconstruction: The Port Royal Experiment.* New York: Oxford University Press, 1964.

Rothman, David J. *Discovery of the Asylum: Social Order and Disorder in the New Republic.* Boston: Little, Brown and Company, 1971.

Rumble, John W. "A Carolina Country Squire in the Old South and the New: The Papers of James F. Sloan." *South Atlantic Quarterly* 81 (Summer 1982): 323–37.

Saville, Julie. *The Work of Reconstruction: From Slave to Wage Laborer in South Carolina, 1860–1868.* New York: Cambridge University Press, 1997.

Schaper, William A. "Sectionalism and Representation in South Carolina." In *Annual Report of the American Historical Association for the Year 1900,* 1:367–83, 419–37. Washington, D.C.: Government Printing Office, 1901.

Schlotterbeck, John T. "Plantation and Farm: Social and Economic Change in Orange and Greene Counties, Virginia, 1716 to 1860." Ph.D. diss., Johns Hopkins University, 1980.

Schultz, Harold S. *Nationalism and Sectionalism in South Carolina, 1852–1860: A Study of the Movement for Southern Independence.* Durham, N.C.: Duke University Press, 1950.

Shapiro, Herbert. "The Ku Klux Klan during Reconstruction: The South Carolina Episode." *Journal of Negro History* 49 (1964): 34–55.

Shore, Laurence. *Southern Capitalists: The Ideological Leadership of an Elite, 1832–1885.* Chapel Hill: University of North Carolina Press, 1986.

Simkins, Francis Butler, and Robert Hilliard Woody. *South Carolina during Reconstruction*. Chapel Hill: University of North Carolina Press, 1932.

Simon, Bryant. "The Appeal of Cole Blease of South Carolina: Race, Class, and Sex in the New South." *Journal of Southern History* 62 (February 1996): 57–86.

Sinha, Manisha. "The Counter-Revolution of Slavery: Class, Politics, and Ideology in Antebellum South Carolina." Ph.D. diss., Columbia University, 1994.

———. *The Counter-Revolution of Slavery: Politics and Ideology in Antebellum South Carolina*. Chapel Hill: University of North Carolina Press, 2000.

Small, Sandra E. "The Yankee Schoolmarm in Freedmen's Schools: An Analysis of Attitudes." *Journal of Southern History* 45 (August 1979): 381–402.

Smith, Alfred Glaze, Jr. *Economic Readjustment of an Old Cotton State: South Carolina, 1820–1860*. Columbia: University of South Carolina Press, 1958.

Smith, Mark M. *Mastered by the Clock: Time, Slavery, and Freedom in the American South*. Chapel Hill: University of North Carolina Press, 1997.

Stagg, J. C. A. "The Problem of Klan Violence: The South Carolina Up-Country, 1868–1871." *Journal of American Studies* 8 (1974): 303–18.

Stampp, Kenneth M. *The Era of Reconstruction, 1865–1877*. New York: Vintage Books, 1965.

Stevens, William Oliver. *Pistols at Ten Paces: The Story of the Code of Honor in America*. Boston: Houghton Mifflin, 1940.

Stoddard, James Alexander. "Backgrounds of Secondary Education in South Carolina." M.A. thesis, University of South Carolina, 1924.

Stokes, Allen H., Jr. "Black and White Labor and the Development of the Southern Textile Industry." Ph.D. diss., University of South Carolina, 1977.

———. "John H. Montgomery: A Pioneer Southern Industrialist." M.A. thesis, University of South Carolina, 1967.

Stover, John F. *The Railroads of the South, 1865–1900: A Study in Finance and Control*. Chapel Hill: University of North Carolina Press, 1955.

Summers, Mark W. *Railroads, Reconstruction, and the Gospel of Prosperity: Aid under the Radical Republicans, 1865–1877*. Princeton, N.J.: Princeton University Press, 1984.

Sydnor, Charles. "The Southerner and the Laws." *Journal of Southern History* 6 (February 1940): 3–24.

Taylor, Rosser H. *Ante-Bellum South Carolina: A Social and Cultural History*. Chapel Hill: University of North Carolina Press, 1942.

Taylor, William R. "Toward a Definition of Orthodoxy: The Patrician South and the Common Schools." *Harvard Educational Review* 36 (1966): 412–26.

Terrill, Tom E. "Eager Hands: Labor for Southern Textiles, 1850–1860." *Journal of Economic History* 36 (March 1976): 84–99.

Thompson, Henry T. *The Establishment of the Public School System of South Carolina*. Columbia, S.C.: R. L. Bryan Company, 1927.

Thornton, J. Mills, III. *Politics and Power in a Slave Society: Alabama, 1800–1860.* Baton Rouge: Louisiana State University Press, 1978.

Tindall, George Brown. *South Carolina Negroes, 1877–1900.* Columbia: University of South Carolina Press, 1952.

Towers, Frank. *The Urban South and the Coming of the Civil War.* Charlottesville: University of Virginia Press, 2004.

Trelease, Allen W. *White Terror: The Ku Klux Klan Conspiracy and Southern Reconstruction.* Baton Rouge: Louisiana State University Press, 1971.

Tucker, Barbara M. *Samuel Slater and the Origins of the American Textile Industry, 1790–1860.* Ithaca, N.Y.: Cornell University Press, 1984.

Underwood, James Lowell. *The Constitution of South Carolina.* Vol. 2. Columbia: University of South Carolina Press, 1986.

Varon, Elizabeth R. *We Mean to Be Counted: White Women and Politics in Antebellum Virginia.* Chapel Hill: University of North Carolina Press, 1998.

Vaughn, William Preston. *Schools for All: The Blacks and Public Education in the South, 1865–1877.* Lexington: University Press of Kentucky, 1974.

Waldrep, George Calvin, III. "Politics of Hope and Fear: The Struggle for Community in the Industrial South." Ph.D. diss., Duke University, 1996.

Wallenstein, Peter. *From Slave South to New South: Public Policy in Nineteenth Century Georgia.* Chapel Hill: University of North Carolina Press, 1987.

Walters, Ronald G. *The Antislavery Appeal: American Abolition after 1830.* Baltimore, Md.: Johns Hopkins University Press, 1976.

Watson, Harry L. "Conflict and Collaboration: Yeomen, Slaveholders, and Politics in the Antebellum South." *Social History* 10 (October 1985): 273–98.

———. *Jacksonian Politics and Community Conflict: The Emergence of the Second Party System in Cumberland County, North Carolina.* Baton Rouge: Louisiana State University Press, 1981.

Weiman, David F. "Petty Commodity Production in the Cotton South: Upcountry Farmers in the Georgia Cotton Economy, 1840–1880." Ph.D. diss., Stanford University, 1983.

Weir, Robert M. *Colonial South Carolina: A History.* Millwood, N.Y.: KTO Press, 1983.

Wells, Jonathan Daniel. *The Origins of the Southern Middle Class, 1800–1861.* Chapel Hill: University of North Carolina Press, 2004.

West, Steven A. "From Yeoman to Redneck in Upstate South Carolina, 1850–1915." Ph.D. diss., Columbia University, 1998.

Williams, Jack K. *Dueling in the Old South: Vignettes of Social History.* College Station: Texas A & M University Press, 1980.

———. *Vogues in Villainy: Crime and Retribution in Ante-Bellum South Carolina.* Columbia: University of South Carolina Press, 1959.

Williams, Lou Faulkner. *The Great South Carolina Ku Klux Klan Trials, 1871–1872.* Athens: University of Georgia Press, 1996.

Williamson, Gustauvus Galloway, Jr. "Cotton Manufacturing in South Carolina, 1865–1892." Ph.D. diss., Johns Hopkins University, 1954.

Williamson, Joel. *After Slavery: The Negro in South Carolina during Reconstruction, 1861–1877.* Chapel Hill: University of North Carolina Press, 1965.

Wood, Gordon S. *Creation of the American Republic, 1776–1787.* Chapel Hill: University of North Carolina Press, 1969.

Wood, Peter H. *Black Majority: Negroes in Colonial South Carolina from 1670 through the Stono Rebellion.* New York: W. W. Norton, 1974.

Woodman, Harold D. *King Cotton and His Retainers: Financing and Marketing the Cotton Crop of the South, 1800–1925.* Lexington: University of Kentucky Press, 1968.

———. *New South—New Law: The Legal Foundations of Credit and Labor Relations in the Postbellum Agricultural South.* Baton Rouge: Louisiana State University Press, 1995.

———. "Post–Civil War Agriculture and the Law." *Agricultural History* 53 (January 1979): 319–37.

Woodward, C. Vann. *Origins of the New South, 1877–1913.* Baton Rouge: Louisiana State University Press, 1951.

Wooster, Ralph A. *The People in Power: Courthouse and Statehouse in the Lower South, 1850–1860.* Knoxville: University of Tennessee Press, 1969.

———. *Politicians, Planters, and Plain Folk: Courthouse and Statehouse in the Upper South, 1850–1860.* Knoxville: University of Tennessee Press, 1975.

Wright, Gavin. "Cheap Labor and Southern Textiles, 1880–1930." *Quarterly Journal of Economics* 96 (November 1981): 605–29.

———. "Cotton Competition and the Post-bellum Recovery of the American South." *Journal of Economic History* (September 1974): 610–35.

———. "'Economic Democracy' and the Concentration of Agricultural Wealth in the Cotton South, 1850–1860." *Agricultural History* 44 (January 1970): 63–93.

———. *Old South, New South: Revolutions in the Southern Economy since the Civil War.* New York: Basic Books, 1986.

———. *The Political Economy of the Cotton South: Households, Markets, and Wealth in the Nineteenth Century.* New York: W. W. Norton, 1978.

Wright, Louis B. *South Carolina: A Bicentennial History.* New York: W. W. Norton, 1976.

Writers' Program. *A History of Spartanburg County.* New York: Band & White, 1940.

Wyatt-Brown, Bertram. "Black Schooling during Reconstruction." In *The Web of Southern Social Relations: Women, Family, and Education*, edited by Walter J.

Fraser, R. Frank Saunders, Jr., and Jon L. Wakelyn, 146–65. Athens: University of Georgia Press, 1985.

———. "Community, Class, and Snopesian Crime: Local Justice in the Old South." In *Class, Conflict, and Consensus: Antebellum Southern Community Studies*, edited by Orville Vernon Burton and Robert C. McMath, Jr., 173–206. Westport, Conn.: Greenwood Press, 1982.

———. *Southern Honor: Ethics and Behavior in the Old South*. New York: Oxford University Press, 1984.

Zimmerman, Hilda Jane. "Penal Systems and Penal Reform in the South since the Civil War." Ph.D. diss., University of North Carolina at Chapel Hill, 1947.

Zuczek, Richard. *State of Rebellion: Reconstruction in South Carolina*. Columbia: University of South Carolina Press, 1996.

Index

abolitionism and abolitionists: free schools as influenced by, 85; southern economy critiqued by, 48; in Spartanburg, 76, 97–98

African Americans: as free, 95, 96, 97; on juries, 219–20; and penitentiary system, 236–38, 241; schooling of, during post-Reconstruction, 203–5; schooling of, during Reconstruction, 193–97, 201–2, 275n15, 276n34. *See also* freedmen; Freedmen's Bureau; slaves and slavery

agricultural production: in antebellum era, 12–16, 31, 46–47; and railroads, 57

alcohol: efforts to restrict sales of, 214; illegal distilling of, 228–32; temperance efforts against, 50, 108–12, 233

Allen, E. S., 240

Anderson, James, 197

Anderson, William C., 123

artisans, attitudes toward, 49

Asheville, N.C., 61, 62, 163, 169

Associated Railroads of the Carolinas, 174

Atlanta, Ga., 163, 167, 174

Atlanta and Charlotte Railroad, 169

Atlanta and Richmond Air-Line Railroad: convict labor used by, 240; effects of, 175, 178, 179; financing and construction of, 167–69; racial violence by workers of, 228; and Republicans, 224; taxes for, 153

Auburn Prison (New York), 105

Ayers, Edward, 241

Bank of the State of South Carolina, 21–24

banks and banking, 21–24

Baptists, 108, 109

Barnett, M. C., 214

Barney, William, 121

Barrett, J. M., 97

Barry, Charles, 154

Bates, B. F., 32, 145, 146

Best, John Hardin, 71

Bivings, James, 25, 103; as railroad supporter, 57; as textile factory owner, 45, 47, 124

Bivingsville textile factory: antebellum development of, 44–46, 50, 51, 54; during Civil War, 124, 125–26; postwar expansion of, 179–80, 182–83

"black codes," 215

Blake, William Kennedy, 171

Blassingame, J. H., 138, 139

Blease, Cole, 245

Blue Ridge Railroad Company: declares bankruptcy, 169, 271n24; efforts of, to buy Spartanburg and Union Railroad, 167, 168; Spartanburg opposition to, 63–64, 65, 165–66, 170

Bobo, Edwin H., 186, 187
Bobo, Simpson, 18, 19, 28, 55, 66, 122; iron-manufacturing involvement of, 29, 40, 41, 179, 184; on jurors, 219, 220; and Ku Klux Klan, 223; as lawyer, 100, 136, 139; and postwar black schooling, 193, 204; as railroad supporter, 56, 61; and religion, 108; during secession crisis, 116, 118, 119; slaveholdings of, 31; as temperance advocate, 109; textile factories involvement of, 42, 45; on violence, 226
Bomar, John, 45, 124, 126, 182, 193
Bomar, John Earle, 14, 21, 136; education views of, 84, 85; and Ku Klux Klan, 227; usury law opposed by, 141, 142
Bomar, Thomas, 243
Bomar, Thomas H., 177
Bond, Bradley, 12
brickyards, 179
Broad River, 11, 53, 164
Brooks, Preston, 114, 116
Brown, Mary Davis, 109
Brown, Richard D., 6
Bryant, Javan, 218
Bryant, William Cullen, 50
Burton, Orville Vernon, 75
Byas, Benjamin, 191
Byrne, Frank, 2, 6, 21, 120

Calhoun, John C., 26
Camp, J. P. F., 191, 218, 220
Campobello, S.C., 67, 172
canals, 52
Cannon, Gabriel, 17, 27, 34, 66, 136, 137; black schoolhouse removal efforts of, 196; Blue Ridge Railroad opposed by, 64; as convict-labor supporter, 238, 239; efforts of, to defeat Republicans, 218; as investor in textile factories, 45, 51; Ku Klux Klan involvement of, 223; Ku Klux Klan violence condemned by, 225, 226, 279n36; martial law prevention efforts of, 227; postwar railroad involvement of, 167, 168, 169, 170, 173; as railroad supporter, 56, 57, 62; as railroad tax supporter, 65; resolution on jurors introduced by, 221; as revenue officers supporter, 232; secession views of, 116, 118; and taxpayers' conventions, 150, 151, 152; usury law opposed by, 141, 142
Cantillon, Richard, 6
Cantrell, Isaac, 222–23
Cantrell, Julius, 230
Caraher, A. P., 148, 217
Cardozo, Francis L., 191
Carlisle, James H., 109, 119, 206, 211
Carlisle, John W., 100, 136, 139, 214
Carlton, David, 85, 210
carriage factories, 178–79
Carson, John, 122
Carson, W. B., 190, 202
Cavis, A. T., 107, 114, 116
Cedar Hill textile factory, 45, 181
Centennial Exposition of 1876, 177–78
Chamberlain, Daniel, 196, 197, 239, 281n87
Chaplin, Joyce, 12, 19
Charleston, S.C., 53, 55, 145, 161; antebellum era interest of, in railroads, 61, 62, 63, 64, 67; postwar interest of, in railroads, 165, 166, 167, 170, 174, 184; public school system in, 77, 257n19
Charlotte and South Carolina Rail Road Company, 56
Cherokee, S.C., 160, 171, 188, 198, 209
Chestnut, John A., 191

Civil Rights Act of 1875, 196
class consciousness, racism used to prevent, 7–8, 134, 147, 244–45
Cleveland, Jesse, 17–18
Cleveland, John B., 174
Clifton Manufacturing Company, 184, 211
Columbia, S.C., 53, 109, 155, 170, 238; interest of, in railroads to upcountry, 55, 56, 57, 67, 167
Committee of Vigilance and Safety, 76, 98; vigilance committees in general, 118–19
Committee on Education, 81, 85
Congaree River, 53, 239
Conner, Sebal, 199
conscription, 128
constitutional convention (1868), 217–19
consumer culture, 18, 146
Converse, Dexter Edgar, 45, 46, 66, 126, 167, 182–84
convict-lease system, 239–41, 281n87. *See also* penitentiary system
Coopersville Iron Works, 40, 124, 125
cotton production: in antebellum era, 12, 13, 14, 31, 57, 251n56; in postwar era, 135, 144, 268n27
cotton trade, 174–75
Court of Common Pleas: debt cases before, 99, 102, 136, 139, 140; in postwar era, 213, 215
Court of General Sessions: cases before, 90–91; during Civil War, 129–30; and increase in property cases, 99–100; in postwar era, 213, 215, 216, 235
Cowpens, S.C., 229, 230
Cowpens Iron Foundry, 17
Crawfordsville textile factory, 45, 124, 179, 181

crop-lien law, 142, 144, 160
Cummings, Anson W., 150, 196–97, 225–26, 227, 238
Curtis, William, 119, 175

Dart, J. L., 203–4
Davis, E. F., 147
Davis, James S. M., 40
Davis, J. B., 173
Davis, Jefferson, 125
Dawkins, Mary, 177–78
Dawkins, Orphelia, 176
Dawkins, Thomas, 29
Dean, Hosea J., 18, 100, 109; as investor in textile factories, 42, 51; as state legislator, 23, 27, 28, 34
DeBow, James D. B., 177
debt, and postwar farmers, 138–40
DeCredico, Mary, 125
DeLarge, R. C., 191
Democratic Party: in antebellum era, 24–25, 26, 114; in postwar era, 5, 160, 205, 206, 218–19
desertion, 128
development, early republic debate over, 251n54
Dibble, Samuel, 207–8
Douglas, Stephen A., 114, 116, 117
Downey, Tom, 2, 43, 51, 254n59
dueling, 89, 234
Duncan, B. O., 191
Duncan, David R., 100, 136, 170, 172, 180–81, 221, 239

economic development, and historiography of antebellum South, 1–4
economy, wartime, 122–28
Edgefield County and District, S.C., 43, 85, 240

education. *See* schools, private; schools, public
Edwards, Oliver E., 18, 34, 68, 100, 116
"Elmore," 57–58
English Manufacturing Company, 184–85
Enoree River, 11, 16, 223
entrepreneurs: definition of, 6; and postwar education, 212; and postwar legal system, 241–42; postwar opportunities for, 163, 188; and religion, 108; secession response of, 113, 118, 120–21; stronger legal structure advocated by, 98–99, 214; and women, 6–7
Evins, John H.: efforts of, to defeat Republicans, 218; integrated schools opposed by, 192; as lawyer, 100, 136; as manufacturing supporter, 180; in military, 121; as railroad supporter, 163, 167, 170; at taxpayers' conventions, 150, 151
Evins, Samuel N., 23, 29, 45

Fair Forest, S.C., 13, 131, 171
Farley, Hugh L., 157, 185
Farrow, James, 34, 114, 137, 214; as lawyer, 28, 32–33, 100, 136; as railroad supporter, 57, 61; as railroad tax supporter, 66–67, 68; secession views of, 116–18, 119; state funding of South Carolina College supported by, 86–87
Farrow, T. Stobo, 141, 159, 192
Feaster, Andrew, 50
fence laws: in antebellum era, 14; in postwar era, 154–60
Finch, Benjamin, 129–30
Finger, Joseph, 17, 45, 51, 108
Fingerville, S.C., 17, 45, 108, 211

Finley, David G., 80
Fleming, William Magill, 224, 227, 230
flour mills, 178
Ford, Lacy, 3–4, 176
Foster, B. B., 16, 119
Foster, H. H., 223
Foster, Joel, 218–19, 225, 226
Foster, Joseph, 17, 122, 145
Foster, Rice, 191, 218
Foster & Judd, 17, 145
Fourteenth Amendment, 212, 217
Fowler, Elias, 148
Fowler, James, 52, 178–79
Fowler, Wallace, 225
Frazier, Charles, 3
free blacks, 95, 96, 97
Freedman, Joseph, 147
freedmen: and postwar courts, 215–17, 219–21; postwar labor arrangements of, 147–49, 161; taxation of, 138
Freedmen's Bureau, 148; courts of, 216–17; and schools, 190, 197, 201
Freehling, William, 20
Free School Act (1811), 73–74, 81. *See also* schools, public
Free Soil Party, 26

Genobles, John, 223, 224
Gentry, John S., 191, 218
Gillespie, Michele, 8
Glenn Springs, S.C., 10, 15, 16, 66, 142, 218
grand juries, 24, 91, 150; blacks as members of, 219–20; and calls for greater legal structure, 102–3, 104; common schooling supported by, 76–77; on concealed weapons, 233–34; on convict-lease law, 240–41; on Ku Klux Klan, 226; penitentiary supported by, 106, 107–8

Grange, 153–54, 269n60
Graniteville Manufacturing Company, 43, 44, 85, 120, 186, 210
Grant, Ulysses, 227
Grassy Pond, S.C., 36, 172
Greenville and Columbia Rail Road Company, 55, 56, 62, 165, 166, 169, 271n24
Greenville and French Broad Railroad, 61, 62, 65, 164, 169, 170
Greenville County and District, S.C., 55, 109, 114, 125, 128
Greenwood and Augusta Railroad, 240
Gregg, William, 43, 44, 46, 85, 120, 210, 255n59
Griffith, H. P., 233
Grimball, Lewis, 136
Grindal Shoals, 54, 55, 254n58
gristmills, 178

Hahn, Steven, 158, 269n60
Hall, Henry B., 232
Hammond, Harry, 161
Hampton, Wade, 207, 232
Harris, David Golightly: on black jurors, 219; and education of children, 202; farming practices of, 13–14; on postwar economy, 134, 139; on postwar violence, 214, 216; railroad commented on by, 61; secession views of, 120; on tenants and laborers, 147, 149, 186; wartime experiences of, 121, 122, 125, 128, 129–30, 131, 132
Harris, Emily, 130–31
Harris, Gwin, 186
Hawkins, Pet, 233
Heaton, Fanny, 234–35
Hendersonville, N.C., 172, 173
Henry, James Edward, 16–17, 18, 25, 27, 42, 57, 75, 76, 97

Hill, James L., 44, 124
Hill, Leonard, 42
Hindus, Michael Stephen, 90, 94
Holmes, Zelotus, 9
Homestead Act, 139–40
honor, 89

immigrant labor, 151–52
Independent Republicans, 151
industrialization: Civil War support for, 125; postwar support for, 177–78. *See also* iron manufacturing; railroads; textile manufacturing
iron manufacturing, 16, 29, 39–41, 124, 179, 273n51
Irwin, William, 222, 224, 225

Jefferies, John R., 147
Jefferson, Thomas, 71, 251n54
Jeter, Thomas, 164
Jillson, Justus K., 193–94, 195, 197, 198, 199
Johnson, Andrew, 80, 137, 164
Johnson, Anthony, 221
Johnson, Michael, 4
Jones (Dr.), 225
Jones, W. M., 209
Judd, David Cook, 17, 83, 145
Julius (freedman), 147

Kansas-Nebraska Act, 114, 115
Kantor, Shawn, 158
Kershaw (Judge), 234
Kilgore, Benjamin F., 16, 119
King, G. H., 129
Kings Mountain Iron Company, 40
Kousser, J. Morgan, 158
Ku Klux Klan, 98, 149, 200; congressional investigation of, 226–27; effectiveness of, 224–25; and entre-

Ku Klux Klan (*continued*)
 preneurs, 223–24, 226, 279n36; and illegal distillers, 230; membership of, 222–23, 242; prosecution of members of, 227–28

Landrum, John G., 109, 119
Laura (freedwoman), 148
Laurens County and District, S.C., 35, 85, 148, 158, 159
law: during Civil War, 129–31; and extralegal authority, 88–90, 235, 242
Lawson's Fork, 39, 45, 50, 54
lawyers: in antebellum era, 18; increasing influence of, 100; in postwar era, 136
Leaphart, Charles, 165
Lee & Twitty, 18, 145
Legg, George W. H., 122, 214
Leitner, Elias C.: on banks, 23, 24; and Bivingsville factory, 44, 45, 50; as grand jury foreman, 77, 104; opposes 1850 secession convention, 27, 28; as river improvement supporter, 54
Leloudis, James, 209
Leslie, C. P., 191
Lewis, Walter I., 203, 205
Lieber, Francis, 106
Limestone Springs, S.C., 175, 229, 230
Limestone Springs Female High School, 82, 83
Lincoln, Abraham, 117, 118
Lipscomb, Edward, 151, 218, 219, 224, 280n50
Lipscomb, Elias, 226
Lipscomb, Elizabeth, 124
Littlejohn, Samuel, 218
livestock, 14, 155; laws regarding, 14, 154–60
Long, Wayne, 6

Louisville, Cincinnati, and Charleston Railroad Company, 55
Lowell factory system, 42–43
Lyle, J. Banks, 140, 225, 228

Mackey, Thomas J., 155–56, 233
magistrates, as common-schooling advocates, 75–76, 262n37
Magistrates and Freeholders Court: during Civil War, 130–31; as counter to abolitionists, 93–94; and jury composition, 92–93; racial-control role of, 94–97; and sentencing, 94, 261n20; and slave owners, 93
Manning, John L., 63
Marion, Francis, 72
McArthur, O. P., 115
McBee, Vardry, 40, 45, 62
McCardell, John, 259n54
McKissick, Edward, 243
Means, A. G., 148, 234
Means, S. C., 124
Melton, C. D., 128, 265n53
Memminger, Christopher G., 170, 257n19
merchants and mercantile activity: in antebellum era, 17–18, 21, 31–32, 51–52; in postwar era, 134, 135, 142, 144, 145–47, 174; and secession, 120
Methodists, 108
middle class, 2; definition of southern, 5–6; farmers as members of, 13; northern influence on, 252n14; and school reform, 82; women as members of, 145–46
Miller, David, 186
Miller, Hugh, 84
Miller, Wilbur, 229
Miller, W. T., 150
Mitchell, Hiram, 18, 51, 145

modernization: definition of, 6; ideology of, 243
Montgomery, John H., 145, 174, 182, 273n65
Moore, John J., 234–35, 242
Moore, Maurice A., 79, 80, 148
Moore, Thomas John, 48, 124, 129, 152, 170, 234
Morgan, Chad, 2, 125
Morgan, Samuel, 45, 180, 181
Myers, John, 238

Nashville convention (1850), 26, 27, 28, 29
National Bank of Spartanburg, 145, 168, 219
National Union Convention (1866), 137
Nelson, Scott, 127, 223, 279n36
Nesbitt Iron Works, 40, 41, 53
North Carolina, 28, 53, 56; support of, for internal improvements, 53, 61, 62, 168, 169, 170

Oakes, James, 30, 251n53
Oeland, P. J., 84, 198
O'Neall, John Belton, 93, 96, 103, 104, 109, 110
Orr, James L., 114, 115, 117, 139, 177, 190
Otterson, Samuel, 27

Pacolet, S.C., 172, 174, 230
Pacolet Manufacturing Company, 182
Pacolet River, 11, 39, 40, 45, 54, 55, 182, 183
Parker, W. F., 227
Patrons of Husbandry, 153–54, 269n60
Peabody Education Fund, 204, 206, 211
Peete, Alfred, 185
Pelot, Lalla, 185, 186

penitentiary system: and blacks, 236, 238, 241; and convict-lease system, 239–41, 281n87; development of, in antebellum south, 105–6; development of, in United States, 105; operation of, in postwar South Carolina, 236, 238; and prison labor, 107; Spartanburg support for, 106–8
Perman, Michael, 151
Perry, Benjamin F., 18, 62, 88, 106, 114, 117, 214
Petty, Charles, 158, 206, 210, 233, 240
Piedmont Railroad, 126–27
planters: attitudes of, toward free schools, 74–75; contrasted with Spartanburg town elites, 4, 25, 30; dependence of, on industrialists and merchants, 51–52; as entrepreneurs, 248n19; and the law, 88, 89, 90; in postwar era, 163; substitute soldiers hired by, 129; and wartime manufacturing, 125
Pocock, J. G. A., 88
Poole, Eva, 193–94
Poole, R. C., 137–38, 220
Poole, Washington, 200
Porcher, Frederick, 78, 81
Presbyterians, 108
Pressley (Judge), 235
Providence, R.I., factory system of, 41, 42
P. Whitin and Sons, 46, 120

Racine, Philip, 93
racism, used to prevent class consciousness, 7–8, 134, 147, 244–45
railroads, 38; during Civil War, 126–27; and competition among, in upcountry, 63–64; early development of, in South Carolina, 55–56; Ku

railroads (*continued*)
  Klux Klan interference with, 226; and manufacturing, 57–59; postwar expansion of, 163–73; state regulation of, 173–74; and taxation, 65–68, 153, 167–68, 171–72
Railroad Tax Act (1860), 65
Ransier, A. J., 191
Reconstruction Acts, 217
Redeemer Democrats, and education, 205
Reid, R. H.: black schooling views of, 193, 194, 202; state school appropriation withheld by, 199–200; white schooling views of, 197–98
Reidville, S.C., 171
Reidville Female Academy, 82
Reidville High School, 17, 190, 202
Reidy, Joseph, 158
religion, 108
republican ideology, 2, 117
Republican Party, 67, 218, 224
Rhett, Robert Barnwell, 26, 115, 117, 125
Rhode Island, immigrants of, to Spartanburg, 16, 17, 41–42
Rice, Benjamin, 157, 158
Richmond and Danville Railroad, 126–27, 167, 169, 172, 173
Richmond and West Point Terminal Company, 173
rivers: calls for improvements in navigation of, 53–54; conflicts over usage of, 54–55
Ruffin, Edmund, 10, 40

sawmills, 179
Say, Jean-Baptiste, 6
schools, private, 75
schools, public: and abolitionism, 85; in antebellum South, 71–73; in antebellum South Carolina, 73–75; attitudes toward, 74; for blacks during Reconstruction, 193–97, 201–2, 275n15, 276n34; for blacks in post-Reconstruction era, 203–5; during Civil War, 131; and economic development, 84, 85; and farmers, 80; funding for, 74, 77–78; historiography of, 71, 189; link of, to economic success, 208–10; northern influence on, 81–83; provisions for, in South Carolina Constitution of 1868, 191–92; and school taxes, 77–79, 206–7, 258n40; and slavery, 82; southern goals for, 83; at textile mills, 210–11; and white laborers, 84; for whites during Reconstruction, 197–201, 202–3; for whites in post-Reconstruction era, 205–6
Schumpeter, Joseph, 6
Scott, Robert K., 192, 217, 221, 224, 231
Scott, Thomas A., 167
Scruggs, Robert, 209–10
secession crisis of 1849–51, 26–30
secession crisis of 1860–61, 113, 117–20
sectionalism, within South Carolina, 4, 19–20
Sickles, Daniel, 139, 215, 217
Simms, Jim, 148
Simms, William Gilmore, 10
Simon, Bryant, 245
Sinha, Manisha, 117
Slater, Samuel, 41
slave owners, 14–16, 127
slaves and slavery, 7–8, 20; during Civil War, 130–31; expansion of, 26, 31; and free schools, 82, 83; increased controls over, 96–97; iron foundry use of, 40–41; and Magistrates and

Freeholders Court, 92–95; textile factory use of, 47
Sloan, James F., 50, 54, 61, 249n13; farming practices of, 12–13, wartime experiences of, 121, 122, 128
Smith, Elihu Penquite, 15, 23, 27, 51, 52, 123, 225
Smith, Eliphus, 123
Smith, George, 154
Smith, Mark, 1
Smith, Robert M., 141, 142, 152, 200, 218, 226
Smith, Whiteford, 131
Smith, William, 14–15
Snetter, E. J., 190
soldiers, 121–22, 128–29
Somers, Robert, 141, 155
South Carolina College, 76, 86–87
South Carolina Constitution (1865), 215
South Carolina Constitution (1868), 139, 150; provisions of, for courts, 219; provisions of, for education, 191–92
South Carolina Convention (1860), 118
South Carolina Cotton Manufactory, 42
South Carolina legislature: apportionment in, 19–20, 74; and free schools, 73, 74, 85–86
South Carolina Manufacturing Company, 19, 51, 55, 219; operations of, 39–40, 124, 179; slaves used by, 29
South Carolina Railroad Company, 55, 166
South Carolina State Institution for the Education of the Deaf, Dumb, and Blind, 195–96
Southern Railway Security Company, 167, 223
Southern Relief Association of New York, 144–45

Spartanburg and Asheville Railroad, 169–72, 173, 178, 239
Spartanburg and Rutherfordton Railroad, 187
Spartanburg and Union Railroad, 17, 29, 38, 113; calls for purchase of stock for, 56–57; calls for western extension of, 61–63; charter for, 56; during Civil War, 126; completion of, 61; convict labor hired by, 239; financial problems of, 60–61; postwar, 164–67, 168; state aid sought for, 58–59, 61–64; town-rural divisions over, 59–60, 65–68
Spartanburg County and District: Civil War mobilization of, 121–22; desire for northern investment in, 33; early settlement of, 11–12; geography of, 10–11, 39; politics of 1850s in, 114–16; postwar economy of, 135–36; postwar politics of, 136–37; during secession crisis of 1860–61, 117–21; and town-rural divisions, 30–31, 34–37, 80, 176–77, 188, 244, 255n72
Spartanburg Female College, 81, 82, 131
Spartanburg High School, 202
Spartanburg Ladies Relief Association, 122
Spartanburg town, 16, 17; expansion of, in antebellum era, 31–34; expansion of, in postwar era, 174–76, 243; Union troops arrive in, 132
Spartanburg, Union and Columbia Railroad, 173
stay law, 138, 139
St. John's College, 131
stock laws: antebellum era, 14; postwar era, 154–160
Stone, Catherine, 51, 52
Sullivan, Charles P., 85

Sumner, Charles, 115, 196
Swedish Iron Manufacturing Company, 41

Tarrant, Sumter, 109
taxation and taxes: in kind, 127; manufacturer exemptions from, 180–81; postwar, 137–38, 149–50, 152–53. *See also* railroads; schools, public
taxpayers' conventions, 150–52
teachers, 82–83
temperance, 50, 108–12, 233; and alcohol in general, 214, 228–32
Tennessee, 28, 56, 61, 62, 63, 80
textile manufacturing: in antebellum era, 16–17, 41–52; calls for regulation of, 186–87; during Civil War, 124–26; postwar expansion of, 179–85; white labor in, during postwar era, 186, 273n65; women and children in, 7
Thompson, Hugh S., 204, 206, 207, 211
Thomson, H. H., 19, 25, 28, 29, 31, 42, 57
Thomson, W. Waddy, 196, 200–201
Tolleson, Alfred, 21, 32, 122, 136
Towers, Frank, 4
Trimmier, Francis M., 144, 148, 238
Trimmier, George, 96, 100, 107
Trimmier, William H., 84, 85, 114, 116
Tucker, Joseph Wofford, 23, 27, 28, 100, 108; northern investment interest of, 32, 33; as railroad supporter, 34, 38, 60; as school-reform supporter, 81–84, 85; state funding of private higher education supported by, 86, 87; state tax for South Carolina College opposed by, 86
Turner, Adolphus P., 230, 231
Turner, Claudius C., 218

Turner, Randolph, 111
Tyger River, 11, 16, 42, 44, 181

Union County and District, S.C.: fence law in, 157, 158, 159; support of, for internal improvements, 53, 54, 56
Unionville, S.C., 148, 217
U.S. Revenue Department: and illegal distilleries, 228–29, 232; revenue officer of, attacked, 230–31
usury laws, 21, 140–42, 160–61, 267n22

Vaucluse Manufacturing Company, 43
Vernon, T. O. P., 29, 96, 99, 110, 215
vigilance committees, 118–19
violence: and class, 89–90; postwar, 214; and race, 216; southern view of, 89

wage labor: southern attitudes toward, 47–49; support for, during Civil War, 125
Walker, Ann, 136
Walker, Joseph, 172, 174–75
Walker, William, 25
Walker, Fleming & Company, 182
Wallace, Daniel, 29, 64, 114
Wallace, Peter M., 23, 27, 110, 144, 148; as convict-labor supporter, 238; as school-reform advocate, 70, 79–80; as textile factory owner, 44, 45
Walnut Street Prison (Pa.), 105
Waters, T. W., 23, 27, 28
weapons: calls for restrictions on, 104, 233–34; and prohibition on concealed pistols, 214
Wells, Jonathan Daniel, 2, 5, 33, 72, 82, 108
West, Steven, 12, 119
Western North Carolina Railroad, 164
Whig Party, 24, 25, 26

White, Thomas, 233
Williams, David R., 74
Wilmington and Manchester Railroad, 167
Wilmot, David, 26
Wilson, John Stanyarne, 186, 187
Wingo, Coy, 191, 218
Winsmith, John C., 15, 56, 161, 214; attacked by Ku Klux Klan, 224; Blue Ridge Railroad opposed by, 63–64; district courts opposed by, 215; railroad tax opposed by, 65–68; supports 1850 secession, 27, 29
Wofford, William, 16, 39
Wofford College, 109, 131, 178, 211
women: education of, 131; and manual labor, 49; in merchant families, 248n21, 250n25; in middle class, 6–7, 18, 145–46; and postwar economy, 136; and railroads, 168; as teachers, 82–83; wartime activities of, 122, 264n29
Woodruff, Andrew B., 141, 142, 150, 151, 152
Woodruff, C. D., 96
Woodward, C. Vann, 1, 243, 245
Wright, Gavin, 163
Wyatt-Brown, Bertram, 89, 275n15

yeomen, 7, 12–14, 25, 30, 38, 104; and the law, 100, 102; in postwar era, 134, 188; and schooling, 198, 202; and secession, 113, 118; and textile factories, 50; and wartime economy, 123
York County and District, S.C., 40, 53, 109, 155, 222